Middle School 2-1

기말고사 완벽대비

적중 100

영어 기출 문제집

중**2**

지학 | 민찬규

Best Collection

구성과 특징

교과서의 주요 학습 내용을 중심으로 학습 영역별 특성에 맞춰 단계별로 다양한 학습 기회를 제공하여 단원별 학습능력 평가는 물론 중간 및 기말고사 시험 등에 완벽하게 대비할 수 있도록 내용을 구성

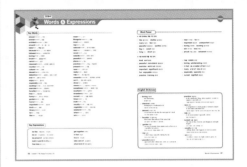

Words & Expressions

Step1 Key Words 단원별 핵심 단어 설명 및 풀이
Key Expression 단원별 핵심 숙어 및 관용어 설명
Word Power 반대 또는 비슷한 뜻 단어 배우기
English Dictionary 영어로 배우는 영어 단어

Step2 실력평가 단원별 수시평가 대비 주관식, 객관식 문제풀이

Step3 서술형 대비 학업성취도 및 수행능력평가 대비 서술형 문제풀이

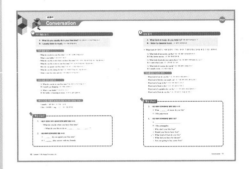

Conversation

Step1 핵심 의사소통 의사소통에 필요한 주요 표현 방법 요약
핵심 Check 기본적인 표현 방법 및 활용능력 확인

Step2 대화문 익히기 상황에 따른 대화문 활용 및 연습

Step3 기본평가 시험대비 기초 학습 능력 평가

Step4 실력평가 단원별 수시평가 대비 주관식, 객관식 문제풀이

Step5 서술형 대비 학업성취도 및 수행능력평가 대비 서술형 문제풀이

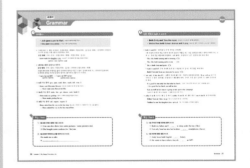

Grammar

Step1 주요 문법 단원별 주요 문법 사항과 예문을 알기 쉽게 설명
핵심 Check 기본 문법사항에 대한 이해 여부 확인

Step2 기본평가 시험대비 기초 학습 능력 평가

Step3 실력평가 단원별 수시평가 대비 주관식, 객관식 문제풀이

Step4 서술형 대비 학업성취도 및 수행능력평가 대비 서술형 문제풀이

Reading

Step1 구문 분석 단원별로 제시된 문장에 대한 구문별 분석과 내용 설명
확인문제 문장에 대한 기본적인 이해와 인지능력 확인

Step2 확인학습A 빈칸 채우기를 통한 문장 완성 능력 확인

Step3 확인학습B 제시된 우리말을 영어로 완성하여 작문 능력 키우기

Step4 실력평가 단원별 수시평가 대비 주관식, 객관식 문제풀이

Step5 서술형 대비 학업성취도 및 수행능력평가 대비 서술형 문제풀이
교과서 구석구석 교과서에 나오는 기타 문장까지 완벽 학습

Composition

   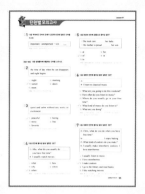

|영역별 핵심문제|

단어 및 어휘, 대화문, 문법, 독해 등 각 영역별 기출문제의 출제 유형을 분석하여 실전에 대비하고 연습할
수 있도록 문제를 배열

|서술형 실전 및 창의사고력 문제|

학교 시험에서 점차 늘어나는 서술형 시험에 집중 대비하고 고득점을 취득하는데 만전을 기하기 위한
학습 코너

|단원별 예상문제|

기출문제를 분석한 후 새로운 시험 출제 경향을 더하여 새롭게 출제될 수 있는 문제를 포함하여 시험에 완벽
하게 대비할 수 있도록 준비

|단원별 모의고사|

영역별, 단계별 학습을 모두 마친 후 실전 연습을 위한 모의고사

INSIGHT on the textbook · · · · · · · · · · · · · · · · · ·   교과서 파헤치기

- 단어Test1~2 영어 단어 우리말 쓰기와 우리말을 영어 단어로 쓰기
- 대화문Test1~2 대화문 빈칸 완성 및 전체 대화문 쓰기
- 본문Test1~5 빈칸 완성, 우리말 쓰기, 문장 배열연습, 영어 작문하기 복습 등 단계별 반복 학습을
  통해 교과서 지문에 대한 완벽한 습득
- 구석구석지문Test1~2 지문 빈칸 완성 및 전문 영어로 쓰기

Happy Others, Happier Me

🎤 의사소통 기능

- 도움 제안하기
  Let me help you.

- 칭찬에 답하기
  I'm glad you like(d) it.

🎤 언어 형식

- 목적격 관계대명사
  Here are two stories **which** I read yesterday.

- to부정사를 목적격보어로 취하는 동사
  She **asked** him **to do** the job. `

Words & Expressions

Key Words

- **activity** [æktívəti] 몡 활동
- **arrow** [ǽrou] 몡 화살, 화살표
- **avoid** [əvɔ́id] 동 피하다
- **basket** [bǽskit] 몡 바구니
- **bus stop** 버스 정류장
- **children's center** 아동 센터
- **coin** [kɔin] 몡 동전
- **confusing** [kənfjúːziŋ] 혱 혼란스러운
- **danger** [déindʒər] 몡 위험
- **decide** [disáid] 동 결심하다
- **different** [dífərənt] 혱 다른
- **disappear** [disəpíər] 동 사라지다
- **effort** [éfərt] 몡 노력
- **explain** [ikspléin] 동 설명하다
- **few** [fju:] 혱 몇몇의
- **forget** [fərgét] 동 잊어버리다
- **frame** [freim] 몡 틀, 테
- **free** [fri:] 혱 무료의
- **glad** [glæd] 혱 기쁜
- **hear** [hiər] 동 듣다
- **map** [mæp] 몡 지도
- **mentee** [mentí:] 몡 멘티
- **mentor** [méntɔːr] 몡 멘토
- **need** [ni:d] 동 필요로 하다
- **outside** [áutsàid] 혱 바깥의, 외부의
- **pay phone** 공중전화
- **plan** [plæn] 동 …하려고 계획하다
- **plastic bag** 비닐봉지
- **possible** [pásəbl] 혱 가능한
- **refrigerator** [rifrídʒərèitər] 몡 냉장고
- **rest** [rest] 동 쉬다, 휴식하다
- **say** [sei] 동 (글·글씨 등이) 쓰이다
- **secret** [síːkrit] 몡 비밀, 비결 혱 비밀의
- **sign** [sain] 몡 표지판
- **soap** [soup] 몡 비누
- **solution** [səlúːʃən] 몡 해결책
- **solve** [sɑlv] 동 해결하다
- **start** [stɑːrt] 동 시작하다
- **sticker** [stíkər] 몡 딱지, 스티커
- **street** [striːt] 몡 거리
- **success** [səksés] 몡 성공
- **trash** [træʃ] 몡 쓰레기
- **volunteer club** 자원 봉사 동아리
- **wonderful** [wʌ́ndərfəl] 혱 훌륭한, 굉장한

Key Expressions

- **come up with** (생각을) 찾아내다, 제시하다
- **during the day** 낮 동안
- **give it a try** 시도하다, 한번 해 보다
- **give out** …을 나누어 주다
- **have to** …해야 한다
- **on one's own** 자기 스스로
- **one day** (과거의) 어느 날
- **put up** 설치하다, 세우다
- **stop -ing** …하는 것을 멈추다
- **thanks to** … 덕분에
- **the other day** 며칠 전에, 지난번, 요전에
- **waste one's time** …의 시간을 낭비하다

Word Power

※ 서로 반대되는 뜻을 가진 어휘
- □ **mentor** 멘토 ↔ m □ **same** 같은 ↔ **different** 다른
- □ **forget** 잊어버리다 ↔ **remember** 기억하다
- □ **success** 성공 ↔ **failure** 실패
- □ **start** 시작하다 ↔ **finish** 끝내다
- □ **danger** 위험 ↔ **safety** 안전

- □ **outside** 바깥의 ↔ **inside** 안쪽의
- □ **possible** 가능한 ↔ **impossible** 불가능한
- □ **free** 한가한 ↔ **busy** 바쁜

※ 동사 – 명사
- □ **succeed** 성공하다 — **success** 성공
- □ **fail** 실패하다 — **failure** 실패

- □ **advise** 충고하다 — **advice** 충고
- □ **solve** 해결하다 — **solution** 해결

English Dictionary

- □ **activity** 활동
  → something that is done as work for a particular purpose 특별한 목적을 위한 일로 이루어지는 것
- □ **arrow** 화살표
  → a mark that is shaped like an arrow and that is used to show direction
  화살과 같은 모양으로 방향을 보여주기 위해 사용되는 표시
- □ **confusing** 혼란스러운
  → difficult to understand 이해하기 어려운
- □ **disappear** 사라지다
  → to stop being visible 보여지는 것이 멈추다
- □ **few** 몇몇의
  → not many, but some 많지 않은, 그러나 약간 있는
- □ **free** 무료의
  → not costing any money 어떠한 돈도 들지 않는
- □ **hear** 듣다
  → to be aware of sounds with your ears
  당신의 귀로 소리를 인식하다
- □ **map** 지도
  → a drawing or plan of the earth's surface or part of it, showing countries, town, rivers, etc.
  국가, 마을, 강 등을 보여주는 지구의 표면 또는 그것의 일부의 그림이나 도면

- □ **mentee** 멘티
  → a person who is advised and helped by a more experienced person
  좀 더 경험이 있는 사람에 의해 조언을 받거나 도움을 받는 사람
- □ **montor** 멘토
  → someone who teaches or gives help and advice to a less experienced and often younger person
  경험이 별로 없거나 종종 어린 사람에게 도움이나 조언을 주거나 가르치는 사람
- □ **refrigerator** 냉장고
  → a device or room that is used to keep things cold
  사물들을 차갑게 유지하기 위해 사용되는 장치나 공간
- □ **secret** 비밀의
  → kept hidden from others 다른 사람들로부터 숨겨진
- □ **sign** 표지판
  → a piece of paper, wood, etc., with words or pictures on it that gives information about something
  어떤 것에 관한 정보를 제공하는 글귀나 사진들이 위에 있는 종이, 나무 등의 조각
- □ **success** 성공
  → the correct or desired result of an attempt
  어떤 시도의 정확하거나 바람직한 결과
- □ **start** 시작하다
  → to begin doing or using something
  무언가를 하거나 사용하기 시작하다

01 다음 영영풀이가 나타내는 말을 고르시오.

> a drawing or plan of the earth's surface or part of it, showing countries, towns, rivers, etc.

① arrow　　　② map
③ effort　　　④ soap
⑤ activity

02 다음 문장에 공통으로 들어갈 말을 고르시오.

> • What does the card _____ ?
> • Will you _____ what you mean simply?
> • I disagree with what you _____ .

① tell　　　② write
③ say　　　④ hear
⑤ listen

03 다음 중 밑줄 친 부분의 뜻풀이가 바르지 <u>않은</u> 것은?

① The <u>sign</u> in the store window says 'OPEN'. 서명
② The moon <u>disappeared</u> behind a cloud.
　　　　　　　　　사라졌다
③ Nobody else knows about this place because it's our <u>secret</u> place.
　　　　　　　　　비밀의
④ The <u>arrow</u> on the sign points north.
　　　화살표
⑤ We did a fun <u>activity</u> at an English camp.
　　　　　　　　활동

04 〔서답형〕 다음 짝지어진 단어의 관계가 같도록 빈칸에 알맞은 말을 쓰시오.

> low: high = _____ : safety

05 다음 주어진 문장의 밑줄 친 free와 같은 의미로 쓰인 것은?

> • Hojun and I planned to give out <u>free</u> stickers today.

① I was so happy because I received <u>free</u> tickets.
② Each student has a <u>free</u> choice of course.
③ What do you like to do in your <u>free</u> time?
④ <u>Free</u> speech is one of the features of democracy.
⑤ Let's set <u>free</u> a bird from a cage.

06 〔서답형〕 다음 문장의 빈칸에 들어갈 말을 보기에서 골라 쓰시오.

> ┌─ 보기 ─┐
> confusing / secret / soap / decide

(1) The road sign was really _____ .
(2) You can _____ if you'll stay here or not.
(3) My sister made the _____ using the natural oil.
(4) The _____ to my health is to exercise regularly.

01 다음 짝지어진 단어의 관계가 같도록 빈칸에 알맞은 말을 쓰시오.

> success : failure = possible : _____

02 다음 대화의 빈칸에 보기에 주어진 단어를 알맞게 채워 넣으시오.

> ┤ 보기 ├
>
> help / try / glad / good / tip

> A: I'm not (A)_____ at science. What can I do?
> B: Let me (B)_____ you. Why don't you start with easier books?
> A: Okay, I'll give it a (C)_____. Thanks for the (D)_____.
> B: No problem. I'm (E)_____ you like it.

03 다음 주어진 우리말과 일치하도록 주어진 단어를 모두 배열하여 문장을 완성하시오.

(1) 그는 집 앞에 'For Sale' 표지판을 세웠다.
(a 'For Sale' / put / in / of / his / he / house / up / sign / front)
➡ _____

(2) 나는 그의 도움 덕택에 이 일을 일찍 끝냈다.
(thanks / this / work / earlier / finished / I / his / to / help)
➡ _____

(3) 우리는 우리 스스로 숙제를 해야 한다.
(on / we / own / our / homework / do / our / have / to)
➡ _____

04 다음 우리말에 맞게 빈칸에 알맞은 말을 쓰시오.

(1) 네 도움 덕분에 우리는 그 일을 마칠 수 있었다.
➡ _____ _____ your help, we could finish the work.

(2) 며칠 전에 엄마는 내게 쿠키를 구워 주셨다.
➡ My mother baked cookies for me _____ _____ _____.

(3) 우리 견본을 좀 나누어 주는 게 어때?
➡ Why don't we _____ _____ some samples?

05 다음 문장의 빈칸에 들어갈 말을 보기에서 골라 쓰시오.

> ┤ 보기 ├
>
> give out / come up with / put up / one day

(1) We'll _____ free umbrellas on a rainy day.

(2) She will _____ a new idea for our club.

(3) We _____ the poster on the window.

(4) _____, all dinosaurs disappeared completely.

06 다음 영영풀이가 나타내는 말을 찾아 쓰시오.

> a piece of paper, wood, etc., with words or pictures on it that gives information about something

➡ _____

Conversation

① 도움 제안하기

Let me help you. 내가 도와줄게.

■ 상대방에게 도움을 제안하고자 할 때 'Let me help you.', 'I'll help you.' 또는 'I'll give you a hand.' 등으로 표현할 수 있다.

도움 요청하기

• Would you help me out? (나를 좀 도와주시겠어요?)
• Could you do something for me? (저를 좀 도와주시겠습니까?)
• Would you give me a hand? (저 좀 도와주시겠어요?)
• Would you mind helping me? (좀 도와주시겠습니까?)

도움 제안하기

• Let me help you. (내가 도와줄게.)
• Would you like me to help you? (내가 너를 도와주길 원하니?)
• Do you need any help? (도움이 필요하세요?)
• Can I give you a hand? (도와 드릴까요?)
• May I help you? (제가 도와드릴까요?)
• How can I help you? (무엇을 도와드릴까요?)
• I'll help you. (제가 도와드릴게요.)

핵심 Check

1. 다음 우리말과 일치하도록 빈칸에 알맞은 말을 쓰시오.

   A: I don't have a bottle-opener. I can't open the bottle.

   B: Let _____ _____ _____. (내가 도와드릴게요.)

2. 다음 우리말과 일치하도록 빈칸에 알맞은 말을 쓰시오.

   A: _____ _____ _____ _____ _____? (도움이 필요하신가요?)

   B: Yes. I can't fix the light. It's too high.

3. 다음 우리말과 일치하도록 빈칸에 알맞은 말을 쓰시오.

   A: I can't swim here. It's too _____. (여기서 수영을 못하겠어요. 너무 깊어요.)

   B: _____ _____. I'll _____ _____. (걱정 마세요. 제가 도와드릴게요.)

② 칭찬에 답하기

> **I'm glad you like it.** 네가 그것을 좋아한다니 나도 기뻐.

■ 'I'm glad you like(d) it.'은 '네가 그것을 좋아한[했]다니 나도 기뻐.' 라는 뜻으로 자신이 상대방에게 해 준 일에 관해 칭찬의 말을 들었을 때 답하는 표현이다.

칭찬에 답하기

- My pleasure. (저도 기뻐요.)
- Not at all. (별 말씀을요.)
- You're welcome. (천만에요.)
- Don't mention it. (별 말씀을요.)
- I'm glad[happy, pleased] to hear that. (그 말을 들으니 기쁩니다.)
- You're so kind to say that. (그렇게 말해 주시다니 참 친절하시군요.)
- Thank you for saying so. (그렇게 말해 주셔서 감사합니다.)

 핵심 Check

4. 다음 우리말과 일치하도록 빈칸에 알맞은 말을 쓰시오.

   A: It's a wonderful picture. I like it. (훌륭한 그림이야. 나는 그게 마음에 들어.)

   B: I'm _____ _____ _____ _____. (네가 그것을 좋아한다니 나도 기뻐.)

5. 다음 우리말과 일치하도록 빈칸에 알맞은 말을 쓰시오.

   A: How nice! I really like this scarf. (멋지다! 나 이 스카프가 정말 마음에 들어.)

   B: _____ _____. (저도 기뻐요.)

6. 다음 우리말과 일치하도록 빈칸에 알맞은 말을 쓰시오.

   A: What a great story! (정말 훌륭한 이야기예요!)

   B: Thank you _____ _____ _____. (그렇게 말해 주시니 감사합니다.)

A. Listen and Speak 1 A

Tom: Hojun and I planned to ❶give out free stickers today, but I think he forgot.

Sora: Really? ❷Let me help you then. Why are you going to give out stickers?

Tom: It's part of our ❸volunteer club activity.

Sora: ❹I see. What does this sticker mean?

Tom: It means that when we smile at ❺each other, the world will become a better place.

Sora: That's a wonderful idea.

Tom: 호준이와 나는 오늘 무료 스티커를 나눠주기로 계획 했는데 호준이가 잊어버린 것 같아.
Sora: 그래? 그럼 내가 도와줄 게. 너희는 스티커를 왜 나 눠주려고 하니?
Tom: 그건 우리 자원봉사 동아 리 활동의 일부야.
Sora: 그렇구나. 이 스티커는 무 엇을 의미하니?
Tom: 그건 우리가 서로에게 미 소 지을 때, 세상이 더 좋 은 곳이 될 거라는 의미야.
Sora: 그거 멋진 아이디어구나.

❶ give out: ~을 나누어 주다
❷ Let me help you then.: 그러면 내가 도와줄게.
❸ volunteer club: 자원봉사 동아리
❹ I see.: 알겠어.
❺ each other: 서로

Check(√) True or False

(1) Sora is going to help Tom.   T ☐ F ☐

(2) Sora already knew the meaning of the sticker.   T ☐ F ☐

B. Real Life Communication

Emily: Welcome back, Brian. Are you feeling better?

Brian: Yes, thanks. I tried to study ❶on my own in the hospital, but it was hard.

Emily: Let me help you. ❷Why don't you join my study group?

Brian: Did you start a ❸study group? That's wonderful.

Emily: Thanks. I think that we can learn better when we teach each other.

Brian: I agree. I'll try hard to be a good member. Thanks for helping me.

Emily: You're welcome. ❹I'm glad you like my idea.

Emily: 돌아온 걸 환영해, Brian. 좀 나아졌니?
Brian: 응, 고마워. 나는 병원에 서 혼자 공부하려고 했는 데, 어려웠어.
Emily: 내가 도와줄게. 우리 스 터디 모임에 함께 하는 게 어때?
Brian: 스터디 모임을 시작했 니? 그거 멋지다.
Emily: 고마워. 나는 우리가 서 로를 가르쳐주면 더 잘 배울 수 있을 거라고 생 각해.
Brain: 맞아. 나는 좋은 구성원 이 되려고 열심히 노력할 게. 도와줘서 고마워.
Emily: 천만에. 내 아이디어를 좋아해줘서 나도 기뻐.

❶ on one's own: 자기 스스로
❷ Why don't you ~?: 너는 ~하는 게 어때?
❸ study group: 공부 모임
❹ I'm glad you like my idea.: 상대방의 칭찬에 대답하는 표현이다.

Check(√) True or False

(3) Brian came back to school from the hospital.   T ☐ F ☐

(4) Brian isn't going to join Emily's study group.   T ☐ F ☐

Listen and Speak 1 B

Mike: Jimin, what are all these things in the box?

Jimin: They're for my ❶mentee at the ❷ children's center. I'm going to give her my old books today.

Mike: Do you teach ❸her every weekend?

Jimin: Yes. I feel happy when I teach her.

Mike: ❹You are a good mentor. Oh, the box looks heavy. Let me help you.

Jimin: Thanks.

❶ mentee (멘티) ↔ mentor (멘토)
❷ children's center: 아동 센터
❸ Jimin의 mentee를 가리킨다.
❹ Jimin을 칭찬하는 표현이다.

Listen and Speak 2 B

Yujin: I read a story about a special boy in India. Do you want to hear about ❶it?

Jack: Sure. Why is he special, Yujin?

Yujin: Many children in his town couldn't go to school and ❷had to work. So he taught ❸them in his house every day.

Jack: That's a great story.

Yujin: I'm glad you like it.

❶ a story about a special boy in India를 가리킨다.
❷ had to: ~해야 했다(have to의 과거형)
❸ many children in his town을 가리킨다.

Listen and Speak 2-A

Alex: Mom, ❶this is for you. I made it with plastic bags.

Mom: That's very cute, Alex. How did you know that I needed a new basket?

Alex: You talked about ❷it when we were having dinner ❸the other day.

Mom: ❹How nice! I really like this basket. It has many different colors.

Alex: I'm glad you like it.

❶ 'This is for you.'는 상대방에게 선물 등을 줄 때 쓰는 표현이다.
❷ a new basket을 가리킨다.
❸ the other day: 며칠 전, 요전날
❹ How nice!: '정말 마음에 든다!'라는 표현으로 감탄문 형식으로 쓰였다. 원래의 표현은 How nice this basket is!이며 '주어+동사' 뒷부분이 생략된 형태이다.

Let's Check

Henry: Your bag looks heavy. Let me help you.

Sujin: Thanks. Where is the ❶bus stop around here?

Henry: ❷It's over there. I'll carry your bag to the bus stop for you.

Sujin: ❸You're very kind.

Henry: ❹No problem. I am going that way, too.

❶ bus stop: 버스 정류장
❷ It's over there.: 그것은 저쪽에 있어.
❸ Henry의 도움에 칭찬하는 표현이다.
❹ '별말씀을요.'의 뜻으로 칭찬에 답하는 표현이다.

● 다음 우리말과 일치하도록 빈칸에 알맞은 말을 쓰시오.

Listen & Speak 1 A

Tom: Hojun and I planned to _____ _____ free stickers today, but I think he forgot.

Sora: Really? _____ _____ _____ _____ _____. Why are you going to give out stickers?

Tom: It's part of our _____ _____ _____.

Sora: I see. What does this sticker _____?

Tom: _____ _____ _____ when we smile at _____ _____, the world will become a _____.

Sora: That's a wonderful idea.

Tom: 호준이와 나는 오늘 무료 스티커를 나눠주기로 계획했는데 호준이가 잊어버린 것 같아.
Sora: 그래? 그럼 내가 도와줄게. 너희는 스티커를 왜 나눠주려고 하니?
Tom: 그건 우리 자원봉사 동아리 활동의 일부야.
Sora: 그렇구나. 이 스티커는 무엇을 의미하니?
Tom: 그건 우리가 서로에게 미소 지을 때, 세상이 더 좋은 곳이 될 거라는 의미야.
Sora: 그거 멋진 아이디어구나.

Listen & Speak 1 B

Mike: Jimin, what are all these things in the box?

Jimin: They're for _____ _____ at the children's center. I'm going to give her my old books today.

Mike: _____ _____ _____ _____ _____ _____ _____?

Jimin: Yes. I feel happy when I teach her.

Mike: _____ _____ _____ _____ _____. Oh, the box looks heavy. Let me help you.

Jimin: Thanks.

Mike: 지민아, 상자에 들어 있는 이게 전부 뭐니?
Jimin: 그건 아동 센터에 있는 내 멘티를 위한 거야. 오늘 내가 보던 책들을 줄 거야.
Mike: 너는 그녀를 주말마다 가르치니?
Jimin: 응. 나는 그녀를 가르칠 때 행복해.
Mike: 넌 좋은 멘토구나. 아, 상자 무거워 보인다. 내가 도와줄게.
Jimin: 고마워.

Listen & Speak 2 A

Alex: Mom, _____ _____ _____ _____. I made it with plastic bags.

Mom: That's very cute, Alex. _____ _____ _____ _____ I needed a new basket?

Alex: You talked about it when we were having dinner _____ _____.

Mom: _____ _____! I really like this basket. It has many different colors.

Alex: _____ _____ _____ _____ _____.

Alex: 엄마, 이거 선물이에요. 제가 비닐봉지로 만들었어요.
Mom: 그것 참 예쁘구나, Alex. 내가 새로운 바구니가 필요한 걸 어떻게 알았니?
Alex: 엄마가 지난번에 저녁 먹을 때 말씀하셨어요.
Mom: 아주 멋지구나! 이 바구니가 아주 좋은 걸. 색깔이 아주 다양하구나.
Alex: 엄마가 좋아하시니 저도 기뻐요.

Listen & Talk 2 B

Yujin: _____ _____ _____ _____ _____ _____ _____ _____ _____ _____. Do you want to hear about it?

Jack: Sure. _____ _____ _____ _____, Yujin?

Yujin: Many children in his town couldn't go to school and _____ _____ _____. So he taught them in his house every day.

Jack: That's a great story.

Yujin: _____ _____ _____ _____ _____.

Real Life Communication

Emily: Welcome back, Brian. _____ _____ _____ _____?

Brian: Yes, thanks. I tried to study _____ _____ _____ in the hospital, but it was hard.

Emily: _____ _____ _____ _____ _____. Why don't you _____ _____ _____ _____?

Brian: Did you start a study group? That's wonderful.

Emily: Thanks. I think that _____ _____ _____ _____ _____ _____ _____ _____ _____.

Brian: I agree. I'll try hard to be a good member. _____ _____ _____ _____.

Emily: You're welcome. I'm glad you like my idea.

Let's Check 1

Henry: Your bag _____ _____. _____ _____ _____ _____.

Sujin: Thanks. _____ _____ _____ _____ _____ _____?

Henry: It's over there. I'll carry your bag to the bus stop for you.

Sujin: You're very kind.

Henry: _____ _____. I am going that way, too.

[01~02] 다음 대화를 읽고 물음에 답하시오.

Henry: Your bag looks heavy. (A)Let me help you.
Sujin: Thanks. Where is the bus stop around here?
Henry: It's over there. I'll carry your bag to the bus stop for you.
Sujin: You're very kind.
Henry: No problem. I am going that way, too.

01 위 대화의 밑줄 친 (A)의 의도로 적절한 것은?

① 도움 요청하기　　　　② 도움 제안하기
③ 도움 거절하기　　　　④ 충고 구하기
⑤ 선호 표현하기

02 위 대화의 내용과 일치하지 <u>않는</u> 것은?

① Sujin's bag looked heavy.
② Henry helped Sujin by carrying her bag.
③ Sujin was looking for the bus stop.
④ Henry was going to the taxi stop.
⑤ Sujin appreciated Henry's help.

[03~04] 다음 대화를 읽고 물음에 답하시오.

Alex: Mom, this is ⓐfor you. I made it ⓑwith plastic bags.
Mom: That's very cute, Alex. How did you know ⓒwhich I needed a new basket?
Alex: You talked about it when we were having dinner the ⓓother day.
Mom: ⓔHow nice! I really like this basket. It has many different colors.
Alex: I'm glad you like it.

03 위 대화의 밑줄 친 ⓐ~ⓔ 중 어법상 <u>틀린</u> 것을 찾아 바르게 고치시오.

➡ _____

04 위 대화의 내용과 일치하지 <u>않는</u> 것은?

① Alex는 엄마에게 바구니를 만들어 드렸다.
② Alex는 비닐봉지로 바구니를 만들었다.
③ Alex가 만든 바구니는 다양한 색을 갖고 있다.
④ Alex와 엄마는 며칠 전 저녁을 먹기 전 새 바구니를 구매했다.
⑤ 엄마는 Alex의 선물이 마음에 들었다.

01 다음 짝지어진 대화가 어색한 것은?

① A: I can't move the table. Can anybody help me?
  B: Let me help you.
② A: What's the matter with you?
  B: How can I help you?
③ A: It's hard for me to build the model airplane.
  B: I'll help you.
④ A: I can't open the window.
  B: Let me give you a hand.
⑤ A: I can't open the bottle.
  B: May I help you?

[02~04] 다음 대화를 읽고 물음에 답하시오.

Tom: Hojun and I planned to give out free stickers today, but I think he forgot.
Sora: Really? (A)내가 도와줄게.(let) Why are you going to give out stickers?
Tom: It's part of our volunteer club activity.
Sora: I see. What does this sticker mean?
Tom: It means that when we smile at each other, the world will become a better place.
Sora: (B)_____

02 위 대화의 밑줄 친 (A)의 우리말을 주어진 단어를 사용하여 영작하시오.

➡ _____

03 위 대화의 빈칸 (B)에 들어갈 말로 어색한 것은?

① What a great idea!
② That sounds good.
③ Excellent!
④ What a pity!
⑤ That's a wonderful idea.

04 위 대화의 내용과 일치하도록 빈칸을 완성하시오.

W: What does the sticker emphasize?
A: It emphasizes the importance of _____.

[05~06] 다음 대화를 읽고 물음에 답하시오.

Yujin: I read a story about a special boy in India. Do you want to hear about it? (A)
Jack: Sure. Why is he special, Yujin? (B)
Yujin: Many children in his town couldn't go to school and had to work. (C)
Jack: That's a great story. (D)
Yujin: I'm glad you like it. (E)

05 다음 (A)~(E) 중 주어진 문장이 들어가기에 적절한 곳은?

So he taught them in his house every day.

① (A) ② (B) ③ (C) ④ (D) ⑤ (E)

06 위 대화를 읽고 대답할 수 없는 것은?

① What did Yujin read?
② Why was the boy in India special?
③ What should many children in India do instead of going to school?
④ What did Jack think about the story about a special boy in India?
⑤ What did Yujin do to help many children in India?

서답형

07 다음 대화의 내용과 일치하도록 Mike의 일기를 완성하시오.

> Mike: Jimin, what are all these things in the box?
> Jimin: They're for my mentee at the children's center. I'm going to give her my old books today.
> Mike: Do you teach her every weekend?
> Jimin: Yes. I feel happy when I teach her.
> Mike: You are a good mentor. Oh, the box looks heavy. Let me help you.
> Jimin: Thanks.

> Mon, June 24th, 2019
> Today, I was impressed with Jimin. She teaches (A)_____ at the children's center every weekend. In addition, she was going to give (B)_____ to her mentee. She said that (C)_____ when she taught her. I thought (D)_____.
> The box looked heavy, so I helped her. I think that helping others makes the world a better place.

➡ (A) _____
　 (B) _____
　 (C) _____
　 (D) _____

[08~09] 다음 대화를 읽고 물음에 답하시오.

> Emily: Welcome back, Brian. Are you feeling better?
> Brian: Yes, thanks. I tried to study on my own in the hospital, but it was hard.
> Emily: Let me help you. Why don't you join my study group?
> Brian: Did you start a study group? That's wonderful.

> Emily: Thanks. I think that we can learn better when we teach each other.
> Brian: I agree. I'll try hard to be a good member. Thanks for helping me.
> Emily: You're welcome. I'm glad you like my idea.

서답형

08 What did Emily suggest to Brain?

➡ _____

서답형

09 Why did Emily start a study group?

➡ _____

　 _____

서답형

10 다음 대화가 자연스럽게 이어지도록 순서대로 배열하시오.

> (A) Okay, I'll give it a try. Thanks for the tip.
> (B) I'm not good at science. What can I do?
> (C) No problem. I'm glad you like it.
> (D) Let me help you. Why don't you start with easier books?

➡ _____

[11~12] 다음 대화를 읽고 물음에 답하시오.

> Aram: I'm very tired. What should I do?
> Jack: Let me help you. I can give you a massage.
> Aram: Thank you for your help.
> Jack: No problem. I'm glad you liked ⓐit.

서답형

11 위 대화의 밑줄 친 ⓐit이 가리키는 것을 영어로 쓰시오.

➡ _____

서답형

12 What did Jack do to make Aram feel better?

➡ _____

[01~02] 다음 대화를 읽고 물음에 답하시오.

Mike: Jimin, what are all these things in the box?

Jimin: They're for my mentee at the children's center. I'm going to give her my old books today.

Mike: Do you teach her every weekend?

Jimin: Yes. (A)_____

Mike: You are a good (B)m_____. Oh, the box looks heavy. Let me help you.

Jimin: Thanks.

01 다음 빈칸 (A)에 들어갈 말을 보기에 주어진 단어를 모두 배열하여 완성하시오.

┌─ 보기 ┤
happy / when / I / her / teach / feel / I
└─

➡ _____

02 위 대화의 빈칸 (B)에 주어진 영영 풀이가 가리키는 말을 쓰시오.

┌─────────────────────────────┐
someone who teaches or gives help and advice to a less experienced and often younger person
└─────────────────────────────┘

➡ m_____

[03~04] 다음 대화를 읽고 물음에 답하시오.

Yujin: I read a story about a special boy in India. Do you want to hear about it?

Jack: Sure. Why is he special, Yujin?

Yujin: Many children in his town couldn't go to school and had to work. So he taught (A)them in his house every day.

Jack: That's a great story.

Yujin: I'm glad you like it.

03 위 대화의 밑줄 친 (A)them이 가리키는 것을 영어로 쓰시오.

➡ _____

04 위 대화의 내용과 일치하도록 Jack의 담화를 완성하시오.

┌─────────────────────────────┐
Jack: Today, Yujin told me a great story about (A)_____. I was wondering why she said that (B)_____. Yujin said the boy taught many children in his town who (C)_____ in his house every day. It was a great story.
└─────────────────────────────┘

➡ (A) _____
   (B) _____
   (C) _____

[05~06] 다음 대화를 읽고 물음에 답하시오.

Tom: Hojun and I planned to give out free stickers today, but I think he forgot.

Sora: Really? Let me help you then. Why are you going to give out stickers?

Tom: It's part of our volunteer club activity.

Sora: I see. What does this sticker mean?

Tom: It means that when we smile at each other, the world will become a better place.

Sora: That's a wonderful idea.

05 What is Sora going to do to help Tom?

➡ _____

06 Tom이 준비한 스티커의 의미를 우리말로 20자 내외로 서술하시오.

➡ _____

Grammar

① 목적격 관계대명사

- I have a friend **whom** I want you to meet. 나는 네가 만나보기를 원하는 친구가 한 명 있어.
- The chair **which** you gave to me was broken. 네가 나에게 준 의자가 망가졌어.

■ 관계대명사는 두 개의 문장을 하나로 이어주는 접속사 역할을 하면서 동시에 대명사 역할을 한다. 전치사의 목적어 혹은 동사의 목적어였던 대명사를 목적격 관계대명사로 만들어 문장을 하나로 이어준다.

- There were many people in the cafe **which** we visited last week. 〈동사의 목적어〉 우리가 지난주에 방문한 카페에는 사람이 많았어.
- Those boys **who(m)** the woman is looking after look very cute. 〈전치사의 목적어〉 그 여자가 돌보고 있는 저 소년들은 매우 귀여워 보인다.

■ 목적격 관계대명사 who(m), which는 that으로 대체할 수 있으며, 생략 가능하다. 관계대명사가 전치사의 목적어로 사용된 경우 전치사는 동사 뒤에 그대로 두거나, 전치사를 관계대명사 앞으로 보낼 수 있다.

- Mr. Pang **who(m)** the children love teaches how to swim to them. 그 아이들이 사랑하는 Pang씨는 그들에게 수영하는 방법을 가르친다.
- She never touched food **which** she didn't like. 그녀는 좋아하지 않는 음식에는 손도 대지 않았다.
- The i-pad **which** I got from my father was my birthday present. 내가 아버지로부터 받은 그 아이패드는 내 생일 선물이었어.
- The areas **which** you have mentioned have some problems. 네가 언급한 그 지역에는 몇 가지 문제점이 있어.
- The missing boy **who(m)** people were looking for came home last night. 사람들이 찾던 그 실종 소년이 어젯밤 집으로 왔다.
- Tell me about the people **who(m)** you cared for in the hospital. 네가 병원에서 돌봤던 사람들에 관해 말해줘.

핵심 Check

1. 다음 우리말과 같도록 빈칸에 알맞은 말을 쓰시오.

   (1) 이것은 그가 작년에 산 집이다.

   ➡ This is the house _____ he bought last year.

   (2) 나는 모두가 천재라고 생각하는 한 남자를 안다.

   ➡ I know a man _____ everyone thinks a genius.

② to부정사를 목적격보어로 취하는 동사

> • Dan **persuaded** me **to buy** the computer for him. Dan은 내가 그를 위해 컴퓨터를 사도록 설득했다.
>
> • Andrea **expected** us **to welcome** her. Andrea는 우리가 그녀를 환영하리라고 기대했다.

■ '동사+목적어+to V' 형태로 목적어가 to부정사의 주체가 되도록 해석한다.

　• I don't **want** her **to see** my portfolio. 나는 그녀가 나의 포트폴리오를 보는 걸 원치 않아.

　• Mom **persuaded** me **to do** my homework first. 엄마는 내가 숙제를 먼저 하도록 설득하셨다.

■ to부정사를 목적격보어로 취하는 동사에는 allow, ask, tell, advise, get, force, require, order, persuade, encourage, enable, cause, need, want, help, would like, teach, expect 등이 있다.

　• Our teacher **encourages** us **to think** of others before us. 우리 선생님은 우리가 우리보다 타인을 먼저 생각하도록 권장하신다.

　• We **would like** you **to have** a cup of tea. 우리는 당신이 차 한 잔 하길 원합니다.

■ to부정사 목적격보어의 부정형은 'not to V'로 표현한다.

　• My lawyer **advised** me **not to say a word**. 나의 변호사는 내게 한마디도 하지 말라고 조언했다.

　• Dad **ordered** me **not to go** out at night. 아빠는 내게 밤에 나가지 말라고 명령하셨다.

■ make, have, let은 원형부정사를 목적격보어로 취하는 사역동사이다. '목적어가 V하게 하다'로 해석한다.

　• She **let** me **go** shopping with my friends. 그녀는 내가 친구들과 함께 쇼핑하러 가게 허락했다.

　• What **made** you **break** the promise? 무엇이 너로 하여금 그 약속을 어기게 만든 거야?

핵심 Check

2. 다음 우리말과 같도록 빈칸에 알맞은 말을 쓰시오.

(1) Julia는 우리가 그와 악수하도록 설득했다.

➡ Julia ＿＿＿＿ us ＿＿＿＿ ＿＿＿＿ hands with him.

(2) 나는 그들이 훨씬 더 많이 먹으리라고 예상한다.

➡ I ＿＿＿＿ them ＿＿＿＿＿＿ much more.

(3) 그 여자는 그녀의 아들에게 늦지 말라고 말했다.

➡ The woman ＿＿＿＿ her son ＿＿＿＿ ＿＿＿＿ ＿＿＿＿ late.

01 다음 문장에서 어법상 <u>어색한</u> 부분을 바르게 고쳐 쓰시오.

(1) The eggs who I bought are very fresh.

_____ ➡ _____

(2) The building which John built were huge.

_____ ➡ _____

(3) I believe that it will enable us continue this work together.

_____ ➡ _____

(4) Will you allow me to passing, please?

_____ ➡ _____

02 괄호 안에 주어진 단어를 어법에 맞게 빈칸에 쓰시오.

(1) The man whom I fell in love with _____ near my house now.
(live)

(2) The race _____ you took part in was very successful. (which)

(3) The police told them _____ calm. (stay)

(4) We encouraged her _____ a new life. (start)

03 주어진 단어를 바르게 배열하여 다음 우리말을 영어로 쓰시오. 필요하다면 단어를 추가하거나 변형하시오.

(1) 이것은 그들이 필요로 했던 테이블이다. (need / this / is / the / they / table)

➡ _____

(2) 그녀는 내가 주관한 어떤 회의에 왔어요. (I / a meeting / she / come / that / run / to)

➡ _____

(3) 우리는 그들이 열심히 일하도록 강요할 수 없어. (hard / can't / them / we / work / force)

➡ _____

(4) 무엇이 네가 그렇게 생각하게 만들었니? (so / think / what / you / make)

➡ _____

01 다음 빈칸에 알맞은 말을 모두 고르시오.

> You can find the things _____ you need in the refrigerator.

① who   ② whom   ③ that
④ which   ⑤ whose

02 다음 빈칸에 들어갈 말로 적절한 것은?

> 이것은 어제 엄마가 내게 사주신 신발이다.
> = These are the shoes _____ yesterday.

① whom my mom bought for her
② which I bought for my mom
③ that was bought for my mom
④ which my mom bought for me
⑤ that was bought to me by mom

03 다음 빈칸에 적절하지 않은 것은?

> _____ to save time.

① The plan enabled us
② He wanted me
③ She encouraged us
④ Our boss made us
⑤ Mom advised us

서답형
04 주어진 단어와 적절한 관계대명사를 이용하여 다음 우리말을 영어로 쓰시오.

> 그는 내가 가진 모든 돈을 쓰도록 허락하지 않았다.
> (allow / use / all / have)

➡ _____
_____

05 다음 밑줄 친 부분 중 생략할 수 없는 것은?

① Is she the girl <u>who</u> you talked about?
② The milk <u>which</u> I bought went bad.
③ This is the letter <u>that</u> he sent me.
④ This is the jacket <u>which</u> you brought.
⑤ It is true <u>that</u> he spread the rumor.

06 다음 우리말을 영어로 바르게 옮긴 것은?

> 부산에 있는 작은 가게들은 사람들로 붐빈다.

① Small shops in Busan was crowded with people.
② There were small shops in Busan.
③ Small shops in Busan are crowded with people.
④ Busan has small shops which are run by many people.
⑤ There are small shops in Busan which many people run.

07 다음 중 빈칸에 들어갈 동사 'play'의 형태가 <u>다른</u> 하나는?

① Mom didn't allow me _____ the piano at night.
② My parents encouraged me _____ the flute in front of the guests.
③ We decided _____ soccer after school.
④ Many radio stations refused _____ the music.
⑤ Are you interested in _____ music on the stage?

08 다음 우리말에 맞게 빈칸에 알맞은 말을 쓰시오.

네가 해야 하는 다음 단계는 그것을 끓이는 것이다.

The next step _____ _____ _____

_____ is _____ _____ it.

09 다음 중 어법상 바르지 <u>않은</u> 것은?

① Some flowers which you picked are on the table.
② Would you like me to speak at the dinner?
③ My advice caused him stop smoking.
④ Is this the yogurt you brought?
⑤ I need you to sign for it.

10 다음 중 어법상 바른 문장의 개수는?

ⓐ The toys in the room is not mine.
ⓑ I don't think that she wanted me do the job.
ⓒ Did you find the key that you were looking for?
ⓓ The car he drives is very old.
ⓔ Ms. Henderson requires us handing in the reports as soon as possible.

① 1개   ② 2개   ③ 3개
④ 4개   ⑤ 5개

11 다음 중 빈칸에 적절하지 <u>않은</u> 것은?

The doctor _____ my dad to drink lots of water.

① advises   ② encourages   ③ tells
④ persuades   ⑤ has

12 다음 두 문장을 하나의 문장으로 만드시오.

• Do you remember those people?
• You met them on holiday.

➡ _____

_____

13 다음 중 보기의 밑줄 친 that과 쓰임이 같은 것은?

┤ 보기 ├
Why aren't you wearing the watch that you borrowed from me?

① Did you know <u>that</u> he came back from Toronto?
② He doesn't know the fact <u>that</u> you don't want to believe it.
③ Most people think <u>that</u> the Beatles is the best pop group.
④ Kelly said <u>that</u> she made some mistakes.
⑤ She is using the pan <u>that</u> I gave to her.

14 다음 중 어법상 옳은 것끼리 바르게 짝지어진 것은?

• A rabbit is an animal [who / which] every child loves.
• Persuade him [tell / to tell] us what he knows.
• He made me [pay / to pay] the bill at the restaurant.

① who – tell – pay
② which – tell – pay
③ who – to tell – to pay
④ which – to tell – pay
⑤ which – to tell – to pay

15 다음 빈칸에 공통으로 들어갈 말로 가장 적절한 것은?

> • Have you noticed _____ many Italian foods have tomatoes in them?
> • The coat _____ the girl is wearing does not look special.

① who   ② which   ③ that
④ whom   ⑤ whose

서답형
16 주어진 단어를 빈칸에 어법에 맞게 쓰시오.

> I want you _____ _____ _____
> _____ _____ because I need a mentor who can help me with math.
> (help / with)

중요
17 다음 중 빈칸에 들어갈 관계대명사의 쓰임이 <u>다른</u> 하나는?

① The students _____ we chose are diligent and honest.
② The candies _____ the shop sells taste good.
③ The performance _____ he saw has been loved by many people.
④ The camera _____ many people love is too expensive.
⑤ A shampoo bottle _____ is in the bathroom is empty.

서답형
18 다음 우리말 의미에 맞게 빈칸에 알맞은 말을 쓰시오.

> 여기에 어제 내가 했던 두 가지 흥미로운 일이 있다.
> Here are two interesting things _____
> _____ _____.

서답형
19 주어진 단어를 활용하여 다음 빈칸에 알맞은 말을 쓰시오.

> 나가, 그렇지 않으면 우리가 너희를 나가게 만들 거야.
> Get out, or _____ _____ _____
> _____ _____ go out. (force)

서답형
20 주어진 어구를 바르게 배열하여 다음 우리말을 영어로 쓰시오.

> 네가 해서는 안 되는 유일한 것은 다른 사람들이 이야기하는 도중에 끼어드는 것이다.
> (cut in / the only thing / you / while / are talking / others / that / should not do / is / to)

➡ _____
_____

21 다음 중 어법상 바르지 <u>않은</u> 것은?

> Can you ①do me a favor? There ②is ③ one thing ④that I need you ⑤do for me.

중요
22 다음 중 빈칸에 들어갈 말로 가장 적절한 것은?

> My parents would like me _____ with them.

① to living   ② living   ③ live
④ to live   ⑤ lives

서답형
23 다음 빈칸에 알맞은 말을 쓰시오.

> 그는 우리에게 삶을 사랑하도록 가르쳤어요.
> He _____ _____ _____ _____
> life.

01 다음 주어진 동사를 문맥과 어법에 맞게 빈칸에 쓰시오.

> know / clean / be / believe / focus

- The elderly are people who _____ old.
- If you want to learn Hangul, let me _____ . I will teach you.
- Do you expect me _____ such a nonsense story?
- Mom got me _____ my room.
- The boss ordered us _____ on the job.

02 다음 대화를 읽고 주어진 단어를 활용하여 Hannah에 관하여 쓰시오.

> **Clark:** Do you know how to play the piano?
> **Hannah:** Yes, I do. My cousin taught me.

(teach / Hannah)

➡ _____

03 주어진 단어를 활용하여 다음 우리말을 영어로 쓰시오.

> 넌 내가 무엇을 하길 원하는 거야?
> (what / want / do)

➡ _____

04 다음 상황을 읽고 빈칸에 알맞은 말을 쓰시오.

> There was a girl who listened to music a little loudly in the library. So Peter said to the girl, "Would you turn down the music?"

➡ Peter asked _____

05 다음 보기와 같이 하나의 문장을 두 개의 문장으로 나누시오.

> ┤ 보기 ├
> Have you been to the place which Mary visited last year?
> ➡ Have you been to the place?
> ➡ Mary visited the place last year.

(1) Kyle has the money he found on the street.
   ➡ _____
   ➡ _____

(2) Is this the book that you are looking for?
   ➡ _____
   ➡ _____

06 주어진 단어를 활용하여 James와 Olivia의 대화 내용을 한 문장으로 요약하시오.

> **Olivia:** I have had a stomachache for a few days.
> **James:** Oh, I'm so sorry. Did you see a doctor?
> **Olivia:** No, I didn't.
> **James:** You should see a doctor.

> (advise)

➡ _____

07 주어진 단어를 바르게 나열하여 다음 우리말을 영어로 쓰시오. 필요하다면 단어를 변형하시오.

> 내가 지원했던 그 일자리를 얻길 원해.
> (to / apply / I / I / that / the / for / job / get / want)

➡ _____

08 대화를 읽고 주어진 단어를 활용하여 빈칸에 알맞은 말을 쓰시오.

> Jason: I want to go shopping with Ann.
> Mom: You can go on Monday.

> allow

➡ Jason's mom _____

_____

09 주어진 문장과 같은 의미가 되도록 빈칸에 알맞은 말을 쓰시오.

> Emma asked me, "Can you play the guitar for me?"

➡ Emma asked me _____

10 주어진 단어를 바르게 배열하여 다음 우리말을 영어로 쓰시오. 필요하다면 단어를 추가하거나 변형하시오.

> 그들이 발달시킨 그 기술은 우리가 안전하게 자동차를 운전하는 것을 가능하게 한다.
> (safely / the / technology / a car / that / develop / they / enable / drive / us / have)

➡ _____

_____

11 주어진 단어를 활용하여 다음 우리말을 영어로 쓰시오. 필요하다면 단어를 변형하시오.

> 나는 John이 공원에서 발견했던 그 고양이를 좋아해.
> (like / find / at the park)

➡ _____

12 주어진 단어를 활용하여 빈칸에 알맞은 말을 쓰시오.

> 독감은 사람들에게 두통을 유발할 수 있다.
> The flu can _____
> (cause / have)

➡ _____

13 다음 두 개의 문장을 하나의 문장으로 연결하시오.

(1) Osaka is the city. My sister visited the city last week.

➡ _____

_____

(2) Robert is an actor. We like him very much.

➡ _____

(3) My dad gave me the wallet. I really wanted to have it.

➡ _____

_____

14 다음 우리말을 영어로 쓰시오.

> 내가 할 수 있는 유일한 것은 조용히 하는 거야.
> = The only thing _____ _____
> _____ _____ _____
> _____ _____ .

15 주어진 단어를 바르게 배열하여 문장을 완성하시오.

> Sandra _____ _____ _____
> _____ a good vacation.
> (have / me / told / to)

Small but Great Ideas

Here are two stories which I read yesterday. Do you want to hear about
목적격 관계대명사(= that) 생략 가능   want의 목적어

them?
= two stories which I read yesterday

Call Someone You Love
Call someone. + You love someone.

New York had many pay phones on its streets. However, nobody really
부정주어로서 문장 전체를 부정의 뜻으로 만들며 '아무도 ～ 않다'라는 뜻

used them. One day, a man came up with an idea. He stuck coins to
어느 날   stick - stuck - stuck

one of the phones. He also put up a sign that said, "Call Someone You
stick A to B: A를 B에 붙이다   He also put up a sign. + The sign said. "Call Someone (who(m)[that]

Love." Soon, many people were using the phone.
You Love."   과거진행형

When they were talking to someone whom they loved, they didn't
= that

stop smiling. His idea became a big success. During the day, all the
stop+Ving: V하는 것을 멈추다

coins disappeared. The man was very happy because his small idea
이유를 나타내는 접속사

gave happiness to many people.
give ～ to ... : ～을 …에게 주다 (3형식)

hear: 듣다
pay phone: 공중전화
one day: (과거의) 어느 날
come up with: (생각이) 떠오르다
put up: 세우다
say: (글·글씨 등이) 쓰이다
sign: 표지판
success: 성공
during the day: 낮 동안
disappear: 사라지다

📎 확인문제

● 다음 문장이 본문의 내용과 일치하면 T, 일치하지 않으면 F를 쓰시오.

1 The first story is about what happened in New York. ☐

2 It was hard to see people using a pay phone. ☐

3 The man stuck a coin to some pay phones. ☐

4 People couldn't call someone they loved because they had no coins. ☐

5 It took several days for all the coins to disappear. ☐

The Red Arrow Man

A few years ago, the maps at bus stops in Seoul were very confusing.
몇 년 전에   주어   the maps 수식

They didn't have enough information. People had to ask others to
=The maps   ask ~ to ... : ~에게 … 해 달라고 요청하다

explain the maps. "Where is this bus stop on the map? Does this bus

go to Gwanghwamun?" Many people often took the wrong bus and
버스를 잘못 탔다

wasted their time.

One day, a young man decided to solve this problem. He bought
(과거의) 어느 날   decided의 목적어

lots of red arrow stickers. Every day he rode his bicycle around the
=many   ride-rode-ridden

city and stuck the stickers on the bus maps. Nobody asked him to do
stick-stuck-stuck

this. He just wanted to help others. Thanks to his effort, people could
버스 지도에 빨간 스티커를 붙이는 일   =other people   ~ 덕분에

understand the maps easily and save time.

arrow: 화살, 화살표
few: 몇몇의
map: 지도
bus stop: 버스 정류장
confusing: 혼란스러운
waste one's time: ~의 시간을 낭비하다
thanks to: ~ 덕택에
understand: 이해하다
easily: 쉽게
save: 절약하다

 확인문제

● 다음 문장이 본문의 내용과 일치하면 T, 일치하지 않으면 F를 쓰시오.

1 People in Seoul were confused by the bus maps. ☐

2 The bus maps had plenty of information in the past. ☐

3 There was someone who forced a young man to stick the stickers. ☐

4 What the man wanted to do was to help others. ☐

5 He borrowed some money to buy arrow stickers. ☐

● 우리말을 참고하여 빈칸에 알맞은 말을 쓰시오.

Small but Great Ideas

1 Here _____ two stories _____ I read yesterday.

2 Do you want _____ _____ about _____?

3 Call Someone _____ _____.

4 New York _____ many pay phones on its streets.

5 _____, _____ really used them.

6 One day, a man _____ _____ _____ an idea.

7 He _____ coins _____ one of the phones.

8 He also _____ _____ a sign _____ _____, "Call Someone You Love."

9 Soon, many people _____ _____ the phone.

10 _____ they were talking to someone _____ _____ _____, they didn't stop _____.

11 His idea became _____ _____ _____.

12 _____ the day, all the coins _____.

13 The man was very happy _____ his small idea gave _____ _____ many people.

작지만 위대한 아이디어

1 여기 내가 어제 읽은 이야기가 두 개 있어.

2 들어볼래?

3 당신이 사랑하는 누군가에게 전화하세요.

4 뉴욕에는 길거리에 공중전화가 많이 있었다.

5 그러나 아무도 그것들을 실제로 사용하지는 않았다.

6 어느 날, 한 남자에게 좋은 아이디어가 떠올랐다.

7 그는 공중전화 하나에 동전들을 붙였다.

8 그는 또한 "당신이 사랑하는 사람에게 전화하세요."라고 쓰인 표지판을 설치했다.

9 곧, 많은 사람들이 그 전화기를 사용하고 있었다.

10 그들이 사랑하는 누군가에게 전화하고 있을 때, 그들은 미소 짓기를 멈추지 않았다.

11 그의 아이디어는 커다란 성공이었다.

12 낮 동안, 모든 동전이 사라졌다.

13 그 남자는 자신의 작은 아이디어가 많은 사람에게 행복을 가져다주었기 때문에 매우 행복했다.

14 The Red _____ _____

15 _____ _____ _____ _____, the maps at bus stops in Seoul _____ very _____.

16 They didn't have _____ _____.

17 People had to _____ _____ _____ _____ the maps.

18 "_____ is this bus stop _____ the map? Does this bus _____ _____ Gwanghwamun?"

19 Many people _____ _____ the wrong bus and _____ their time.

20 One day, a young man _____ _____ _____ this problem.

21 He bought _____ _____ _____ _____ _____ _____.

22 Every day he _____ his bicycle _____ the city and _____ the stickers _____ the bus maps.

23 Nobody _____ _____ _____ _____ this.

24 He just _____ _____ _____ others.

25 _____ _____ his effort, people could understand the maps _____ and _____ _____.

14 빨간 화살표 청년

15 몇 년 전에, 서울의 버스 정류장의 지도는 매우 혼란스러웠다.

16 지도에는 충분한 정보가 없었다.

17 사람들은 다른 사람들에게 지도를 설명해 달라고 요청해야 했다.

18 "이 버스 정류장은 지도의 어디에 있는 건가요? 이 버스가 광화문으로 가나요?"

19 많은 사람이 종종 버스를 잘못 타서 시간을 낭비하곤 했다.

20 어느 날, 한 젊은 청년이 이 문제를 해결해 보기로 했다.

21 그는 빨간 화살표 스티커를 많이 샀다.

22 매일 그는 자전거를 타고 서울 시내를 돌아다니며 버스 지도에 스티커를 붙였다.

23 아무도 그 청년에게 이 일을 하라고 요청하지 않았다.

24 그는 단지 다른 사람들을 돕고 싶었다.

25 그의 노력 덕분에, 사람들은 지도를 쉽게 이해하고 시간을 절약할 수 있었다.

● 우리말을 참고하여 본문을 영작하시오.

여기 내가 어제 읽은 이야기가 두 개 있어.

1 ➡ _____

들어볼래?

2 ➡ _____

당신이 사랑하는 누군가에게 전화하세요.

3 ➡ _____

뉴욕에는 길거리에 공중전화가 많이 있었다.

4 ➡ _____

그러나 아무도 그것들을 실제로 사용하지는 않았다.

5 ➡ _____

어느 날, 한 남자에게 좋은 아이디어가 떠올랐다.

6 ➡ _____

그는 공중전화 하나에 동전들을 붙였다.

7 ➡ _____

그는 또한 "당신이 사랑하는 사람에게 전화하세요."라고 쓰인 표지판을 설치했다.

8 ➡ _____

곧, 많은 사람들이 그 전화기를 사용하고 있었다.

9 ➡ _____

그들이 사랑하는 누군가에게 전화하고 있을 때, 그들은 미소 짓기를 멈추지 않았다.

10 ➡ _____

그의 아이디어는 커다란 성공이었다.

11 ➡ _____

낮 동안, 모든 동전이 사라졌다.

12 ➡ _____

13 그 남자는 자신의 작은 아이디어가 많은 사람에게 행복을 가져다주었기 때문에 매우 행복했다.

➡ _____

14 빨간 화살표 청년

➡ _____

15 몇 년 전, 서울의 버스 정류장의 지도는 매우 혼란스러웠다.

➡ _____

16 지도에는 충분한 정보가 없었다.

➡ _____

17 사람들은 다른 사람들에게 지도를 설명해 달라고 요청해야 했다.

➡ _____

18 "이 버스 정류장은 지도의 어디에 있는 건가요? 이 버스가 광화문으로 가나요?"

➡ _____

19 많은 사람이 종종 버스를 잘못 타서 시간을 낭비하곤 했다.

➡ _____

20 어느 날, 한 젊은 청년이 이 문제를 해결해 보기로 했다.

➡ _____

21 그는 빨간 화살표 스티커를 많이 샀다.

➡ _____

22 매일 그는 자전거를 타고 서울 시내를 돌아다니며 버스 지도에 스티커를 붙였다.

➡ _____

23 아무도 그 청년에게 이 일을 하라고 요청하지 않았다.

➡ _____

24 그는 단지 다른 사람들을 돕고 싶었다.

➡ _____

25 그의 노력 덕분에, 사람들은 지도를 쉽게 이해하고 시간을 절약할 수 있었다.

➡ _____

[01~08] 다음 글을 읽고 물음에 답하시오.

Here are two stories which I read yesterday. Do you want to hear (A)[from / about] ⓐ them?

Call Someone You Love

New York had many pay phones on its streets. ⓑ_____, nobody really used (B)[it / them]. ① One day, a man came up with an idea. He stuck coins to one of the phones. ② He also put up a sign that said, "Call Someone You Love." ③ When they were talking to someone ⓒ_____ they loved, they didn't stop smiling. ④ His idea became a big success. (C)[During / While] the day, all the coins disappeared. ⑤ The man was very happy because his small idea gave happiness ⓓ_____ many people.

서답형

01 밑줄 친 ⓐ가 가리키는 것을 6단어의 영어로 쓰시오.

➡ _____

02 다음 중 빈칸 ⓑ에 들어갈 말로 가장 적절한 것은?

① Therefore　　② As a result
③ In addition　　④ For example
⑤ However

서답형

03 빈칸 ⓒ에 알맞은 말을 모두 쓰시오.

➡ _____

중요
04 다음 중 빈칸 ⓓ에 들어갈 말로 가장 적절한 것은?

① in　　② to　　③ on
④ for　　⑤ by

05 ①~⑤ 중 주어진 문장이 들어가기에 가장 적절한 곳은?

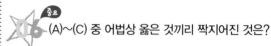
Soon, many people were using the phone.

①　　②　　③　　④　　⑤

중요
06 (A)~(C) 중 어법상 옳은 것끼리 짝지어진 것은?

① from – it – During
② about – it – During
③ from – them – While
④ about – them – During
⑤ from – it – while

07 다음 중 위 글을 읽고 답할 수 있는 것은?

① How many pay phones were there on New York streets?
② Why did nobody use the pay phones?
③ Who stuck coins to a pay phone?
④ How many coins were stuck to a pay phone?
⑤ How many coins did each person use?

서답형

08 주어진 단어를 이용하여 다음 질문에 완전한 문장의 영어로 답하시오.

Q: What did the sign say?
A: _____ (it)

➡ _____

[09~15] 다음 글을 읽고 물음에 답하시오.

The Red Arrow Man

(A)[A few / A little] years ago, the maps ⓐ_____ bus stops in Seoul were very (B)[confusing / confused]. They didn't have enough information. People had to ask others to explain the maps. "Where is this bus stop on the map? Does this bus go to Gwanghwamun?" Many people often took the wrong bus and ⓑ_____ (C)[its / their] time.

One day, a young man decided to solve this problem. He bought lots of red arrow stickers. Every day he rode his bicycle around the city and stuck the stickers on the bus maps. Nobody asked him ⓒto do this. He just wanted to help others. ⓓ_____ his effort, people could understand the maps easily and ⓔsave time.

09 다음 중 빈칸 ⓐ에 들어갈 말과 같은 것은?

① Did you turn _____ the light in the livingroom?
② I was surprised _____ the news.
③ Dad will pick you _____ at five.
④ Please take care _____ yourself.
⑤ Do you mind waiting _____ a little while?

서답형
10 빈칸 ⓑ에 밑줄 친 ⓔ의 반의어를 어법에 맞게 쓰시오.

➡ _____

서답형
11 밑줄 친 ⓒ가 의미하는 것을 우리말로 쓰시오.

➡ _____
_____

12 다음 중 빈칸 ⓓ에 들어갈 말로 가장 적절한 것은?

① Despite   ② Instead of
③ Thanks to   ④ At last
⑤ Depending on

중요
13 (A)~(C) 중 어법상 옳은 것끼리 짝지어진 것은?

① A few – confusing – its
② A little – confused – its
③ A few – confusing – their
④ A little – confused – their
⑤ A few – confused – their

서답형
14 Write the reason why people often took the wrong bus in Seoul. Use the words 'because', 'there', and 'on the maps.'

➡ _____
_____

15 다음 중 위 글의 내용과 일치하지 않는 것은?

① People needed some explanation about the maps.
② There were people who took the wrong bus because of the maps.
③ A young man had an idea to solve the problem of the maps.
④ Somebody wanted the young man to stick the stickers.
⑤ A young man used his bicycle in order to stick the stickers.

[16~22] 다음 글을 읽고 물음에 답하시오.

Here are two stories which I read yesterday. Do you want ⓐ_____ about them?

Call Someone You Love
New York had many pay phones ⓑ_____ its streets. However, nobody really used them. One day, a man came up with an idea. He stuck coins to one of the phones. He also put up a sign (A)that said, "Call Someone You Love." (B)Soon, many people were using (C)the phone. When they were ⓒ_____ to someone whom they loved, they didn't stop smiling. His idea became a big success. During the day, all the coins disappeared. The man was very happy because his small idea gave happiness to many people.

서답형
16 주어진 단어를 어법과 문맥에 맞게 빈칸 ⓐ와 ⓒ에 쓰시오.

> talk / hear

➡ ⓐ _____ ⓒ _____

17 다음 중 빈칸 ⓑ에 들어갈 말과 같은 것은?
① Are you interested _____ studying English?
② She was not satisficd _____ the result.
③ Ms. Han wanted us to pay attention _____ her class.
④ He likes to take care _____ plants.
⑤ He is the person you can depend _____.

서답형
18 다음과 같이 풀이되는 단어를 위 글에서 찾아 쓰시오.

> to stop being visible

➡ _____

19 다음 중 밑줄 친 (A)와 쓰임이 다른 하나는?
① Is he the boy that you talked with?
② The man and his dog that are running together look happy.
③ Do you remember the story that Miranda told you?
④ I want to say that he is my hero.
⑤ Kyle showed me the watch that was really expensive.

20 다음 중 밑줄 친 (B)를 대신하여 쓰일 수 있는 것은?
① For a long time   ② Before long
③ Hardly   ④ Still
⑤ Lately

서답형
21 다음은 밑줄 친 (C)를 설명하는 문장이다. 빈칸에 알맞은 말을 쓰시오.

> the phone _____ the man _____ _____ _____.

22 다음 중 위 글의 내용과 일치하지 않는 것은?
① I read a couple of stories yesterday.
② Many pay phones were on the streets in New York.
③ Not everyone used pay phones.
④ A man stuck some coins to a pay phone.
⑤ All the coins were used during the day.

서답형

23 다음 주어진 문장과 자연스럽게 연결되도록 (A)~(C)를 바르게 나열하시오.

New York had many pay phones on its streets.

(A) He also put up a sign that said, "Call Someone You Love." Soon, many people were using the phone.

(B) However, nobody really used them. One day, a man came up with an idea. He stuck coins to one of the phones.

(C) When they were talking to someone whom they loved, they didn't stop smiling. His idea became a big success.

➡ _____

[24~30] 다음 글을 읽고 물음에 답하시오.

The Red Arrow Man

A few years ago, the maps at bus stops in Seoul were very ⓐ_____. They didn't have enough information. ⓑPeople had to ask others explain the maps. "Where is this bus stop ⓒ_____ the map? Does this bus go to Gwanghwamun?" Many people often took ①the wrong bus and wasted their time.

One day, a young man decided to ②solve this problem. He bought lots of red arrow stickers. Every day he rode his bicycle around the city and ③stuck the stickers ⓓ_____ the bus maps. ④Nobody asked him to do this. He just wanted to ⑤bother others. Thanks to his effort, people could understand the maps easily and save time.

24 다음 중 빈칸 ⓐ에 들어갈 말로 가장 적절한 것은?

① rare
② confusing
③ easy
④ familiar
⑤ common

서답형

25 밑줄 친 ⓑ에서 어법상 바르지 않은 것을 찾아 바르게 고쳐 쓰시오.

➡ _____

26 빈칸 ⓒ와 ⓓ에 공통으로 들어갈 말로 가장 적절한 것은?

① at
② by
③ on
④ under
⑤ about

중요

27 ①~⑤ 중 글의 흐름상 어색한 것은?

①   ②   ③   ④   ⑤

서답형

28 다음 질문에 완전한 문장의 영어로 답하시오.

Q: What was the problem with the bus maps in Seoul?

➡ _____

29 다음 중 위 글을 읽고 알 수 없는 것은?

① 서울 버스 정류장의 지도에 부족했던 것
② 사람들이 버스를 잘못 탄 이유
③ 광화문으로 가는 버스 번호
④ 청년이 산 스티커 모양
⑤ 청년이 자전거를 타고 돌아다니며 한 일

서답형

30 글의 내용에 맞게 다음 빈칸에 알맞은 말을 쓰시오.

Thanks to the young man's effort, people in _____ could take the _____ bus and _____.

[01~09] 다음 글을 읽고 물음에 답하시오.

ⓐHere are two stories which I read yesterday. Do you want to hear about them?

ⓑCall Someone You Love
New York had many pay phones on its streets. However, nobody really used ⓒthem. One day, a man came up with an idea. He stuck coins to one of the phones. He also put up a sign that said, "Call Someone You Love." Soon, many people were using the phone. When they were talking to someone whom they loved, ⓓthey didn't stop smiling. His idea became a big success. During the day, all the coins disappeared. The man was very (A)_____ because ⓔhis small idea gave (B)_____ to ⓕmany people.

01 주어진 단어를 어법에 맞게 빈칸 (A)와 (B)에 쓰시오.

happy

➡ (A) _____ (B) _____

02 적절한 대명사를 이용하여 밑줄 친 ⓐ를 두 개의 문장으로 나누어 쓰시오.

➡ _____
➡ _____

03 밑줄 친 ⓑ에는 생략된 단어가 있다. 생략하지 않은 문장으로 다시 쓰시오.

➡ _____

04 밑줄 친 ⓒ가 가리키는 것을 위 글에서 찾아 쓰시오.

➡ _____

05 주어진 동사를 이용하여 밑줄 친 ⓓ와 같은 의미의 문장을 쓰시오.

keep

➡ _____

06 다음은 밑줄 친 ⓔ의 의미를 영어로 쓴 것이다. 적절한 관계대명사를 이용하여 빈칸에 알맞은 말을 쓰시오.

sticking _____ to one of the phones
_____ _____ _____

07 적절한 관계대명사를 이용하여 밑줄 친ⓕ를 설명하는 문장을 완성하시오.

many people _____ used the phone with _____.

08 글의 내용에 맞게 다음 대화의 빈칸에 알맞은 말을 쓰시오.

A: What did a man _____ to one of the pay phones?
B: He _____ _____ to one of them. I think he wanted people _____ _____ the phone to call _____ they loved.

09 글의 내용에 맞게 다음 빈칸에 알맞은 말을 쓰시오.

The man stuck coins to one of the phones as well as _____ _____ _____ _____.

[10~18] 다음 글을 읽고 물음에 답하시오.

The Red Arrow Man

A few years ago, the maps at bus stops in Seoul were very confusing. ⓐThey didn't have enough information. People had to ask others to explain the maps. "Where is this bus stop on the map? Does this bus go to Gwanghwamun?" Many people often took the wrong bus and wasted their time.

One day, a young man decided to solve this problem. He bought lots of red arrow stickers. Every day he rode his bicycle around the city and stuck the stickers on the bus maps. ⓑNobody asked him to do this. He just wanted to help others. Thanks to his effort, people could understand the maps easily and save time.

10 밑줄 친 ⓐ가 가리키는 것을 위 글에서 찾아 쓰시오.

➡ _____

11 다음은 밑줄 친 ⓑ와 같은 의미의 문장이다. 적절한 관계대명사를 이용하여 빈칸에 알맞은 말을 쓰시오.

There was no one _____ _____
_____ _____ _____ _____ .

12 Why did people have to ask others to explain the maps at bus stops in Seoul?

➡ It was because _____
_____

13 글의 내용에 맞게 다음 물음에 완전한 문장의 영어로 답하시오.

Q: What did the young man stick on the bus maps?

➡ _____

14 주어진 단어를 이용하여 다음 우리말을 영어로 쓰시오.

그의 노력은 사람들이 지도를 쉽게 이해하는 것을 가능하게 했다. (enable)

➡ _____
_____

15 글의 내용에 맞게 다음 빈칸에 알맞은 말을 쓰시오.

The color of the stickers _____ the young man bought _____ _____ .

16 다음은 위 글을 요약한 것이다. 빈칸에 알맞은 말을 쓰시오.

The bus maps in Seoul were very _____. So, a young man stuck red arrow stickers on _____. Thanks to him, people didn't have to _____ their time.

17 주어진 단어를 이용하여 다음 우리말을 영어로 쓰시오.

나는 버스 정류장의 지도들이 충분한 정보를 가지길 원했다. (want)

➡ _____
_____

18 Write the reason why the man stuck red arrow stickers on bus maps every day. Use the phrase 'it's because'.

➡ _____

Real Life Communication B

A: I'm not good at science. What can I do?
be good at: ~을 잘하다

B: Let me help you. Why don't you start with easier books?
~하는 게 어때?(= How about ~?= Let's~)

A: Okay, I'll give it a try. Thanks for the tip.
한번 해 보다

B: No problem. I'm glad you like it.

구문해설 • try: 시도 • tip: 조언

A: 나는 과학을 잘 못해. 어떻게 해야 할까?

B: 내가 도와줄게. 더 쉬운 책으로 시작하는 게 어때?

A: 응, 한번 시도 해볼게. 조언 고마워.

B: 괜찮아. 네가 좋아하니 기뻐.

Let's Write

Be a Mentor!

My name is Semi and I'm in the second grade. I want to help my mentee with
　　　　　　　　　　　　　　　2학년에　　　　　　to부정사를 목적어로 취하는 동사
her homework. I can meet my mentee after school. I'll ask my mentee to be on
　　　　　　　　　　　　　　　　　　　　　　　ask+목적어+to부정사: 목적어가 V하도록 요청하다
time. I think a good mentor can be a good friend. So I want to become a good
　　　　　　think의 목적어가 되는 명사절　　　　　그래서
friend whom my mentee can trust.
목적격 관계대명사로 생략 가능

구문해설 • grade: 점수, 학년 • mentor: 멘토(경험 없는 사람에게 오랜 기간에 걸쳐 조언과 도움을 베풀어 주는 선배)
• mentee: 멘티(멘토로부터 상담이나 조언을 받는 사람) • after school: 방과 후에
• be on time: 시간을 지키다

멘토가 되세요!

제 이름은 세미이고 저는 2학년입니다. 저는 제 멘티의 숙제를 돕고 싶습니다. 저는 방과 후에 제 멘티를 만날 수 있습니다. 저는 제 멘티에게 시간을 지키라고 요청할 것입니다. 저는 좋은 멘토는 좋은 친구가 될 수 있다고 생각합니다. 그래서 저는 제 멘티가 믿을 수 있는 좋은 친구가 되고 싶습니다.

Culture & Life

Do you see toys inside the bars of soap? Children in South Africa wash their
　　　　　　　　　　toys를 수식하는 형용사구
hands more often to get the toys. Washing your hands can prevent many health
　　　　　　　　to부정사의 부사적 용법 중 '목적'　　동명사(주어)
problems. Thanks to this idea, fewer children are getting sick.
　　　　　　　~ 덕분에　　　　　few의 비교급

구문해설 • bar: 바, 막대 • inside: ~ 안에 • South Africa: 남아프리카 • get: 얻다 • prevent: 예방하다
• get sick: 병에 걸리다

비누들 안에 들어 있는 장난감이 보이나요? 남아프리카의 어린이들은 장난감을 갖기 위해 더 자주 손을 씻습니다. 손을 씻는 것은 많은 건강 문제를 막을 수 있습니다. 이 아이디어 덕분에, 병에 걸리는 어린이들이 줄어들고 있습니다.

영역별 핵심문제

01 다음 영영풀이가 가리키는 것을 고르시오.

> a device or room that is used to keep things cold

① toaster   ② refrigerator

③ closet   ④ stove

⑤ blender

02 다음 중 밑줄 친 부분의 뜻풀이가 바르지 <u>않은</u> 것은?

① They <u>plan</u> to go abroad after graduating from high school. ~할 계획이다

② You need much <u>effort</u> to finish the project.　여유

③ Each student found out a different <u>solution</u> to the problem. 해결책

④ Where should we put our <u>trash</u>? 쓰레기

⑤ I put my jeans in the <u>basket</u>. 바구니

03 다음 우리말에 맞게 빈칸에 알맞은 말을 쓰시오.

(1) 너의 시간을 낭비하지 마라.
➡ Don't _____ _____ _____.

(2) 너는 그 문제를 네 스스로 해결해야 한다.
➡ You should solve the problem _____ _____ _____.

(3) 그는 컴퓨터 게임을 멈추고 나를 바라보았다.
➡ He _____ _____ computer games and looked at me.

04 다음 짝지어진 단어의 관계가 같도록 빈칸에 알맞은 말을 쓰시오.

> teacher : student = mentor : _____

05 다음 문장의 빈칸에 들어갈 말을 보기에서 골라 쓰시오.

> ┤ 보기 ├─
> the other day / come up with / on your own

(1) We can _____ _____ _____ creative ideas.

(2) _____ _____ _____, I came across my English teacher on the street.

(3) I can't believe you made it _____ _____ _____.

06 다음 주어진 문장의 밑줄 친 rest와 <u>다른</u> 의미로 쓰인 것은?

> • The riders can take a <u>rest</u> at the parking lot.

① It is important for me to have an hour for <u>rest</u> during work.

② We needed a <u>rest</u> for a while because we didn't stop working.

③ You look so tired. Get some <u>rest</u>.

④ You'd better stop singing for a while and try to <u>rest</u>.

⑤ The <u>rest</u> of students spent time reading the books in the library.

Conversation

[07~09] 다음 대화를 읽고 물음에 답하시오.

Tom: Hojun and I planned to give out free stickers today, but I think he forgot.

Sora: Really? (A)Let me help you then. Why are you going to give out stickers?

Tom: It's part of our volunteer club activity.

Sora: I see. What does this sticker mean?

Tom: It means that when we smile at each other, the world will become a better place.

Sora: That's a wonderful idea.

07 위 대화의 밑줄 친 (A)와 바꾸어 쓸 수 있는 것은?

① Can you help me then?
② Let me give you a hand then.
③ I need your help then.
④ Would you help me then?
⑤ I wonder if you can help me then.

08 위 대화에서 다음 영영풀이가 뜻하는 말을 찾아 쓰시오.

> a person who does a job without being paid for it

➡ _____

09 위 대화의 내용과 일치하지 않는 것은?

① Hojun과 Tom은 함께 봉사활동을 할 계획이었다.
② Sora가 Hojun 대신 Tom을 도와 줄 것이다.
③ Tom은 무료 스티커를 나누어 줄 계획이다.
④ 스티커는 우리가 서로 웃을 때 세상은 더 좋은 곳이 될 것이라는 것을 의미한다.
⑤ Sora는 Tom과 같은 봉사 동아리에서 활동하고 있다.

[10~12] 다음 대화를 읽고 물음에 답하시오.

Mike: Jimin, what are all these things in the box?

Jimin: (A) I'm going to give her my old books today.

Mike: (B) Do you teach her every weekend?

Jimin: (C) Yes. I feel ⓐhappy when I teach her.

Mike: (D) You are a good mentor. Oh, the box looks heavy. Let me help you.

Jimin: (E) Thanks.

10 위 대화의 (A)~(E) 중 주어진 문장이 들어가기에 적절한 곳은?

> They're for my mentee at the children's center.

① (A) ② (B) ③ (C) ④ (D) ⑤ (E)

11 위 대화의 밑줄 친 ⓐ와 바꾸어 쓸 수 없는 것은? (2개)

① delighted   ② pleased
③ joyful   ④ amazing
⑤ discouraged

12 위 대화의 내용과 일치하지 않는 것은?

① Jimin teaches her mentee at the children's center.
② Jimin is going to give her old books to her mentee.
③ Jimin meets her mentee every weekend.
④ Mike is going to give his hand to Jimin.
⑤ Mike is going to read some books at the children's center.

[13~15] 다음 대화를 읽고 물음에 답하시오.

Alex: Mom, this is for you. I made it with plastic bags. ⓐ

Mom: That's very cute, Alex. ⓑ

Alex: You talked about it when we were having dinner the other day. ⓒ

Mom: How nice! I really like this basket. It has many different colors. ⓓ

Alex: I'm glad you like it. ⓔ

13 위 대화의 ⓐ~ⓔ 중 주어진 문장이 들어가기에 적절한 곳은?

How did you know that I needed a new basket?

① ⓐ ② ⓑ ③ ⓒ ④ ⓓ ⑤ ⓔ

14 What did Alex make for her mom?

➡ _____

15 When did Alex's mom talk about a new basket?

➡ _____

_____

16 다음 대화가 자연스럽게 이어지도록 순서대로 배열하시오.

(A) I'm glad you like it.

(B) That's a great story.

(C) Sure. Why is he special, Yujin?

(D) I read a story about a special boy in India. Do you want to hear about it?

(E) Many children in his town couldn't go to school and had to work. So he taught them in his house every day.

➡ _____

Grammar

17 다음 빈칸에 들어갈 말로 가장 적절한 것은?

The man warned us _____ the house. Because the roof of the house leaks.

① buy ② not buying
③ buying ④ not to buy
⑤ not to buying

18 다음 빈칸에 알맞은 말을 쓰시오.

Korea is one of the countries ⓐ_____ lacks water. So teachers advise us ⓑ_____ water when we take a shower. Because saving water is the most important thing that we can do now.

➡ ⓐ _____ ⓑ _____

19 다음 대화의 빈칸에 들어갈 말이 바르게 짝지어진 것은?

A: I want you _____ me what Katie's favorite flower is.

B: Tulips are the flowers _____ Katie likes most.

① tell – whose ② telling – which
③ to tell – that ④ to tell – what
⑤ telling – what

20 다음 중 빈칸에 공통으로 들어갈 말로 가장 적절한 것은?

• The novel _____ she wrote ten years ago is going to be published again.

• Ann, _____ hat do you like better, this or that?

① which ② that ③ who
④ whose ⑤ whom

21 다음 중 어법상 바르지 않은 것은?

① The poor management caused the disease to spread fast.
② Slow music helps us to stay calm and think carefully.
③ The teacher ordered us not to make any troubles.
④ I would like you accept my apology.
⑤ Don't let her stay alone in the park at night.

22 다음 우리말을 영어로 옮길 때 빈칸에 알맞은 말을 쓰시오.

• 그녀에게 이 편지를 복사하라고 요청해 주겠니?
= Can you _____ _____ _____ this letter?

23 다음 중 어법상 바르지 않은 것은?

The bananas ①which my friend ② wanted ③me ④to taste yesterday ⑤ was very sweet.

24 밑줄 친 부분 중 생략할 수 없는 것은?

① He is the boy that my mom always compares with me.
② The tree that you planted grows well.
③ Did you think about the suggestion that I made?
④ I want to become a good friend that my friends can trust.
⑤ There are kids that have been left alone all day.

25 다음 빈칸에 적절하지 않은 것은?

My mentor _____ me to do my best.

① persuaded   ② wanted
③ advised   ④ told
⑤ said

Reading

[26~29] 다음 글을 읽고 물음에 답하시오.

Here ①are two stories which I read yesterday. Do you want to hear about them?

Call Someone You Love
New York had many pay phones on its streets. However, (A)[everybody / nobody] really used ②them. One day, a man (B)[came up with / came down with] an idea. He ③stuck coins to one of the phones. He also put up a sign that said, "Call Someone You Love." Soon, many people were ④used the phone. When they were talking to someone ⓐ _____, they didn't stop ⑤smiling. His idea became a big success. During the day, all the coins (C)[appeared / disappeared]. The man was very happy because his small idea gave happiness to many people.

26 알맞은 관계대명사를 이용하여 빈칸 ⓐ에 들어갈 말을 세 단어로 쓰시오.

➡ _____

27 (A)~(C)에서 글의 흐름상 적절한 것끼리 바르게 짝지은 것은?

① everybody – came up with – appeared
② nobody – came up with – disappeared
③ everybody – came down with – appeared
④ nobody – came down with – disappeared
⑤ everybody – came up with – disappeared

28 ①~⑤ 중 어법상 틀린 것을 찾아 바르게 고치시오.

➡ _____

29 다음 중 글을 읽고 답할 수 <u>없는</u> 것은?

① What idea did a man come up with?
② Where were the pay phones in New York?
③ When did people start to use the pay phone?
④ What did people keep doing while using the pay phone?
⑤ How many phone calls did people make?

[30~34] 다음 글을 읽고 물음에 답하시오.

The Red Arrow Man
A few years ago, the maps at bus stops in Seoul were very confusing. They didn't have enough information. People had to ask others (A)_____ the maps. "Where is this bus stop on the map? Does this bus go to Gwanghwamun?" Many people often ⓐtook the wrong bus and wasted their time.
One day, a young man decided (B)_____ this problem. ① Every day he rode his bicycle around the city and stuck the stickers on the bus maps. ② Nobody asked him (C)_____ this. ③ He just wanted to help others. ④ Thanks to his effort, people could understand the maps easily and save time. ⑤

30 주어진 단어를 문맥과 어법에 맞게 빈칸 (A)~(C)에 쓰시오.

(solve / explain / do)

➡ (A) _____ (B) _____ (C) _____

31 ①~⑤ 중 다음 문장이 들어가기에 가장 적절한 곳은?

He bought lots of red arrow stickers.

①   ②   ③   ④   ⑤

32 다음 중 밑줄 친 ⓐ와 의미가 같은 것은?

① Do you take sugar in your coffee?
② I will take the black jacket.
③ Katherine forgot to take her purse with her.
④ What are you going to take to get there?
⑤ Can you take my hand for a moment?

33 다음 중 위 글의 내용과 일치하지 <u>않는</u> 것은?

① The maps at bus stops in Seoul made people confused a few years ago.
② There wasn't enough information on the maps.
③ People in Seoul took the wrong bus all the time.
④ The young man stuck stickers on his own.
⑤ The man thought that his effort would help other people.

34 위 글의 내용에 맞게 다음 물음에 완전한 문장의 영어로 답하시오.

Q: What happened to people because of the bus maps?

➡ _____
_____

[01~03] 다음 대화를 읽고 물음에 답하시오.

> Tom: Hojun and I planned to give out ⓐfree stickers today, but I think he forgot.
>
> Sora: (A) Why are you going to give out stickers?
>
> Tom: (B) It's part of our volunteer club activity.
>
> Sora: (C) I see. What does this sticker mean?
>
> Tom: (D) It means that when we smile at each other, the world will become a better place.
>
> Sora: (E) That's a wonderful idea.

✎ 출제율 90%

01 위 대화의 (A)~(E) 중 주어진 문장이 들어가기에 적절한 곳은?

> Really? Let me help you then.

① (A) ② (B) ③ (C) ④ (D) ⑤ (E)

✎ 출제율 95%

02 위 대화의 밑줄 친 ⓐfree와 같은 의미로 쓰인 것은?

① They are fighting for free speech.

② Jane felt free like a bird.

③ I usually listen to music in my free time.

④ Please feel free to contact me.

⑤ We don't have to pay for the drinks because they're all free.

✎ 출제율 90%

03 위 대화를 읽고 대답할 수 없는 것은?

① What did Hojun and Tom plan to do today?

② Why did Tom want to give out stickers?

③ What did the stickers mean?

④ Which club did Tom belong to?

⑤ Why didn't Hojun appear to do his volunteer club activity?

[04~05] 다음 대화를 읽고 물음에 답하시오.

> Alex: Mom, this is for you. I made it with plastic bags.
>
> Mom: That's very cute, Alex. How did you know that I needed a new basket?
>
> Alex: You talked about it when we were having dinner the other day.
>
> Mom: (A)How nice! I really like this basket. It has many different colors.
>
> Alex: (B)엄마가 좋아하시니 저도 기뻐요. (glad)

✎ 출제율 95%

04 위 대화의 밑줄 친 (A)와 바꾸어 쓸 수 있는 것을 <u>모두</u> 고르시오.

① How nice the basket is!

② How much is it?

③ What do you think about it?

④ How is the basket?

⑤ What a nice basket!

✎ 출제율 90%

05 위 대화의 밑줄 친 우리말 (B)를 주어진 단어를 사용하여 영작하시오.

➡ _____

[06~07] 다음 대화를 읽고 물음에 답하시오.

> Yujin: I read a story about a special boy in India. Do you want to hear about it?
>
> Jack: Sure. Why is he special, Yujin?
>
> Yujin: Many children in his town couldn't go to school and had to work. So he taught them in his house every day.
>
> Jack: (A)_____
>
> Yujin: I'm glad you like it.

06 위 대화의 빈칸 (A)에 들어갈 말로 <u>어색한</u> 것은?

① It's so touching.
② What a beautiful story!
③ How wonderful it is!
④ That's a great story.
⑤ I'm sorry to hear that.

07 위 대화의 내용과 일치하도록 빈칸을 완성하시오.

> Q: Why was the boy in India special?
> A: Because he taught (A)_____
> _____ who (B)_____
> _____ in his house
> every day.

[08~10] 다음 대화를 읽고 물음에 답하시오.

Emily: Welcome back, Brian. Are you feeling ⓐbetter?
Brian: Yes, thanks. I tried to study on my own in the hospital, but it was hard.
Emily: Let me help you. (A)Why don't you join my study group? (how)
Brian: Did you start a study group? That's ⓑwonderful.
Emily: Thanks. I think that we can learn ⓒbetter when we teach each other.
Brian: I ⓓdisagree. I'll try hard to be a good member. Thanks for helping me.
Emily: You're welcome. I'm ⓔglad you like my idea.

08 위 대화의 밑줄 친 (A)와 바꾸어 쓸 수 있는 말을 주어진 단어를 사용하여 쓰시오.

➡ _____

09 위 대화의 밑줄 친 ⓐ~ⓔ 중 대화의 흐름상 <u>어색한</u> 말을 찾아 바르게 고치시오.

➡ _____

10 위 대화의 내용과 일치하지 <u>않는</u> 것은?

① Brian은 몸이 좋지 않았었다.
② Emily는 스터디 모임을 시작했다.
③ Emily는 서로 가르쳐 주면 더 잘 배울 수 있을 것이라고 생각한다.
④ Emily는 Brain에게 스터디 모임에 함께 할 것을 제안하였다.
⑤ Brain은 Emily와 함께 병원에서 공부하였다.

11 다음 빈칸에 들어갈 말이 바르게 짝지어진 것은?

> • The thing _____ Ann asked me _____ is preparing for the party.

① which – do
② that – doing
③ what – to do
④ which – to do
⑤ that – did

12 다음 우리말을 영어로 옮길 때 빈칸에 들어갈 말로 가장 적절한 것은?

> 내가 답변해 주기를 원하는 질문이 뭐니?
> What is the question _____?

① that you want to ask
② which you want me to answer
③ that you want to answer
④ which I want to answer
⑤ that I want you to answer

13 다음 중 어법상 바르지 <u>않은</u> 것은?

① I want you to consider the option.
② The cup that is on the table is mine.
③ Men who work hard is diligent.
④ Molly will ask you to help her.
⑤ Don't tell me to join the club.

14 주어진 단어를 활용하여 다음 우리말을 영어로 쓰시오. (출제율 85%)

> 내가 사고 싶은 차는 미니밴(minivan)이야.
> (that)

➡ _____

15 다음 두 문장을 하나의 문장으로 쓰시오. (출제율 90%)

(1) He gave some candies to the little kids. He saw them.

➡ _____

(2) There was a festival. Many people took part in the festival.

➡ _____

(3) The dish was not that expensive. You broke it.

➡ _____

16 다음 상황을 읽고 빈칸에 알맞은 말을 쓰시오. (출제율 95%)

> I felt a little cold. When I looked around, I found that the window was open. Jimmy sat next to the window. So I asked Jimmy _____ _____ _____ _____.

17 다음 중 보기의 밑줄 친 that과 쓰임이 같은 것은? (출제율 100%)

> ┌─ 보기 ─┐
> The fact that you lied to me never changes.

① Jack is the man that saved my life.
② The train that you took is slow.
③ I heard the news that you won the game.
④ The pen that you bought is here.
⑤ Always cook the foods that you eat.

[18~21] 다음 글을 읽고 물음에 답하시오.

Here are two stories which I read yesterday. Do you want to hear about them?

Call Someone You Love
New York had many pay phones on its streets. However, nobody really used them. One day, a man came up with an idea. He stuck coins to one of the phones. He also put up a sign ⓐ_____ said, "Call Someone You Love." Soon, many people were using the phone. When they were talking to someone whom they loved, they didn't stop smiling. His idea became a big success. During the day, all the coins disappeared. The man was very happy because his small idea gave happiness to many people.

18 빈칸 ⓐ에 알맞은 말을 모두 쓰시오. (출제율 90%)

➡ _____

19 다음 중 글의 내용과 일치하는 것의 개수는? (출제율 95%)

> ⓐ There are many public telephones in New York.
> ⓑ People in New York enjoy using a public phone.
> ⓒ It is difficult to know who stuck the coins to the phone.
> ⓓ People used all the coins during the day.
> ⓔ The man thought his idea failed in the end.

① 1개   ② 2개   ③ 3개
④ 4개   ⑤ 5개

📝 출제율 90%

20 다음 중 위 글에 이어질 내용으로 가장 적절한 것은?

① what I did yesterday
② another story I wrote
③ another interesting story I heard
④ the other story I read
⑤ other people I called

📝 출제율 95%

21 글의 내용에 맞게 빈칸에 알맞은 말을 쓰시오.

> His small idea gave happiness to many people, so _____.

📝 출제율 90%

22 주어진 문장과 자연스러운 연결이 되도록 (A)~(D)를 바르게 나열하시오.

> A few years ago, the maps at bus stops in Seoul were very confusing.

(A) "Where is this bus stop on the map? Does this bus go to Gwanghwamun?" Many people often took the wrong bus and wasted their time.

(B) Every day he rode his bicycle around the city and stuck the stickers on the bus maps. Nobody asked him to do this. He just wanted to help others.

(C) One day, a young man decided to solve this problem. He bought lots of red arrow stickers.

(D) They didn't have enough information. People had to ask others to explain the maps.

➡ _____

[23~25] 다음 글을 읽고 물음에 답하시오.

The Red Arrow Man

A few years ago, the maps at bus stops in Seoul were very confusing. They didn't have enough information. People had to ask others to explain the maps. "Where is this bus stop on the map? Does this bus go to Gwanghwamun?" Many people often took the wrong bus and wasted their time.

One day, a young man decided to solve this problem. He bought lots of red arrow stickers. Every day he rode his bicycle around the city and stuck the stickers on the bus maps. Nobody asked him to ⓐdo this. He just wanted to help others. Thanks to his effort, people could understand the maps easily and save time.

📝 출제율 90%

23 위 글의 밑줄 친 ⓐdo this가 가리키는 것을 우리말로 간단히 쓰시오.

➡ _____

📝 출제율 95%

24 다음 중 위 글의 내용과 일치하지 않는 것은?

① The maps at bus stops in Seoul were not easy to understand.
② The stickers that the man bought were arrow shapes.
③ The young man had his bike.
④ What the man wanted was to help other people.
⑤ The man stuck the stickers every weekend.

📝 출제율 85%

25 What happened after the young man's effort? Answer in English with a full sentence.

➡ _____

_____

[01~03] 다음 대화를 읽고 물음에 답하시오.

Mike: Jimin, what are all these things in the box?

Jimin: They're for my mentee at the children's center. I'm going to give her my old books today.

Mike: Do you teach her every weekend?

Jimin: Yes. I feel happy when I teach her.

Mike: You are a good mentor. Oh, the box looks heavy. Let me help you.

Jimin: Thanks.

01 What is Jimin going to give to her mentee today?

➡ _____

02 How does Jimin feel when she teaches her mentee?

➡ _____

03 What is Mike going to do to help Jimin?

➡ _____

04 다음 빈칸에 알맞은 말을 쓰시오.

> The dentist told me _____ _____ my mouth. But I was so scared that I couldn't open it.

05 주어진 단어를 활용하여 다음 우리말을 영어로 쓰시오.

> 너는 우리가 도서관에서 대출한 그 책을 가지고 있니?
> (have / which / check out / from)

➡ _____
_____

06 주어진 단어를 활용하여 다음 문장과 같은 의미의 문장을 쓰시오.

> My mom let me stay out late.
> (allow)

➡ _____

07 다음 상황을 읽고 주어진 단어를 활용하여 빈칸을 알맞게 채우시오.

> Paul: Jimmy, would you get in line, please? We are all waiting in line here.

> ask

➡ Paul _____.

08 적절한 관계대명사를 이용하여 다음 우리말을 영어로 쓰시오.

> 네가 읽고 있는 책은 흥미롭니?

➡ _____

09 다음 우리말에 맞도록 빈칸에 알맞은 말을 쓰시오.

> 어제 네가 길에서 이야기하고 있었던 소년은 누구였니?
> Who was the boy _____ _____
> _____ on the street yesterday?

Call Someone You Love

New York had many pay phones on its streets. However, nobody really used them. One day, ⓐa man came up with an idea. He stuck coins ①to one of the ②phones. He also put up a sign that ③said, "Call Someone You Love." Soon, many people were using the phone. When they were talking to someone whom they loved, they didn't stop ④to smile. His idea became ⑤a big success. During the day, all the coins disappeared. The man was very happy because his small idea gave happiness to many people.

10 ①~⑤ 중 어법상 틀린 것을 골라 바르게 고치시오.

➡ _____

11 다음은 밑줄 친 ⓐ와의 대화이다. 빈칸에 알맞은 말을 쓰시오.

> A: What are you doing?
> B: I am _____ _____ to this pay phone.
> A: Why?
> B: It will enable people _____ _____ someone _____ _____. And people will have an interest in using pay phones.
> A: What a great idea!

12 글의 내용에 맞도록 다음 물음의 대답을 완성하시오.

> Q: Why was the man happy?
> A: It's because _____.

➡ _____

The Red Arrow Man

A few years ago, the maps at bus stops in Seoul were very confusing. They didn't have enough information. People had to ask others to explain the maps. "Where is this bus stop on the map? Does this bus go to Gwanghwamun?" Many people often took the wrong bus and wasted their time.

One day, a young man decided to solve this problem. He bought lots of red arrow stickers. Every day he rode his bicycle around the city and stuck the stickers on the bus maps. Nobody asked him to do this. He just wanted to help others. Thanks to his effort, people could understand the maps easily and save time.

13 다음 우리말에 맞게 빈칸에 알맞은 말을 쓰시오.

> 그가 그 문제를 해결하기 위하여 산 것들은 빨간 화살표 스티커였다.
> The things _____ _____ _____
> _____ _____ were red arrow stickers.

14 What did people have to do to take the right bus in Seoul? Answer in English with a full sentence.

➡ _____

창의사고력 서술형 문제

01 다음 대화의 내용과 일치하도록 Brian의 일기를 완성하시오.

Emily: Welcome back, Brian. Are you feeling better?
Brian: Yes, thanks. I tried to study on my own in the hospital, but it was hard.
Emily: Let me help you. Why don't you join my study group?
Brian: Did you start a study group? That's wonderful.
Emily: Thanks. I think that we can learn better when we teach each other.
Brian: I agree. I'll try hard to be a good member. Thanks for helping me.
Emily: You're welcome. I'm glad you like my idea.

⬇

Tue, May 28th, 2019
I was happy to come back to school. Emily welcomed me very warmly. We talked about lots of things including study. While I was in the hospital, I tried to study (A)_____ but it was hard. When I talked about it to Emily, she gave me a hand. She suggested (B)_____. She started it because she thought that (C)_____. I agreed to her idea. I decided to (D)_____. I really appreciated her.

02 알맞은 관계대명사를 이용하여 다음 사물이나 직업을 설명하는 문장을 완성하시오.

a painter / a purse / a baker / a chair

(1) _____

(2) _____

(3) _____

(4) _____

03 주어진 동사로 여러 가지 문장을 쓰시오.

ask / encourage / force / enable / allow / tell

(1) _____

(2) _____

(3) _____

(4) _____

(5) _____

단원별 모의고사

01 다음 짝지어진 단어의 관계가 같도록 빈칸에 알맞은 말을 쓰시오.

> same : different = inside : _____

02 다음 영영풀이가 가리키는 것을 고르시오.

> a person who is advised and helped by more experienced person

① mentee　　　② teacher
③ mentor　　　④ professor
⑤ president

03 다음 우리말을 주어진 단어를 이용하여 영작하시오.

(1) 박쥐는 대개 낮 동안에 잠을 잔다. (mostly, during)

➡ _____

(2) 나는 나의 엄마에게 전화하기 위해 공중전화를 사용했다. (pay, call, mom)

➡ _____

(3) 그는 회의에서 좋은 아이디어를 생각해 냈다. (came, great)

➡ _____

[04~06] 다음 대화를 읽고 물음에 답하시오.

Alex: Mom, this is for you. I made it with plastic bags.
Mom: That's very cute, Alex. How did you know that I needed a new basket?
Alex: You talked about it when we were having dinner the other day.
Mom: (A)_____ nice! I really like this basket. It has many different colors.
Alex: I'm glad you like it.

04 위 대화의 빈칸 (A)와 바꾸어 쓸 수 없는 것은?

① Why　　　② How
③ What　　　④ When
⑤ Where

05 위 대화를 통해 알 수 있는 엄마의 심경으로 적절한 것은?

① lonely　　　② happy
③ nervous　　　④ upset
⑤ dissatisfied

06 위 대화를 읽고 대답할 수 없는 것은?

① What did Alex make for his mom?
② What did Alex use to make his gift for his mom?
③ How did Alex know that his mother needed a new basket?
④ How did Alex feel when his mother liked his gift?
⑤ Where did Alex learn how to make a basket?

[07~09] 다음 대화를 읽고 물음에 답하시오.

Emily: Welcome back, Brian. Are you feeling better?
Brian: Yes, thanks. I tried to study (A)[of / on] my own in the hospital, but it was hard.
Emily: Let me help you. Why don't you join my study group?
Brian: Did you start a study group? That's wonderful.
Emily: Thanks. I think (B)[which / that] we can learn better when we teach each other.

Brian: I agree. I'll try hard to be a good member. Thanks for helping me.

Emily: (D)_____ I'm glad you (C)[like / to like] my idea.

07 위 대화의 괄호 (A)~(C)에서 알맞은 말을 고르시오.

➡ (A)_____, (B)_____, (C)_____

08 위 대화의 빈칸 (D)에 들어가기에 어색한 것은?

① Don't mention it.
② It's my pleasure.
③ Not at all.
④ You're welcome.
⑤ Don't blame me.

09 위 대화를 읽고 대답할 수 없는 것은?

① What did Brian try to do in the hospital?
② What did Emily start?
③ What did Emily suggest to Brian?
④ What did Emily think about a study group?
⑤ What did Emily and Brain learn in a study group?

[10~11] 다음 대화를 읽고 물음에 답하시오.

Henry: Your bag looks heavy. Let me help you.

Sujin: Thanks. Where is the bus stop around here?

Henry: It's over there. I'll carry your bag to the bus stop for you.

Sujin: You're very kind.

Henry: No problem. I am going that way, too.

10 What was Sujin looking for?

➡ _____

11 How did Henry help Sujin?

➡ _____

12 다음 중 짝지어진 대화가 어색한 것은?

① A: I made this picture frame for you.
   B: Thanks. It's wonderful.
② A: Sounds great. I like your story.
   B: I'm glad you like it.
③ A: You're so kind to say like that.
   B: My pleasure.
④ A: I really appreciate your help.
   B: Don't mention it.
⑤ A: I enjoyed baking this cake for you.
   B: I'm sorry to hear that.

13 다음 중 빈칸에 공통으로 들어갈 말로 가장 적절한 것은?

• The dog _____ you take care of has a long tail.
• The children _____ she is looking at look excited.

① that   ② which   ③ whose
④ who   ⑤ what

14 다음 빈칸에 알맞은 말을 쓰시오.

I don't like to eat vegetables. But my mother wants me _____ _____ them.

15 다음 중 빈칸에 들어갈 말로 적절하지 <u>않은</u> 것은?

> I _____ you to answer the phone.

① would like   ② want
③ ask   ④ allow
⑤ make

16 주어진 어구를 활용하여 다음 우리말을 영어로 쓰시오.

> 나는 많은 사람들이 아주 좋아할 영화를 만들고 싶어.
> (a movie / will love)

➡ _____

17 주어진 어구를 바르게 배열하여 다음 우리말을 영어로 쓰시오. 필요하다면 단어를 추가하시오.

> 그 선생님은 우리에게 정각에 오라고 말씀하셨다.
> (on / the teacher / be / us / time / told)

➡ _____

[18~21] 다음 글을 읽고 물음에 답하시오.

Call Someone You Love
New York had many pay phones on its streets. However, nobody really used them. One day, a man came up with an idea. He stuck coins to one of the phones. He also put up a sign that said, "Call Someone You Love." Soon, many people were using the phone. When they were talking to someone whom they loved, they didn't stop (A)smiling. His idea became a big success. During the day, all the coins disappeared. The man was very happy (B) _____ his small idea gave happiness to many people.

18 밑줄 친 (A)와 쓰임이 <u>다른</u> 하나는?

① I am tired of <u>hearing</u> the noise.
② Do you mind <u>opening</u> the door?
③ Norman finished <u>reading</u> the paper.
④ What are they <u>doing</u> now?
⑤ The boys practiced <u>playing</u> soccer after school.

19 다음 중 빈칸 (B)에 들어갈 말로 적절한 것을 <u>모두</u> 고르면?

① though   ② until   ③ as
④ if   ⑤ because

20 다음 중 글의 내용과 일치하는 것은?

① Everybody used play phones in New York.
② A man stuck coins to a pay phone in New York.
③ A man talked with people about using pay phones.
④ People started to use the pay phone after having a conversation with the man.
⑤ Many coins were left at night.

21 주어진 어구를 바르게 배열하여 위 글을 요약하는 문장을 완성하시오.

> (thanks to / when / someone they loved / many people in New York / a man's idea / became happy / they called).

➡ _____
_____
_____

[22~25] 다음 글을 읽고 물음에 답하시오.

The Red Arrow Man

A few years ago, the maps at bus stops in Seoul (A)[was / were] very confusing. They didn't have enough information. People had to ask others to explain the maps. "Where is this bus stop on the map? Does this bus go to Gwanghwamun?" Many people (B)[often took / took often] the wrong bus and wasted their time.

One day, a young man decided to solve this problem. He bought ⓐ_____ red arrow stickers. Every day he rode his bicycle around the city and stuck (C)[it / them] on the bus maps. Nobody asked him to do this. He just wanted to help others. Thanks to his effort, people could understand the maps easily and save time.

22 다음 중 빈칸 ⓐ에 들어갈 말로 적절하지 <u>않은</u> 것은?

① lots of   ② many
③ a lot of   ④ a number of
⑤ much

23 (A)~(C)에서 어법상 옳은 것끼리 바르게 짝지은 것은?

① was – often took – it
② were – often took – them
③ was – took often – it
④ were – took often – it
⑤ was – took often – them

24 다음 중 위 글을 읽고 답할 수 있는 것의 개수는?

ⓐ What was the matter with the maps at bus stops in Seoul?
ⓑ How many bus stops were there in Seoul a few years ago?
ⓒ What bus did people take to go to Gwanghwamun?
ⓓ What did the man do to solve the problem?
ⓔ Why did people often take the wrong bus?

① 1개   ② 2개   ③ 3개
④ 4개   ⑤ 5개

25 위 글의 내용에 맞게 빈칸에 알맞은 말을 쓰시오.

The young man wanted to help _____ _____ _____ the maps easily.

For a Healthy Summer

🎤 의사소통 기능

- 유감·동정 표현하기
  I'm sorry to hear that.

- 당부하기
  Make sure you wear a hat.

🎤 언어 형식

- something+형용사
  I want **something cold** to drink.

- 현재완료
  I've finished my dinner.

Words & Expressions

Key Words

- **advice** [ædváis] 명 충고, 조언
- **bite** [bait] 명 (벌레에) 물린 상처 동 (벌레가) 물다
- **brush** [brʌʃ] 동 ~을 닦다
- **blood** [blʌd] 명 피
- **bug** [bʌg] 명 벌레
- **bump** [bʌmp] 명 혹, 타박상
- **buzz** [bʌz] 동 윙윙거리다
- **empty** [émpti] 동 비우다
- **female** [fíːmeil] 형 암컷의, 여성의
- **food poisoning** 식중독
- **happen** [hǽpən] 동 일어나다, 발생하다
- **healthy** [hélθi] 형 건강한
- **itch** [itʃ] 동 가렵다
- **itchy** [ítʃi] 형 가려운
- **lay** [lei] 동 (알을) 낳다
- **male** [meil] 형 수컷의, 남성의
- **million** [míljən] 명 100만, 다수
- **miss** [mis] 동 놓치다, 빼먹다
- **mosquito** [məskíːtou] 명 모기
- **pack** [pæk] 동 (가방을) 싸다
- **pointed** [pɔ́intid] 형 뾰족한
- **prevent** [privént] 동 예방하다, 방지하다
- **protein** [próutin] 명 단백질
- **reduce** [ridjúːs] 동 줄이다
- **scratch** [skrætʃ] 동 긁다
- **sense** [sens] 동 느끼다, 감지하다
- **sharp** [ʃɑːrp] 형 날카로운
- **sink** [siŋk] 명 (부엌의) 수채 동 가라앉다
- **sleeve** [sliːv] 명 (옷의) 소매, 소맷자락
- **standing** [stǽndiŋ] 형 괴어 있는
- **stomach** [stʌ́mək] 명 위, 복부, 배
- **strange** [streindʒ] 형 이상한
- **sunburn** [sʌ́nbərn] 명 햇볕에 탐, 그을림
- **sunscreen** [sʌ́nskrìːn] 명 자외선 차단제
- **sure** [ʃuər] 형 확실한
- **sweat** [swet] 명 땀 동 땀을 흘리다
- **sweaty** [swéti] 형 땀에 젖은
- **thirsty** [θə́ːrsti] 형 목마른
- **tiny** [táini] 형 아주 작은
- **trash** [træʃ] 명 쓰레기
- **useful** [júːsfəl] 형 유용한
- **wipe** [waip] 명 닦아내는 천[솜]
- **worried** [wə́ːrid] 형 걱정[근심]하는

Key Expressions

- **at that moment** 그때에
- **do better** 더 잘하다
- **feed on** ~을 먹고살다
- **for a while** 당분간
- **go for a walk** 산책 가다
- **I'd love to** ~하고 싶다
- **keep ... in mind** ~을 명심하다
- **lose (~) by** ~(점, 골 등) 차로 (경기에서) 지다
- **stay away from** ~에서 떨어져 있다, 멀리하다
- **suffer from** ~으로 고통받다
- **take ~ to ...** ~을 …로 데려가다[가져가다]

Word Power

※ 서로 반대되는 뜻을 가진 어휘

☐ **male** 수컷의, 남성의 ↔ **female** 암컷의, 여성의

☐ **sharp** 예민한, 날카로운 ↔ **dull** 무딘, 둔한

☐ **empty** 텅 빈 ↔ **full** 가득 찬

☐ **healthy** 건강한 ↔ **unhealthy** 건강하지 못한

☐ **tiny** 아주 작은 ↔ **huge** 거대한

☐ **useful** 유용한 ↔ **useless** 쓸모없는

※ 질병을 나타내는 어휘

☐ **stomachache** 복통

☐ **toothache** 치통

☐ **cough** 기침

☐ **fever** 열

☐ **sore throat** 인후염

☐ **headache** 두통

☐ **cold** 감기

☐ **cancer** 암

☐ **earache** 귀앓이

☐ **runny nose** 콧물

English Dictionary

☐ **bite** 물린 상처
→ a wound made by biting
물려서 만들어진 상처

☐ **bump** 혹, 타박상
→ an area of skin that is raised because it was hit, bitten, etc.
맞거나 물려서 부푼 피부의 한 부분

☐ **buzz** 윙윙거리다
→ to make a low, continuous sound of a flying insect
날아다니는 곤충이 낮고 지속적인 소리를 내다

☐ **happen** 일어나다, 발생하다
→ to take place especially without being planned
특히 계획된 것 없이 발생하다

☐ **itch** 가렵다
→ to have an unpleasant feeling on your skin that makes you want to scratch
피부 위에 당신이 긁고 싶도록 만드는 불쾌한 느낌을 갖다

☐ **lay** (알을) 낳다
→ to produce an egg outside the body
몸 밖에 알을 생산하다

☐ **miss** 놓치다, 빼먹다
→ to fail to do, take, make, or have something
무언가를 하거나 가져가거나 만들거나 소유하지 못하다

☐ **mosquito** 모기
→ a small flying insect that bites the skin of people and animals to suck their blood
사람이나 동물의 피부를 물어 그들의 피를 빠는 작은 날아다니는 곤충

☐ **pack** (가방을) 싸다
→ to put something into a bag so that you can take it with you
무언가를 가방에 넣어 갖고 갈 수 있게 하다

☐ **prevent** 방지하다, 막다
→ to stop something from happening or existing
무언가가 발생하거나 존재하는 것을 막다

☐ **protein** 단백질
→ a substance found in foods such as meat, milk, eggs, and beans
고기, 우유, 계란, 그리고 콩과 같은 음식에서 발견되는 물질

☐ **scratch** 긁다
→ to rub your skin with something sharp
날카로운 무언가로 당신의 피부를 문지르다

☐ **sense** 느끼다, 감지하다
→ to become aware of something even though you can't see it, hear it, etc.
비록 당신이 보거나 들을 수 없지만 무언가를 알아차리게 되다

☐ **sunburn** 햇볕에 탐, 그을림
→ a condition in which your skin becomes sore and red from too much sunshine
너무 많은 햇빛으로 당신의 피부가 쓰리고 붉어진 상태

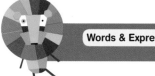
서답형

01 다음 짝지어진 단어의 관계가 같도록 빈칸에 알맞은 말을 쓰시오.

man : woman = male : _____

서답형

02 다음 영영풀이가 가리키는 것을 고르시오.

to rub your skin with something sharp

① scratch　　② prevent
③ bite　　④ buzz
⑤ pack

 중요

03 다음 중 밑줄 친 부분의 뜻풀이가 바르지 않은 것은?

① Almost 5 <u>million</u> people have watched this program. 백만
② Students learn safety rules to <u>prevent</u> the accident. 예방하다
③ Athletes are working out hard in a <u>sweat</u>. 달콤한
④ I felt hungry and <u>thirsty</u> after walking for an hour. 목마른
⑤ Eggs are one of the major sources of <u>protein</u>. 단백질

서답형

04 다음 우리말에 맞게 빈칸에 알맞은 말을 쓰시오.

(1) 나의 머리에 혹이 있다.
➡ There's a _____ on my head.
(2) 등이 가렵다.
➡ My back _____.
(3) 나를 위해 내 등을 좀 긁어 주시겠어요?
➡ Will you _____ my back for me?

서답형

05 다음 우리말에 맞게 빈칸에 알맞은 말을 쓰시오.

(1) 그 때에, 조그만 무언가가 그에게로 날아왔다.
➡ _____ _____ _____, something tiny flew at him.
(2) 나는 공원에 산책하러 갔다.
➡ I _____ _____ _____ in the park.
(3) 펭귄은 물고기를 먹고 산다.
➡ Penguins _____ _____ fish.

서답형

06 다음 문장의 빈칸에 들어갈 말을 보기에서 골라 쓰시오.

┌─ 보기 ─┐
tiny / sweaty / protein / standing / pointed
└─────────┘

(1) We were hot and _____ after playing basketball.
(2) This dog's ears are large and _____.
(3) Meat is an excellent source of _____.
(4) She's wearing a dress with a pattern of _____ roses.
(5) We can find mosquitos near _____ water.

07 다음 주어진 문장의 밑줄 친 pointed와 같은 의미로 쓰인 것은?

I need a <u>pointed</u> pencil to draw a picture.

① He <u>pointed</u> at a spot on the map.
② We don't like being <u>pointed</u> at.
③ My child <u>pointed</u> out animals in the book.
④ This bird has a <u>pointed</u> beak.
⑤ She <u>pointed</u> to the restroom.

01 다음 짝지어진 단어의 관계가 같도록 빈칸에 알맞은 말을 쓰시오.

> tiny : huge = _____ : full

02 다음 영영풀이가 가리키는 것을 쓰시오.

> a small flying insect that bites the skin of people and animals to suck their blood

➡ _____

03 다음 문장의 빈칸에 들어갈 말을 보기에서 골라 쓰시오.

> ┤ 보기 ├
> lay / strange / buzzing / prevent

(1) A mosquito is _____ around me.

(2) Brush your teeth after meals to _____ tooth problems.

(3) Do you know whether the frogs _____ eggs or not?

(4) I met someone _____ on my way home.

04 다음 우리말에 맞게 빈칸에 알맞은 말을 쓰시오.

(1) 나는 네가 다음번에 더 잘 할 것이라고 확신한다.
➡ I'm sure that you'll _____ _____ next time.

(2) 너의 충고를 명심할게.
➡ I'll _____ your advice _____ _____.

(3) 나는 두통으로 고통 받고 있다.
➡ I'm _____ _____ the headache.

05 다음 우리말에 맞게 주어진 단어를 사용하여 영작하시오.

(1) 우리 당분간 여기에 머무르는 게 어때? (while, why)
➡ _____

(2) 나는 한국으로 돌아가고 싶다. (love, back)
➡ _____

(3) 많은 사람들이 식중독으로 고통 받았다. (suffered)
➡ _____

06 다음 우리말과 일치하도록 주어진 어구를 모두 배열하여 완성하시오.

(1) 만약 네가 그 개에게서 뼈를 가져가면, 그가 너를 물을 것이다. (if로 시작할 것)
(you / from / he / the bone / if / take / will / bite / the dog / you)
➡ _____

(2) 너무 덥고 땀이 나기 때문에 나는 여름을 좋아하지 않는다. (I로 시작할 것)
(don't / get / because / I / sweaty / too / like / hot / summer / I / and)
➡ _____

(3) 눈병을 예방하기 위해 항상 비누로 손을 씻어라. (to로 시작할 것)
(prevent / always / an eye disease / with / soap / your / wash / to / hands)
➡ _____
_____

교과서

Conversation

① 유감·동정 표현하기

> **I'm sorry to hear that.** (그것 참 안됐네요.)

- 'I'm sorry to hear that.'은 '그것 참 안됐네요.'라는 뜻으로 좋지 못한 소식을 들었을 때, 유감이나 동정을 표현하는 말이다.

유감·동정 표현하기

- That's too bad. (그것 참 안됐군요.)
- That's a pity. (그것 참 안됐군요.)
- What a pity! (가엾어라!)
- That's terrible. (끔찍한 일이군요.)
- That's a shame. (유감이군요.)

핵심 Check

1. 다음 우리말과 일치하도록 빈칸에 알맞은 말을 쓰시오.

   (1) **A:** I lost my wallet. (나는 지갑을 잃어버렸어요.)

   B: I'm _____ _____ _____ that. (그것 참 안됐군요.)

   (2) **A:** I'm not feeling well. (몸 상태가 좋지 않아요.)

   B: That's _____ _____. (그것 참 안됐군요.)

   (3) **A:** My stomach hurts! I think I have food poisoning. (배가 아파요! 나 식중독인거 같아요!)

   B: _____ _____. How about going to see a doctor? (끔찍한 일이야. 의사에게 가는 게 어때?)

② 당부하기

> **Make sure you wear a hat.** (반드시 모자를 쓰세요.)

■ 'Make sure (that) you ~.'는 '반드시 ~해라.'라는 뜻으로 당부를 하는 표현이다. 비슷한 표현으로 'Make sure to ~. / Don't forget to ~.' 등이 있다. 이에 대한 응답 표현으로 'Okay, I will.' 또는 'I'll keep that in mind.' 등이 있다.

당부하기

- Make sure you wear sunscreen when you go outside.
  (밖에 나갈 때 반드시 자외선 차단제를 바르세요.)

- Don't forget to wash your hands before you touch food.
  (음식에 손대기 전에 손을 씻는 것을 잊지 마세요.)

- Remember to empty your trash can more often.
  (당신의 쓰레기통을 더 자주 비워야 하는 것을 기억하세요.)

- Keep in mind that you should take an umbrella with you.
  (우산을 가져가야 한다는 것을 명심하세요.)

 핵심 Check

2. 다음 우리말과 일치하도록 빈칸에 알맞은 말을 쓰시오.

(1) **A:** ＿＿＿＿＿ ＿＿＿＿＿ you avoid standing water. (반드시 괴어 있는 물은 피하세요.)

   B: Okay, I will. (알겠어요. 그렇게 할게요.)

(2) **A:** ＿＿＿＿＿ ＿＿＿＿＿ to put a green tea bag on the itchy area. (가려운 부위에 녹차 티백을 올려놓는 것을 잊지 마세요.)

   B: Okay, I'll try that. (알겠어요. 시도해 볼게요.)

(3) **A:** Remember to wear a long sleeve. (긴소매를 입어야 한다는 것을 기억하세요.)

   B: ＿＿＿＿＿ ＿＿＿＿＿ ＿＿＿＿＿ ＿＿＿＿＿ ＿＿＿＿＿. (명심할게요.)

A. Listen & Speak 2 –B

Sujin: Dad, do we have any bug spray?

Dad: Yes, ❶it's under the sink. Why?

Sujin: ❷There are a lot of fruit flies around the trash.

Dad: Oh no! What did you put in the trash?

Sujin: Some fruit waste.

Dad: Fruit flies love sweet things. ❸Make sure you don't put fruit waste in the trash can.

Sujin: I'll keep ❹that in mind. I think we should also empty our trash can more often.

Dad: That's a good idea.

Sujin: 아빠, 우리 벌레 퇴치 스프레이가 있나요?
Dad: 응, 그것은 싱크대 밑에 있단다. 왜?
Sujin: 쓰레기 주변에 많은 초파리가 있어요.
Dad: 오 안돼! 쓰레기에 무엇을 넣었니?
Sujin: 약간의 과일 쓰레기요.
Dad: 초파리는 달콤한 것들을 좋아해. 쓰레기통에 과일 쓰레기를 버리지 않도록 하렴.
Sujin: 명심할게요. 제 생각에 우리는 또한 쓰레기통을 좀 더 자주 비워야 할 것 같아요.
Dad: 좋은 생각이구나.

❶ it은 bug spray를 가리킨다.
❷ there are+복수 명사 / there is+단수 명사
❸ 'Make sure ~'는 '반드시 ~해라.'라는 당부의 표현이다.
❹ that은 과일 쓰레기를 쓰레기통에 넣지 말라는 것을 가리킨다.

Check(√) True or False

(1) The bug spray is under the sink. T ☐ F ☐

(2) Sujin kept in mind that she should not put fruit waste in the trash can. T ☐ F ☐

B. Real Life Communication

Ms. Wheeler: Junsu, ❶what happened to your face?

Junsu: I got a lot of mosquito ❷bites.

Ms. Wheeler: ❸I'm sorry to hear that. How did it happen?

Junsu: It happened when I went camping last weekend.

Ms. Wheeler: Oh dear. Don't scratch ❹them!

Junsu: I know, but ❺they're really itchy.

Ms. Wheeler: Clean ❻them with cool water. That'll help. Also, make sure you wear long sleeves when you go camping.

Junsu: Okay, thank you.

Ms. Wheeler: 준수야, 얼굴이 왜 그러니?
Junsu: 모기에 많이 물렸어요.
Ms. Wheeler: 그것 참 안됐구나. 어쩌다 그랬니?
Junsu: 지난 주말에 캠핑 갔다가 그랬어요.
Ms. Wheeler: 이런 참. 물린 곳을 긁지 마라.
Junsu: 알아요, 하지만 정말 가려워요.
Ms. Wheeler: 물린 곳을 찬물로 닦으렴. 도움이 될 거야. 또한 캠핑 갈 때에는 긴 소매 옷을 입도록 해.
Junsu: 네, 감사합니다.

❶ 'what happened to ~?'는 '~에 무슨 일이 있었니?'라는 의미이다
❷ bite는 (벌레에) 물린 상처를 뜻한다.
❸ I'm sorry to hear that.은 유감이나 동정을 나타내며 'That's too bad.'와 바꾸어 쓸 수 있다.
❹,❺,❻ them과 they 모두 mosquito bites를 가리킨다.

Check(√) True or False

(3) Junsu went camping last weekend. T ☐ F ☐

(4) Junsu suffered from a lot of mosquito bites on his face. T ☐ F ☐

 Listen & Speak 1-A (1)

Brian: You look worried, Jimin. ❶What's wrong?

Jimin: I'm worried ❷because my cat is sick.

Brian: I'm sorry to hear that. ❸Why don't you take her to an animal doctor?

Jimin: Okay, I will.

❶ What's wrong?은 '무슨 일이니?'라는 의미로 'What happened?'와 바꾸어 쓸 수 있다.
❷ 'because+주어+동사'로 이어지는 반면에 'because of+명사(구)'가 이어진다.
❸ 'Why don't you ~?'는 '~하는 게 어때?'라고 제안하는 표현이다.

Listen & Speak 1-A (2)

Jane: How was the soccer game with Minsu's class, Alex?

Alex: We ❶lost by three goals.

Jane: I'm sorry to hear that. I hope you ❷do better next time.

Alex: I hope so, too.

❶ lose by ... ···점, ···골 등 차로 (경기에서) 지다
❷ do better: 더 잘하다

Listen & Speak 1-B

Tom: Let's go swimming this weekend, Yujin.

Yujin: I'd love to, but I can't.

Tom: ❶Why not?

Yujin: I have an eye problem. The doctor told me to ❷stop swimming for a while.

Tom: I'm sorry to hear that. Maybe we can go next weekend.

Yujin: I really hope so.

❶ 수영을 못가는 이유를 질문하고 있는 표현이다.
❷ stop+~ing: ~하는 것을 멈추다, stop+to부정사: ~하기 위해 멈추다
for a while: 당분간

 Listen & Speak 2-A (1)

Emma: Tim, look at your face! You got ❶ sunburn.

Tim: Yes, it hurts a lot. I went swimming at the beach without sunscreen.

Emma: Oh dear! ❷Make sure you wear sunscreen next time.

❶ sunburn: 햇볕에 탐, 그을림
❷ 'Make sure ~.'는 당부하는 표현으로 'keep in mind ~', 'Don't forget to ~.' 또는 'Remember ~.'와 바꾸어 쓸 수 있다.

Listen & Speak 2-A (2)

Mom: Hojun, do you want to go shopping with me?

Hojun: Sorry, Mom. I'm going to play baseball with Alex this afternoon.

Mom: Okay. No problem. Just make sure you wear a hat. It's going to be very hot this afternoon.

Hojun: ❶Okay, I will.

❶ 당부하기에 대한 대답으로 'I'll keep that in mind.'로 대답할 수도 있다.

Listen & Speak 2-A (3)

Mike: Did you ❶pack for the school trip tomorrow, Sue?

Sue: Yes. Now I'm checking my list again. I don't want to ❷miss anything.

Mike: Make sure you take an umbrella with you. It might rain tomorrow.

Sue: Okay, thank you.

❶ pack: (가방을) 싸다
❷ miss: 놓치다, 빼먹다

● 다음 우리말과 일치하도록 빈칸에 알맞은 말을 쓰시오.

해석

Listen & Speak 1–A (1)

Brian: You look _____, Jimin. What's wrong?

Jimin: I'm _____ because _____ _____ _____ _____.

Brian: _____ _____ _____ _____ _____. Why don't you take her to an animal doctor?

Jimin: Okay, _____ _____.

Listen & Speak 1–A (2)

Jane: _____ was the soccer game with Minsu's class, Alex?

Alex: We _____ _____ three goals.

Jane: _____ _____ _____ _____ _____. I hope _____ _____ _____ _____ _____.

Alex: I hope so, too.

Listen & Speak 1-B

Tom: Let's go swimming this weekend, Yujin.

Yujin: I'd love to, but _____ _____.

Tom: _____ _____?

Yujin: I have an eye problem. The doctor told me _____ _____ _____ _____ _____ _____.

Tom: I'm sorry to _____ _____. Maybe we can go _____ _____.

Yujin: I really _____ _____.

Listen & Speak 2–A (1)

Emma: Tim, look at your face! You got _____.

Tim: Yes, it hurts _____ _____. I went swimming at the beach _____ _____.

Emma: Oh dear! _____ _____ you wear sunscreen next time.

해석

Listen & Speak 2-A (2)

Mom: Hojun, do you want to go shopping with me?

Hojun: Sorry, Mom. I'm going to play baseball with Alex this afternoon.

Mom: Okay. No problem. _____ _____ _____ _____

_____ _____ _____. It's going to be very hot this afternoon.

Hojun: Okay, _____ _____.

Listen & Speak 2-B

Sujin: Dad, do we have _____ bug spray?

Dad: Yes, it's under _____ _____. Why?

Sujin: There are a lot of _____ _____ around the trash.

Dad: Oh no! What did you _____ in the _____?

Sujin: Some fruit waste.

Dad: Fruit flies love sweet things. _____ _____ _____

_____ _____ _____ _____ _____ _____

_____ _____.

Sujin: I'll _____ that _____ _____. I think we should also

_____ _____ _____ _____ more often.

Dad: That's a good idea.

Real Life Communication

Ms. Wheeler: Junsu, _____ _____ to your face?

Junsu: I got a lot of _____ _____.

Ms. Wheeler: _____ _____ _____ _____ _____. _____

did it happen?

Junsu: It happened when I _____ _____ last weekend.

Ms. Wheeler: Oh dear. _____ _____ _____!

Junsu: I know, but they're really _____.

Ms. Wheeler: Clean them _____ cool water. That'll help. Also,

_____ _____ _____ _____ _____

when you go camping.

Junsu: Okay, thank you.

01 다음 대화의 빈칸에 들어갈 말로 적절한 것은?

> Jane: How was the soccer game with Minsu's class, Alex?
> Alex: _____
> Jane: I'm sorry to hear that. I hope you do better next time.
> Alex: I hope so, too.

① We beat his class.
② We lost by three goals.
③ We were so happy to win the game.
④ It was a tough game but we won.
⑤ Minsu was a really good player.

02 다음 대화가 자연스럽게 이어지도록 순서대로 배열하시오.

> (A) Okay, I will.
> (B) Hojun, do you want to go shopping with me?
> (C) Sorry, Mom. I'm going to play baseball with Alex this afternoon.
> (D) Okay. No problem. Just make sure you wear a hat. It's going to be very hot this afternoon.

➡ _____

[03~04] 다음 대화를 읽고 물음에 답하시오.

> Brian: You look worried, Jimin. What's wrong?
> Jimin: I'm worried because my cat is sick.
> Brian: (A)_____ Why don't you take her to an animal doctor?
> Jimin: Okay, I will.

03 위 대화의 빈칸 (A)에 들어갈 말로 어색한 것은?

① That's too bad.　　② That's really sad.
③ That's a pity.　　④ What a relief.
⑤ I'm sorry to hear that.

04 위 대화의 내용과 일치하지 않는 것은?

① Jimin was concerned about her cat.
② Jimin's cat was sick.
③ Brian felt sorry to hear about Jimin's cat.
④ Brian advised Jimin to take her cat to the vet.
⑤ Brian was going to take Jimin to a doctor.

01 다음 대화의 빈칸에 들어갈 말로 어색한 것을 고르시오.

> Emma: Tim, look at your face! You got sunburn.
>
> Tim: Yes, it hurts a lot. I went swimming at the beach without sunscreen.
>
> Emma: Oh dear! _____

① Don't forget to wear sunscreen next time.
② Make sure you wear sunscreen next time.
③ Remember to wear sunscreen next time.
④ Keep in mind that you should wear sunscreen next time.
⑤ You don't have to wear sunscreen next time.

[02~03] 다음 대화를 읽고 물음에 답하시오.

> Tom: (a)Let's go swimming this weekend, Yujin.
>
> Yujin: I'd love to, but I can't.
>
> Tom: Why not?
>
> Yujin: I have an eye problem. (A)_____
>
> Tom: I'm sorry to hear that. Maybe we can go next weekend.
>
> Yujin: I really hope so.

서답형

02 위 대화의 빈칸 (A)에 들어갈 말을 주어진 어구를 모두 배열하여 완성하시오.

> ┌ 보기 ┐
> for / to / stop / a while / the doctor / me / told / swimming

➡ _____

03 위 대화의 밑줄 친 (a)와 바꾸어 쓸 수 있는 것을 모두 고르시오.

① Why don't we go swimming this weekend, Yujin?
② Do you want to go swimming this weekend, Yujin?
③ How about going swimming this weekend, Yujin?
④ Do you like going swimming this weekend, Yujin?
⑤ Why do you go swimming this weekend, Yujin?

[04~05] 다음 대화를 읽고 물음에 답하시오.

> Brian: You look worried, Jimin. What's wrong?
>
> Jimin: I'm worried because my cat is sick.
>
> Brian: I'm sorry to hear that. (A)Why don't you take her to an animal doctor? (how)
>
> Jimin: Okay, I will.

서답형

04 위 대화의 밑줄 친 (A)와 의미가 같도록 주어진 단어를 활용하여 다시 쓰시오.

➡ _____

05 위 대화에서 Jimin의 심경으로 적절한 것은?

① pleased   ② anxious
③ nervous   ④ excited
⑤ encouraged

[06~07] 다음 대화를 읽고 물음에 답하시오.

> Mom: Hojun, do you want to go shopping with me?
> Hojun: Sorry, Mom. I'm going to play baseball with Alex this afternoon.
> Mom: Okay. No problem. (A)Just make sure you wear a hat. (mind, should, keep) It's going to be very hot this afternoon.
> Hojun: Okay, I will.

서답형

06 위 대화의 밑줄 친 (A)와 의미가 같도록 주어진 단어를 사용하여 다시 쓰시오.

➡ _____

07 위 대화의 내용과 일치하는 것은?

① Hojun wants to go shopping with his mom.
② Hojun is going to play baseball with Alex tomorrow.
③ Hojun's mom kept in mind that she should wear a hat.
④ The weather is going to be bad this afternoon.
⑤ Hojun will wear a hat when he plays baseball with Alex.

[08~10] 다음 대화를 읽고 물음에 답하시오.

> Sujin: Dad, do we have any bug spray?
> Dad: Yes, it's under the sink. Why?
> Sujin: (A) There are a lot of fruit flies around the trash.
> Dad: (B) Oh no! What did you put in the trash?
> Sujin: (C) Some fruit waste.
> Dad: (D) Fruit flies love sweet things. Make sure you don't put fruit waste in the trash can.
> Sujin: (E) I think we should also empty our trash can more often.
> Dad: That's a good idea.

08 위 대화의 (A)~(E) 중 주어진 문장이 들어가기에 가장 적절한 곳은?

I'll keep that in mind.

① (A) ② (B) ③ (C) ④ (D) ⑤ (E)

서답형

09 위 대화에서 다음 영영풀이가 가리키는 말을 찾아 쓰시오.

to remove everything that is in a container, etc.

➡ _____

서답형

10 위 대화의 내용과 일치하도록 아래의 빈칸을 완성하시오.

<How to prevent fruit flies> Don't put (A)_____ in the trash can. (B)_____ more often.

[11~12] 다음 대화를 읽고 물음에 답하시오.

> Jane: How was the soccer game with Minsu's class, Alex?
> Alex: (A)We lost by three goals.
> Jane: (B)That's too bad. (hear) I hope you do better next time.
> Alex: I hope so, too.

11 위 대화의 밑줄 친 (A)에서 알 수 있는 Alex의 심경으로 적절한 것은?

① pleased   ② discouraged
③ excited   ④ joyful
⑤ surprised

서답형

12 위 대화의 밑줄 친 (B)와 의미가 같도록 주어진 단어를 사용하여 다시 쓰시오.

➡ _____

01 다음 대화의 우리말을 주어진 단어를 사용하여 영어로 옮기시오.

> Sora: You look upset, Minu. What's wrong?
> Minu: I lost my hat. It was my favorite.
> Sora: 그거 참 안됐네요. (sorry) Why don't you go to the Lost and Found Center?
> Minu: That's a good idea.

➡ _____

[02~03] 다음 대화를 읽고 물음에 답하시오.

> Emma: Tim, look at your face! You got sunburn.
> Tim: Yes, it hurts a lot. I went swimming at the beach without sunscreen.
> Emma: Oh dear! _____

02 위 대화의 빈칸에 들어갈 말을 〈보기〉의 단어를 배열하여 완성하시오.

┌─ 보기 ─────────────────┐
│ wear / next / sunscreen / make / time │
│ / sure / you │
└────────────────────────┘

➡ _____

03 Why did Tim get sunburn? Answer in English.

➡ _____

_____

[04~05] 다음 대화를 읽고 물음에 답하시오.

> Ms. Wheeler: Junsu, what happened to your face?
> Junsu: I got a lot of mosquito bites.
> Ms. Wheeler: I'm sorry to hear that. How did it happen?

> Junsu: It happened when I went camping last weekend.
> Ms. Wheeler: Oh dear. Don't scratch them!
> Junsu: I know, but they're really itchy.
> Ms. Wheeler: Clean them with cool water. That'll help. Also, make sure you wear long sleeves when you go camping.
> Junsu: Okay, thank you.

04 Where did Junsu get the mosquito bites? Answer in English.

➡ _____

05 위 대화의 내용과 일치하도록 빈칸을 완성하시오.

┌────────────────────────────┐
│ When you got bitten by mosquitos │
│ ■ Make sure _____ . │
└────────────────────────────┘

➡ _____

06 다음 대화가 자연스럽게 이어지도록 순서대로 배열하시오.

┌────────────────────────────┐
│ Dad, do we have any bug spray? │
│ (A) Some fruit waste. │
│ (B) Yes, it's under the sink. Why? │
│ (C) Oh no! What did you put in the trash? │
│ (D) There are a lot of fruit flies around the trash. │
│ (E) Fruit flies love sweet things. Make sure you don't put fruit waste in the trash can. │
└────────────────────────────┘

➡ _____

교과서

Grammar

> • I want to eat **something sweet.** 나는 달콤한 뭔가를 먹고 싶어.
> • Is there **anyone nice** like you? 너처럼 친절한 사람이 있니?

■ '-body, -thing, -one'으로 끝나는 부정대명사는 형용사가 뒤에서 수식한다. 이러한 대명사에는 somebody, something, someone, anybody, anything, anyone, nobody, nothing, no one, everything 등이 있다.

- I need **someone reliable**. 나는 어떤 믿을 만한 사람이 필요해.

- Do you have **anything bigger** than this? 이것보다 더 큰 어떤 것을 가지고 있나요?

- Henna wants **somebody cute** like Tom. Henna는 Tom처럼 귀여운 누군가를 원한다.

- I want to see **something colorful** and **beautiful**. 나는 다채롭고 아름다운 무언가를 보고 싶어.

■ 위의 대명사를 to부정사와 형용사가 동시에 수식할 때 어순은 '대명사+형용사+to부정사'이다.

- She doesn't have **anyone kind to talk** with. 그녀에게는 함께 대화할 친절한 사람이 없어.

- Mike wanted to meet **someone brave to be** admired. Mike는 존경 받을 만한 용감한 누군가를 만나기를 원했다.

- There is **something important to deal** with. 처리해야 할 중요한 무언가가 있다.

핵심 Check

1. 다음 우리말과 같도록 빈칸에 알맞은 말을 쓰시오.

(1) 뜰에 이상한 무언가가 있어.

➡ There is ＿＿＿＿＿ ＿＿＿＿＿ in the yard.

(2) 나는 가지고 놀기에 재미있는 것이 있어.

➡ I have ＿＿＿＿＿ fun ＿＿＿＿＿ ＿＿＿＿＿ ＿＿＿＿＿.

(3) 차가운 마실 것 좀 주시겠어요?

➡ Can I have anything ＿＿＿＿＿ ＿＿＿＿＿ ＿＿＿＿＿?

② 현재완료

> • I **have** just **finished** my project. 나는 나의 프로젝트를 막 끝냈어.
> • **Have** you **seen** the movie star in person? 너는 그 영화배우를 직접 본 적이 있니?

■ 현재완료는 과거의 사건이 현재까지 영향을 미칠 때 사용한다. 'have[has]+p.p.'의 형태로, 부정형은 'have[has] not+p.p.'이며, 의문형은 'Have[Has]+주어+p.p. ~?'로 나타낸다.

  • I **haven't returned** the book yet. 나는 아직 그 책을 반납하지 않았다.

  • **Have** you ever **been** to Busan before? 전에 부산에 가 본 적이 있니?

■ 현재완료는 '완료, 경험, 계속, 결과' 네 가지 용법으로 쓰인다. 완료 용법은 'just, already, yet' 등과 같은 부사와 주로 함께 쓰이며, 경험은 'ever, never, once, before' 등과 같은 부사와 함께 쓰인다. 'How long ~?'으로 묻는 질문이나 'for+기간', 'since+특정 시점'은 현재완료의 계속적 용법에 속한다. 결과적 용법은 특별한 부사(구)와 어울리지 않고 과거에 발생한 사건으로 인하여 현재까지 영향을 미치고 있는 상태를 나타낼 때 쓴다.

  • I **have drawn** a picture of myself once. 나는 자화상을 그려 본 적이 한 번 있다.

  • **Have** you **caught** a butterfly before? 너는 전에 나비를 잡아 본 적이 있니?

  • My grandfather **has owned** the restaurant since 2012. 할아버지는 2012년 이래로 그 식당을 소유하고 계신다.

  • Jason **has gone** to Budapest. Jason은 부다페스트에 가고 없다. 〈결과〉

※ have[has] been to와 have[has] gone to의 사용에 유의하자. '~에 가 본 적이 있다'는 경험은 have[has] been to로 표현하고, '~에 가고 없다'는 결과는 have[has] gone to로 표현한다.

■ 현재완료는 과거의 일이 현재까지 영향을 미칠 때 쓰는 시제이므로 과거를 나타내는 부사(구)인 yesterday, last year, ~ago 및 의문부사 when과 함께 쓸 수 없다.

  • I **met** Tom last week. 나는 지난주에 Tom을 만났어.

  • When **did** you make the cake? 너 그 케이크를 언제 만들었니?

핵심 Check

2. 주어진 동사를 어법에 맞게 쓰시오.

  (1) _____ you ever _____ your own ice cream? (make)
  (2) I _____ _____ awake since last night. (be)
  (3) There _____ _____ a lot of snow on the ground since New Year's Day. (be)
  (4) My parents _____ _____ a lot. (travel)

01 다음 문장에서 어법상 <u>어색한</u> 부분을 고치시오.

(1) Is there wrong anything with it?

_____ ➡ _____

(2) I want something to eat healthy.

_____ ➡ _____

(3) They have talked about it last month.

_____ ➡ _____

(4) Jina played the piano since she was a child.

_____ ➡ _____

02 주어진 동사를 현재완료 시제로 어법에 맞게 쓰시오.

(1) He _____ his shoes yet. (polish)

(2) I am looking for Jane. _____ you _____ her today? (see)

(3) There is something I _____ you yet. (tell)

(4) Mona _____ the newspaper. (just, read)

(5) Jack _____ the suit many times. (wear)

03 주어진 단어를 바르게 배열하여 다음 우리말을 영어로 쓰시오. 필요하다면 단어를 변형하거나 추가하시오.

(1) 나는 차가운 마실 것이 필요해. (need / something / I / cold / drink)

➡ _____

(2) 우리는 프랑스에 두 번 가 봤어. (twice / have / we / be / France / to)

➡ _____

(3) 읽기에 재미있는 것이 있니? (read / you / fun / do / anything / have)

➡ _____

(4) 이 게임을 해 본 적이 있니? (play / game / you / have / this / ever)

➡ _____

1 다음 중 빈칸에 들어갈 말로 가장 적절한 것은?

> We _____ Gloria since last year.

① don't meet   ② haven't met
③ met   ④ will meet
⑤ meet

02 다음 우리말을 영어로 바르게 옮긴 것은?

> 그녀의 어머니는 이전에 한국에 가 본 적이 있다.

① Her mother has gone to Korea before.
② Her mother has been in Korea ago.
③ Her mother has been to Korea before.
④ Her mother has wanted to be in Korea.
⑤ Her mother has visited Korea many times.

3 다음 빈칸에 들어갈 말이 바르게 짝지어진 것은?

> A: Ron _____ away on holiday now.
> B: Oh, where _____ he _____?

① was – has – gone   ② be – did – go
③ was – did – go   ④ is – has – gone
⑤ is – does – go

서답형
04 주어진 단어를 활용하여 다음 대화의 우리말을 영어로 쓰시오.

> A: 그녀가 나에게 중요한 무언가를 말해 주었어.
> (something)
> B: What was it?

➡ _____

05 다음 빈칸에 들어갈 말로 가장 적절한 것은?

> 너에게 소개할 특별한 사람이 있어.
> I have _____.

① to introduce someone special to you
② special someone to introduce to you
③ someone special to introduce to you
④ to introduce special someone to you
⑤ someone special to you to introduce

06 다음 문장의 밑줄 친 부분과 쓰임이 같은 것은?

> Have you ever used this machine?

① My aunt has just knitted a sweater.
② We have already painted the wall.
③ The boy has studied English for a year.
④ They have never ridden a horse.
⑤ How long have you been here?

7 다음 중 어법상 옳은 문장은?

① There is interesting nothing here.
② I have gone to Jeju-do.
③ She said she needed something fun.
④ Have you seen her yesterday?
⑤ We want something to talk.

서답형
08 다음 대화의 우리말을 영어로 쓰시오.

> A: What time are the Kims coming?
> B: 그들은 이미 도착했어.

➡ _____

⭐ 중요
9 다음 빈칸 (A)~(C)에 들어갈 말이 바르게 짝지어진 것은?

> • Jane   __(A)__   her car key an hour ago.
> • I haven't heard from her   __(B)__   a long time.
> • Jimmy   __(C)__   the book several times until now.

	(A)	(B)	(C)
①	has lost	since	read
②	lost	ago	has read
③	lost	for	has read
④	lost	since	has read
⑤	has lost	since	has read

10 다음 중 어법상 틀린 문장은?

① Ms. Hong has been in Hong Kong for a month.
② Do you have anything interesting to see?
③ I have just finished my report.
④ The students have already packed their bags.
⑤ I think you need something to cat warm.

11 다음 우리말을 영어로 바르게 옮기지 않은 것은?

① 나는 키 큰 누군가가 필요해.
   → I need someone tall.
② 나는 그녀를 한동안 보지 못했어.
   → I haven't seen her for a while.
③ 그녀는 어제 새 차를 샀다.
   → She has bought a new car yesterday.
④ 그는 멍청한 짓을 저질렀다.
   → He did something stupid.
⑤ Bing 가족은 방금 이곳에 도착했다.
   → The Bings have just arrived here.

12 주어진 어구를 이용하여 다음 우리말을 영어로 쓰시오.

> 하기에 위험한 것은 없어.
> ➡ There is nothing _____.

13 다음 빈칸에 들어갈 말이 바르게 짝지어진 것은?

> A: Have you _____ finished your homework?
> B: No, I haven't finished it _____.

① since – yet
② already – yet
③ for – since
④ ever – already
⑤ already – ago

⭐ 중요
14 다음 중 어법상 바르지 않은 것은?

> A: How long ①have you played the piano?
> B: I ②have played the piano ③for 20 years. I ④have learned how to play it ⑤when I was six years old.

①   ②   ③   ④   ⑤

15 다음 빈칸에 들어갈 말이 바르게 짝지어진 것은?

> A: Have you met _____ at the party?
> B: No, I _____ no one yet.

① interesting someone – met
② anyone interesting – met
③ interesting anyone – have met
④ someone interesting – meet
⑤ anyone interesting – have met

16 주어진 단어를 활용하여 다음 우리말을 영어로 쓰시오.

> 나는 함께 일할 근면한 사람이 필요해요.
> (diligent)

➡ _____

17 다음 빈칸에 들어갈 말이 바르게 짝지어진 것을 고르시오.

> Julia and Grace are very close friends.
> Julia ＿＿＿ Grace since she was 12 years
> old. So Julia ＿＿＿ Grace very well.

① knows – knows
② knew – knows
③ knew – has known
④ has known – knows
⑤ has known – knew

18 다음 중 어법상 어색한 것은?

① Has anything interesting happened?
② Mary had a date with someone very handsome.
③ I want to try on something larger.
④ There is nothing to eat in the fridge.
⑤ Tell me special everything.

19 다음 밑줄 친 두 문장을 하나의 문장으로 바르게 바꾼 것은?

> A: Where is your sister?
> B: She went out. She is not here.

① She has been here.
② She has not been here.
③ She has gone out.
④ She wasn't here.
⑤ She was here.

서답형
20 주어진 단어를 바르게 배열하여 다음 우리말을 영어로 쓰시오.

> 나는 뭔가 다른 일을 해 보고 싶어.
> (different / do / something / want / I / to)

➡ ＿＿＿＿＿＿＿＿＿＿＿＿＿＿＿＿＿

21 주어진 문장을 영어로 바르게 옮긴 것은?

> 돌보아야 할 사람이 있나요?

① Do you have someone to look at?
② Do you have anyone to look for?
③ Is there someone to take care?
④ Is there anyone to take care of?
⑤ Do you know there is someone to take care of?

22 다음 빈칸에 들어갈 말이 바르게 짝지어진 것은?

> • Tim has been in Seoul ＿＿＿ last Sunday.
> • Tim has been in Seoul ＿＿＿ two days.
> • Tim has not left Seoul ＿＿＿.

① for　　　since　　　already
② since　　for　　　yet
③ already　for　　　already
④ for　　　since　　　ago
⑤ since　　for　　　ago

23 다음 중 어법상 바르지 않은 것은?

① I haven't heard from her for a long time.
② Julia has just bought a new house.
③ Robert used the desk for ten years until now.
④ I have seen the ad a lot lately.
⑤ Jacob has been in Canada since October.

서답형
24 주어진 단어를 활용하여 다음 우리말을 영어로 쓰시오.

> 저는 가지고 놀 새로운 것이 필요해요.
> (something / play with)

➡ ＿＿＿＿＿＿＿＿＿＿＿＿＿＿＿＿＿

01 다음 두 문장을 하나의 문장으로 쓰시오.

It started to rain last night. It still rains.

➡ _____

02 다음 대화의 빈칸에 알맞은 말을 쓰시오.

A: I have a car.
B: How long _____ your car?
A: I _____ it since March.

➡ _____

03 다음 빈칸에 알맞은 말을 세 단어의 영어로 쓰시오.

There isn't any food in the house. We have got _____.

➡ _____

04 주어진 단어를 이용하여 어법에 맞게 빈칸에 알맞은 말을 쓰시오.

A: _____ to Vietnam? (be, ever)
B: Yes, I have.
A: When _____ there? (go)
B: Five years ago.

➡ _____

05 다음 우리말을 영어로 쓰시오.

너는 유명한 누군가를 만난 적이 있니?

➡ _____

06 주어진 동사를 문맥이나 어법에 맞게 빈칸에 쓰시오.

happen go have be teach

(1) Kyle _____ many different jobs until now.
(2) Your friend was here just now, but I think she _____ somewhere else.
(3) The horrible accident _____ long time ago.
(4) The weather _____ cold for a long time. It's still cold.
(5) My aunt _____ students math in 2015.

07 주어진 단어를 활용하여 다음 밑줄 친 우리말을 영어로 쓰시오.

I like her. So 나는 그녀의 기분을 다치게 할 어떠한 것도 하고 싶지 않아.
(want / anything / hurt)

➡ _____

08 다음 대화의 빈칸에 알맞은 말을 쓰시오.

A: I am so bored. I need something _____ _____ _____.
B: How about seeing this movie? I think it will be interesting as much as you want.

09 주어진 단어를 활용하여 다음 대화의 밑줄 친 @, ⓑ를 어법에 맞게 영어로 쓰시오.

> A: @따뜻한 마실 것이 있나요? (there / drink)
> B: ⓑ지금 막 커피를 끓였어요. (make some coffee) Do you want some?
> A: Sure.

➡ @ _____

ⓑ _____

10 주어진 단어를 이용하여 다음 문장을 현재완료 시제로 표현하시오.

> • Amelia moved to this city in 2016.
> • It's the year 2020 now.
> • (for / since)

➡ _____

➡ _____

11 다음 대화의 빈칸에 알맞은 말을 쓰시오.

> A: Do you know when Jenny arrived in Canada?
> B: I heard that _____ Canada two days ago.
> A: Then she _____ in Canada for two days.

12 주어진 단어를 활용하여 다음 우리말을 영어로 쓰시오.

> 그 박물관에 가 본 적이 있니? (ever, be)

➡ _____

13 주어진 단어를 활용하여 다음 우리말을 영어로 쓰시오.

> 그 잡지에는 읽을 만한 중요한 것이 없다. (there / nothing)

➡ _____

14 주어진 단어를 활용하여 다음 밑줄 친 우리말을 영어로 쓰시오.

> A: I need to sit down. 편안하게 앉을 만한 것이 있나요? (there / sit on)
> B: There is a couch on the corner.

➡ _____

15 다음 대화의 빈칸에 알맞은 말을 세 단어의 영어로 쓰시오.

> A: I need something _____.
> B: Then, how about wearing my coat? It will make you feel warm.

16 우리말에 맞게 주어진 단어를 활용하여 다음 대화를 영어로 쓰시오.

> A: _____
> (너는 영어를 얼마나 오랫동안 배워 왔니?)
> B: _____
> (나는 8개월째 영어를 배우고 있어.)
> (learn)

An Interview with Mrs. Mosguito

It was a hot summer evening. Seojun went for a walk in the park.
비인칭 주어로 날짜, 요일, 날씨 등을 표현함.

Soon, he was sweating.
과거진행형

Seojun: I'm thirsty. I want something cold to drink.
-body, -thing, -one'으로 끝나는 대명사는 형용사가 뒤에서 수식. to drink는 to부정사의 형용사적 용법으로 앞의 something cold를 수식.

At that moment, something tiny flew at him and bit his arm.
tiny는 something을 뒤에서 수식.

Mrs. Mosquito: Hey, catch me if you can.
if you can catch me

Seojun: Who are you? What have you done to me?
have done은 완료 용법의 현재완료

Mrs. Mosquito: I'm a mosquito. I've just finished my dinner.
just는 '방금, 막'이란 뜻으로 현재완료와 함께 쓰임.

Seojun: Where are you from? How did you find me?

Mrs. Mosquito: I'm from a nearby river. I was looking for some
근처의, 가까운 곳의   look for: ~을 찾다

blood to drink there. Then I smelled something sweaty
to drink는 to부정사의 형용사적 용법으로 some blood를 수식

and found you here.

Seojun: How could you smell me from the river?

Mrs. Mosquito: Mosquitoes can sense heat and smell very well.

That's why we have survived for millions of years.
그래서   현재완료(계속)   'for+기간'은 '~ 동안'

Seojun: Do all mosquitoes drink blood like you?
~처럼(전치사)

Mrs. Mosquito: No. Only female mosquitoes like me drink blood.
오직, 단지

Male mosquitoes only feed on fruit and plant juice.

mosquito: 모기
go for a walk: 산책 가다
sweat: 땀을 흘리다
buzz: 윙윙거리다
at that moment: 그때에
tiny: 아주 작은
sweaty: 땀 냄새가 나는
sense: 느끼다, 감지하다
million: 100만, 다수
female: 암컷의, 여성의
male: 수컷의, 남성의
feed on: ~을 먹고 살다

 확인문제

● 다음 문장이 본문의 내용과 일치하면 T, 일치하지 않으면 F를 쓰시오.

1   Seojun was sweating and felt thirsty. ☐

2   Mrs. Mosquito came from a nearby river. ☐

3   All mosquitoes drink blood. ☐

Seojun: That's interesting. So why do you drink blood?
<small>흥미를 유발할 때 Ving</small>

Mrs. Mosquito: I need the protein in blood to lay my eggs.
<small>to부정사의 부사적 용법 중 목적(~하기 위해서)을 나타냄.</small>

Seojun: How do you drink blood? Do you have sharp teeth?
<small>tooth의 복수형</small>

Mrs. Mosquito: No, I don't have teeth. But I have a long and pointed mouth. So I can drink your blood easily.

Seojun: After you bit me, I got a bump. It itches.
<small>a bump를 가리킴</small>

Mrs. Mosquito: I'm sorry to hear that. Make sure you don't scratch it. Also, clean it with alcohol wipes.
<small>to부정사의 부사적 용법 중 감정의 원인: ~해서   당부하는 표현</small>
<small>a bump를 가리킴</small>

Seojun: Alcohol wipes? I've never tried that before.
<small>과거부터 현재까지의 경험을 나타내는 현재완료 구문 '결코 ~한 적이 없다'</small>

Mrs. Mosquito: It will reduce the itchiness.
<small>Cleaning it with alcohol wipes를 가리킴</small>

Seojun: Okay, I'll try that at home. Thanks.
<small>알코올 솜으로 닦는 것</small>

Mrs. Mosquito: I have to go. See you soon.

Seojun: Where are you going?

Mrs. Mosquito: I'm going back to the river.
<small>go back to: ~로 돌아가다</small>

Seojun: Wait! A lot of people have suffered from your bites. How can we prevent them?
<small>과거부터 현재까지 계속되는 상황을 나타내는 현재완료 구문</small>
<small>= your bites</small>

Mrs. Mosquito: Stay cool and wear long sleeves.
<small>~하게 지내다</small>

Seojun: Thanks. I'll keep your advice in mind.

protein: 단백질
lay: (알을) 낳다
pointed: 뾰족한
bump: 타박상, 혹
itch: 가렵다
scratch: 긁다
wipe: 닦아내는 천이나 솜
suffer from: ~로부터 고통 받다
prevent: ~을 예방하다
sleeve: (옷의) 소매, 소맷자락
keep~in mind: ~을 명심하다

확인문제

● 다음 문장이 본문의 내용과 일치하면 T, 일치하지 않으면 F를 쓰시오.

1 In order to lay eggs, mosquitoes need protein. ☐

2 Mosquitoes have many teeth. ☐

3 Mrs. Mosquito wanted Seojun to scratch. ☐

4 Mrs. Mosquito wanted to go back to the river after the conversation. ☐

5 Mrs. Mosquito gave no advice to Seojun. ☐

● 우리말을 참고하여 빈칸에 알맞은 말을 쓰시오.

1 _____ was a hot summer _____.

2 Seojun _____ _____ _____ _____ in the park.

3 Soon, he was _____.

4 Seojun: I'm _____. I want something _____ _____ _____.

5 At that moment, _____ _____ flew _____ him and _____ his arm.

6 Mrs. Mosquito: Hey, catch me _____ _____ _____.

7 Seojun: Who are you? What _____ _____ _____ to me?

8 Mrs. Mosquito: I'm a mosquito. I've _____ _____ my dinner.

9 Seojun: Where are you _____? _____ did you _____ me?

10 Mrs. Mosquito: I'm _____ a _____ river.

11 I _____ _____ _____ some blood _____ _____ there.

12 Then I smelled _____ _____ and found you here.

13 Seojun: How could you _____ _____ from the river?

14 Mrs. Mosquito: Mosquitoes can _____ _____ and _____ very well.

15 That's _____ we _____ _____ for millions of years.

16 Seojun: Do all mosquitoes drink blood _____ _____?

17 Mrs. Mosquito: No. Only _____ mosquitoes like me _____ _____.

18 Male mosquitoes only _____ _____ fruit and plant juice.

---

1 무더운 여름날의 저녁이었습니다.

2 서준이는 공원에 산책을 갔습니다.

3 곧, 그는 땀을 흘리고 있었습니다.

4 서준: 목말라. 뭔가 시원한 것을 마시고 싶어.

5 그때에, 뭔가 조그마한 것이 그에게로 날아와서 그의 팔을 물었습니다.

6 모기: 이봐, 나를 잡을 수 있으면 잡아 봐.

7 서준: 너는 누구니? 나한테 무슨 짓을 한 거지?

8 모기: 나는 모기야. 난 방금 저녁 식사를 마쳤어.

9 서준: 너는 어디에서 왔니? 너는 어떻게 나를 찾은 거야?

10 모기: 나는 근처 강에서 왔어.

11 나는 그곳에서 마실 피를 찾던 중이었지.

12 그러다가 땀 냄새를 맡았고, 여기서 너를 발견했어.

13 서준: 너는 어떻게 강에서부터 내 냄새를 맡을 수 있었지?

14 모기: 모기들은 열과 냄새를 매우 잘 감지해.

15 그래서 우리가 수백만 년 동안 살아남은 거야.

16 서준: 모든 모기가 너처럼 피를 마셔?

17 모기: 아니. 오직 나와 같은 암컷 모기만이 피를 마셔.

18 수컷 모기들은 과일과 식물의 즙만을 먹고 살아.

19 Seojun: That's _____. So why do you drink blood?

20 Mrs. Mosquito: I need _____ _____ in blood _____ _____ my eggs.

21 Seojun: _____ do you drink blood? Do you have _____ _____?

22 Mrs. Mosquito: No, I don't have _____.

23 But I have _____ _____ and _____ _____.

24 _____ I can drink your blood _____.

25 Seojun: After you _____ me, I _____ _____ _____. It _____.

26 Mrs. Mosquito: I'm sorry _____ _____ _____.

27 _____ _____ you don't scratch _____.

28 Also, _____ _____ with alcohol wipes.

29 Seojun: Alcohol wipes? I've _____ _____ _____ _____.

30 Mrs. Mosquito: It will reduce _____ _____.

31 Seojun: Okay, I'll _____ _____ at home. Thanks.

32 Mrs. Mosquito: I _____ _____ _____. See you soon.

33 Seojun: _____ are you _____?

34 Mrs. Mosquito: I'm _____ _____ to the river.

35 Seojun: Wait! A lot of people _____ _____ from your bites.

36 How can we _____ _____?

37 Mrs. Mosquito: Stay _____ and _____ long _____.

38 Seojun: Thanks. I'll _____ your advice _____.

---

19 서준: 그거 재미있네. 그럼 너는 왜 피를 마시는 거야?

20 모기: 알을 낳으려면 핏속의 단백질이 필요해.

21 서준: 너는 피를 어떻게 마시는 거야? 날카로운 이빨이 있니?

22 모기: 아니, 나는 이빨이 없어.

23 하지만 길고 뾰족한 입이 있지.

24 그래서 나는 너의 피를 쉽게 마실 수 있는 거야.

25 서준: 네가 나를 문 다음, 부어오른 자국이 생겼어. 가려워.

26 모기: 그 말을 들으니 미안하군.

27 그것을 긁지 않도록 해.

28 또한, 그것을 알코올 솜으로 닦아.

29 서준: 알코올 솜? 나는 전에 그것을 한 번도 해 보지 않았어.

30 모기: 그것은 가려움을 줄여 줄 거야.

31 서준: 알았어. 집에서 해 볼게. 고마워.

32 모기: 나는 이제 가야겠어. 다음에 보자.

33 서준: 너는 어디로 가는데?

34 모기: 강으로 돌아가려고.

35 서준: 기다려! 많은 사람이 모기에 물려서 괴로워하고 있어.

36 어떻게 하면 모기에 물리는 것을 막을 수 있지?

37 모기: 시원하게 지내고 소매가 긴 옷을 입어.

38 서준: 고마워. 너의 충고를 명심할게.

● 우리말을 참고하여 본문을 영작하시오.

1 무더운 여름날의 저녁이었습니다.

➡ _____

2 서준이는 공원에 산책을 갔습니다.

➡ _____

3 곧, 그는 땀을 흘리고 있었습니다.

➡ _____

4 서준: 목말라. 뭔가 시원한 것을 마시고 싶어.

➡ Seojun: _____

5 그때에, 뭔가 조그마한 것이 그에게로 날아와서 그의 팔을 물었습니다.

➡ _____

6 모기: 이봐, 나를 잡을 수 있으면 잡아 봐.

➡ Mrs. Mosquito: _____

7 서준: 너는 누구니? 나한테 무슨 짓을 한 거지?

➡ Seojun: _____

8 모기: 나는 모기야. 난 방금 저녁 식사를 마쳤어.

➡ Mrs. Mosquito: _____

9 서준: 너는 어디에서 왔니? 너는 어떻게 나를 찾은 거야?.

➡ Seojun: _____

10 모기: 나는 근처 강에서 왔어.

➡ Mrs. Mosquito: _____

11 나는 그곳에서 마실 피를 찾던 중이었지.

➡ _____

12 그러다가 땀 냄새를 맡았고, 여기서 너를 발견했어.

➡ _____

13 서준: 너는 어떻게 강에서부터 내 냄새를 맡을 수 있었지?

➡ Seojun: _____

14 모기: 모기들은 열과 냄새를 매우 잘 감지해.

➡ Mrs. Mosquito: _____

15 그래서 우리가 수백만 년 동안 살아남은 거야.

➡ _____

16 서준: 모든 모기가 너처럼 피를 마셔?

➡ Seojun: _____

17 모기: 아니. 오직 나와 같은 암컷 모기만이 피를 마셔.

➡ Mrs. Mosquito: _____

18 수컷 모기들은 과일과 식물의 즙만을 먹고 살아.

➡ _____

19 서준: 그거 재미있네. 그럼 너는 왜 피를 마시는 거야?

➡ Seojun: _____

20 모기: 알을 낳으려면 핏속의 단백질이 필요해.

➡ Mrs. Mosquito: _____

21 서준: 너는 피를 어떻게 마시는 거야? 날카로운 이빨이 있니?

➡ Seojun: _____

22 모기: 아니, 나는 이빨이 없어.

➡ Mrs. Mosquito: _____

23 하지만 길고 뾰족한 입이 있지.

➡ _____

24 그래서 나는 너의 피를 쉽게 마실 수 있는 거야.

➡ _____

25 서준: 네가 나를 문 다음, 부어오른 자국이 생겼어. 가려워.

➡ Seojun: _____

26 모기: 그 말을 들으니 미안하군.

➡ Mrs. Mosquito: _____

27 그것을 긁지 않도록 해.

➡ _____

28 또한, 그것을 알코올 솜으로 닦아.

➡ _____

29 서준: 알코올 솜? 나는 전에 그것을 한 번도 해 보지 않았어.

➡ Seojun: _____

30 모기: 그것은 가려움을 줄여 줄 거야.

➡ Mrs. Mosquito: _____

31 서준: 알았어, 집에서 해 볼게. 고마워.

➡ Seojun: _____

32 모기: 나는 이제 가야겠어. 다음에 보자.

➡ _____

33 서준: 너는 어디로 가는데?

➡ Seojun: _____

34 모기: 강으로 돌아가려고.

➡ Mrs. Mosquito: _____

35 서준: 기다려! 많은 사람이 모기에 물려서 괴로워하고 있어.

➡ Seojun: _____

36 어떻게 하면 모기에 물리는 것을 막을 수 있지?

➡ _____

37 모기: 시원하게 지내고 소매가 긴 옷을 입어.

➡ Mrs. Mosquito: _____

38 서준: 고마워. 너의 충고를 명심할게.

➡ Seojun: _____

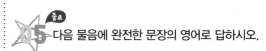

Reading 시험대비 실력평가

[01~07] 다음 글을 읽고 물음에 답하시오.

It was a hot summer evening. Seojun went for a walk in the park. Soon, he was ⓐ_____.

Seojun: I'm thirsty. I want something (A)[to drink cold / cold to drink].

At that moment, something tiny flew (B)[at / by] him and bit his arm.

Mrs. Mosquito: Hey, catch me ⓑif you can.

Seojun: Who are you? What have you done to me?

Mrs. Mosquito: I'm a mosquito. I've just finished my dinner.

Seojun: ⓒ_____ How did you find me?

Mrs. Mosquito: I'm from a nearby river. I was looking for some blood to drink there. Then I smelled (C)[sweaty something / something sweaty] and found you here.

01 다음과 같이 풀이되는 단어를 빈칸 ⓐ에 어법에 맞게 쓰시오.

> to produce a clear liquid from your skin when you are hot or nervous

➡ _____

02 다음 중 밑줄 친 ⓑ와 쓰임이 다른 하나는?

① Call me if you have time.
② If it is fine, we will go out together.
③ Jane wanted to know if you would go with us.
④ I will do that if you want me to do it instead of you.
⑤ If she arrives here in time, there will be no trouble.

03 위 글의 흐름상 빈칸 ⓒ에 들어갈 말로 가장 적절한 것은?

① What did you do?
② Where are you going?
③ Where are you from?
④ Why did you do?
⑤ What happened to you?

04 According to the passage, which one is wrong about Mrs. Mosquito?

① She bit Seojun in the evening.
② She was looking for blood.
③ She drank Seojun's blood.
④ She found Seojun by smelling him.
⑤ She had dinner with Seojun.

05 다음 물음에 완전한 문장의 영어로 답하시오.

> Q: What was Mrs. Mosquito doing near the river?

➡ _____

06 (A)~(C)에서 어법상 옳은 것끼리 바르게 짝지어진 것은?

① to drink cold - at - sweaty something
② cold to drink - by - something sweaty
③ cold to drink - at - something sweaty
④ cold to drink - by - sweaty something
⑤ to drink cold - at - something sweaty

07 When and where did the above story happen? Answer in English.

➡ _____

[08~13] 다음 대화를 읽고 물음에 답하시오.

Mrs. Mosquito: I'm ⓐ_____ a nearby river. I was looking for some blood to drink there. Then I smelled something sweaty and found you here.

Seojun: How could you smell me ⓑ_____ the river?

Mrs. Mosquito: Mosquitoes can sense heat and smell very well. That's why we have survived for millions of years.

Seojun: Do all mosquitoes ⓒ_____ like you?

Mrs. Mosquito: No. Only female mosquitoes like me drink blood. Male mosquitoes only feed on fruit and plant juice.

Seojun: That's interesting. So why do you drink blood?

Mrs. Mosquito: I need the protein in blood ⓓto lay my eggs.

 08 빈칸 ⓐ와 ⓑ에 공통으로 들어갈 말로 가장 적절한 것은?

① at   ② by   ③ from
④ on   ⑤ in

서답형
09 빈칸 ⓒ에 들어갈 말을 위 대화에서 찾아 쓰시오.

➡ _____

10 다음 중 밑줄 친 ⓓ와 쓰임이 같은 것은?

① Do you have a pen to write with?
② It is my duty to tell the truth.
③ We went to the mart to buy a bottle of water.
④ Linda hoped to see him again someday.
⑤ To make people laugh is hard for me.

11 다음 중 위 대화를 읽고 알 수 <u>없는</u> 것은?

① Seojun was sweating when Mrs. Mosquito found him.
② There has been mosquitoes for millions of years.
③ There is protein in human blood.
④ Female mosquitoes lay eggs.
⑤ Female mosquitoes can also feed on plant juice.

 12 다음 중 위 대화에 나오는 어휘의 풀이가 <u>아닌</u> 것은?

① to eat something as food
② to produce an egg outside the body
③ wet with sweat
④ to make the low, continuous sound of a flying insect
⑤ a substance found in foods such as meat, milk, eggs, and beans

서답형
13 위 대화의 내용에 맞게 빈칸에 알맞은 말을 쓰시오.

Q: Do you know why female mosquitoes drink blood?
A: Yes, I do. It's because _____.

➡ _____

[14~18] 다음 대화를 읽고 물음에 답하시오.

Seojun: That's ①<u>interesting</u>. So why do you drink blood?

Mrs. Mosquito: I need the protein in blood ②to lay my eggs.

Seojun: How do you drink blood? Do you have sharp ③<u>teeth</u>?

Mrs. Mosquito: No, I don't have teeth. But I can drink your blood easily ⓐ_____ I have a long and ④pointed mouth.

Seojun: After you ⑤bite me, I got a bump. It itches.

Mrs. Mosquito: I'm sorry to hear that. Make sure you don't scratch it. Also, clean it with alcohol wipes.

Seojun: Alcohol wipes? ⓑI've never tried that before.

Mrs. Mosquito: ⓒIt will reduce the itchiness.

14 다음 중 빈칸 ⓐ에 들어갈 말로 가장 적절한 것은?

① after ② since ③ when
④ so ⑤ if

15 다음 중 밑줄 친 문장 ⓑ에서 쓰인 현재완료와 그 용법이 같은 것은?

① He has already heard about the party at school.
② They have just arrived from New York.
③ We haven't found the clue yet.
④ Miranda has gone on her summer vacation.
⑤ I have met Frank once in Seoul.

서답형
16 주어진 단어를 활용하여 밑줄 친 ⓒ가 가리키는 것을 쓰시오.

(clean / the bump)

➡ _____

17 위 대화의 밑줄 친 ①~⑤ 중 어법상 바르지 않은 것은?

① ② ③ ④ ⑤

18 다음 중 위 대화를 읽고 답할 수 없는 것은?

① Is there any reason Mrs. Mosquito drinks blood?
② How does Mrs. Mosquito feel after she heard that Seojun got a bump?
③ Where did Mrs. Mosquito bite Seojun?
④ Why did Seojun get a bump?
⑤ Why does Mrs. Mosquito need protein?

[19~24] 다음 대화를 읽고 물음에 답하시오.

Seojun: Alcohol wipes? ⓐI've never tried that before.

Mrs. Mosquito: It will reduce the itchiness.

Seojun: Okay, I'll try that at home. Thanks.

Mrs. Mosquito: I have to go. See you soon.

Seojun: Where are you going?

Mrs. Mosquito: I'm going back to the river.

Seojun: Wait! A lot of people have suffered ⓑ_____ your bites. How can we prevent ⓒthem?

Mrs. Mosquito: Stay cool and wear long sleeves.

Seojun: Thanks. ⓓ너의 충고를 명심할게.

19 다음 중 밑줄 친 ⓐ와 쓰임이 같은 것은?

① I have known her since I was six.
② We haven't seen you for a long time.
③ Jane has studied French since last year.
④ Julia has stayed in California for a year.
⑤ Jason has seen the movie two times.

20 다음 중 빈칸 ⓑ에 들어갈 말과 같은 것은?

① Would you pick _____ the trash, please?
② Don't give _____. You can try it again.
③ Were you surprised _____ the news?
④ I look forward _____ seeing you again.
⑤ Do you know where he came _____?

21 밑줄 친 ⓒ가 가리키는 것을 위 대화에서 찾아 쓰시오.

➡ _____

서답형
22 주어진 단어를 이용하여 밑줄 친 우리말 ⓓ를 영어로 쓰시오.

> keep, advice

➡ _____

23 다음 중 위 대화의 내용과 일치하지 <u>않는</u> 것은?

① Alcohol wipes can help reduce the itchiness.
② Seojun feels thankful to Mrs. Mosquito.
③ Mrs. Mosquito was from the river.
④ Staying cool helps people to prevent themselves from mosquito bites.
⑤ Seojun will not wear long sleeves to prevent mosquito bites.

서답형
24 '의문사+to부정사'를 이용하여 위 대화의 내용에 맞게 빈칸에 알맞은 말을 쓰시오.

> Mrs. Mosquito advises Seojun on _____ _____ _____ mosquito bites.

[25~28] 다음 글을 읽고 물음에 답하시오.

My family and I moved to Korea when I was 8. (A)_____ We have visited many great places here. Today is the first day of summer vacation. Tomorrow, we are going to visit Jeju. I have (B)[never gone to / never been to] Jeju. So I'm very (C)[exciting / excited]. I have just finished (D)[packing / to pack], and I'm ready to go. I hope we have a wonderful time in Jeju.

*I = Kate

서답형
25 다음 두 문장을 하나의 문장으로 만들어 빈칸 (A)에 들어갈 말을 쓰시오.

> We moved to Korea six years ago.
> We still live in Korea.

➡ _____

26 다음 중 위 글을 읽고 답할 수 있는 것은?

① How many members are there in Kate's family?
② How many places has Kate visited?
③ When is Kate going to go to Jeju?
④ What is Kate going to do in Jeju?
⑤ How is Kate going to go to Jeju?

중요
27 (B)~(D)에서 어법상 옳은 것끼리 바르게 짝지어진 것은?

① never gone to – exciting – packing
② never been to – exciting – to pack
③ never gone to – excited – packing
④ never been to – excited – packing
⑤ never gone to – excited – to pack

서답형
28 What is Kate going to do on the second day of summer vacation?

➡ _____

Reading **89**

[01~04] 다음 글을 읽고 물음에 답하시오.

It was a hot summer evening. Seojun went for a walk in the park. Soon, he was sweating.

Seojun: I'm thirsty. (A)뭔가 차가운 것을 마시고 싶어.

At that moment, something tiny flew at him and bit his arm.

Mrs. Mosquito: Hey, catch me (B)if you can.

Seojun: Who are you? What have you done to me?

Mrs. Mosquito: I'm a mosquito. I've just finished my dinner.

Seojun: Where are you from? How did you find me?

Mrs. Mosquito: I'm from a nearby river. I was looking for some blood to drink there. Then I smelled something sweaty and found you here.

1 밑줄 친 우리말 (A)를 영어로 쓰시오.

➡ _____ _____

02 밑줄 친 (B)를 생략되지 않은 문장으로 쓰시오.

➡ _____

3 According to the passage, what has Mrs. Mosquito done to Seojun? Answer in English with a full sentence.

➡ _____

04 글의 내용에 맞게 빈칸에 알맞은 말을 쓰시오.

Walking in a hot summer made Seojun _____.

[05~08] 다음 대화를 읽고 물음에 답하시오.

Seojun: How do you drink blood? Do you have sharp teeth?

Mrs. Mosquito: No, I don't have teeth. But I have a long and pointed mouth. So I can drink your blood easily.

Seojun: After you bit me, I got a bump. It itches.

Mrs. Mosquito: I'm sorry to hear that. Make sure you don't scratch it. Also, clean it with alcohol wipes.

Seojun: Alcohol wipes? (A)나는 전에 그것을 한 번도 해 보지 않았어.

Mrs. Mosquito: It will reduce the itchiness.

05 다음 빈칸에 적절한 말을 쓰시오.

Cleaning the bump with alcohol wipes will be helpful in _____.

6 주어진 단어를 활용하여 밑줄 친 우리말 (A)를 영어로 쓰시오.

try, that

➡ _____

07 위 대화의 내용에 맞게 빈칸에 알맞은 말을 쓰시오.

When she heard that Seojun got a bump and it itches, Mrs. Mosquito told him not _____. Also she advised him _____.

08 위 대화의 내용에 맞게 빈칸에 알맞은 말을 쓰시오.

The mosquito's mouth is long and _____.

[09~12] 다음 대화를 읽고 물음에 답하시오.

Mrs. Mosquito: Mosquitoes can sense heat and smell very well. That's why we have survived for millions of years.

Seojun: Do all mosquitoes drink blood like you?

Mrs. Mosquito: No. Only female mosquitoes like me drink blood. Male mosquitoes only feed on fruit and plant juice.

Seojun: That's (A)_____. So why do you drink blood?

Mrs. Mosquito: I need the protein in blood to lay my eggs.

09 주어진 단어를 어법에 맞게 빈칸 (A)에 쓰시오.

(interest)

➡ _____

10 다음 빈칸에 들어갈 말을 위 대화에서 찾아 쓰시오.

Mrs. Mosquito is talking about what mosquitoes _____ _____, and _____ female mosquitoes drink blood.

11 What does Mrs. Mosquito need to lay her eggs? Answer in English with a full sentence.

➡ _____

12 위 대화의 내용에 맞게 빈칸에 알맞은 말을 쓰시오.

Hi, we are the mosquito couple. My wife and I eat different things. I eat _____, however, my wife feed on _____.

[13~16] 다음 대화를 읽고 물음에 답하시오.

Seojun: Alcohol wipes? ①I've never tried that before.

Mrs. Mosquito: It will reduce the itchiness.

Seojun: Okay, I'll try that ②at home. Thanks.

Mrs. Mosquito: I ③have to go. See you soon.

Seojun: Where are you going?

Mrs. Mosquito: I'm going back to the river.

Seojun: Wait! (A)많은 사람들이 모기에 물려서 괴로워하고 있어. How can we prevent them?

Mrs. Mosquito: Stay cool and wear ④long sleeves.

Seojun: Thanks. I'll keep your ⑤advise in mind.

13 주어진 어구를 이용하여 밑줄 친 우리말 (A)를 영어로 쓰시오.

have / suffer from / your bites

➡ _____

14 위 대화의 내용에 맞게 빈칸에 알맞은 말을 쓰시오.

_____ _____ _____ _____ _____ _____ can prevent people from being bitten by mosquitoes.

15 Where is Mrs. Mosquito from? Answer in English with a full sentence.

➡ _____

16 ①~⑤ 중 어법상 틀린 것을 찾아 바르게 고쳐 쓰시오.

➡ _____

해석

Let's check

Sora: You look upset, Minu. What's wrong?
　　　　　　　　　　　　= What's the matter (with you)?

Minu: I lost my hat. It was my favorite.
　　　　　　　　잃어버린 모자를 가리킨다.

Sora: I'm sorry to hear that. Why don't you go to the Lost and Found Center?
　　　　　　　　　　　　= How about ～? = What about ～? 모두 제안하는 표현이다.

Minu: That's a good idea.

구문해설 • the Lost and Found Center: 분실물 센터

Sora: 너 속상해 보인다, 민우야. 무슨 일이니?

Minu: 내 모자를 잃어버렸어. 내가 가장 좋아하는 거였는데.

Sora: 그것 참 안됐구나. 분실물 센터에 가보는 게 어때?

Minu: 좋은 생각이다.

Let's Write

Summer Health Guide

Sunburn

Have you ever suffered from sunburn? Here are some useful tips to prevent
　　　경험을 묻는 현재완료　　　　　　some useful tips에 수일치

sunburn in summer.

1. Wear sunscreen.

2. Wear a hat

Be smart and enjoy the hot weather.
명령문: ～해라

구문해설 • suffer from: ～으로 고통 받다 • here are ～: 여기에 ～이 있다 • prevent: 예방하다
　　　　 • wear: 바르다

여름철 건강 관리 수칙

햇볕 화상

햇볕 화상으로 고통 받은 적이 있나요? 여기 여름에 햇볕 화상을 예방할 수 있는 유용한 팁이 있습니다.

1. 선크림을 바르세요.

2. 모자를 쓰세요.

현명하게 무더운 날씨를 즐기세요.

Culture & Life

In summer, some people in Korea wear thin and light pants to stay cool.
　　　　　　　　　　　　　　　　　　　　　　목적을 나타내는 부사적 용법의 to부정사

They call them "refrigerator pants." Refrigerator pants come in colorful
　　call: 5형식 동사　them=thin and light pants

patterns. Some of them look very stylish.
　　　　　　　　look+형용사: ～하게 보이다

구문해설 • thin: 얇은 • light: 가벼운 • call A B: A를 B라고 부르다 • pattern: 무늬 • stylish: 세련된

여름철에 몇몇 한국 사람들은 시원함을 유지하기 위해 얇고 가벼운 바지를 입는다. 그들은 그것을 '냉장고 바지'라고 부른다. 화려한 무늬를 가진 냉장고 바지들이 나온다. 어떤 것들은 매우 세련되어 보인다.

영역별 핵심문제

Words & Expressions

01 다음 짝지어진 단어의 관계가 같도록 빈칸에 알맞은 말을 쓰시오.

> forget : remember = thick : _____

02 다음 영영풀이가 가리키는 것을 고르시오.

> an area of skin that is raised because it was hit or bitten

① bite   ② sleeve

③ sunburn   ④ bump

⑤ buzz

03 다음 우리말에 맞게 빈칸에 알맞은 말을 쓰시오.

(1) 너는 벽난로에서 떨어져 있어야 한다.
➡ You should _____ _____ _____ the fireplace.

(2) 그녀는 그녀의 장난감을 그녀의 방으로 가져갔다.
➡ She _____ her toy _____ her room.

(3) 우리는 1점 차로 경기에서 졌다.
➡ We _____ the game _____ one point.

04 다음 주어진 우리말에 맞게 영작하시오.

(1) 새들은 곤충을 먹고 산다.
➡ _____

(2) 여왕개미의 일은 알을 낳는 것이다.
➡ _____

(3) 나는 위험을 감지했다. (3 단어)
➡ _____

05 다음 중 밑줄 친 부분의 뜻풀이가 바르지 않은 것은?

① The crocodile has pointed teeth. 뾰족한

② You'd better wear long sleeves when you go camping. 바지

③ This bird can lay one egg a year. 낳다

④ Children are picking up the trash on the road. 쓰레기

⑤ You should wear a hat to avoid a sunburn. 햇볕에 탐

06 다음 주어진 문장의 밑줄 친 lay와 같은 의미로 쓰인 것은?

> Mosquitoes lay eggs in high temperatures.

① These hens are not laying well.

② Did he lay his hand on my shoulder?

③ The hunters are laying a trap in the forest.

④ Mike lay on a sofa.

⑤ She lay in her bed and slept like a baby.

07 다음 문장에 공통으로 들어갈 말을 고르시오.

> • The football player is suffering _____ a knee injury.
> • I tried to stay away _____ flowers because of allergy.

① on   ② for   ③ from

④ by   ⑤ to

Conversation

[08~10] 다음 대화를 읽고 물음에 답하시오.

Ms. Wheeler: Junsu, what happened to your face?

Junsu: I got a lot of mosquito bites.

Ms. Wheeler: I'm sorry to hear that. How did it happen?

Junsu: It happened when I went camping last weekend.

Ms. Wheeler: Oh dear. Don't scratch ⓐthem!

Junsu: I know, but they're really itchy.

Ms. Wheeler: Clean ⓐthem with cool water. That'll help. Also, make sure you wear long sleeves when you go camping.

Junsu: Okay, thank you.

08 위 대화에서 다음 영영풀이가 가리키는 말을 찾아 쓰시오.

> to take place especially without being planned

➡ _____

09 위 대화의 밑줄 친 ⓐthem이 공통으로 가리키는 것을 찾아 쓰시오.

➡ _____

10 위 대화의 내용과 일치하지 <u>않는</u> 것은?

① Junsu went camping last weekend.

② Junsu got a lot of mosquito bites on his face.

③ Junsu is suffering from mosquito bites because they are itchy.

④ Junsu should take a shower with cool water not to get bitten by mosquitoes.

⑤ Ms. Wheeler advises Junsu that he should wear long sleeves when he goes camping.

[11~12] 다음 대화를 읽고 물음에 답하시오.

Sujin: Dad, do we have any bug spray?

Dad: Yes, it's under the sink. Why?

Sujin: There ⓐare a lot of fruit flies around the trash.

Dad: Oh no! What did you put ⓑin the trash?

Sujin: Some fruit waste.

Dad: Fruit flies love sweet things. ⓒTo make sure you don't put fruit waste in the trash can.

Sujin: I'll keep ⓓthat in mind. I think we should also ⓔempty our trash can more often.

Dad: That's a good idea.

11 위 대화의 밑줄 친 ⓐ~ⓔ 중 어법상 어색한 것을 골라 바르게 고치시오.

➡ _____

12 위 대화를 읽고 대답할 수 <u>없는</u> 것은?

① What did Sujin put in the trash?

② Where was the bug spray?

③ Why did Sujin need the bug spray?

④ What do fruit flies love?

⑤ What should Sujin do to reduce the trash?

[13~14] 다음 대화를 읽고 물음에 답하시오.

Emma: Tim, look at your face! You got sunburn.

Tim: Yes, it hurts a lot. I went swimming at the beach without sunscreen.

Emma: Oh dear! Make sure you wear sunscreen next time.

13 위 대화에서 다음 영영풀이가 가리키는 말을 찾아 쓰시오.

> a condition in which your skin becomes sore and red from too much sunshine

➡ _____

14 What did Emma tell Tim to do?

➡ _____

15 다음 대화의 내용과 일치하도록 Tom의 일기를 완성하시오.

> **Tom:** Let's go swimming this weekend, Yujin.
>
> **Yujin:** I'd love to, but I can't.
>
> **Tom:** Why not?
>
> **Yujin:** I have an eye problem. The doctor told me to stop swimming for a while.
>
> **Tom:** I'm sorry to hear that. Maybe we can go next weekend.
>
> **Yujin:** I really hope so.

⬇

> Mon, June 24th, 2019
> Today, I suggested (A)_____
> _____ to Yujin. Unfortunately,
> she said she couldn't join me because of
> (B)_____. She told me that she
> should (C)_____. I
> was sorry to hear that. I hoped we could
> go together next weekend.

[16~17] 다음 대화를 읽고 물음에 답하시오.

> **Jane:** How was the soccer game with Minsu's class, Alex?
>
> **Alex:** We lost by three goals.
>
> **Jane:** I'm sorry to hear that. I hope you do better next time.
>
> **Alex:** I hope so, too.

16 With whose class did Alex's class play the soccer game?

➡ _____

17 What did Alex hope to do next time?

➡ _____

Grammar

18 다음 우리말을 영어로 옮길 때 빈칸에 들어갈 말로 가장 적절한 것은?

> 그것은 나에게 생각할 다른 무언가를 줄 거야.
> It will give me _____.

① something to think about different
② something different to think with
③ differently thinking about something
④ different something to think
⑤ something different to think about

19 다음 중 어법상 바르지 않은 것은?

> **Joe:** I ①have had ②a cold ③since over a week.
>
> **Mary:** Why don't you ④go ⑤see a doctor?

①   ②   ③   ④   ⑤

20 다음 우리말을 영어로 바르게 옮기지 않은 것은?

① 나는 재미있는 무언가를 하길 원해.
→ I want to do something fun.
② 그들은 전에 그 박물관에 가 본 적이 있니?
→ Have they been to the museum before?
③ 난 데리고 올 사람이 없어.
→ I have no one to bring.
④ Jason은 여름 휴가 갔어.
→ Jason has gone on summer vacation.
⑤ Jessica는 지난주부터 아파.
→ Jessica was sick since last week.

21 다음 빈칸에 들어갈 말로 적절하지 않은 것은?

> The children have played basketball together _____.

① already   ② before   ③ once
④ many times   ⑤ yesterday

22 주어진 단어를 이용하여 다음 우리말을 영어로 쓰시오.

> 너는 뭔가 이상한 것을 발견했니? (find)

➡ _____

23 다음 문장을 읽고 알 수 있는 것을 모두 고르시오.

> Grace has left the hospital already.

① Grace was in the hospital.
② Grace likes to go to the hospital.
③ Grace has gone to the hospital.
④ Grace is not in the hospital now.
⑤ Grace has been to the hospital several times.

24 다음 문장의 현재완료와 그 쓰임이 다른 하나는?

> Has Sarah started her new job yet?

① I haven't met my new neighbor yet.
② Joe has just read the book.
③ Becky has already had dinner.
④ Mom has driven the car for a month.
⑤ They have already checked the list.

25 다음 문항에서 어법상 틀린 것을 찾아 바르게 고치시오.

> Steve's grandmother has died two years ago.

➡ _____

26 다음 중 어법상 바르지 않은 것은?

① Yuna is cooking something healthy.
② Ian is planning something special for summer.
③ Jiho hasn't cleaned his room yet.
④ Jenny has lost her card the other day.
⑤ I have never learned judo before.

27 주어진 단어를 활용하여 다음 대화의 우리말을 영어로 쓰시오.

> A: 영화는 아직 시작하지 않았어. (start)
> B: Then how about buying something to eat?

➡ _____

Reading

[28~31] 다음 글을 읽고 물음에 답하시오.

ⓐIt was a hot summer evening. Seojun went for a walk in the park. Soon, he was sweating.

Seojun: I'm thirsty. I want something cold to drink.

At that moment, something tiny flew at him and bit his arm.

Mrs. Mosquito: Hey, catch me if you can.

Seojun: Who are you? ⓑWhat have you done to me?

Mrs. Mosquito: I'm a mosquito. I've just finished my dinner.

Seojun: Where are you from? How did you find me?

Mrs. Mosquito: I'm from a nearby river. I was looking for some blood to drink there. Then I smelled something sweaty and found you here.

28 다음 중 밑줄 친 ⓐ와 쓰임이 다른 하나는?

① It was dark outside.

② It is Sunday today.

③ It was rainy then.

④ It is not my fault.

⑤ It is two miles from here to the beach.

29 다음 중 밑줄 친 문장 ⓑ와 현재완료의 쓰임이 다른 하나는?

① Stella has done her homework already.

② Matt has just met Mina in the church.

③ We have seen this movie before.

④ They have already had lunch.

⑤ Have you finished your homework yet?

30 다음 중 위 글을 읽고 답할 수 없는 것은?

① Why was Seojun sweating?

② How did Seojun feel when he was walking?

③ Where did Mrs. Mosquito come from?

④ Where is Seojun from?

⑤ What did Mrs. Mosquito do to Seojun?

31

Where did Mrs. Mosquito smell something sweaty? Answer in English with a full sentence.

➡ _____

[32~36] 다음 대화를 읽고 물음에 답하시오.

Seojun: That's interesting. So why do you drink blood?

Mrs. Mosquito: I need the protein in blood to lay my eggs. ①

Seojun: How do you drink blood? Do you have sharp teeth?

Mrs. Mosquito: No, I don't have teeth. ② But I have a long and pointed mouth. So I can drink your blood easily. ③

Seojun: After you bit me, I got a bump. It itches.

Mrs. Mosquito: I'm sorry to hear that. ④ Also, clean it with alcohol wipes.

Seojun: Alcohol wipes? I've never tried that before.

Mrs. Mosquito: It will reduce the itchiness. ⑤

Seojun: Okay, I'll try that at home. Thanks.

32 ①~⑤ 중 다음 주어진 문장이 들어가기에 가장 적절한 곳은?

Make sure you don't scratch it.

①   ②   ③   ④   ⑤

33 다음 중 위 대화의 내용과 일치하지 않는 것은?

① Seojun wonders why Mrs. Mosquito drinks blood.

② Mrs. Mosquito can drink blood easily with its mouth.

③ Seojun has never cleaned a bump with alcohol wipes before.

④ Seojun wants to know how to use alcohol wipes.

⑤ Mrs. Mosquito bit Seojun.

34 위 대화의 내용에 맞게 다음 빈칸에 알맞은 말을 쓰시오.

Q: How can Mrs. Mosquito drink blood easily?

A: She can drink blood easily thanks to

_____.

35 다음과 같이 풀이되는 단어를 위 대화에서 찾아 쓰시오.

an area of skin that is raised because it was hit, bitten, etc.

➡ _____

36

According to the dialog, what will Seojun do when he goes home? Answer in English. Use the words 'clean' and 'with.'

➡ _____

출제율 90%

01 다음 문장에 공통으로 들어갈 말을 고르시오.

> • Can I use your phone _____ a while?
> • I often go _____ a walk, listening to music.

① from ② by
③ for ④ off
⑤ during

[02~03] 다음 대화를 읽고 물음에 답하시오.

Sujin: Dad, do we have any bug spray?
Dad: Yes, it's under the sink. Why?
Sujin: There are a lot of fruit flies around the trash.
Dad: Oh no! What did you put in the trash?
Sujin: Some fruit waste.
Dad: Fruit flies love sweet things. Make sure you don't put fruit waste in the trash can.
Sujin: I'll keep (A)that in mind. I think we should also empty our trash can more often.
Dad: That's a good idea.

출제율 90%

02 위 대화의 밑줄 친 (A)that이 가리키는 내용을 우리말로 간략히 쓰시오.

➡ _____

출제율 95%

03 위 대화의 내용과 일치하지 않는 것은?

① Sujin looked for the bug spray because of lots of fruit flies.
② Sujin put some fruit waste in the trash.
③ Fruit flies like sweet things, so Sujin should not put fruit waste in the trash can.
④ It is a good way to empty the trash can more often to prevent fruit flies.
⑤ Sujin makes sure that she should put fruit trash in the trash can.

[04~05] 다음 대화를 읽고 물음에 답하시오.

Jane: (A)[What / How] was the soccer game with Minsu's class, Alex?
Alex: We lost (B)[by / off] three goals.
Jane: I'm sorry to hear that. I hope you do (C) [much / better] next time.
Alex: I hope so, too.

출제율 100%

04 위 대화의 (A)~(C)에 들어갈 말로 적절한 것끼리 짝지어진 것은?

	(A)	(B)	(C)
①	What	by	much
②	What	off	much
③	How	by	much
④	How	off	better
⑤	How	by	better

출제율 90%

05 위 대화의 내용과 일치하도록 빈칸을 완성하시오.

> Alex was depressed after the soccer game with Minsu's class because his class _____ _____. Jane encouraged him to _____ next time.

[06~08] 다음 대화를 읽고 물음에 답하시오.

Brian: You look ⓐworried, Jimin. What's ⓑ wrong?
Jimin: I'm worried ⓒbecause of my cat is sick.
Brian: I'm sorry ⓓto hear that. Why don't you ⓔtake her to an animal doctor?
Jimin: Okay, I will.

출제율 90%

06 위 대화의 밑줄 친 ⓐ~ⓔ 중 어법상 어색한 것을 찾아 바르게 고치시오.

➡ _____

07 What's the matter with Jimin?

➡ _____

08 What is Jimin going to do after talking with Brian?

➡ _____

[09~10] 다음 대화를 읽고 물음에 답하시오.

Tom: Let's go swimming this weekend, Yujin.

Yujin: I'd love to, but I can't.

Tom: Why not?

Yujin: I have an eye problem. The doctor told me to stop swimming for a while.

Tom: I'm sorry to hear that. Maybe we can go next weekend.

Yujin: I really hope so.

09 What did Tom suggest to Yujin?

➡ _____

10 Why couldn't Yujin go swimming with Tom?

➡ _____

11 다음 우리말을 주어진 단어를 배열하여 영어로 쓰시오. 필요하다면 단어를 추가하거나 변형하시오.

그녀는 그녀를 도울 힘 센 누군가가 필요하다. (her / she / help / need / strong / someone)

➡ _____

12 다음 주어진 문장의 빈칸에 들어갈 말과 같은 말이 들어가는 것은?

Mr. and Mrs. Hanson have been together _____ they were in college.

① The weather has been fine _____ a long time.
② I have been waiting for the bus _____ fifteen minutes.
③ We haven't eaten anything _____ breakfast.
④ Jacob has known the boys _____ a year.
⑤ They have lived in this town _____ several months.

13 다음 우리말을 영어로 바르게 옮긴 것은?

그들은 런던을 방문한 적이 없다.

① They have gone to London.
② They have never gone to London.
③ They have been to London
④ They have never visited London.
⑤ They have just visited London.

14 다음 중 어법상 옳은 문장의 개수는?

ⓐ Did you see strange anyone on the street?
ⓑ I'm ready now. I have finished my work.
ⓒ Where have you been last night?
ⓓ She said she needed something sweet to eat.
ⓔ What time did Kelly go out?

① 1개   ② 2개   ③ 3개
④ 4개   ⑤ 5개

출제율 90%

15 주어진 단어를 활용하여 빈칸에 알맞은 말을 쓰시오.

> A: What does your friend do?
>
> B: He is a sculptor. He _____ (win) many prizes for his work.
>
> A: _____ (you / see) any of his sculptures?
>
> B: Yes, I _____ (see) some of his works last week.

출제율 100%

16 다음 중 현재완료의 용법이 <u>다른</u> 하나는?

① How long have you played the guitar?

② The Roberts have been married for 15 years.

③ Have you known Linda for a long time?

④ This house has been empty for many years.

⑤ Have you ever talked with July seriously?

출제율 90%

17 다음 대화의 빈칸에 알맞은 말을 쓰시오.

> A: I want something _____ _____ _____. Do you have anything like that?
>
> B: I have some cold milk.

[18~20] 다음 글을 읽고 물음에 답하시오.

> Mrs. Mosquito: I'm from a nearby river. I was looking for some blood to drink there. Then I smelled something sweaty and found you here.
>
> Seojun: How could you smell me from the river?
>
> Mrs. Mosquito: Mosquitoes can sense heat and smell very well. (A)[That's because / That's why] we have survived (B)[for / since] millions of years.

> Seojun: Do all mosquitoes drink blood like you?
>
> Mrs. Mosquito: No. Only female mosquitoes like me drink blood. Male mosquitoes only feed on fruit and plant juice.
>
> Seojun: That's interesting. So why do you drink blood?
>
> Mrs. Mosquito: I need the protein in blood to (C) [lie / lay] my eggs.

출제율 90%

18 (A)~(C)에서 어법상 옳은 것끼리 바르게 짝지어진 것은?

① That's because	for	lay
② That's why	for	lie
③ That's because	since	lay
④ That's why	for	lay
⑤ That's because	since	lie

출제율 95%

19 다음 중 위 글의 내용과 일치하지 <u>않는</u> 것은?

① Mrs. Mosquito wanted to drink blood.

② Mrs. Mosquito smelled something sweaty from the nearby river.

③ All mosquitoes drink blood.

④ Female mosquitoes drink blood because they need protein in blood.

⑤ Male mosquitoes eat plant juice as food.

출제율 90%

20 위 글의 내용에 맞게 빈칸에 알맞은 말을 주어진 단어를 활용하여 쓰시오.

> Mosquitoes are good at _____ _____ _____ _____. (sense)

[21~25] 다음 글을 읽고 물음에 답하시오.

Seojun: How do you drink blood? Do you have sharp teeth?

Mrs. Mosquito: No, I don't have teeth. But I have a long and pointed mouth. ⓐ _____ I can drink your blood easily.

Seojun: After you bit me, I got ①a bump. ②It itches.

Mrs. Mosquito: I'm sorry to hear that. Make sure you don't scratch ③it. Also, clean ④it with alcohol wipes.

Seojun: Alcohol wipes? ⓑI've never tried that before.

Mrs. Mosquito: ⑤It will reduce the itchiness.

Seojun: Okay, I'll try that at home. Thanks.

Mrs. Mosquito: I have to go. See you soon.

Seojun: Where are you going?

Mrs. Mosquito: I'm going back to the river.

출제율 90%

21 다음 중 빈칸 ⓐ에 들어갈 말로 가장 적절한 것은?

① That's because
② However
③ That's why
④ But
⑤ On the other hand

출제율 100%

22 다음 중 밑줄 친 ⓑ의 현재완료와 그 쓰임이 다른 하나는?

① Jane has been to France once.
② He has heard the music before.
③ Mina has gone to her home.
④ We have visited there many times.
⑤ Have you played the golf before?

출제율 95%

23 밑줄 친 ①~⑤ 중 가리키는 것이 다른 하나는?

①　　　②　　　③　　　④　　　⑤

출제율 90%

24 다음 중 위 글을 읽고 답할 수 없는 것은?

① Why does Mrs. Mosquito feel sorry?
② What will reduce the itchiness?
③ What is Seojun going to do at home?
④ How long is Mrs. Mosquito's mouth?
⑤ What did Seojun get after Mrs. Mosquito bit him?

출제율 90%

25 주어진 어구를 이용하여 다음 물음에 완전한 문장으로 답하시오.

> **Q:** How can you reduce the itchiness when you get a mosquito bite? (the area / with / can)

➡ _____

_____

[01~03] 다음 대화를 읽고 물음에 답하시오.

Sujin: Dad, do we have any bug spray?

Dad: Yes, it's under the sink. Why?

Sujin: There are a lot of fruit flies around the trash.

Dad: Oh no! What did you put in the trash?

Sujin: Some fruit waste.

Dad: Fruit flies love sweet things. Make sure you don't put fruit waste in the trash can.

Sujin: I'll keep that in mind. I think we should also empty our trash can more often.

Dad: That's a good idea.

01 Where is the bug spray?

➡ _____

02 Why is Sujin looking for the bug spray?

➡ _____

03 What should Sujin do to prevent fruit flies?

➡ _____

_____

04 주어진 단어를 바르게 배열하여 다음 대화를 완성하시오. (필요하다면 단어를 추가하시오.)

> A: Do you have a special plan for today?
> B: No. (nothing / do / have / special / I)

➡ _____

05 다음 대화가 자연스럽게 이어지도록 순서대로 배열하시오.

> (A) Why not?
> (B) I'd love to, but I can't.
> (C) I have an eye problem. The doctor told me to stop swimming for a while.
> (D) I'm sorry to hear that. Maybe we can go next weekend.
> (E) Let's go swimming this weekend, Yujin.

➡ _____

06 주어진 단어를 활용하여 빈칸에 알맞은 말을 쓰시오.

> A: Do you know Jason's sister?
> B: I _____ (see) her a few times, but I _____ (never / speak) to her until now. _____ (you / ever / speak) to her?
> A: Yes. I _____ (meet) her at a party last month. She is very kind.

07 주어진 단어를 활용하여 다음 우리말을 영어로 쓰시오.

> 나는 함께 얘기할 어떤 재미있는 사람이 필요해. (funny / someone)

➡ _____

08 다음 우리말을 6단어의 영어로 이루어진 문장으로 쓰시오.

> 나는 너에게 결코 거짓말을 한 적이 없어.

➡ _____

09 다음 빈칸에 알맞은 말을 쓰시오.

> Nick has been sick _____ a long time. He has been in the hospital _____ October.

10 다음 빈칸에 알맞은 말을 두 단어로 쓰시오.

> Don't do _____.
> 위험한 일은 하지 마.

[11~16] 다음 대화를 읽고 물음에 답하시오.

Seojun: Who are you? What have you done to me?

Mrs. Mosquito: I'm a mosquito. I've just finished my dinner.

Seojun: ①Where are you from? How did you find me?

Mrs. Mosquito: I'm from ②a nearby river. I ③was looking for some blood to drink there. Then I smelled (A)sweaty something and found you here.

Seojun: How could you smell me from the river?

Mrs. Mosquito: Mosquitoes can sense heat and smell very well. That's why we ④have survived for millions of years.

Seojun: Do all mosquitoes drink blood like you?

Mrs. Mosquito: No. Only female mosquitoes like me ⑤drinks blood. Male mosquitoes only feed on fruit and plant juice.

11 밑줄 친 (A)를 올바르게 고치시오.

➡ _____

12 위 대화의 내용에 맞게 다음 물음에 완전한 문장의 영어로 답하시오.

> Q: How did Mrs. Mosquito find Seojun?

➡ _____

13 모기들이 수백만 년 동안 살아남은 이유를 영어로 쓰시오. (8 words)

➡ _____

14 위 대화의 내용에 맞게 다음 빈칸에 알맞은 말을 쓰시오.

> A: I got a mosquito bite.
> B: Oh, that must be a _____ mosquito. I heard that _____ mosquitoes just eat fruit and plant juice.

15 ①~⑤ 중 어법상 틀린 것을 골라 바르게 고쳐 쓰시오.

➡ _____

16 주어진 단어를 바르게 배열하여 암컷 모기와 수컷 모기의 차이를 한 문장으로 쓰시오.

> (on / female / male / feed / mosquitoes / mosquitoes / blood / unlike)

➡ _____

_____

01 다음 대화의 내용과 일치하도록 빈칸을 완성하시오.

> Mike: Did you pack for the school trip tomorrow, Sue?
> Sue: Yes. Now I'm checking my list again. I don't want to miss anything.
> Mike: Make sure you take an umbrella with you. It might rain tomorrow.
> Sue: Okay, thank you.

⬇

> Sue was checking her list again after (A)_____ because she didn't want to miss anything. At that time, Mike reminded her to (B)_____ because it might rain tomorrow.

02 현재완료의 완료, 계속, 경험, 결과 용법을 이용하여 자신의 이야기를 <보기>와 같이 쓰시오.

보기
> • I have just made some cookies.
> • I have driven a car for ten years.
> • I have been to Japan with my family.
> • I have lost my backpack in the zoo.

(1) _____

(2) _____

(3) _____

(4) _____

03 '-body, -thing, -one'으로 끝나는 부정대명사와 주어진 형용사를 이용하여 여름에 할 수 있는 다양한 말을 써 보시오.

> cold   cool   funny   scary

(1) _____

(2) _____

(3) _____

(4) _____

단원별 모의고사

01 다음 문장의 빈칸에 들어갈 말을 보기에서 골라 쓰시오.

> ┤ 보기 ├
>
> at that moment / go for a walk /
> keep in mind / lose by

(1) Ann and Jane usually _____
after meals.

(2) _____, the phone rang.

(3) Tim's team will _____ a
score of 2-1.

(4) _____ that you should wear
the sunscreen.

[02~03] 다음 대화를 읽고 물음에 답하시오.

Tom: Let's go swimming this weekend, Yujin.

Yujin: (A) I'd love to, but I can't.

Tom: (B) Why not?

Yujin: (C) The doctor told me to stop
swimming for a while.

Tom: (D) I'm sorry to hear that. Maybe we can
go next weekend.

Yujin: (E) I really hope so.

02 위 대화의 (A)~(E) 중 주어진 문장이 들어가기에 적절한 곳은?

> I have an eye problem.

① (A) ② (B) ③ (C) ④ (D) ⑤ (E)

03 위 대화의 내용과 일치하지 <u>않는</u> 것은?

① Tom suggested going swimming this
weekend to Yujin.

② Yujin wished to go swimming but she
couldn't.

③ Yujin had an eye problem.

④ The doctor said that Yujin should not
swim for a while.

⑤ Yujin made a plan to go swimming next
weekend.

04 다음 대화의 (A)~(C)에 들어갈 알맞은 말을 고르시오.

Brian: You look (A)[worrying / worried],
Jimin. What's wrong?

Jimin: I'm sad (B)[because / because of]
my cat is sick.

Brian: I'm sorry (C)[hearing / to hear] that.
Why don't you take her to an animal
doctor?

Jimin: Okay, I will.

	(A)	(B)	(C)
①	worrying	because	hearing
②	worrying	because of	hearing
③	worried	because	hearing
④	worried	because of	to hear
⑤	worried	because	to hear

[05~06] 다음 대화를 읽고 물음에 답하시오.

Mike: Did you pack for the school trip
tomorrow, Sue?

Sue: Yes. Now I'm checking my list again. I
don't want to miss anything.

Mike: (A)_____ It might
rain tomorrow.

Sue: Okay, thank you.

05 위 대화의 빈칸에 들어갈 말을 〈보기〉에 주어진 단어를 배
열하여 완성하시오.

> ┤ 보기 ├
>
> with / make / you / take / an /
> umbrella / you / sure

➡ _____

06 위 대화를 읽고 대답할 수 없는 것은?

① What is Sue checking now?
② What is Sue going to do tomorrow?
③ What might be the weather like tomorrow?
④ What is Mike asking Sue do to?
⑤ What did Sue miss?

[07~08] 다음 대화를 읽고 물음에 답하시오.

Amy: I have a mosquito bite. It's really itchy.
Brian: I'm sorry to hear that. Hold a green tea bag on the itchy area. That'll help.
Amy: Okay, I'll try that.
Brian: (A)_____(prevent) more bites, make sure you stay cool and avoid (B)_____ (sweat).
Amy: Good idea. Thanks.

07 위 대화의 빈칸 (A)와 (B)에 주어진 단어를 적절한 형태로 쓰시오.

➡ (A) _____, (B) _____

08 What can Amy do to relieve the itchiness?

➡ _____

[09~10] 다음 대화를 읽고 물음에 답하시오.

Ms. Wheeler: Junsu, what happened to your face?
Junsu: (A) I got a lot of mosquito bites.
Ms. Wheeler: (B) How did it happen?
Junsu: (C) It happened when I went camping last weekend.
Ms. Wheeler: (D) Oh dear. Don't scratch them!
Junsu: (E) I know, but they're really itchy.

Ms. Wheeler: Clean them with cool water. That'll help. Also, make sure you wear long sleeves when you go camping.
Junsu: Okay, thank you.

09 위 대화의 (A)~(E) 중에서 주어진 문장이 들어가기에 적절한 곳을 고르시오.

I'm sorry to hear that.

① (A)   ② (B)   ③ (C)   ④ (D)   ⑤ (E)

10 위 대화의 내용과 일치하도록 빈칸을 완성하시오.

Junsu: I'm suffering from (A)_____ _____ on my face. I got them when I went camping last weekend. They are really (B)_____. Ms. Wheeler advised me to (C)_____. Moreover, I keep in mind that (D)_____ _____when I go camping.

11 다음 대화가 자연스럽게 이어지도록 순서대로 배열하시오.

(A) I hope so, too.
(B) We lost by three goals.
(C) How was the soccer game with Minsu's class, Alex?
(D) I'm sorry to hear that. I hope you do better next time.

➡ _____

12 다음 주어진 그림을 보고 빈칸에 알맞은 말을 쓰시오.

A: Make sure _____.
B: Okay. I'll keep that in mind.

➡ _____

13 다음 중 어법상 바르지 <u>않은</u> 것은?

① Dan arrived here an hour ago.
② I have read this novel for last Friday.
③ Do you have anything cold to drink?
④ Have you met each other before?
⑤ Clara is drawing something funny.

14 다음 두 문장을 하나의 문장으로 표현하시오.

Claire is studying medicine at the university. She started studying medicine two years ago.

➡ _____
_____

15 다음 빈칸에 들어갈 말로 가장 적절한 것은?

Where _____? I have been looking for you all afternoon.

① are you going
② have you gone
③ have you been
④ were you going
⑤ do you want to go

16 다음 대화의 빈칸에 들어갈 말이 바르게 짝지어진 것은?

A: Would you like something _____?
B: No, thanks. I _____.

① eating – had lunch
② to eat – have just had lunch
③ eating – haven't had lunch yet
④ to eat – didn't have lunch
⑤ to eat – have had lunch an hour ago

17 주어진 단어를 활용하여 다음 우리말을 영어로 쓰시오.

내게는 해야 할 더 중요한 일이 있어요.
(have / important / do)

➡ _____

[18~21] 다음 글을 읽고 물음에 답하시오.

It was a hot summer evening. Seojun went for a walk in the park. Soon, he was sweating.

Seojun: I'm thirsty. I want something cold to drink.

At that moment, (A)<u>뭔가 조그마한 것이 그에게로 날아 왔다</u> and bit his arm. (tiny, fly)

Mrs. Mosquito: Hey, catch me if you can.

Seojun: Who are you? What have you done to me?

Mrs. Mosquito: I'm a mosquito. I've just finished my dinner.

Seojun: Where are you from? How did you find me?

Mrs. Mosquito: I'm from a nearby river. I was looking for some blood to drink there. Then I smelled something sweaty and found you here.

18 밑줄 친 우리말 (A)를 주어진 단어를 이용하여 영어로 쓰시오.

➡ _____

19 다음 중 위 글의 내용과 일치하지 <u>않는</u> 것은?

① Seojun was walking in the park.
② It happened in a hot summer evening.
③ Mrs. Mosquito bit Seojun's leg.
④ Mrs. Mosquito had dinner by drinking blood.
⑤ Seojun wanted to drink something cold.

20 다음 중 위 글에서 찾아볼 수 <u>없는</u> 것은?

① 무더운 여름날 저녁
② 땀을 흘리는 서준
③ 강에서 마실 물을 찾는 모기
④ 땀 냄새를 감지한 모기
⑤ 갈증을 느끼는 서준

21 다음은 근처 강에서 모기가 한 말이다. 빈칸에 들어갈 말을 위 글에서 찾아 쓰시오.

| Oh, I am so hungry. I need _____. |

➡ _____

[22~25] 다음 글을 읽고 물음에 답하시오.

My family and I moved to Korea when I was 8. We have lived in Korea for 6 years. (A)We have visited many great places here. Today is the first day of summer vacation. Tomorrow, we are going to visit Jeju. I have never been to Jeju. So I'm very excited. I have just finished packing, and I'm ready to go. I hope we have a wonderful time in Jeju.

*I = Kate

22 다음 중 밑줄 친 (A)와 같은 의미의 문장은?

① We have met many people in Korea.
② We have been to many places in Korea.
③ We hoped to go back to the place we lived in.
④ We have gone to many great places in Korea.
⑤ We think there are many great places to see in Korea.

23 다음 중 위 글의 내용과 일치하지 <u>않는</u> 것은?

① Kate lives in Korea with her family.
② Kate moved to Korea six years ago.
③ She is going to visit Jeju.
④ Kate feels excited to visit Jeju.
⑤ Kate has not packed yet.

24 According to the passage, how old is Kate now?

➡ _____

25 위 글의 내용에 맞게 빈칸에 알맞은 말을 쓰시오.

| Kate has lived in Korea _____ she was eight. |

I Don't Have a Clue

의사소통 기능

- 설명 요청하기
  Can you explain how to use the buttons?

- 열거하기
  First, fold the paper in half. Second, turn it over.
  Then, draw a face.

언어 형식

- 수동태
  The cheese **was eaten by** a mouse.

- 조동사의 수동태
  Bright stars **can be seen** at night.

Words & Expressions

교과서

Key Words

□ **accident**[ǽksidənt] 명 사고

□ **bat**[bæt] 명 배트, 방망이

□ **bean**[biːn] 명 콩

□ **block**[blɑk] 명 구역, 블록

□ **bottom**[bátəm] 명 맨 아래 (부분)

□ **button**[bʌ́tən] 명 단추

□ **candle**[kǽndl] 명 양초

□ **clue**[kluː] 명 단서, 실마리

□ **congratulation**[kəngrætʃuléiʃən] 명 축하

□ **cross**[krɔːs] 동 건너다

□ **delete**[dilíːt] 동 삭제하다

□ **detective**[ditéktiv] 명 탐정, 형사

□ **disappear**[dìsəpíər] 동 사라지다

□ **dragon**[drǽɡən] 명 용

□ **enter**[éntər] 동 입장하다, 들어가다

□ **escape**[iskéip] 동 탈출하다

□ **explain**[ikspléin] 동 설명하다

□ **finally**[fáinəli] 부 마침내

□ **fold**[fould] 동 접다

□ **half**[hæf] 명 반, 절반

□ **hide**[haid] 동 숨기다, 숨다

□ **inside**[ìnsáid] 전 ~의 안에, ~의 내부에

□ **lie**[lai] 동 거짓말하다

□ **luckily**[lʌ́kili] 부 다행히

□ **none**[nʌn] 대 하나도 ~ 않다

□ **outside**[áutsàid] 전 ~ 밖에 부 밖으로, 밖에

□ **prize**[praiz] 명 상

□ **riddle**[rídl] 명 수수께끼

□ **safely**[séifli] 부 안전하게

□ **scene**[siːn] 명 장면

□ **solve**[sɑlv] 동 해결하다

□ **somewhere**[sʌ́mhwɛər] 부 어딘가에

□ **space**[speis] 명 공간, 우주

□ **stamp**[stæmp] 명 우표

□ **straight**[streit] 부 똑바로, 일직선으로

□ **strange**[streindʒ] 형 이상한

□ **suspect**[səspékt] 명 용의자

□ **thief**[θiːf] 명 도둑

□ **throw**[θrou] 동 던지다

□ **triangle**[tráiæŋgl] 명 삼각형

□ **twice**[twais] 부 두 번, 두 배

□ **win**[win] 동 얻다, 이기다

Key Expressions

□ **at the time of**: ~이 일어나던 때에

□ **catch a thief**: 도둑을 잡다

□ **fill A with B**: A를 B로 채우다

□ **for free**: 공짜로

□ **help yourself**: 마음껏 드세요

□ **make it to** ~: ~에 이르는 데 성공하다

□ **turn over**: ~을 뒤집다

□ **write down**: ~을 적다

Word Power

※ 서로 반대되는 뜻을 가진 단어

- □ **appear** 나타나다 ↔ **disappear** 사라지다
- □ **top** 맨 위 ↔ **bottom** 맨 아래쪽
- □ **throw** 던지다 ↔ **catch** 잡다
- □ **win** 이기다 ↔ **lose** 지다
- □ **dark** 어두운 ↔ **bright** 밝은

- □ **inside** ~의 안에 ↔ **outside** ~의 밖에
- □ **safe** 안전한 ↔ **dangerous** 위험한
- □ **special** 특별한 ↔ **general** 일반적인
- □ **straight** 똑바른, 일직선의 ↔ **curved** 굽은
- □ **fold** 접다 ↔ **unfold** 펴다

English Dictionary

- □ **accident** 사고
  → an event in which a car, train, plane, etc. is damaged and often someone is hurt
  자동차, 기차, 비행기 등이 손상되고 때로는 누군가가 다치는 사건

- □ **bat** 방망이, 배트
  → a long wooden stick with a special shape that is used in some sports and games
  몇몇 스포츠와 게임에서 사용되는 특별한 모양을 가진 긴 나무 막대

- □ **bean** 콩
  → a seed or a pod that comes from a climbing plant and is cooked as food
  덩굴나무에서 나오며 음식으로 요리되는 씨앗 또는 꼬투리

- □ **bottom** 맨 아래 (부분)
  → the flat surface on the lowest side of an object
  물체의 가장 낮은 부분의 평평한 표면

- □ **clue** 단서, 실마리
  → an object or piece of information that helps someone solve a crime or mystery
  누군가가 범죄나 미스터리를 풀도록 도와주는 물체나 정보

- □ **cross** 건너다
  → to go from one side of something such as a road, river, room, etc. to the other
  길, 강, 방 등과 같은 무언가의 한 쪽에서 다른 쪽으로 가다

- □ **delete** 삭제하다
  → to remove something that has been written down or stored in a computer
  적어 놓았거나 컴퓨터에 저장해 놓은 무언가를 제거하다

- □ **detective** 탐정
  → someone who is paid to discover information about someone or something
  누군가 또는 무언가에 대한 정보를 발견하도록 돈을 받는 사람

- □ **enter** 입장하다
  → to go or come into a place
  한 장소로 들어가거나 들어오다

- □ **escape** 탈출하다
  → to leave a place when someone is trying to catch you or stop you, or when there is a dangerous situation
  누군가가 당신을 잡으려 하거나 당신을 멈출 때, 또는 위험한 상황이 있을 때 한 장소를 떠나다

- □ **half** 반, 절반
  → exactly or about 50% of an amount, time, distance, number, etc.
  양, 시간, 거리, 수 등의 정확히 또는 거의 50%

- □ **riddle** 수수께끼
  → a question that is deliberately very confusing and has a humorous or clever answer
  의도적으로 매우 혼란스럽게 하는 그리고 재미있거나 재기 넘치는 대답을 갖는 질문

- □ **suspect** 용의자
  → someone who is thought to be guilty of a crime
  어떤 범죄의 죄가 있다고 생각되는 사람

- □ **thief** 도둑
  → someone who steals things from another person or place
  다른 사람이나 장소로부터 물건들을 훔치는 사람

01 다음 짝지어진 단어의 관계가 같도록 빈칸에 알맞은 말을 쓰시오.

> agree: disagree = appear : _____

02 다음 영영풀이가 가리키는 것을 고르시오.

> to remove something that has been written down or stored in a computer

① enter ② delete ③ shift
④ throw ⑤ cross

03 다음 중 밑줄 친 부분의 뜻풀이가 바르지 <u>않은</u> 것은?

① Clues can be found <u>somewhere</u> inside the room. 어딘가에
② <u>Luckily</u>, he wasn't badly hurt. 다행히
③ The thief <u>escaped</u> from the police station. 탈출했다
④ Where did you <u>hide</u> your gold? 찾다
⑤ The players are dragons and <u>seahorses</u>. 해마

04 다음 우리말에 맞게 빈칸에 알맞은 말을 쓰시오.

(1) 나는 셜록 홈즈가 위대한 탐정들 중 한 명이었다고 생각한다.
➡ I think Sherlock Holmes was one of the greatest _____.
(2) 수건을 반으로 접으세요.
➡ _____ the towel in _____.
(3) 그는 1분 만에 수학 퍼즐을 해결했다.
➡ He _____ the math puzzle in just one minute.

05 다음 문장의 빈칸에 들어갈 말을 〈보기〉에서 골라 쓰시오.

> ┤ 보기 ├
> made it to / turn over / help yourself /
> for free

(1) The soccer team _____ the finals.
(2) I got this T-shirt _____.
(3) You should _____ the sweet potato before it burns.
(4) _____ to anything you like on the table.

06 다음 주어진 문장의 밑줄 친 suspects와 같은 의미로 쓰인 것은?

> The detective met some <u>suspects</u> and asked questions.

① The spoiled food is <u>suspected</u> of causing food poisoning.
② Who is the <u>suspect</u> in the crime?
③ I <u>suspected</u> that he stole my wallet.
④ The police <u>suspect</u> that he is a spy.
⑤ We <u>suspected</u> him to be a liar.

07 다음 문장에 공통으로 들어갈 말을 고르시오.

> • There is enough space for three people to _____ down.
> • I don't want to _____ to my parents anymore.
> • I promise not to _____ again.

① explain ② solve ③ throw
④ win ⑤ lie

01 다음 짝지어진 단어의 관계가 같도록 빈칸에 알맞은 말을 쓰시오.

> top : bottom = inside : _____

02 다음 우리말에 맞게 빈칸에 알맞은 말을 쓰시오.

(1) 너는 이것을 일주일에 두 번 볼 수 있다.
➡ You can see this _____ in a week.

(2) 그녀는 사고가 일어나던 때에 아침을 만들고 있었다.
➡ She was making breakfast _____ _____ of the accident.

(3) 당신은 우리 가게에서 일곱 가지 상품을 무엇이든 무료로 고를 수 있다.
➡ You can choose any seven items from our store _____.

03 다음 우리말을 주어진 어구를 배열하여 영작하시오.

(1) 그 이야기를 제게 설명해 주실 수 있나요?
(you / me / to / the story / can / explain)
➡ _____

(2) 너는 하루에 두 번 약을 먹어야 한다.
(twice / a day / the pills / should / you / take)
➡ _____

(3) 나는 빵을 삼각형으로 잘랐다.
(triangles / the bread / into / I / cut)
➡ _____

04 다음 우리말에 맞게 빈칸에 알맞은 말을 쓰시오.

(1) 그녀는 어제 차 사고를 당했다.
➡ She got in a car _____ yesterday.

(2) Mary가 게임하는 중에 다쳤니?
➡ Did Mary get _____ during the game?

(3) 경찰이 오후에 용의자를 심문할 것이다.
➡ The police will _____ the suspect in the afternoon.

(4) 네 컴퓨터에 공간을 만들기 위해 모든 사진을 지워야 한다.
➡ You should _____ all of the pictures on your computer to make more space.

05 다음 우리말을 주어진 단어를 이용하여 영작하시오.

(1) 경찰은 도둑을 잡을 수 있을 것이라고 확신했다. (catch, sure)
➡ _____

(2) 페이지를 넘겨 그림을 보세요. (turn, look)
➡ _____

(3) 이 병을 물로 채워 주시겠어요? (would, fill, with)
➡ _____

06 다음 대화의 빈칸을 완성하시오.

> A: Try to solve this riddle.
> B: Sure.
> A: This has three to four legs but it can't walk. Can you explain why?
> B: Yes! It's because it's a _____.

1 설명 요청하기

Can you explain how to use the buttons? (버튼 사용법을 설명해 줄 수 있니?)

- 'Can you explain ~?'은 '너는 ~을 설명해 줄 수 있니?'라는 뜻으로, 상대방에게 설명을 요청할 때 쓰는 표현이다. 'Can you explain' 다음에 'how to ~' 표현을 사용하여 어떤 절차나 방법을 물어볼 수 있다.

설명 요청하기

- I don't get it. Can you explain why? (이해가 안돼요. 이유를 설명해 줄 수 있나요?)
- Can you show me how to use this machine? (어떻게 이 기계를 사용할 수 있는지 보여줄 수 있나요?)
- Can you tell me how to draw this character? (이 캐릭터를 어떻게 그릴 수 있는지 말해 줄래요?)
- Let me know how to make the cookies. (쿠키 만드는 법을 알려 주세요.)

핵심 Check

1. 다음 우리말과 일치하도록 빈칸에 알맞은 말을 쓰시오.

   (1) **A:** Can you _____ a little bit more? (좀 더 설명을 해 주시겠습니까?)

   B: No problem. (그럼요.)

   (2) **A:** _____ how to use the copier. (복사기 사용법 좀 알려 주세요.)

   B: Sure. Look at this. (물론이지. 여기를 봐.)

   (3) **A:** _____? (어제 무슨 일이 일어났었는지 말해줄 수 있니?)

   B: Well, I got hurt in a car accident. (차 사고로 다쳤어.)

2 열거하기

First, fold the paper in half. Second, turn it over. Then, draw a face.
(먼저, 종이를 반으로 접어. 두 번째로, 뒤집어. 그러고 나서, 얼굴을 그려.)

■ 서수를 사용하여 어떤 절차의 순서를 열거할 수 있다. 이때, 'Second, Third' 대신에 'Next, Then'을 쓸 수 있다.

열거하기

• First, draw a circle. Second, put a star inside. Then, put a triangle on top of the circle.
(첫째로, 원을 그리세요. 둘째, 안에 별을 놓으세요. 그러고 나서, 원의 맨 위에 삼각형을 놓으세요.)

• First, he looked around the school. Then, he met some suspects and asked questions. Finally, he found the thief. (첫째로, 그는 학교를 둘러봤어. 그러고 나서, 몇몇의 용의자를 만나서 질문을 했지. 마침내, 그는 도둑을 찾았어.)

핵심 Check

2. 다음 우리말과 일치하도록 빈칸에 알맞은 말을 쓰시오.

(1) **A:** Can you explain how to make a taco? (타코 만드는 법을 설명해 주실 수 있어요?)

B: _____, fill your tortilla with vegetables and meat. _____, add some sauce on the top. (먼저, 토르티야를 채소와 고기로 채워. 그 다음, 위에 약간의 소스를 추가하렴.)

(2) **A:** _____, the farmer buys a fox, a duck, and a bag of beans. _____, the farmer needs to cross a river. (먼저 농부는 여우, 오리, 콩 자루를 하나씩 사. 그러고 나서, 농부는 강을 건너야 해.)

B: What's the problem? (뭐가 문제인데?)

(3) **A:** _____, fold a paper in half to make a triangle. _____, fold the top of the triangle to the bottom line. _____, fold both ends of the bottom line to the top to make ears. _____, turn it over and draw a face. (먼저, 종이를 반으로 접어서 세모를 만들어. 두 번째로, 세모의 꼭대기를 맨 아랫선 쪽으로 접어. 세 번째로, 맨 아랫선 양쪽 끝을 위로 접어서 귀를 만들어. 그러고 나서, 그것을 뒤집어서 얼굴을 그려.)

B: That sounds easy. (쉽구나.)

Listen and Speak 2-B

Jane: Minsu, do you know the TV show about the student ❶detective?

Minsu: Yes. I love ❷that show, but I didn't see ❷it this week. What was ❷it about?

Jane: Well, all of the bikes at school disappeared.

Minsu: So, what did ❸he do?

Jane: ❹First, he looked around the school. ❹Then, he met some suspects and ❺asked questions. ❹Finally, he found the thief. The thief was....

Minsu: No, don't tell me! I'll watch it later.

Jane: 민수야, 학생 탐정이 나오는 TV쇼를 아니?
Minsu: 응, 나는 그 쇼를 아주 좋아하지만 이번 주에는 못 봤어. 무슨 내용이었어?
Jane: 음, 학교의 모든 자전거들이 사라졌어.
Minsu: 그래서 그가 무엇을 했어?
Jane: 첫째로, 그는 학교를 둘러봤어. 그러고 나서, 몇몇의 용의자를 만나서 질문을 했지. 마침내, 그는 도둑을 찾았어. 도둑은...
Minsu: 안 돼, 말하지 마! 내가 나중에 볼 거야.

❶ detective: 탐정
❷ that show와 it 모두 the TV show about the student detective를 가리킨다.
❸ he는 the student detective를 가리킨다.
❹ 학생 탐정이 한 일을 열거하고 있다.
❺ met과 병렬구조이다.

Check(√) True or False

(1) Minsu loves the TV show about the student detective.　　T ☐ F ☐

(2) Jane knows who the thief was.　　T ☐ F ☐

Real Life Communication

Emily: Junsu, do you want to solve a riddle?

Junsu: Sure, what is ❶it?

Emily: There is a farmer. First, the farmer buys a fox, a duck, and a bag of beans. Then, the farmer needs to cross a river.

Junsu: What's the problem?

Emily: The boat can only hold the farmer and one more thing.

Junsu: ❷Are you saying that the farmer can take only one thing ❸at a time?

Emily: Yes. Also, the fox will eat the duck or the duck will eat the beans if the farmer isn't there. Can you explain how to move everything across the river safely?

Junsu: Hmm ....

Emily: 준수야, 수수께끼 하나 풀어볼래?
Junsu: 물론이지, 뭔데?
Emily: 한 농부가 있어. 먼저 농부는 여우, 오리, 콩 자루를 하나씩 사. 그러고 나서, 농부는 강을 건너야 해.
Junsu: 뭐가 문제인데?
Emily: 보트는 단지 농부와 한 가지만 더 옮길 수 있어.
Junsu: 농부가 한 번에 오직 한 가지만 옮길 수 있다는 말이니?
Emily: 응. 또한 만약 농부가 없다면 여우가 오리를 먹거나, 오리가 콩을 먹을 거야. 전부를 강 건너로 안전하게 옮길 방법을 설명할 수 있겠니?
Junsu: 음....

❶ it은 riddle(수수께끼)을 가리킨다.
❷ 자신의 이해를 한 번 더 점검하고 있다.
❸ at a time: 한 번에

Check(√) True or False

(3) The farmer should cross a river with only one thing.　　T ☐ F ☐

(4) Without the farmer, the fox will eat the beans.　　T ☐ F ☐

Listen and Speak 1-A

Jimin: Do you want to play the new game ❶that I bought?

Brian: Sure, what is it, Jimin?

Jimin: It's ❷like a soccer game but the players are dragons and ❸seahorses. You need to use these buttons to play.

Brian: That sounds fun. ❹Can you explain how to use the buttons?

Jimin: Sure.

❶ that은 목적격 관계대명사로 which로 바꾸어 쓸 수 있다.
❷ like는 전치사로 '~와 같은'을 뜻한다.
❸ seahorse: 해마
❹ 버튼 사용법에 대한 설명을 요청하는 표현이다. how to+동사원형: ~하는 방법

Listen and Speak 2 -A

Tom: Yujin, ❶look at my paper fox.

Yujin: That's cute. How did you make ❷it?

Tom: First, ❸fold a paper ❹in half to make a triangle. Second, fold the top of the triangle to the bottom line. Third, fold both ends of the bottom line to the top to make ears. Then, ❺turn it over and draw a face.

Yujin: That sounds easy.

❶ look at: ~을 보다
❷ it은 Tom's paper fox를 가리킨다.
❸ 동사로 시작하는 명령문이다.
❹ in half: 반으로
❺ turn over: 뒤집다

Listen and Speak 1-B

Jack: Kelly, here's a riddle. You can see this twice in a week, once in a year, but never in a day. What is this?

Kelly: ❶I have no idea.

Jack: It's the letter "E."

Kelly: ❷I don't get it. Can you explain why?

Jack: Well, there are two "E"s in the word "week," one "E" in the word "year" but no "E"s in the word "day."

Kelly: Aha! ❸Now I get it.

❶ I have no idea. = I don't know.
❷ I don't get it. = I don't understand.
❸ I get it. = I understand. = I see.

Let's Check

Minjun: Wow! Something smells really good, Mom. What is it?

Mom: We're going to have tacos for dinner. ❶Help yourself.

Minjun: Can you explain how to make a taco?

Mom: First, ❷fill your tortilla with vegetables and meat. Then, add some sauce on the top.

Minjun: ❸Sounds delicious!

Mom: Would you like some cheese?

Minjun: No, thanks.

❶ Help yourself.: 마음껏 드세요.
❷ fill A with B: A를 B로 채우다
❸ Sounds delicious.: 맛있을 거 같아요.

● 다음 우리말과 일치하도록 빈칸에 알맞은 말을 쓰시오.

Listen & Speak 1 - A

Jimin: Do you want to play the new game _____ I _____?

Brian: Sure, what is it, Jimin?

Jimin: It's _____ a soccer game but the players are _____ and _____. You _____ _____ _____ these buttons _____ _____.

Brian: That _____ fun. _____ _____ _____ _____ _____ _____ the buttons?

Jimin: Sure.

해석

Jimin: 내가 산 새로운 게임을 하고 싶니?
Brian: 물론이야. 그게 뭐니, 지민아?
Jimin: 축구 시합 같은 것인데 선수들이 용과 해야야. 게임을 하려면 이 버튼들을 사용해야 해.
Brian: 재밌을 거 같아. 버튼 사용법을 설명해 줄 수 있니?
Jimin: 물론이지.

Listen & Speak 1 - B

Jack: Kelly, here's a _____. You can see this _____ in a week, _____ in a year, but _____ _____ _____ _____ _____ _____.
What is this?

Kelly: _____ _____ _____ _____ _____.

Jack: It's the letter "E."

Kelly: I don't _____ _____. _____ _____ _____ _____ _____?

Jack: Well, there are two "E"s in the word "week," one "E" in the word "year" but no "E"s in the word "day."

Kelly: Aha! Now I _____ _____.

Jack: Kelly, 수수께끼가 있어. 넌 이것을 1주에 두 번, 1년에 한 번 볼 수 있어, 하지만 1일에는 전혀 볼 수가 없어. 이게 뭐게?
Kelly: 전혀 모르겠어.
Jack: 알파벳 'E'야.
Kelly: 이해가 안 가. 이유를 설명해 줄 수 있니?
Jack: 음, 단어 week에는 'E'가 2개 있고, 단어 year에는 'E'가 1개 있고, 단어 day에는 'E'가 없잖아.
Kelly: 아! 이제 이해했다.

Listen & Speak 2 - A

Tom: Yujin, _____ _____ my paper fox.

Yujin: That's cute. _____ _____ _____ _____ _____ _____ _____?

Tom: _____, fold a paper _____ _____ to make a triangle. _____, fold the top of the triangle to the _____ _____. _____, fold _____ _____ of the bottom line to the top to make ears. _____, _____ it _____ and draw a face.

Yujin: That sounds _____.

Tom: 유진아, 내 종이 여우를 봐.
Yujin: 귀엽다. 어떻게 만들었니?
Tom: 먼저, 종이를 반으로 접어서 세모를 만들어. 두 번째로, 세모의 꼭대기를 맨 아랫선 쪽으로 접어. 세 번째로, 맨 아랫선 양쪽 끝으로 위로 접어서 귀를 만들어. 그리고 나서, 그것을 뒤집어서 얼굴을 그려.
Yujin: 쉽구나.

Listen & Talk 2 - B

Jane: Minsu, do you know the TV show about the student _____?

Minsu: Yes. I love that show, but I _____ _____ it _____ _____. What was it _____?

Jane: Well, _____ _____ the bikes at school _____.

Minsu: So, what _____ he _____?

Jane: _____, he _____ _____ the school. _____, he met some _____ and asked questions. _____, he found the _____. The thief was ....

Minsu: No, _____ _____ me! I'll _____ it _____.

Real Life Communication

Emily: Junsu, do you want to _____ a riddle?

Junsu: Sure, what is it?

Emily: There is a farmer. _____, the farmer buys a fox, a duck, and _____ _____ _____ _____. Then, the farmer _____ _____ _____ _____ _____.

Junsu: What's the problem?

Emily: The boat can only _____ the farmer and _____ _____ thing.

Junsu: Are you saying that the farmer can _____ only one thing _____ _____ _____?

Emily: Yes. Also, the fox will eat the duck or the duck will eat the beans if the farmer isn't there. _____ _____ _____ _____ _____ _____ _____ _____ the river safely?

Junsu: Hmm ....

Let's Check

Minjun: Wow! Something _____ really _____, Mom. What is it?

Mom: We're _____ _____ have tacos _____ _____. _____ _____.

Minjun: _____ _____ _____ _____ _____ _____ _____ _____ a taco?

Mom: _____, _____ your tortilla _____ vegetables and meat. _____, add some sauce _____ _____ _____.

Minjun: Sounds _____!

Mom: _____ you _____ some cheese?

Minjun: No, _____.

해석

Jane: 민수야, 학생 탐정이 나오는 TV 쇼를 아니?

Minsu: 응, 나는 그 쇼를 아주 좋아하지만 이번 주에는 못 봤어. 무슨 내용이었어?

Jane: 음, 학교의 모든 자전거들이 사라졌어.

Minsu: 그래서 그가 무엇을 했어?

Jane: 첫째로, 그는 학교를 둘러 봤어. 그리고 나서, 몇몇의 용의자를 만나서 질문을 했지. 마침내, 그는 도둑을 찾았어. 도둑은....

Minsu: 안 돼, 말하지 마! 내가 나중에 볼 거야.

Emily: 준수야, 수수께끼 하나 풀어볼래?

Junsu: 물론이지, 뭔데?

Emily: 한 농부가 있어. 먼저 농부는 여우, 오리, 콩 자루를 하나씩 사. 그리고 나서, 농부는 강을 건너야 해.

Junsu: 뭐가 문제인데?

Emily: 보트는 단지 농부와 한 가지만 더 옮길 수 있어.

Junsu: 농부가 한 번에 오직 한 가지만 옮길 수 있다는 말이니?

Emily: 응. 또한 만약 농부가 없다면 여우가 오리를 먹거나, 오리가 콩을 먹을 거야. 전부를 강 건너로 안전하게 옮길 방법을 설명할 수 있겠니?

Junsu: 음....

Minjun: 와! 뭔가 정말 좋은 냄새가 나요, 엄마. 뭐예요?

Mom: 우리는 저녁 식사로 타코를 먹을 거야. 맘껏 먹거렴.

Minjun: 타코 만드는 법을 설명해 주실 수 있어요?

Mom: 먼저, 토르티야를 채소와 코기로 채워. 그 다음, 위에 약간의 소스를 추가하렴.

Minjun: 맛있을 것 같아요!

Mom: 치즈 좀 줄까?

Minjun: 아뇨, 괜찮아요.

01 다음 대화가 자연스럽게 이어지도록 주어진 문장을 알맞게 배열하시오.

> (A) Sure, what is it, Jimin?
> (B) That sounds fun.
> (C) It's like a soccer game but the players are dragons and seahorses. You need to use these buttons to play.
> (D) Do you want to play the new game that I bought?

➡ _____

[02~04] 다음 대화를 읽고 물음에 답하시오.

Tom: Yujin, look at my paper fox.

Yujin: That's cute. How did you make it?

Tom: First, fold a paper in half to make a triangle. (A)둘째, fold the top of the triangle to the bottom line. (B)셋째, fold both ends of the bottom line to the top to make ears. Then, turn it over and draw a face.

Yujin: That sounds easy.

02 위 대화에서 다음의 영영풀이가 가리키는 말을 찾아 쓰시오.

> a shape that is made up of three lines and three angles

➡ _____

03 위 대화에서 (A)와 (B)의 우리말을 영어로 쓰시오.

➡ (A) _____, (B) _____

04 위 대화의 내용과 일치하지 않는 것은?

① Yujin은 Tom에게 종이 여우 만드는 법에 대해 물어보았다.
② 종이 여우를 만들기 위해 먼저 종이를 반으로 접어서 세모를 만들어야 한다.
③ 두 번째로, 맨 아랫선을 사용하여 세모로 접어야 한다.
④ 세 번째로, 맨 아랫선 양쪽 끝을 위로 접어 귀를 만든다.
⑤ 네 번째로, 귀를 만든 면을 뒤집어 얼굴을 그린다.

[01~02] 다음 대화를 읽고 물음에 답하시오.

Jimin: Do you want to play the new game that I bought?

Brian: Sure, what is it, Jimin?

Jimin: It's like a soccer game but the players are dragons and seahorses. You need to use these buttons to play.

Brian: That sounds fun. (A)Can you explain how to use the buttons?

Jimin: Sure.

01 위 대화의 밑줄 친 (A)와 의도가 <u>다른</u> 것은? (2개)

① Would you show me how to use the buttons?

② Do you understand how to use the buttons?

③ Can you tell me how to use the buttons?

④ Let me know how to use the buttons, please.

⑤ Why don't you explain how to use the buttons?

02 위 대화의 내용과 일치하지 <u>않는</u> 것은?

① Jimin bought the new game.

② Brian wants to play soccer with Jimin on the playground.

③ The game is similar to a soccer game.

④ The dragons and seahorses are the players in the new game.

⑤ The buttons are used to play the game.

[03~04] 다음 대화를 읽고 물음에 답하시오.

Jack: Kelly, here's a riddle. You can see this twice in a week, once in a year, but never in a day. What is this?

Kelly: I have no idea.

Jack: It's the letter "(A)_____."

Kelly: (B)I don't get it. Can you explain why?

Jack: Well, there are two "(A)_____"s in the word "week," one "(A)_____" in the word "year" but no "(A)_____"s in the word "day."

Kelly: Aha! Now I get it.

서답형

03 위 대화의 빈칸 (A)에 공통으로 들어갈 수수께끼의 답을 쓰시오.

➡ _____

04 위 대화의 밑줄 친 (B)와 바꾸어 쓸 수 있는 말은?

① Not at all.

② I don't understand.

③ It doesn't matter.

④ I can't believe this.

⑤ It's not fair.

[05~07] 다음 대화를 읽고 물음에 답하시오.

Tom: Yujin, look at my paper fox.

Yujin: That's cute. How did you make (A)it?

Tom: First, fold a paper in half to make a triangle. Second, fold the top of the triangle to the bottom line. Third, fold both ends of the bottom line to the top to make ears. Then, turn it over and draw a face.

Yujin: That sounds easy.

서답형

05 위 대화에서 밑줄 친 (A)it이 가리키는 것을 찾아 쓰시오.

➡ _____

서답형
06 To make the paper fox, what should Yujin do after making a triangle by folding a paper in half?

➡ _____

_____

서답형
07 What should Yujin make just before drawing a face?

➡ _____

[08~09] 다음 대화를 읽고 물음에 답하시오.

Jane: Minsu, do you know the TV show about the student detective?
Minsu: (A) Yes. I love that show, but I didn't see it this week. What was it about?
Jane: (B) Well, all of the bikes at school disappeared.
Minsu: (C) So, what did he do?
Jane: (D) Then, he met some suspects and asked questions. Finally, he found the thief. The thief was ....
Minsu: (E) No, don't tell me! I'll watch it later.

중요
08 위 대화의 (A)~(E) 중 주어진 문장이 들어가기에 가장 적절한 곳은?

First, he looked around the school.

① (A) ② (B) ③ (C) ④ (D) ⑤ (E)

09 위 대화를 읽고 대답할 수 없는 것은?

① What show does Minsu like?
② What happened at school?
③ Who was the thief who had stolen all the bikes at school?
④ What did the student detective do to catch the thief?
⑤ Why didn't Minsu want to know who the thief was?

[10~13] 다음 대화를 읽고 물음에 답하시오.

Minjun: Wow! Something smells really good, Mom. What is it?
Mom: We're going to have tacos for dinner. (A)Help yourself.
Minjun: (B)타코 만드는 법을 설명해 주실 수 있어요?
Mom: First, fill your tortilla (a)____ vegetables and meat. Then, add some sauce on the top.
Minjun: Sounds (b)_____!
Mom: (C)Would you like some cheese?
Minjun: No, thanks.

서답형
10 위 대화의 밑줄 친 (A)의 의미를 우리말로 간략히 쓰시오.

➡ _____

서답형
11 위 대화의 밑줄 친 (B)의 우리말을 〈보기〉에 주어진 단어를 배열하여 완성하시오.

┌─ 보기 ─┐

make / how / a taco / can / to / you / explain

➡ _____

12 위 대화의 밑줄 친 (C)와 바꾸어 쓸 수 있는 것은?

① Do you want some cheese?
② Do you like cheese?
③ Have you tried some cheese?
④ Do you know some cheese?
⑤ Do you mind if I have some cheese?

서답형
13 위 대화의 빈칸 (a)에는 알맞은 전치사를, (b)에는 대화의 흐름에 어울리는 d로 시작되는 단어를 쓰시오.

➡ (a)_____, (b) _____

[01~04] 다음 대화를 읽고 물음에 답하시오.

Emily: Junsu, do you want to solve a riddle?

Junsu: Sure, what is it?

Emily: There is a farmer. First, the farmer buys a fox, a duck, and a bag of beans. Then, the farmer needs to cross a river.

Junsu: What's the problem?

Emily: The boat can only hold the farmer and one more thing.

Junsu: Are you saying that the farmer can take only one thing at a time?

Emily: Yes. Also, the fox will eat the duck or the duck will eat the beans if the farmer isn't there. Can you explain (A)옮길 방법 everything across the river safely?

Junsu: Hmm ....

01 What did the farmer buy before crossing the river?

➡ _____

02 How many things could the farmer load on the boat at a time?

➡ _____

03 What will happen to the fox and the duck if the farmer isn't there?

➡ _____

04 밑줄 친 우리말 (A)를 move를 이용하여 3 단어의 영어로 쓰시오.

➡ _____

05 다음 대화가 자연스럽게 이어지도록 순서대로 배열하시오.

(A) Can you explain how to make a taco?

(B) We're going to have tacos for dinner. Help yourself.

(C) First, fill your tortilla with vegetables and meat. Then, add some sauce on the top.

(D) Wow! Something smells really good, Mom. What is it?

➡ _____

06 다음 대화를 읽고 대화의 내용과 일치하도록 빈칸 (A)~(C)를 명령문 형태로 완성하시오.

Tom: Yujin, look at my paper fox.

Yujin: That's cute. How did you make it?

Tom: First, fold a paper in half to make a triangle. Second, fold the top of the triangle to the bottom line. Third, fold both ends of the bottom line to the top to make ears. Then, turn it over and draw a face.

Yujin: That sounds easy.

⬇

How to make a paper fox
Fold a paper in half to make a triangle.
(A) _____
(B) _____ _____
(C) _____

Grammar

① 수동태

> The author **wrote** many books. 그 작가는 많은 책을 썼다. 〈능동태〉
> Many books **were written by** the author. 많은 책이 그 작가에 의해 쓰여졌다. 〈수동태〉

■ 수동태는 'be+p.p.+by'의 형태로, 행동의 주체보다는 행동의 대상에 초점을 맞춘다. 'by+행위자'는 동작의 주체가 일반인이거나 막연한 사람일 때, 그리고 동작의 주체가 명확하지 않을 때 생략한다.

- Jerry **was taken** to the hospital **by** Tom. Jerry는 Tom에 의해 병원으로 데려가졌다.
- Nelson **is loved by** many people. Nelson은 많은 사람들에게 사랑받는다.
- All the flowers **were planted** yesterday. 어제 모든 꽃들이 심어졌다.

■ 4형식 문장의 수동태는 두 가지 형태를 갖는다. 직접목적어를 주어로 한 수동태에서는 간접목적어에 특정한 전치사를 쓴다. 전치사 to를 쓰는 동사는 'give, tell, teach, show, bring' 등이고, 전치사 for를 쓰는 동사는 'buy, make, cook, get' 등이며, 전치사 of를 쓰는 동사는 'ask'가 있다.

- A picture **was given to** me. 사진 한 장이 내게 주어졌다.
- A chicken soup **was cooked for** Jimmy. Jimmy를 위해 닭고기 수프가 요리되었다.

■ 5형식 문장의 목적격 보어가 원형부정사인 경우, 수동태 문장에서는 to부정사로 바뀐다. 그 외에는 모든 목적격 보어를 그대로 쓸 수 있다.

- Mom **allowed** me **to hang** out with my friends. 엄마는 내가 친구들과 놀도록 허락하셨다.
  (= I **was allowed to hang** out with my friends by Mom.)
- He **made** me **do** the job. 그는 내가 그 일을 하게 했다.
  (= I **was made to do** the job by him.)

■ by 이외의 전치사를 사용하는 수동태에 유의한다.

- Jane **is interested in** playing tennis. Jane은 테니스를 치는 것에 흥미가 있다.
- Cheese **is made from** milk. 치즈는 우유로 만들어진다.
- Katherine **was surprised at** the news. Katherine은 그 소식을 듣고 놀랐다.

핵심 Check

1. 다음 우리말과 같도록 빈칸에 알맞은 말을 쓰시오.

   (1) 우리는 그 벽을 칠했다.

   ➡ The wall ＿＿＿＿ ＿＿＿＿ ＿＿＿＿ us.

   (2) 나는 그에게서 영어를 배웠다.

   ➡ I ＿＿＿＿ ＿＿＿＿ English by him.

② 조동사의 수동태

> • We **can delay** the plan. 우리는 그 계획을 연기할 수 있다. 〈능동태〉
>
> • The plan **can be delayed**. 그 계획은 연기될 수 있다. 〈수동태〉

■ 조동사의 수동태는 '조동사+be+p.p.+by ~'의 형태로, 수동태 구문 앞에 조동사를 넣어 사용한다.
   • A pizza **will be delivered**. 피자가 배달될 것이다.
   • Many messages **must be deleted**. 많은 메시지들이 지워져야 한다.
   • Any puzzle **can be solved** by Jason. 어떠한 퍼즐이든 Jason에 의해 해결될 수 있어.

■ 조동사 수동태의 부정문은 조동사 뒤에 not을 붙여 '주어+조동사+not+be+p.p.(+by 행위자)'를 쓴다. 의문문은 '조동사+주어+be+p.p.(+by 행위자)?' 형태로 쓴다.
   • The information **will not be provided**. 그 정보는 제공되지 않을 것입니다.
   • It **cannot be completed** in an ordinary way. 그것은 평범한 방법으로 완성될 수 없다.
   • **Will** the bike **be bought** by Jerry? Jerry가 그 자전거를 살까?
   • **Can** the book **be borrowed** by any student? 어떤 학생이건 그 책을 빌릴 수 있나요?
   • **Should** the car **be parked** by me? 내가 그 차를 주차해야만 하나요?

핵심 Check

2. 다음 우리말을 능동태와 수동태로 쓰시오.

(1) 나는 그 방을 청소할 거야.
   ➡ I _____.
   ➡ The room _____.

(2) 우리는 우리의 숙제를 해야만 한다.
   ➡ We _____.
   ➡ Our homework _____.

(3) 그가 그녀를 도와 줄 거야.
   ➡ He _____.
   ➡ She _____.

01 다음 문장에서 어법상 <u>어색한</u> 부분을 바르게 고치시오.

(1) My sweater made in England.

_____ ➡ _____

(2) The building will complete next month.

_____ ➡ _____

(3) Careless driving is caused many accidents.

_____ ➡ _____

(4) The window can't open by me.

_____ ➡ _____

02 주어진 동사를 어법에 맞게 빈칸에 쓰시오.

(1) The car _____ last weekend. (steal)

(2) The letter should _____ by this Friday. (send)

(3) Hundreds of people _____ the place every day. (visit)

(4) The Olympic Games _____ every four years. (hold)

(5) Karl _____ as a great teacher now. (look up to)

(6) The children will _____ with toys. (play)

(7) Badminton can _____ by two or four people. (play)

03 주어진 단어를 바르게 배열하여 다음 우리말을 영어로 쓰시오. 필요하다면 단어를 변형하거나 추가하시오.

(1) 그 교실은 매일 청소된다. (clean / every day / the classroom)

➡ _____

(2) 이 건물은 언제 지어졌니? (when / build / this building / was)

➡ _____

(3) 우리는 그에게서 표를 받지 못했다. (tickets / give / were / we / not / him / by)

➡ _____

(4) 이것은 오늘 밤이 되기 전에 되어져야만 해. (tonight / this / do / must / before)

➡ _____

(5) 그 문은 10분 후에 닫힐 겁니다. (10 minutes / the door / close / will / in)

➡ _____

01 다음 괄호 안의 동사의 알맞은 형태를 고르시오.

> Two people (injure) in the accident yesterday.

① injure   ② injured

③ is injured   ④ was injured

⑤ were injured

02 다음 빈칸에 들어갈 말로 가장 적절한 것은?

> Meat _____ in a refrigerator, or it will spoil.

① was kept   ② keeps

③ kept   ④ must be kept

⑤ must keep

03 주어진 문장과 같은 의미의 문장은?

> You should return these books by next Wednesday.

① You return these books by next Wednesday.

② These books should return by next Wednesday.

③ These books should be returned by you by next Wednesday.

④ Next Wednesday is returned by you these books.

⑤ These books are going to be returned by you by next Wednesday.

서답형
04 다음 두 문장이 같은 의미가 되도록 빈칸에 알맞은 말을 쓰시오.

> The noise did not wake me up.
> = I _____ by the noise.

05 다음 중 우리말을 영어로 바르게 옮기지 <u>않은</u> 것은?

① 그 사진은 내 남동생이 찍은 거야.
   → The picture was taken by my brother.

② 그 나무를 너의 부모님이 심으셨니?
   → Was the tree planted by your parents?

③ 나는 아침마다 오렌지 주스를 마셔.
   → I drink orange juice every morning.

④ 우리는 그 노래를 불렀다.
   → The song sang by us.

⑤ 그가 상자를 옮길 거야.
   → The box will be moved by him.

06 다음 빈칸에 들어갈 말이 바르게 짝지어진 것은?

> My car _____ last month, but the next day it _____ by the police.

① is lost – is found

② lost – found

③ was lost – was found

④ was lost – was founded

⑤ was lost – will be found

07 다음 중 밑줄 친 부분을 생략할 수 <u>없는</u> 것은?

① The moon can be seen <u>by us</u> at night.

② Lots of bikes are ridden <u>by people</u> in China.

③ My pencil case was stolen <u>by someone</u>.

④ BTS is loved <u>by people</u> all over the world.

⑤ The vase was broken <u>by Thomson</u>.

서답형

08 주어진 문장을 수동태로 쓰시오.

> She will cook the fish.

➡ _____

09 다음 빈칸에 들어갈 말로 가장 적절한 것은?

> The hospital was _____ down for a day.

① shutting ② shutted ③ shut
④ shuted ⑤ shutten

서답형

10 주어진 어구를 바르게 배열하여 다음 우리말을 영어로 쓰시오. 필요하다면 단어를 변형하시오.

> 그 편지가 올바른 주소로 보내질까?
> (the right address / the letter / send / will / to / be)

➡ _____

중요

11 다음 중 빈칸에 들어갈 단어 play의 형태가 다른 하나는?

① The game is _____ on a court.
② Boys are _____ on the playground.
③ The role is _____ by a British actor.
④ The audio is _____ from the beginning.
⑤ A violin is _____ with a bow.

서답형

12 주어진 단어를 활용하여 다음 우리말을 영어로 쓰시오.

> 너희들은 그 선생님에게 벌 받을 거야.
> (punish)

➡ _____

13 다음 우리말을 영어로 바르게 옮긴 것은?

> Julia의 친구들은 그녀에 대해 좋게 말한다.

① Julia's friends speak well with her.
② Julia is spoken well with her friends.
③ Julia's friends are spoken well of by her.
④ Julia is spoken well of by her friends.
⑤ Julia is talked about by her friends.

중요

14 다음 빈칸에 들어갈 말로 가장 적절한 것은?

> It was cold, so the heater was turned _____ Jason.

① on at ② at by ③ on by
④ off by ⑤ into by

15 다음 중 어법상 바르지 않은 것은?

① The woman typed all the reports.
② My father was born in Canada.
③ A book must be written by him by tomorrow.
④ The glass was filled with chocolate milk.
⑤ James is interested by taking pictures.

중요

16 다음 중 수동태로의 전환이 바르지 않은 것은?

① Someone ate my sandwich.
　→ My sandwich was eaten by someone.
② Mom made me a candy bar.
　→ A candy bar was made for me by Mom.
③ Ms. Han runs a restaurant.
　→ A restaurant is ran by Ms. Han.
④ A stranger spoke to me.
　→ I was spoken to by a stranger.
⑤ Melisa prepared an interview.
　→ An interview was prepared by Melisa.

서답형

17 다음 대화의 빈칸에 알맞은 말을 쓰시오.

> A: Who takes care of your children while you are here?
> B: My children ＿＿＿＿＿＿＿＿＿ my mother.

18 다음 빈칸에 공통으로 들어갈 말로 가장 적절한 것은?

> • The restaurant is crowded ＿＿＿ many people.
> • Are you satisfied ＿＿＿ your birthday present?

① at   ② by   ③ from
④ about   ⑤ with

서답형

19 주어진 문장을 수동태로 바르게 전환하시오.

> They sell stamps in a post office.

➡ ＿＿＿＿＿＿＿＿＿＿＿＿＿＿＿＿＿

서답형

20 다음 우리말을 수동태를 활용하여 영어로 쓸 때 다섯 번째로 오는 단어는?

> 많은 사람들이 이 공연을 볼 거야.

➡ ＿＿＿＿＿＿＿＿＿＿＿＿＿＿＿＿＿

서답형

21 다음 문장을 능동태는 수동태로, 수동태는 능동태로 전환하시오.

(1) I saw him dancing.

➡ ＿＿＿＿＿＿＿＿＿＿＿＿＿

(2) Jack will buy the cake.

➡ ＿＿＿＿＿＿＿＿＿＿＿＿＿

(3) Did you drink the juice?

➡ ＿＿＿＿＿＿＿＿＿＿＿＿＿

중요

22 다음 중 어법상 바르지 않은 것은?

① The car was repaired by a man.
② A terrible accident was happened last night.
③ The illness was cured by a doctor.
④ A boy was hit by a truck.
⑤ The package was delivered by a young girl.

23 다음 중 빈칸에 들어갈 말로 가장 적절한 것은?

> Do your brothers help you?
> = ＿＿＿＿＿＿＿＿＿＿＿＿ your brothers?

① Do you help   ② Are you helping
③ Were you helped   ④ Are you helped
⑤ Are you helped by

중요

24 다음 빈칸에 공통으로 들어갈 말로 가장 적절한 것은?

> • Were the pants bought ＿＿＿ you?
> • Was the chocolate made ＿＿＿ his mother?

① for   ② to   ③ about
④ of   ⑤ in

서답형

25 주어진 문장과 같은 의미가 되도록 빈칸에 알맞은 말을 쓰시오.

> I will take care of your cats.
> = Your cats ＿＿＿＿＿＿＿＿＿＿ .

서답형

26 주어진 단어를 활용하여 다음 우리말을 다섯 단어의 영어 문장으로 쓰시오.

> 이 다리는 수리되어야만 해. (repair)

➡ ＿＿＿＿＿＿＿＿＿＿＿＿＿＿＿＿＿

01 다음 문장을 수동태로 쓰시오.

We will not give up the project.

➡ _____

02 다음 문장에서 어법상 틀린 것을 바르게 고쳐 올바른 문장으로 다시 쓰시오.

My parents will be used the treadmill.

➡ _____

03 다음 대화의 빈칸에 알맞은 말을 쓰시오.

A: How many solutions will they offer?
B: As far as I know, three solutions _____ _____ _____ by them.

04 같은 의미의 문장이 되도록 빈칸에 알맞은 말을 쓰시오.

David put on the pants.
= The pants _____ .

05 괄호 안에 주어진 단어를 어법에 맞게 고쳐 쓰시오.

A: You are going to throw a party for Jenny, right?
B: Yes. A cake will (make) by me, some balloons will (buy) by James, some friends will (invite).

➡ _____

06 주어진 동사를 어법과 내용에 맞게 빈칸에 쓰시오.

arrest / cut / serve / laugh at / eat

(1) Julia _____ by her classmates. She was really embarrassed.
(2) Don't worry. I'm sure that the suspect will _____ by the police.
(3) My dog _____ all the pizza on the table last night.
(4) The news that tuition fees will _____ in half makes me happy.
(5) The cook _____ customers himself. So they feel satisfied.

07 다음 대화의 빈칸에 알맞은 말을 쓰시오.

A: Who will write a script for our play?
B: A script _____ by Colin. He is good at writing.

08 주어진 단어를 활용하여 다음 우리말을 영어로 쓰시오.

이 집은 언제 지어졌니? (build)

➡ _____

09 같은 의미의 문장이 되도록 빈칸에 알맞은 말을 쓰시오.

Someone should tell James the news
= James _____ .

10 다음 각 문장을 능동태는 수동태로, 수동태는 능동태로 전환하시오.

(1) The company may offer Chris a job.
  ➡ _____
  ➡ _____

(2) You must send this letter before June 1.
  ➡ _____

(3) The electric light bulb was invented by Thomas Edison in 1879.
  ➡ _____

(4) I will divide the class into two sections.
  ➡ _____

(5) Rice is grown in many countries by people.
  ➡ _____

11 두 문장이 같은 의미가 되도록 빈칸에 알맞은 말을 쓰시오.

We must wear seat belts during takeoff and landing.
= Seat belts _____ during takeoff and landing.

12 주어진 단어를 활용하여 대화를 완성하시오.

A: Andy, your chores (should, finish) by the time I get home.
B: Don't worry, Dad. I'll do everything you told me to do.

  ➡ _____

13 주어진 단어를 어법에 맞게 빈칸에 쓰시오.

Jim is wearing a gold band on his fourth finger. He (marry).

  ➡ _____

14 주어진 단어를 어법에 맞게 빈칸에 쓰시오.

introduce / originate / grow

Bananas _____ in Asia but now _____
_____ by people all around the world.
They _____ to the Americas in 1516.

15 주어진 어휘를 활용하여 문장을 완성하시오.

When we are in the middle school, we _____ (require / to wear uniforms).

  ➡ _____

16 같은 의미의 문장이 되도록 빈칸에 알맞은 말을 쓰시오.

Timmy dropped a plate after dinner last night.
= A plate _____ .

17 다음 문장을 수동태로 전환하시오.

(1) You must not bring food into the lab.
  ➡ _____

(2) You should turn off cell phones.
  ➡ _____

(3) We cannot explain UFO sightings.
  ➡ _____

Reading

The Great Escape

Welcome to the Escape Tower. You will enter the first room in our
~에 들어가다(타동사)

tower. You need to solve some riddles to escape. Clues can be found
~해야 한다(= have to. should)   ~하기 위해서(to부정사의 부사적 용법)   조동사의 수동태는 '조동사+be+p.p.' 형태임

somewhere inside the room. So, are you ready to think like Sherlock
~처럼 생각하다

Holmes?

Room #1

Mr. Doodle was hit by a car on Sunday afternoon. Luckily, he wasn't
~에 의해 …되다   문장 수식 부사: 운 좋게도

badly hurt, but he didn't see the driver. Three suspects were questioned
(= A police officer questioned three suspects.)

by a police officer. Ms. A said she was reading a book at the time of

the accident. Mr. B said he was walking his dog. Ms. C said she was
said (that): 명사절 접속사 that 생략

making breakfast. Who hit Mr. Doodle? Can you explain why? Do you

have the answer? Write it down. Then you can move to the next room.
down이 부사이고 목적어가 인칭대명사이므로 it이 동사와 부사 사이에 위치함

Clue The accident happened in the afternoon.
자동사(수동태 불가능)

Congratulations! You made it to the second room. However, the

second room is much harder to escape than the first one. Good luck!
비교급 강조 부사 '훨씬' (= still. far. even. a lot)   =room

---

escape: 탈출하다
riddle: 수수께끼
clue: 단서
somewhere: 어딘가에
be ready to: ~할 준비가 되어 있다
hurt: 다친
suspect: 용의자
question: 심문하다
at the time of: ~이 일어나던 때에
accident: 사고
write down: 적다
make it to: ~에 이르는 데 성공하다

📎 **확인문제**

● 다음 문장이 본문의 내용과 일치하면 T, 일치하지 않으면 F를 쓰시오.

1 You should solve some riddles to escape from the tower. ☐

2 Clues will be given to you by the tower manager. ☐

3 The car accident happened on Saturday afternoon. ☐

4 If you write down the answer to the first riddle, you can escape from the tower. ☐

Room #2

Jay gets an email from his favorite clothing store. The title reads "You
won our Lucky Day event!" Jay is surprised. He quickly opens it.

JayJr@kmail.com

You won our 'Lucky Day' event!

Congratulations!

You have won a special prize. During our Lucky Day event, you
can choose any seven items from our store for free! Come to our store
on November 31. We can't wait to see you.

Truly yours,

Kay Brown

However, Jay thinks that the event isn't real and deletes the
email. Can you explain why?

Clue There are usually 30 or 31 days in a month.
Do you have the answer? Write it down and then you are free to go!

title: 제목
win: 얻다, 이기다
event: 행사, 이벤트
for free: 무료로
delete: 삭제하다
real: 진실한, 사실의
write down: ~을 적다

📎 **확인문제**

● 다음 문장이 본문의 내용과 일치하면 T, 일치하지 <u>않으면</u> F를 쓰시오.

1　Jay gets many emails from his favorite clothing store. ☐

2　Jay is surprised at the title of the email. ☐

3　Seven items can be chosen by Jay on November 30. ☐

4　Jay wants to meet Kay Brown. ☐

5　Jay thinks the event is not true. ☐

6　Jay deletes the email before reading it. ☐

● 우리말을 참고하여 빈칸에 알맞은 말을 쓰시오.

The Great Escape

1 Welcome _____ the Escape Tower.

2 You will _____ _____ _____ _____ in our tower.

3 You need _____ _____ _____ _____ to escape.

4 Clues can _____ _____ somewhere _____ the room.

5 So, _____ you ready _____ _____ like Sherlock Holmes?

Room # 1

6 Mr. Doodle _____ _____ _____ a car _____ Sunday afternoon.

7 _____, he wasn't _____ _____, but he didn't _____ the driver.

8 Three suspects _____ _____ _____ a police officer.

9 Ms. A said she was _____ _____ _____ at the time of _____ _____.

10 Mr. B said he _____ _____ his dog.

11 Ms. C said she _____ _____ _____.

12 _____ _____ Mr. Doodle? Can you _____ why?

13 Do you have the answer? _____ _____ _____.

14 Then you can _____ _____ the next room.

15 **Clue** The accident _____ _____ the afternoon.

16 Congratulations! You _____ _____ _____ the second room.

대탈출

1 '탈출탑'에 오신 것을 환영합니다.

2 당신은 저희 탑의 첫 번째 방에 들어갈 것입니다.

3 당신은 탈출하기 위하여 몇 개의 수수께끼를 풀어야 합니다.

4 단서들은 방 어딘가에서 발견될 수 있습니다.

5 그러면 당신은 셜록 홈스처럼 생각할 준비가 되었나요?

방 # 1

6 Doodle씨는 일요일 오후에 차에 치였습니다.

7 다행히 그는 심하게 다치지 않았으나 그는 운전자를 보지 못했습니다.

8 세 명의 용의자들이 경찰에게 심문을 받았습니다.

9 A씨는 사고가 일어난 시간에 책을 읽고 있었다고 말했습니다.

10 B씨는 그의 개를 산책시키고 있었다고 말했습니다.

11 C씨는 아침을 만들고 있었다고 말했습니다.

12 누가 Doodle씨를 치었을까요? 왜 그런지 설명할 수 있나요?

13 답을 가지고 있나요? 적어 보세요.

14 그런 다음, 당신은 다음 방으로 갈 수 있습니다.

15 단서: 사건은 오후에 일어났습니다.

16 축하합니다! 당신은 두 번째 방에 오는 데 성공하셨습니다.

17 However, the second room is _____ _____ _____

_____ _____ the first one. Good luck!

Room #2

18 Jay _____ an email _____ his favorite clothing store.

19 The title _____ "You _____ our Lucky Day event!"

20 Jay is _____. He quickly opens it.

21 JayJr@kmail.com

You _____ our 'Lucky Day' event!

22 _____! You _____ _____ a special prize.

23 _____ our Lucky Day event, you can _____ any seven items

_____ our store _____ _____!

24 Come _____ our store _____ November 31.

25 We can't _____ _____ _____ you.

26 _____ _____, Kay Brown

27 _____, Jay thinks that the event _____ _____ and

_____ the email.

28 _____ you explain _____?

29 **Clue** _____ _____ _____ 30 or 31 _____ in a month.

30 Do you _____ _____ _____?

31 Write _____ down and then you _____ _____

_____!

17 그러나 두 번째 방은 첫 번째 방 보다 탈출하기 훨씬 더 어렵습니다. 행운을 빕니다!

방 # 2

18 Jay는 그가 가장 좋아하는 옷 가게로부터 이메일을 받습니다.

19 제목은 "당신은 '행운의 날' 행사에 당첨되었습니다!"라고 적혀 있습니다.

20 Jay는 놀랍니다. 그는 재빨리 그것을 엽니다.

21 JayJr@kmail.com
당신은 우리의 '행운의 날' 행사에 당첨되었습니다!

22 축하합니다! 당신은 특별한 상품을 받게 되었습니다.

23 '행운의 날' 행사 동안, 당신은 우리 가게에서 일곱 가지 상품을 아무거나 무료로 선택할 수 있습니다!

24 11월 31일에 우리 가게로 오세요.

25 우리는 몹시 당신을 보기를 기대합니다.

26 안녕히 계십시오, Kay Brown

27 그러나 Jay는 그 행사가 사실이 아니라고 생각하고 이메일을 삭제합니다.

28 왜 그런지 설명할 수 있나요?

29 단서: 한 달은 주로 30일 또는 31일이 있습니다.

30 답을 가지고 계신가요?

31 그것을 적으면, 당신은 자유롭게 가실 수 있습니다!

● 우리말을 참고하여 본문을 영작하시오.

The Great Escape

1 '탈출 탑'에 오신 것을 환영합니다.

➡ _____

2 당신은 저희 탑의 첫 번째 방에 들어갈 것입니다.

➡ _____

3 당신은 탈출하기 위하여 몇 개의 수수께끼를 풀어야 합니다.

➡ _____

4 단서들은 방 어딘가에서 발견될 수 있습니다.

➡ _____

5 그러면 당신은 셜록 홈스처럼 생각할 준비가 되었나요?

➡ _____

Room #1

6 Doodle씨는 일요일 오후에 차에 치였습니다.

➡ _____

7 다행히 그는 심하게 다치지 않았으나 그는 운전자를 보지 못했습니다.

➡ _____

8 세 명의 용의자들이 경찰에게 심문을 받았습니다.

➡ _____

9 A씨는 사고가 일어난 시간에 책을 읽고 있었다고 말했습니다.

➡ _____

10 B씨는 그의 개를 산책시키고 있었다고 말했습니다.

➡ _____

11 C씨는 아침을 만들고 있었다고 말했습니다.

➡ _____

12 누가 Doodle씨를 치었을까요? 왜 그런지 설명할 수 있나요?

➡ _____

13 답을 가지고 있나요? 적어 보세요.

➡ _____

14 그런 다음, 당신은 다음 방으로 갈 수 있습니다.

➡ _____

15 단서: 사건은 오후에 일어났습니다.

➡ _____

16 축하합니다! 당신은 두 번째 방에 오는 데 성공하셨습니다.

➡ _____

17 그러나 두 번째 방은 첫 번째 방보다 탈출하기 훨씬 더 어렵습니다. 행운을 빕니다!

➡ _____

Room #2

18 Jay는 그가 가장 좋아하는 옷 가게로부터 이메일을 받습니다.

➡ _____

19 제목은 "당신은 '행운의 날' 행사에 당첨되었습니다!"라고 적혀 있습니다.

➡ _____

20 Jay는 놀랍니다. 그는 재빨리 그것을 엽니다.

➡ _____

21 JayJr@kmail.com
당신은 우리의 '행운의 날' 행사에 당첨되었습니다!

➡ JayJr@kmail.com _____

22 축하합니다! 당신은 특별한 상품을 받게 되었습니다.

➡ _____

23 '행운의 날' 행사 동안, 당신은 우리 가게에서 일곱 가지 상품을 아무거나 공짜로 선택할 수 있습니다!

➡ _____

24 11월 31일에 우리 가게로 오세요.

➡ _____

25 우리는 몹시 당신을 보기를 기대합니다.

➡ _____

26 안녕히 계십시오, Kay Brown

➡ _____

27 그러나 Jay는 그 행사가 사실이 아니라고 생각하고 이메일을 삭제합니다.

➡ _____

28 왜 그런지 설명할 수 있나요?

➡ _____

29 단서: 한 달은 주로 30일 또는 31일이 있습니다.

➡ _____

30 답을 가지고 계신가요?

➡ _____

31 그것을 적으면, 당신은 자유롭게 가실 수 있습니다!

➡ _____

[01~03] 다음 글을 읽고 물음에 답하시오.

Welcome to the Escape Tower. You will enter the first room in our tower. You need (A)to solve some riddles to escape. Clues can be found somewhere inside the room. So, are you ready to think like Sherlock Holmes?

서답형

01 다음과 같이 풀이되는 단어를 위 글에서 찾아 쓰시오.

something that helps a person find something, understand something, or solve a mystery or puzzle

➡ _____

02 다음 중 위 글의 내용과 일치하지 않는 것은?

① There are some riddles to solve.

② In order to escape, you need to solve some riddles.

③ It is necessary to find clues inside the room.

④ Clues are hidden inside the room.

⑤ Sherlock Holmes used to think many things in the tower.

03 다음 중 밑줄 친 (A)와 쓰임이 같은 것은?

① Is there anything to eat?

② She hopes to meet you someday.

③ Bradley woke up early not to be late.

④ Kathy is happy to see him.

⑤ He must be generous to buy you shoes.

[04~08] 다음 글을 읽고 물음에 답하시오.

Room #1

Mr. Doodle (A)_____ by a car on Sunday afternoon. ①Unfortunately, he wasn't badly hurt, but he didn't see the driver. Three suspects were questioned by ②a police officer. Ms. A said she was reading a book at the time of the accident. Mr. B said he was walking his dog. Ms. C said she was making breakfast. ③Who hit Mr. Doodle? Can you explain why? Do you have the answer? Write it down. Then you can ④move to the next room.

Clue: The accident happened ⑤in the afternoon.

Congratulations! You made it to the second room. However, the second room is much harder to escape than the first one. Good luck!

04 다음 중 빈칸 (A)에 들어갈 말로 가장 적절한 것은?

① is hit   ② hit   ③ hits

④ was hit   ⑤ can be hit

05 다음 중 위 글을 읽고 답할 수 없는 것은?

① When was Mr. Doodle hit by a car?

② Why didn't Mr. Doodle see the driver?

③ What was Ms. A doing on Sunday afternoon?

④ What was Mr. B doing at the time of the accident?

⑤ How many people were questioned by a police officer?

서답형

06 ①~⑤ 중 글의 흐름상 어색한 것은?

①   ②   ③   ④   ⑤

서답형

07 How many suspects are there? Answer in English with a full sentence.

➡ _____

서답형

08 다음 물음에 완전한 문장의 영어로 답하시오.

> Q: After you escape from the first room, where do you have to go?

➡ _____

[09~14] 다음 글을 읽고 물음에 답하시오.

Room #2

Jay gets an email from his favorite clothing store. The title reads "You won our Lucky Day event!" Jay (A)_____(surprise). He quickly opens (B)it.

JayJr@kmail.com

You won our 'Lucky Day' event!

Congratulations!

You have won a special prize. During our Lucky Day event, you can choose any seven items from our store for free! Come to our store (C)_____ November 31. We can't wait to see you.

Truly yours,
Kay Brown

However, Jay thinks (D)that the event isn't real and deletes the email. Can you explain why?

Clue: There are usually 30 or 31 days in a month.

서답형

09 빈칸 (A)에 괄호 안에 주어진 동사를 어법에 맞게 쓰시오.

➡ _____

서답형

10 밑줄 친 (B)가 가리키는 것을 위 글에서 찾아 쓰시오.

➡ _____

11 다음 중 빈칸 (C)에 들어갈 말로 가장 적절한 것은?

① in   ② at   ③ on   ④ by   ⑤ to

12 다음 중 밑줄 친 (D)와 쓰임이 다른 하나는?

① Did you just say that she loves me?
② The fact that you stole it doesn't change.
③ Jason knew that they couldn't arrive in time.
④ Where is the box that came yesterday?
⑤ It is impossible that they come together.

서답형

13 According to the email, what can Jay do during their Lucky Day event? Answer in English with eleven words.

➡ _____

중요

14 다음 중 위 글의 내용과 일치하지 않는 것은?

① Jay's favorite clothing store sent an email to Jay.
② The email that the clothing store sent had no title.
③ The person who sent Jay an email is Kay Brown.
④ Jay didn't believe what the email said.
⑤ The email was deleted by Jay.

[15~22] 다음 글을 읽고 물음에 답하시오.

Welcome to the Escape Tower. You will enter the first room in our tower. You need to solve some riddles to escape. ⓐClues can be found somewhere inside the room. So, are you ready to think like Sherlock Holmes?

Room #1

Mr. Doodle was hit by a car on Sunday afternoon. Luckily, he wasn't badly hurt, but he didn't see the driver. Three suspects were questioned by a police officer. Ms. A said she was reading a book ⓑ_____ the time of the accident. Mr. B said he was walking his dog. Ms. C said she (A)[was making / was made] breakfast. Who hit Mr. Doodle? Can you explain why? Do you have the answer? Write (B)[it / them] down. Then you can move to the next room.

Clue: The accident (C)[happened / was happened] in the afternoon.

서답형

15 밑줄 친 ⓐ와 같은 의미의 문장이 되도록 빈칸에 알맞은 말을 쓰시오.

You _____.

16 다음 중 빈칸 ⓑ에 들어갈 말로 가장 적절한 것은?

① on   ② at   ③ to   ④ in   ⑤ by

중요

17 (A)~(C)에서 어법상 옳은 것끼리 바르게 짝지어진 것은?

① was making – it – happened
② was making – them – happened
③ was making – it – was happened
④ was made – them – happened
⑤ was made – them – was happened

서답형

18 위 글의 내용에 맞게 빈칸에 알맞은 말을 쓰시오.

Q: Did Mr. Doodle see the driver?
A: No. The driver _____ Mr. Doodle.

서답형

19 What was Ms. A doing when Mr. Doodle was hit by a car? Answer in English with a full sentence.

➡ _____

_____

20 다음 중 위 글의 내용과 일치하지 않는 것은?

① Solving some riddles lets you get away from the room.
② A car hit Mr. Doodle on Sunday.
③ Mr. Doodle was hardly hurt.
④ According to Ms. C, she was making breakfast when Mr. Doodle was hit by a car.
⑤ Mr. B has a dog.

서답형

21 위 글의 내용에 맞게 빈칸에 알맞은 말을 쓰시오.

If the right answer _____, you can move to the next room.

서답형

22 다음과 같이 풀이되는 단어를 위 글에서 찾아 쓰시오.

a sudden event that is not planned and that causes damage or injury

➡ _____

[23~30] 다음 글을 읽고 물음에 답하시오.

Congratulations! You made it to the second room. (A)_____, the second room is much harder to escape than the first one. Good luck!

Room #2

Jay gets an email (B)_____ his favorite clothing store. The title reads "You won our Lucky Day event!" Jay is surprised. He quickly opens it.

JayJr@kmail.com

You won our 'Lucky Day' event!

Congratulations!

You have won a special prize. During our Lucky Day event, you can choose any seven items from our store (C)for free! Come to our store on November 31. We can't wait to see you.

Truly yours,
Kay Brown

However, Jay thinks that the event isn't real and deletes the email. Can you explain why?

Clue: There are usually 30 or 31 days in a month.

Do you have the answer? Write it down and then (D)당신은 자유롭게 가실 수 있습니다!

23 다음 중 빈칸 (A)에 들어갈 말로 가장 적절한 것은?

① Therefore
② For example
③ However
④ On the other hand
⑤ As a result

24 다음 중 빈칸 (B)에 들어갈 말로 가장 적절한 것은?

① to
② about
③ in
④ from
⑤ by

25 밑줄 친 (C)의 의미로 가장 적절한 것은?

① freely
② for yourself
③ at no cost
④ with paying money
⑤ for anything

26 주어진 단어를 활용하여 밑줄 친 우리말 (D)를 영어로 쓰시오.

free

➡ _____

27 글의 내용에 맞게 다음 물음에 대한 대답을 완성하시오.

Q: By whom is the email deleted?
A: It _____.

28 다음 중 위 글을 읽고 답할 수 없는 것은?

① From whom did Jay get an email?
② What is the title of the email?
③ How many items can Jay choose from the store on the event day?
④ What does Jay think about the email?
⑤ When did Jay get the email?

29 글의 내용에 맞게 빈칸에 알맞은 말을 쓰시오.

Q: Why doesn't Jay believe the email?
A: It's because the event is _____ but there are only _____ in November.

30 글의 내용에 맞게 빈칸에 알맞은 말을 세 단어로 쓰시오.

The second room is not as _____ as the first room.

[01~03] 다음 글을 읽고 물음에 답하시오.

Welcome to the Escape Tower. (A)You will enter into the first room in our tower. You need to solve some riddles to escape. You can find clues somewhere inside the room. So, are you ready to think like Sherlock Holmes?

01 What do you need to do to escape from the tower? Answer in English with a full sentence.

➡ _____

02 밑줄 친 (A)에서 틀린 곳을 고쳐 다시 쓰시오.

➡ _____

03 글의 내용에 맞게 빈칸에 알맞은 말을 쓰시오.

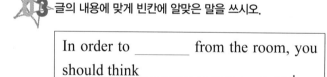

> In order to _____ from the room, you should think _____.

[04~08] 다음 글을 읽고 물음에 답하시오.

Room #1

(A)Mr. Doodle was hit by a car on Sunday afternoon. Luckily, he wasn't badly hurt, but (B) he didn't see the driver. Three suspects were questioned by a police officer. Ms. A said she was reading a book at the time of the accident. Mr. B said he was walking his dog. Ms. C said she was making breakfast. Who hit Mr. Doodle? Can you explain why? Do you have the answer? Write it down. Then you can move to the next room.

Clue: The accident happened in the afternoon.

Congratulations! You made it to the second room. However, (C)두 번째 방은 첫 번째 방보다 탈출하기가 훨씬 더 어렵습니다. Good luck!

04 밑줄 친 (A)를 능동태로 전환하시오.

➡ _____

05 다음은 밑줄 친 문장 (B)와 같은 의미의 문장이다. 빈칸에 알맞은 말을 쓰시오.

> The driver _____.

06 What was the second suspect doing when Mr. Doodle was hit by a car?

➡ _____

07 According to the passage, what happened to Mr. Doodle on Sunday afternoon? Answer in English.

➡ _____

08 주어진 어구를 바르게 배열하여 밑줄 친 우리말 (C)를 영어로 쓰시오.

> (the first one / the second room / than / is / harder / escape / much / to)

➡ _____

_____

[09~13] 다음 글을 읽고 물음에 답하시오.

Room #2

Jay gets an email from his favorite clothing store. The title reads "You won our Lucky Day event!" Jay is surprised. (A)He quickly opens it.

JayJr@kmail.com

You won our 'Lucky Day' event!

Congratulations!

You have won a special prize. During our Lucky Day event, you can choose any seven items from our store for free! Come to our store on November 31. We can't wait to see you.

Truly yours,

Kay Brown

However, Jay thinks that the event isn't real and deletes the email. Can you explain why?

Clue: (B)한 달은 주로 30일 또는 31일이 있습니다.

Do you have the answer? Write it down and then you are free to go!

09 다음 빈칸에 알맞은 말을 써서 밑줄 친 (A)와 같은 의미의 문장을 만드시오.

It _____.

10 주어진 단어를 활용하여 밑줄 친 우리말 (B)를 영어로 쓰시오.

| there |

➡ _____

11 According to the email, what did Jay win?

➡ _____

12 What does Jay do after reading the email? Answer in English with a full sentence.

➡ _____

13 글의 내용에 맞게 빈칸에 알맞은 말을 쓰시오.

Q: What surprises Jay?

A: He _____ the title of the email.

[14~17] 다음 글을 읽고 물음에 답하시오.

It was last Sunday. Dohun was at home. Suddenly, (A)he heard a sound in the next room. When he went into the room, the window was broken. When he looked outside, Sujin was holding a baseball bat and Ted was throwing a ball to his dog. (B)Who broke the window? How can it be explained?

14 밑줄 친 (A)를 수동태로 전환하시오.

➡ _____

15 When was the window broken? Answer in English with five words.

➡ _____

16 밑줄 친 (B)와 같은 의미의 문장이 되도록 빈칸에 알맞은 말을 쓰시오.

By whom _____?

17 What was Sujin holding? Answer in English with a full sentence.

➡ _____

Listen and Speak 1-C

A: Try to solve this riddle.
try to: ~하려고 노력하다 try ~ing: 시험 삼아 ~해 보다

B: Sure.

A: Four people are under one umbrella, but nobody gets wet.
nobody는 부정대명사로 3인칭 단수 취급하여 동사에 -s가 붙는다.

Can you explain why?
=why nobody gets wet

B: Yes! It's because it's a sunny day!
A가 말한 내용   비인칭 주어

구문해설 • riddle: 수수께끼 • wet: 젖은 • explain: 설명하다

A: 이 수수께끼를 풀어봐.
B: 그래.
A: 4명의 사람들이 하나의 우산 아래 있는데 아무도 젖지 않아. 이유를 설명할 수 있겠니?
B: 응! 왜냐하면 맑은 날이기 때문이야.

Let's Write

It was last Sunday. Dohun was at home. Suddenly, he heard a
비인칭 주어

sound in the next room. When he went into the room, the
sound를 수식하는 형용사구

window was broken.
행위자가 불분명 할 때 'by+행위자' 생략

When he looked outside, Sujin was holding a baseball bat and
과거진행형

Ted was throwing a ball to his dog. Who broke the window?
~에게

How can it be explained?
주체가 행위의 대상이 되므로 수동태를 씀

구문해설 • suddenly: 갑자기 • break: ~을 깨뜨리다 (-broke-broken) • hold: ~을 쥐다, 잡다
• throw: ~을 던지다 • explain: ~을 설명하다

지난 일요일이었다. 도훈이는 집에 있었다. 갑자기, 그는 옆 방에서 나는 어떤 소리를 들었다. 그가 그 방으로 갔을 때, 창문이 깨져 있었다. 도훈이가 밖을 보았을 때, 수진이는 야구 방망이를 들고 있었고 Ted는 그의 개에게 공을 던지고 있었다. 누가 창문을 깼을까? 그것은 어떻게 설명될 수 있을까?

Culture & Life

This is the famous riddle of the Sphinx. Oedipus needs to solve it to go into
need to V: V할 필요가 있다   부사적 용법(목적)

Thebes. This is the question that the Sphinx asks him.
목적격 관계대명사

Which creature walks on four legs in the morning, two legs in the afternoon,
의문형용사로 creature 수식

and three legs in the evening?

구문해설 • famous: 유명한 • solve: 해결하다 • question: 질문 • creature: 생명체

이것은 스핑크스의 유명한 수수께끼이다. 오이디푸스는 Thebes에 들어가기 위해 그것을 풀어야 한다. 이것은 스핑크스가 그에게 묻는 질문이다.

어느 생명체가 아침에는 네 다리로 걷고, 오후에는 두 다리로 걷고, 저녁에는 세 다리로 걷는가?

Words & Expressions

01 다음 영영풀이가 가리키는 것을 고르시오.

> someone who steals things from another person or place

① detective   ② liar
③ thief   ④ police
⑤ prosecutor

02 다음 중 밑줄 친 부분의 뜻풀이가 바르지 <u>않은</u> 것은?

① She was reading a book at the time of the <u>accident</u>. 사고
② Sujin was holding a baseball <u>bat</u>. 방망이
③ The duck will eat the <u>beans</u>. 콩
④ Do not <u>cross</u> the river by yourself without your parents. 건너다
⑤ Did you watch this week's TV show about the student <u>detective</u>? 회장

03 다음 우리말과 일치하도록 주어진 단어를 사용하여 영작하시오.

(1) 첫 번째, 원을 그리세요. (draw)
➡ _____

(2) 두 번째, 원 안에 별을 놓으세요. (put, inside)
➡ _____

(3) 그리고 나서 원의 맨 위에 삼각형을 놓으세요. (then)
➡ _____

04 다음 문장의 빈칸에 들어갈 말을 〈보기〉에서 골라 쓰시오. 필요하면 어형 변화를 하시오.

> ┤ 보기 ├
> delete / clue / suspect / escape

(1) The thief _____ from the police station last week.
(2) The _____ lied to the police officer.
(3) The detective looked for _____ at the scene.
(4) Don't open emails with strange titles. _____ them at once.

05 다음 우리말에 맞게 빈칸에 알맞은 말을 쓰시오.

(1) 나는 이 도시를 떠날 준비가 되어 있다.
➡ I'm _____ leave this city.
(2) 나는 축제가 일어나던 때에 아팠었다.
➡ I was ill _____ the festival.
(3) 여기에 당신의 주소를 적으세요.
➡ _____ your address here.

06 다음 주어진 문장의 밑줄 친 cross와 같은 의미로 쓰인 것은?

> My parents needed to <u>cross</u> a river.

① I want to <u>cross</u> the road as soon as possible.
② I drew a <u>cross</u> on the map to mark my office.
③ I want to have a <u>cross</u> as a small tattoo on my hand.
④ You can mark it by a <u>cross</u>.
⑤ My mother always keeps her <u>cross</u> necklace.

Conversation

[07~08] 다음 대화를 읽고 물음에 답하시오.

Jimin: Do you want to play the new game ⓐ what I bought?
Brian: Sure, what is it, Jimin?
Jimin: It's ⓑlike a soccer game but the players are dragons and seahorses. You need to use these buttons ⓒto play.
Brian: That sounds ⓓfun. Can you explain how ⓔto use the buttons?
Jimin: Sure.

07 위 대화의 밑줄 친 ⓐ~ⓔ 중 어법상 어색한 것을 찾아 바르게 고치시오.

➡ _____

08 위 대화를 읽고 대답할 수 없는 것은?

① What are Jimin and Brian going to do?
② What type of game are Jimin and Brian going to play?
③ What role do dragons and seahorses play in the game?
④ Why does Brian need to know how to use the buttons?
⑤ Why did Jimin buy the game similar to a soccer game?

[09~10] 다음 대화를 읽고 물음에 답하시오.

Jack: Kelly, here's a riddle. You can see this twice in a week, once in a year, but never in a day. What is this?
Kelly: (A) I have no idea.
Jack: (B) It's the letter "E."
Kelly: (C) Can you explain why?
Jack: (D) Well, there are two "E"s in the word "week," one "E" in the word "year" but no "E"s in the word "day."
Kelly: (E) Aha! Now I get it.

09 위 대화에서 다음 영영풀이가 나타내는 말을 찾아 쓰시오.

> a difficult question that is asked as a game and that has a surprising or funny answer

➡ _____

10 위 대화의 (A)~(E) 중 주어진 문장이 들어가기에 적절한 곳은?

> I don't get it.

① (A)　② (B)　③ (C)　④ (D)　⑤ (E)

[11~12] 다음 대화를 읽고 물음에 답하시오.

Tom: Yujin, ⓐlook at my paper fox.
Yujin: That's cute. How did you make it?
Tom: First, fold a paper ⓑin half to make a triangle. Second, fold the top of the triangle to the bottom line. (A)Third, fold both ends of the bottom line to the top ⓒ to make ears. Then, ⓓturn it over and ⓔ drawing a face.
Yujin: That sounds easy.

11 위 대화의 ⓐ~ⓔ 중 어법상 어색한 것을 찾아 바르게 고치시오.

➡ _____

12 위 대화의 (A)와 바꾸어 쓸 수 있는 것은?

① Next　② Besides　③ After
④ Before　⑤ Close

[13~14] 다음 대화를 읽고 물음에 답하시오.

Minjun: Wow! Something smells really good, Mom. What is it?
Mom: We're going to have tacos for dinner. Help yourself. (A)

Minjun: Can you explain how to make a taco? (B)

Mom: First, fill your tortilla with vegetables and meat. (C)

Minjun: Sounds delicious! (D)

Mom: Would you like some cheese? (E)

Minjun: No, thanks.

13 위 대화의 (A)~(E) 중 주어진 문장이 들어가기에 적절한 곳은?

> Then, add some sauce on the top.

① (A)　② (B)　③ (C)　④ (D)　⑤ (E)

14 위 대화의 내용과 일치하지 <u>않는</u> 것은?

① 민준이는 좋은 냄새를 맡았다.

② 엄마와 민준이는 저녁식사로 타코를 먹을 것이다.

③ 타코를 만들 때 토르티야와 채소와 고기가 필요하다.

④ 타코 위에 약간의 소스를 추가하여 만든다.

⑤ 민준이는 치즈를 더 원한다.

Grammar

15 다음 중 빈칸에 들어갈 말이 <u>다른</u> 하나는?

① The mountain is covered _____ snow.

② Helen is not satisfied _____ the result.

③ My eyes were filled _____ tears.

④ Terry was surprised _____ his letter.

⑤ He was pleased _____ many gifts.

16 다음 중 어법상 바르지 <u>않은</u> 것은?

① Windows are made of glass.

② The store will be closed at 9 o'clock.

③ Something sad happened last night.

④ A postcard was given to me by Jane.

⑤ Hundreds of people were died in the tornado.

17 다음 빈칸에 들어갈 말로 가장 적절한 것은?

> People made fun of him
> = He _____ people.

① was made fun　② is made fun

③ was made fun of　④ made fun of

⑤ was made fun of by

18 주어진 단어를 활용하여 다음 우리말을 영어로 쓰시오.

> 언제 그 음식이 배달될까? (deliver)

➡ _____

19 다음 중 문장의 전환이 바르지 <u>않은</u> 것은?

① The students use the computer.
　→ The computer is used by the students.

② Does Vicky help you?
　→ Are you helped by Vicky?

③ They asked me a question.
　→ A question was asked to me by them.

④ Stars can be seen at night.
　→ We can see stars at night.

⑤ Is this umbrella carried by you?
　→ Do you carry this umbrella?

20 다음 빈칸에 들어갈 말이 바르게 짝지어진 것은?

> • Vietnam _____ in Southeast Asia.
> • I think life will _____ on other planets.

① located – existed

② locates – exist

③ located – be existed

④ is located – exist

⑤ is located – be existed

21 다음 밑줄 친 ①~⑤ 중 어법상 틀린 것은?

According to our teacher, ①all of our compositions ②should write ③in ink. He won't accept ④papers ⑤written in pencil.

22 다음 문장을 수동태로 전환하시오.

Studying English interests us.

➡ _____

23 다음 문장과 같은 의미의 문장을 모두 고르시오.

Mr. Kim teaches students Korean.

① Students are taught to Korean by Mr. Kim.
② Students are taught Korean by Mr. Kim.
③ Korean teaches students to Mr. Kim.
④ Korean is taught to students by Mr. Kim.
⑤ Korean is taught students by Mr. Kim.

24 다음 중 어법상 옳은 문장의 개수는?

ⓐ The pencil will sharpen by Tom.
ⓑ Did the flowers picked up?
ⓒ Your dog was taken from a hospital.
ⓓ Can the concert be canceled?
ⓔ The piano played by James these days.

① 1개 ② 2개 ③ 3개 ④ 4개 ⑤ 5개

25 다음 중 빈칸에 들어갈 말로 가장 적절한 것은?

Shakespeare wrote *Romeo and Juliet*.
= *Romeo and Juliet* _____ Shakespeare.

① is written   ② was written
③ is written by   ④ was written by
⑤ were written by

26 다음 각 문장을 능동태는 수동태로, 수동태는 능동태로 전환하시오.

(1) We must pick up trash.

➡ _____

(2) Kelly is looked down on by Peter.

➡ _____

Reading

[27~30] 다음 글을 읽고 물음에 답하시오.

Welcome to the Escape Tower. You will enter the first room in our tower. You need to solve some riddles (A)to escape. Clues can be found somewhere inside the room. So, are you ready to think like Sherlock Holmes?

Room #1

Mr. Doodle was hit by a car on Sunday afternoon. ① But he didn't see the driver. ② Three suspects were questioned by a police officer. ③ Ms. A said she was reading a book at the time of the accident. Mr. B said he was walking his dog. ④ Ms. C said she was making breakfast. Who hit Mr. Doodle? ⑤ Can you explain why? Do you have the answer? Write it down. Then you can move to the next room.

Clue: The accident happened in the afternoon.

27 다음 중 주어진 문장이 들어가기에 가장 적절한 곳은?

Luckily, he wasn't badly hurt.

①   ②   ③   ④   ⑤

28 다음 중 밑줄 친 (A)와 쓰임이 같은 것은?

① Jason told them not to do it again.
② I just did it to help your mother.
③ Helen needs something to wear.
④ It was easy to handle the situation.
⑤ Tamia was happy to hear the news.

29 According to the clue, when did the accident happen?

➡ _____

30 다음 탐정 수첩에서 위 글의 내용과 일치하지 <u>않는</u> 것을 <u>두 개</u> 찾아 바르게 고쳐 쓰시오.

> First Riddle
> • Mr. Doodle was hit by a bike.
> • The accident happened on Sunday afternoon.
> • Ms. A was reading a book and Mr. B was walking his dog. Ms. C was making dinner.

➡ _____

➡ _____

[31~34] 다음 글을 읽고 물음에 답하시오.

Congratulations! You made it to the second room. However, the second room is much harder to escape than the first one. Good luck!
Room #2
Jay gets an email from his favorite clothing store. The (A)_____ reads "(B)<u>You won our Lucky Day event!</u>" Jay is surprised. He quickly opens it.
JayJr@kmail.com
You won our 'Lucky Day' event!
Congratulations!
You have won a special prize. During our Lucky Day event, you can choose any seven items from our store for free! Come to our store on November 31. We can't wait to see you.
Truly yours,
Kay Brown
However, Jay thinks that the event isn't real and deletes the email. Can you explain why?
Clue: There are usually 30 or 31 days in a month.
Do you have the answer? Write it down and then you are free to go!

31 다음과 같이 풀이되는 말을 빈칸 (A)에 쓰시오.

> the name given to something such as a book, song, or movie to identify or describe it

➡ _____

32 밑줄 친 (B)를 수동태로 전환하시오.

➡ _____

33 다음 중 위 글을 읽고 답할 수 <u>있는</u> 것은?

① How hard it was to escape from the first room?
② Where is Jay's favorite clothing store?
③ When did Jay get the email?
④ When did Kay Brown send the email to Jay?
⑤ What do you have to do if you have the answer?

34 다음 중 위 글의 내용과 일치하지 <u>않는</u> 것은?

① The first room is much easier to escape than the second room.
② Jay has his favorite clothing store.
③ Jay deletes the email because he doesn't like the special prize.
④ Jay opens the email with surprise.
⑤ You are free to go if you solve the riddle.

[01~02] 다음 대화를 읽고 물음에 답하시오.

Emily: Junsu, do you want to solve a riddle?

Junsu: Sure, what is it?

Emily: There is a farmer. First, the farmer buys a fox, a duck, and a bag of beans. Then, the farmer needs to cross a river.

Junsu: What's the problem?

Emily: The boat can only hold the farmer and one more thing.

Junsu: (A)Are you saying that the farmer can take only one thing at a time?

Emily: Yes. Also, the fox will eat the duck or the duck will eat the beans if the farmer isn't there. Can you explain how to move everything across the river safely?

Junsu: Hmm ....

출제율 90%

01 위 대화의 밑줄 친 (A)와 바꾸어 쓸 수 있는 것은?

① Do you mean that the farmer can take only one thing at a time?

② Why do you say that the farmer can take only one thing at a time?

③ Why do you think the farmer must take only one thing at a time?

④ Do you know that the farmer can take only one thing at a time?

⑤ Have you heard about that the farmer can take only one thing at a time?

출제율 100%

02 위 대화의 내용과 일치하지 않는 것은?

① Emily는 준수에게 수수께끼를 내주었다.

② 농부는 여우한 마리, 오리 한 마리, 콩 한 자루를 샀다.

③ 농부는 강을 건너야 한다.

④ 배는 한 번에 농부와 두 가지 더 옮길 수 있다.

⑤ 농부가 없다면 오리가 콩을 먹거나 여우가 오리를 먹을 수 있다.

[03~04] 다음 대화를 읽고 물음에 답하시오.

Jane: Minsu, do you know the TV show about the student detective?

Minsu: Yes. I love that show, but I didn't see it this week. What was it about?

Jane: Well, all of the bikes at school disappeared.

Minsu: So, what did he do?

Jane: First, he looked around the school. Then, he met some (A)_____s and asked questions. (B)Finally, he found the thief. The thief was ....

Minsu: No, don't tell me! I'll watch it later.

출제율 90%

03 위 대화의 빈칸 (A)에 다음의 영영풀이가 가리키는 말을 고르시오.

a person who is believed to be possibly guilty of committing a crime

① lawyer　　　　② suspect

③ victim　　　　④ merchant

⑤ prosecutor

출제율 95%

04 위 대화의 밑줄 친 (B)와 바꾸어 쓸 수 있는 것을 모두 고르시오.

① Though　　　　② Eventually

③ Nevertheless　　④ At last

⑤ Initially

[05~06] 다음 대화를 읽고 물음에 답하시오.

Jack: Kelly, here's a riddle. You can see this twice in a week, once in a year, but never in a day. What is this?

Kelly: I have no idea.

Jack: It's the letter "E."

Kelly: I don't get it. (A)이유를 설명해 줄 수 있니?

Jack: Well, there are two "E"s in the word "week," one "E" in the word "year" but no "E"s in the word "day."

Kelly: Aha! Now I get it.

출제율 90%

05 위 대화에서 밑줄 친 (A)의 우리말을 4단어로 영작하시오.

➡ _____

출제율 85%

06 위 대화의 내용과 일치하는 것을 고르시오.

① Kelly solved the riddle with the help of Jack.

② Kelly asked Jack to give him a hint for the answer.

③ Kelly didn't understand the answer at first.

④ The riddle Jack gave to Kelly is about the diary.

⑤ Jack was confused when he got to know the answer to the riddle.

[07~08] 다음 대화를 읽고 물음에 답하시오.

Minjun: Wow! Something smells really good, Mom. What is it?

Mom: We're going to have tacos for dinner. (A)맘껏 먹으렴.

Minjun: Can you explain how to make a taco?

Mom: First, fill your tortilla with vegetables and meat. Then, add some sauce on the top.

Minjun: Sounds delicious!

Mom: Would you like some cheese?

Minjun: No, thanks.

출제율 95%

07 위 대화의 밑줄 친 (A)의 우리말을 두 단어로 영작하시오.

➡ _____

출제율 90%

08 위 대화의 내용과 일치하도록 민준이의 일기를 완성하시오.

Sun, Sep 8th, 2019

I had (A)_____ for dinner with Mom. It was so delicious. I wondered how to make tacos. Mom told me that (B)_____ first, and then (C)_____.

Next time, I'll try to make them by myself.

출제율 100%

09 다음 대화가 자연스럽게 이어지도록 순서대로 배열하시오.

(A) That sounds easy.

(B) Look at my paper fox.

(C) That's cute. How did you make it?

(D) First, fold a paper in half to make a triangle. Second, fold the top of the triangle to the bottom line. Third, fold both ends of the bottom line to the top to make ears. Then, turn it over and draw a face.

➡ _____

출제율 90%

10 다음 대화에서 수수께끼의 답이 'E'가 되는 이유를 우리말로 설명하시오.

Jack: Kelly, here's a riddle. You can see this twice in a week, once in a year, but never in a day. What is this?

Kelly: I have no idea.

Jack: It's the letter "E."

Kelly: I don't get it. Can you explain why?

Jack: Well, there are two "E"s in the word "week," one "E" in the word "year" but no "E"s in the word "day."

Kelly: Aha! Now I get it.

➡ _____

11 다음 중 밑줄 친 부분을 생략할 수 있는 것은?

① Was the vase broken <u>by Katherine</u>?
② The door was locked <u>by my parents</u>.
③ The gold mine was discovered <u>by someone</u> in 1890.
④ The water was boiled <u>by your sister</u>.
⑤ A doll was made <u>by my friend</u>.

12 다음 중 문장의 전환이 바르지 <u>않은</u> 것은?

① Julia will help the poor.
　= The poor will be helped by Julia.
② I must do my homework.
　= My homework must be done by me.
③ Bob drew many paintings.
　= Many paintings were drawn by Bob.
④ The result disappointed me.
　= I was disappointed by the result.
⑤ Brad gave me some chocolate.
　= Some chocolate was given to me by Brad.

13 주어진 단어를 활용하여 다음 우리말을 영어로 쓰시오.

식탁이 차려지고 양초들에 불이 켜졌다.
(the table / set / light)

➡ _____

14 빈칸에 들어갈 말이 바르게 짝지어진 것은?

• The building _____ by the earthquake last year.
• The plane _____ behind a cloud.

① was damaged – was disappeared
② is damaged – was disappeared
③ damaged – disappeared
④ is damaged – is disappeared
⑤ was damaged – disappeared

15 다음 우리말과 같은 의미의 문장을 모두 고르시오.

그 소녀는 공에 맞았다.

① The ball hit the girl.
② The ball was hit by the girl.
③ The girl was hit the ball.
④ The girl hit the ball.
⑤ The girl was hit by the ball.

16 다음 빈칸에 알맞은 말을 쓰시오.

Someone will deliver the package to your apartment.
= The package _____ to your apartment.

17 다음 각 문장을 수동태로 전환하시오.

(1) Someone told the kids to leave.
➡ _____
(2) Thomas heard me singing in my room.
➡ _____

[18~22] 다음 글을 읽고, 물음에 답하시오.

　Welcome to the Escape Tower. You will enter the first room in our tower. You need to solve some riddles to escape. Clues can be found somewhere inside the room. So, are you ready to think like Sherlock Holmes?
　Room #1
　Mr. Doodle was hit by a car on Sunday afternoon.
　(A) Who hit Mr. Doodle? Can you explain why? Do you have the answer? Write it down. Then you can move to the next room.

(B) Ms. A said she was reading a book at the time of the accident. Mr. B said he was walking his dog. Ms. C said she was making breakfast.

(C) ⓐLuckily, he wasn't badly hurt, but he didn't see the driver. Three suspects were questioned by a police officer.

Clue: The accident happened in the afternoon.
Congratulations! ⓑ당신은 두 번째 방에 오는 데 성공하셨습니다. However, the second room is much harder to escape than the first one. Good luck!

18 자연스러운 글이 되도록 (A)~(C)를 바르게 나열한 것은?

① (A)-(C)-(B)　② (B)-(A)-(C)
③ (B)-(C)-(A)　④ (C)-(A)-(B)
⑤ (C)-(B)-(A)

19 다음 중 밑줄 친 ⓐLuckily를 대신하여 쓰일 수 있는 것은?

① Especially　② Recently
③ Fortunately　④ Suddenly
⑤ Particularly

20 주어진 어구를 바르게 배열하여 밑줄 친 우리말 ⓑ를 영어로 쓰시오.

(the second / you / to / made / room / it)

➡ _____

21 위 글의 내용에 맞게 빈칸에 알맞은 말을 각각 두 단어로 쓰시오.

A: Do you know that there were _____ in Mr. Doodle's accident?
B: Yes. Actually a police officer _____.

22 다음 중 위 글의 내용과 일치하지 않는 것은?

① Clues for riddles can be found inside the room.
② Mr. Doodle didn't know who hit him.
③ Ms. A was reading a book on Sunday afternoon.
④ Mr. B was with his dog when Mr. Doodle was hit by a car.
⑤ The second room is as difficult to escape as the first room.

[23~25] 다음 글을 읽고 물음에 답하시오.

It was last Sunday. Dohun was at home. Suddenly, he (A)[heard / was heard] a sound in the next room. When he went into the room, the window (B)[broke / was broken]. When he looked outside, Sujin was holding a baseball bat and Ted was throwing a ball to his dog. Who (C)[broke / was broken] the window? How can it be explained?

23 (A)~(C)에서 어법상 옳은 것끼리 바르게 짝지은 것은?

① was heard – broke – broke
② was heard – broke – was broken
③ heard – broke – broke
④ heard – was broken – was broken
⑤ heard – was broken – broke

24 What was Ted doing when Dohun looked outside? Answer in English with a full sentence.

➡ _____

25 다음 중 글의 내용과 일치하지 않는 것은?

① 도훈은 지난 일요일에 집에 있었다.
② 누군가가 창문을 깼다.
③ 도훈이가 있던 방의 창문이 깨졌다.
④ 도훈은 창문이 깨진 것을 보고 밖을 보았다.
⑤ 도훈은 창문이 깨지는 소리를 들었다.

[01~03] 다음 대화를 읽고 물음에 답하시오.

Jimin: Do you want to play the new game that I bought?

Brian: Sure, what is it, Jimin?

Jimin: It's like a soccer game but the players are dragons and seahorses. You need to use these buttons to play.

Brian: That sounds fun. (A)<u>버튼 사용법을 설명해 줄 수 있니?</u>

Jimin: Sure.

01 위 대화의 밑줄 친 (A)의 우리말을 주어진 〈보기〉의 단어를 모두 배열하여 영어로 쓰시오.

┌─ 보기 ─┐

the buttons / how / use / the / can / to / you / explain

➡ _____

02 What are Jimin and Brian going to do together?

➡ _____

03 How can Jimin and Brian play the game?

➡ _____

[04~05] 다음 대화를 읽고 물음에 답하시오.

Jane: Minsu, do you know the TV show about the student detective?

Minsu: Yes. I love that show, but I didn't see it this week. What was it about?

Jane: Well, all of the bikes at school disappeared.

Minsu: So, what did he do?

Jane: First, he looked around the school. Then, he met some suspects and asked questions. Finally, he found the thief. The thief was ....

Minsu: No, don't tell me! I'll watch it later.

04 What was the TV show that Minsu had missed about?

➡ It(=The TV show) was about the case that
_____

05 What did the student detective do to find the thief?

➡ _____
_____

06 다음 문장을 수동태로 전환하시오.

(1) Someone already made the coffee.

➡ _____

(2) Did you return the book?

➡ _____

(3) I will invite my friends.

➡ _____

07 다음 빈칸에 알맞은 말을 쓰시오.

Wild animals attacked the villagers.
= The villagers _____ wild animals.

08 다음 대화의 빈칸에 알맞은 말을 쓰시오.

A: Who will make the decision?
B: The decision _____ our CEO.

09 주어진 어구를 활용하여 다음 우리말을 영어로 쓰시오.

> 실종 소녀가 어제 경찰에 의해 발견되었다.
> (the missing girl, the police)

➡ _____

10 주어진 단어를 어법에 맞게 활용하여 빈칸에 알맞은 말을 쓰시오.

> A: Is the train going to be late?
> B: No. It _____ (expect) to be on time.

[11~13] 다음 글을 읽고 물음에 답하시오.

 Welcome to the Escape Tower. You will enter the first room in our tower. You need to solve some riddles to escape. Clues can be found somewhere inside the room. So, are you ready to think like Sherlock Holmes?
Room #1
 Mr. Doodle was hit by a car on Sunday afternoon. (A)Lucky, he wasn't badly hurt, but he didn't see the driver. (B)A police officer questioned three suspects. Ms. A said she was reading a book at the time of the accident. Mr. B said he was walking his dog. Ms. C said she was making breakfast. Who hit Mr. Doodle? Can you explain why? Do you have the answer? Write it down. Then you can move to the next room.
Clue: The accident happened in the afternoon.

11 밑줄 친 (A)를 알맞은 형으로 고치시오.

➡ _____

12 밑줄 친 (B)와 같은 의미의 문장을 완성하시오.

> Three suspects _____ .

13 Where can you find clues? Answer in English. (7 words)

➡ _____

[14~16] 다음 글을 읽고 물음에 답하시오.

 It was last Sunday. Dohun was at home. Suddenly, he heard a sound in the next room. When he went into the room, (A)the window was broken. When he looked outside, Sujin was holding a baseball bat and Ted was throwing a ball to his dog. Who broke the window? (B) How can it be explained?

14 빈칸에 알맞은 말을 써서 밑줄 친 (A)와 같은 의미의 문장을 완성하시오.

> someone _____

15 Where was Dohun last Sunday? Answer in English with a full sentence.

➡ _____

16 주어진 문장의 빈칸에 알맞은 말을 써 넣어 밑줄 친 (B)와 같은 의미의 문장을 완성하시오.

> How can you _____ who broke the window?

창의사고력 서술형 문제

01 다음 대화의 내용과 일치하도록 빈칸을 완성하시오.

> Jane: Minsu, do you know the TV show about the student detective?
> Minsu: Yes. I love that show, but I didn't see it this week. What was it about?
> Jane: Well, all of the bikes at school disappeared.
> Minsu: So, what did he do?
> Jane: First, he looked around the school. Then, he met some suspects and asked questions. Finally, he found the thief. The thief was ....
> Minsu: No, don't tell me! I'll watch it later.

⬇

> I was fascinated by the TV show about the student detective. I was happy when I heard that Minsu also loved that show. This week, the episode was so exciting. The show was about the crime that (A)_____. I also had the experience of losing my bike, so it was more interesting. When I talked about it to Minsu, he said that he (B)_____ this episode. I told him what (C)_____ had done to find the thief. I know who (D)_____ was, but Minsu didn't want to know it. He said he would watch it later.

02 다음은 Mr. Doodle 사고의 용의자 심문 내용이다. 빈칸에 알맞은 말을 쓰시오.

> A police officer: Ms. A, you said you were reading a book at the time of the accident. Where (A)_____ by you?
> Ms. A: I read the book at a cafe.
> A police officer: Okay. Then Mr. B, nobody saw you walk your dog. It means you (B)_____ to walk your dog by anyone. How can you prove it?
> Mr. B: I went to a pet shop to buy my dog a gum. Ask the clerk who worked on Sunday.
> A police officer: I'll check that out. Ms. C, you said you were making something. What (C)_____ you?
> Ms. C: Breakfast was made by me.

03 주어진 동사와 수동태를 활용하여 다양한 문장을 쓰시오.

> send see show eat borrow

(1) _____

(2) _____

(3) _____

(4) _____

(5) _____

단원별 모의고사

01 다음 짝지어진 단어의 관계가 같도록 빈칸에 알맞은 말을 쓰시오.

> win : lose = s_____ : dangerous

02 다음 영영풀이가 가리키는 것을 고르시오.

> an object or piece of information that helps someone solve a crime or mystery

① clue
② accident
③ fact
④ prize
⑤ scene

03 다음 문장의 빈칸에 들어갈 말을 〈보기〉에서 골라 쓰시오.

> ┤ 보기 ├
>
> case / candle / triangle / hide

(1) The thief couldn't _____ under the table because there wasn't enough space.
(2) The _____ was solved by the police.
(3) The _____ will be put inside the box.
(4) Fold the opposite corners together to form a _____.

04 다음 문장에 공통으로 들어갈 말을 고르시오.

> • The police officer found the clues in the _____ of the crime.
> • The movie opens with a _____ in the Museum of Modern Art.
> • I was fascinated by a beautiful _____.

① prize
② scene
③ bean
④ space
⑤ stamp

[05~07] 다음 대화를 읽고 물음에 답하시오.

Jane: Minsu, do you know the TV show about the student detective?

Minsu: Yes. I love that show, but I didn't see it this week. What was it about?

Jane: Well, all of the bikes at school (A)[appeared / disappeared].

Minsu: So, what did he do?

Jane: First, he looked around the school. Then, he met some (B)[suspects / suspends] and asked questions. Finally, he found the (C)[thief / chief]. The thief was ....

Minsu: No, don't tell me! I'll watch it later.

05 위 대화에서 다음의 영영풀이가 가리키는 말을 찾아 쓰시오.

> a police officer who investigates crimes and catches criminals

➡ _____

06 위 대화의 흐름상 (A)~(C)에 들어갈 말로 적절한 것끼리 바르게 짝지어진 것은?

	(A)	(B)	(C)
①	appeared	suspects	thief
②	appeared	suspends	chief
③	disappeared	suspects	chief
④	disappeared	suspends	thief
⑤	disappeared	suspects	thief

07 위 대화의 내용과 일치하지 <u>않는</u> 것은?

① Minsu missed the TV show about the student detective this week.
② Jane told Minsu about the episode of the TV show.
③ The TV show dealt with the crime of stealing bikes.
④ The student detective investigated the school and some suspects.
⑤ Minsu asked Jane to let him know who the thief was.

[08~10] 다음 대화를 읽고 물음에 답하시오.

Emily: Junsu, do you want to solve a riddle?

Junsu: Sure, what is it?

Emily: There is a farmer. First, the farmer buys a fox, a duck, and a bag of beans. Then, the farmer needs to cross a river.

Junsu: What's the problem?

Emily: The boat can only hold the farmer and one more thing.

Junsu: Are you saying that the farmer can take only one thing at a time?

Emily: Yes. Also, the fox will eat the duck or the duck will eat the beans if the farmer isn't there. (A)전부를 강 건너로 안전하게 옮길 방법을 설명할 수 있겠니?

Junsu: Hmm ....

08 위 대화의 밑줄 친 우리말 (A)를 〈보기〉에 주어진 단어를 모두 배열하여 완성하시오.

┌── 보기 ──
explain / to / the / across / river / can / how / move / you / safely / everything
└────────

➡ _____

_____

09 위 대화를 읽고 대답할 수 <u>없는</u> 질문은?

① What is the riddle Emily gave to Junsu?

② What did the farmer buy?

③ Why should the farmer cross the river?

④ Why shouldn't the farmer leave the fox and the duck together?

⑤ How many things could the boat hold at a time?

10 위 대화에서 제시된 수수께끼의 해결책을 완성하시오.

Junsu: First, the farmer crosses the river with the duck. Second, he comes back and takes (A)_____. Third, he leaves the fox and comes back with (B)_____. Then, he leaves the duck and takes (C)_____. Next, the farmer should leave the beans with the fox. Then, he comes back and crosses the river with (D)_____.

11 다음 대화가 자연스럽게 이어지도록 순서대로 배열하시오.

(A) It's the letter "E."

(B) I have no idea.

(C) I don't get it. Can you explain why?

(D) Well, there are two "E"s in the word "week," one "E" in the word "year" but no "E"s in the word "day."

(E) Kelly, here's a riddle. You can see this twice in a week, once in a year, but never in a day. What is this?

➡ _____

12 다음 짝지어진 대화가 <u>어색한</u> 것은?

① A: Did I draw it correctly?
B: No, you didn't.

② A: Where did you hide your gold?
B: It is in the building on your right.

③ A: Can you explain how to buy a train ticket?
B: First, choose the station. Then, put in the money.

④ A: Would you like some cheese?
B: No, thanks.

⑤ A: How did you make it?
B: That sounds interesting.

13 다음 빈칸에 들어갈 말로 가장 적절한 것은?

> I will not forget their stories.
> = Their stories _____ .

① are not be able to be forgotten
② is not forgotten by me
③ won't be forgot to me
④ don't have to be forgotten by me
⑤ won't be forgotten by me

14 다음 중 어법상 바르지 <u>않은</u> 것은?

① What happened to you last night?
② This key is belonged to your brother.
③ The party will be held in Jin's garden.
④ A job at a local bank was offered to me.
⑤ This symptom can't be explained.

15 다음 문장을 수동태로 전환하시오.

> Hundreds of fans surrounded the rock star outside the theater.

➡ _____

_____

16 다음 빈칸에 들어갈 말로 가장 적절한 것은?

> The noise annoys me.
> = I _____ the noise.

① am annoyed to
② am annoyed of
③ am annoyed in
④ am annoyed with
⑤ am annoyed from

17 주어진 단어를 어법에 맞게 활용하여 문장을 완성하시오.

> Hudson's house burned down. The fire _____ . (cause / lightning)

➡ _____

[18~23] 다음 글을 읽고 물음에 답하시오.

Room #2
 Jay gets an email ①from his favorite clothing store. The title reads "You won our Lucky Day event!" Jay is ②surprised. He quickly opens it.
JayJr@kmail.com
You won our 'Lucky Day' event!
Congratulations!
You have won a special prize. ③During our Lucky Day event, (A)you can choose any seven items from our store for free! Come to our store on November 31. We can't wait to see you.

Truly yours,
Kay Brown
 However, Jay thinks that the event isn't real and ④delete the email. Can you explain why?
Clue There are usually 30 or 31 days ⑤in a month.
 Do you have the answer? Write it down and then you are free to go!

18 밑줄 친 문장 (A)를 우리말로 옮기시오.

➡ _____

_____

19 ①~⑤ 중 어법상 바르지 <u>않은</u> 것은?

①   ②   ③   ④   ⑤

20 다음 중 위 글의 내용과 일치하는 것은?

① Jay deletes the email because he isn't interested in shopping.
② The email was sent to Jay from Jay's favorite shoe store.
③ The email has no title at all.
④ Jay opens the email as soon as he sees it.
⑤ Jay is looking forward to going shopping at the store.

21 다음은 위 사건의 탐정 수첩이다. 글의 내용과 일치하지 않는 것을 두 군데 찾아 바르게 고치시오.

Second Riddle
• Jay will get a special prize.
• The event is on November 30.
• Jay kept his email because it was not true.

➡ _____

➡ _____

22 다음 물음에 완전한 문장의 영어로 답하시오.

Q: How many items are free during the Lucky Day event?

➡ _____

23 다음 중 위 글을 읽고 답할 수 <u>없는</u> 것은?

① Where does Jay get email from?
② Why is Jay surprised?
③ How many people get the email besides Jay?
④ When is the 'Lucky Day' event?
⑤ What do we have to do if we know the answer?

[24~25] 다음 글을 읽고 물음에 답하시오.

It was last Sunday. Dohun was at home. Suddenly, he heard a sound in the next room. When he went into the room, the window was broken. When he looked outside, Sujin was holding a baseball bat and Ted was throwing a ball to his dog. Who broke the window? (A)
_____

24 다음 중 위 글에서 찾아볼 수 <u>없는</u> 것은?

① Dohun who was resting at home on Sunday
② a noise from the next room
③ a ball which was thrown to Dohun's home
④ a girl who was holding a baseball bat
⑤ Dohun looking outside to see who broke the window

25 주어진 단어를 바르게 배열하여 빈칸 (A)에 들어갈 말을 완성하시오. 필요하다면 어형을 변형하시오.

(be / how / explain / it / can)

➡ _____

INSIGHT
on the textbook

교과서 파헤치기

※ 다음 영어를 우리말로 쓰시오.

01	rest	22	trash
02	avoid	23	secret
03	pay phone	24	disappear
04	activity	25	different
05	arrow	26	frame
06	danger	27	outside
07	say	28	children's center
08	effort	29	coin
09	success	30	solve
10	possible	31	map
11	volunteer club	32	free
12	plan	33	plastic bag
13	solution	34	sign
14	mentee	35	come up with
15	wonderful	36	during the day
16	street	37	on one's own
17	explain	38	give it a try
18	confusing	39	put up
19	refrigerator	40	stop -ing
20	need	41	thanks to
21	forget	42	have to
		43	one day

※ 다음 우리말을 영어로 쓰시오.

01	딱지, 스티커		22	쓰레기	
02	바구니		23	냉장고	
03	동전		24	설명하다	
04	표지판		25	노력	
05	혼란스러운		26	결심하다	
06	비밀; 비밀의		27	피하다	
07	해결하다		28	쓰레기	
08	몇몇의		29	위험	
09	버스 정류장		30	쉬다, 휴식하다	
10	아동 센터		31	성공	
11	사라지다		32	공중전화	
12	틀, 테		33	해결책	
13	무료의		34	잊어버리다	
14	비누		35	며칠 전에, 지난번	
15	기쁜		36	~을 나누어 주다	
16	듣다		37	(생각을) 찾아내다, 제시하다	
17	지도		38	낮 동안	
18	다른		39	~하는 것을 멈추다	
19	멘토		40	자기 스스로	
20	바깥의, 외부의		41	설치하다, 세우다	
21	비닐봉지		42	~ 덕분에	
			43	시도하다, 한번 해 보다	

※ 다음 영영풀이에 알맞은 단어를 <보기>에서 골라 쓴 후, 우리말 뜻을 쓰시오.

1 _____ : not many, but some: _____

2 _____ : difficult to understand: _____

3 _____ : to begin doing or using something: _____

4 _____ : to stop being visible: _____

5 _____ : not costing any money: _____

6 _____ : kept hidden from others: _____

7 _____ : something that is done as work for a particular purpose: _____

8 _____ : to be aware of sounds with your ears: _____

9 _____ : the correct or desired result of an attempt: _____

10 _____ : a device or room that is used to keep things cold: _____

11 _____ : a mark that is shaped like an arrow and that is used to show direction:
_____

12 _____ : a person who is advised and helped by more experienced person:
_____

13 _____ : a piece of paper, wood, etc., with words or pictures on it that gives information
about something: _____

14 _____ : to stop working or doing an activity for a time and sit down or lie down
to relax: _____

15 _____ : a drawing or plan of the earth's surface or past of it, showing countries,
towns, rivers, etc.: _____

16 _____ : someone who teaches or gives help and advice to a less experienced and
often younger person: _____

보기			
start	activity	mentor	few
map	confusing	sign	refrigerator
hear	free	arrow	mentee
disappear	secret	rest	success

※ 다음 우리말과 일치하도록 빈칸에 알맞은 말을 쓰시오.

Listen & Speak 1 A

Tom: Hojun and I _____ _____ _____ _____ free stickers today, but I _____ he _____.

Sora: Really? _____ _____ _____ _____ _____. Why are you _____ to _____ _____ stickers?

Tom: It's _____ of our _____ _____ _____.

Sora: I see. What does this sticker _____?

Tom: _____ _____ _____ when we _____ _____ _____ _____, the world will _____ _____ _____ _____.

Sora: That's a _____ _____.

Tom: 호준이와 나는 오늘 무료 스티커를 나눠주기로 계획했는데 호준이가 잊어버린 것 같아.
Sora: 그래? 그럼 내가 도와줄게. 너희는 스티커를 왜 나눠주려고 하니?
Tom: 그건 우리 자원봉사 동아리 활동의 일부야.
Sora: 그렇구나. 이 스티커는 무엇을 의미하니?
Tom: 그건 우리가 서로에게 미소 지을 때, 세상이 더 좋은 곳이 될 거라는 의미야.
Sora: 그거 멋진 아이디어구나.

Listen & Speak 1 B

Mike: Jimin, what are all these things _____ _____ _____?

Jimin: They're for _____ _____ at the children's center. I'm _____ _____ _____ her my old books today.

Mike: _____ _____ _____ _____ _____ _____ _____?

Jimin: Yes. I _____ _____ when I _____ her.

Mike: _____ _____ _____ _____ _____. Oh, the box _____ _____. _____ me _____ you.

Jimin: Thanks.

Mike: 지민아, 상자에 들어 있는 이게 전부 뭐니?
Jimin: 그건 아동 센터에 있는 내 멘티를 위한 거야. 오늘 내가 보던 책들을 줄 거야.
Mike: 너는 그녀를 주말마다 가르치니?
Jimin: 응. 나는 그녀를 가르칠 때 행복해.
Mike: 넌 좋은 멘토구나. 아, 상자 무거워 보인다. 내가 도와줄게.
Jimin: 고마워.

Listen & Speak 2 A

Alex: Mom, _____ _____ _____ _____ _____. I _____ it _____ plastic bags.

Mom: That's very cute, Alex. _____ _____ _____ _____ I _____ a new basket?

Alex: You _____ _____ it when we were having dinner _____ _____ _____.

Mom: _____ _____! I really like this basket. It has _____ _____ _____.

Alex: _____ _____ _____ _____ _____ _____.

Alex: 엄마, 이거 선물이에요. 제가 비닐봉지로 만들었어요.
Mom: 그것 참 예쁘구나, Alex. 내가 새로운 바구니가 필요한 걸 어떻게 알았니?
Alex: 엄마가 지난번에 저녁 먹을 때 말씀하셨어요.
Mom: 아주 멋지구나! 이 바구니가 아주 좋은 걸. 색깔이 아주 다양하구나.
Alex: 엄마가 좋아하시니 저도 기뻐요.

Listen & Speak 2 B

Yujin: _____ _____ _____ _____ _____ _____ _____

_____ _____ _____ _____ . Do you want to _____

_____ it?

Jack: Sure. _____ _____ _____ _____ , Yujin?

Yujin: Many children in his town _____ _____ to school and

_____ _____ _____ . So he _____ them in his house

_____ _____ .

Jack: That's a _____ _____ .

Yujin: _____ _____ _____ _____ _____ .

Real Life Communication

Emily: Welcome back, Brian. _____ _____ _____ _____ ?

Brian: Yes, thanks. I _____ _____ study _____ _____

_____ in the hospital, _____ it was hard.

Emily: _____ _____ _____ _____ _____ . Why don't you _____

_____ _____ _____ _____ ?

Brian: Did you start a _____ _____ ? That's wonderful.

Emily: Thanks. I think that _____ _____ _____ _____

_____ _____ _____ _____ _____ _____ .

Brian: I agree. I'll _____ _____ to be a good member. _____

_____ _____ _____ .

Emily: You're _____ . I'm _____ you _____ my idea.

Let's Check 1

Henry: Your bag _____ _____ . _____ _____ _____

_____ .

Sujin: Thanks. _____ _____ _____ _____ _____ _____

_____ _____ ?

Henry: It's _____ _____ . I'll _____ your bag to the bus stop for

you.

Sujin: You're _____ _____ .

Henry: _____ _____ . I am _____ that way, _____ .

※ 다음 우리말에 맞도록 대화를 영어로 쓰시오.

Listen & Speak 1 A

Tom: _____

Sora: _____

Tom: _____

Sora: _____

Tom: _____
_____

Sora: _____

해석

Tom: 호준이와 나는 오늘 무료 스티커를 나눠주기로 계획했는데 호준이가 잊어버린 것 같아.
Sora: 그래? 그럼 내가 도와줄게. 너희는 스티커를 왜 나눠주려고 하니?
Tom: 그건 우리 자원봉사 동아리 활동의 일부야.
Sora: 그렇구나. 이 스티커는 무엇을 의미하니?
Tom: 그건 우리가 서로에게 미소 지을 때, 세상이 더 좋은 곳이 될 거라는 의미야.
Sora: 그거 멋진 아이디어구나.

Listen & Speak 1 B

Mike: _____

Jimin: _____
_____

Mike: _____

Jimin: _____

Mike: _____

Jimin: _____

Mike: 지민아, 상자에 들어 있는 이게 전부 뭐니?
Jimin: 그건 아동 센터에 있는 내 멘티를 위한 거야. 오늘 내가 보던 책들을 줄 거야.
Mike: 너는 그녀를 주말마다 가르치니?
Jimin: 응. 나는 그녀를 가르칠 때 행복해.
Mike: 넌 좋은 멘토구나. 아, 상자 무거워 보인다. 내가 도와줄게.
Jimin: 고마워.

Listen & Speak 2 A

Alex: _____

Mom: _____

Alex: _____

Mom: _____

Alex: _____

Alex: 엄마, 이거 선물이에요. 제가 비닐봉지로 만들었어요.
Mom: 그것 참 예쁘구나, Alex. 내가 새로운 바구니가 필요한 걸 어떻게 알았니?
Alex: 엄마가 지난번에 저녁 먹을 때 말씀하셨어요.
Mom: 아주 멋지구나! 이 바구니가 아주 좋은 걸. 색깔이 아주 다양하구나.
Alex: 엄마가 좋아하시니 저도 기뻐요.

Listen & Speak 2 B

Yujin: _____

Jack: _____

Yujin: _____

_____

Jack: _____

Yujin: _____

Real Life Communication

Emily: _____

Brian: _____

Emily: _____

Brian: _____

Emily: _____

Brian: _____

Emily: _____

Let's Check 1

Henry: _____

Sujin: _____

Henry: _____

Sujin: _____

Henry: _____

Yujin: 내가 인도의 특별한 소년에 대한 이야기를 읽었어. 들어 볼래?

Jack: 그래. 왜 그가 특별하다는 거니, 유진아?

Yujin: 그 소년의 마을에 있는 많은 아이들이 학교에 갈 수 없었고 일을 해야만 했어. 그래서 그가 매일 자신의 집에서 아이들을 가르쳤다는 거야.

Jack: 그거 멋진 이야기구나.

Yujin: 네가 좋아하니 나도 기뻐.

Emily: 돌아온 걸 환영해, Brian. 좀 나아졌니?

Brian: 응, 고마워. 나는 병원에서 혼자 공부하려고 했는데, 어려웠어.

Emily: 내가 도와줄게. 우리 스터디 모임에 함께 하는 게 어때?

Brian: 스터디 모임을 시작했니? 그거 멋지다.

Emily: 고마워. 나는 우리가 서로를 가르쳐주면 더 잘 배울 수 있을 거라고 생각해.

Brian: 맞아. 나는 좋은 구성원이 되려고 열심히 노력할게. 도와줘서 고마워.

Emily: 천만에. 내 아이디어를 좋아해 줘서 나도 기뻐.

Henry: 가방이 무거워 보이네요. 제가 도와 드릴게요.

Sujin: 고마워요. 이 근처에 버스 정류장이 어디 있나요?

Henry: 저쪽에 있어요. 버스 정류장까지 가방을 들어 드릴게요.

Sujin: 정말 친절하군요.

Henry: 별말씀을요. 저도 그쪽으로 가는 길인 걸요.

※ 다음 우리말과 일치하도록 빈칸에 알맞은 것을 골라 쓰시오.

1 Here _____ two stories _____ I _____ yesterday.
    A. read   B. which   C. are

2 Do you _____ to _____ _____ them?
    A. about   B. hear   C. want

3 _____ Someone _____ _____.
    A. Love   B. You   C. Call

4 New York _____ many _____ phones _____ its _____.
    A. streets   B. on   C. pay   D. had

5 _____, _____ really _____ them.
    A. used   B. nobody   C. however

6 _____ day, a man came _____ _____ an idea.
    A. with   B. up   C. one

7 He _____ coins _____ one _____ the phones.
    A. of   B. to   C. stuck

8 He also _____ _____ a sign _____ said, "Call Someone You Love."
    A. that   B. up   C. put

9 Soon, _____ people _____ _____ the phone.
    A. using   B. were   C. many

10 _____ they were _____ to someone _____ they loved, they didn't stop _____.
    A. smiling   B. whom   C. talking   D. when

11 _____ idea _____ a big _____.
    A. success   B. became   C. his

12 _____ the day, _____ the coins _____.
    A. disappeared   B. all   C. during

13 The man was very happy _____ his small idea _____ _____ to many people.
    A. happiness   B. gave   C. because

---

1 여기 내가 어제 읽은 이야기가 두 개 있어.

2 들어볼래?

3 당신이 사랑하는 누군가에게 전화하세요.

4 뉴욕에는 길거리에 공중전화가 많이 있었다.

5 그러나 아무도 그것들을 실제로 사용하지는 않았다.

6 어느 날, 한 남자에게 좋은 아이디어가 떠올랐다.

7 그는 공중전화 하나에 동전들을 붙였다.

8 그는 또한 "당신이 사랑하는 사람에게 전화하세요."라고 쓰인 표지판을 설치했다.

9 곧, 많은 사람들이 그 전화기를 사용하고 있었다.

10 그들이 사랑하는 누군가에게 전화하고 있을 때, 그들은 미소 짓기를 멈추지 않았다.

11 그의 아이디어는 커다란 성공이었다.

12 낮 동안, 모든 동전이 사라졌다.

13 그 남자는 자신의 작은 아이디어가 많은 사람에게 행복을 가져다주었기 때문에 매우 행복했다.

14 The Red _____ _____

A. Man   B. Arrow

15 A _____ years _____, the maps at bus stops in Seoul _____ very _____.

A. confusing   B. were   C. ago   D. few

16 They _____ have _____ _____.

A. information   B. enough   C. didn't

17 People _____ to ask _____ to _____ the maps.

A. explain   B. others   C. had

18 "_____ is this bus stop _____ the map? Does this bus _____ _____ Gwanghwamun?"

A. to   B. go   C. on   D. where

19 Many people _____ _____ the wrong bus and _____ their time.

A. wasted   B. took   C. often

20 _____ day, a young man _____ _____ _____ this problem.

A. solve   B. to   C. decided   D. one

21 He _____ _____ of red _____ stickers.

A. arrow   B. lots   C. bought

22 Every day he _____ his bicycle _____ the city and _____ the stickers _____ the bus maps.

A. on   B. stuck   C. around   D. rode

23 Nobody _____ him _____ _____ this.

A. do   B. to   C. asked

24 He _____ wanted to _____ _____.

A. others   B. help   C. just

25 _____ to his effort, people _____ understand the maps _____ and _____ time.

A. save   B. easily   C. could   D. thanks

---

14 빨간 화살표 청년

15 몇 년 전에, 서울의 버스 정류장의 지도는 매우 혼란스러웠다.

16 지도에는 충분한 정보가 없었다.

17 사람들은 다른 사람들에게 지도를 설명해 달라고 요청해야 했다.

18 "이 버스 정류장은 지도의 어디에 있는 건가요? 이 버스가 광화문으로 가나요?"

19 많은 사람이 종종 버스를 잘못 타서 시간을 낭비하곤 했다.

20 어느 날, 한 젊은 청년이 이 문제를 해결해 보기로 했다.

21 그는 빨간 화살표 스티커를 많이 샀다.

22 매일 그는 자전거를 타고 서울 시내를 돌아다니며 버스 지도에 스디기를 붙였다.

23 아무도 그 청년에게 이 일을 하라고 요청하지 않았다.

24 그는 단지 다른 사람들을 돕고 싶었다.

25 그의 노력 덕분에, 사람들은 지도를 쉽게 이해하고 시간을 절약할 수 있었다.

※ 다음 우리말과 일치하도록 빈칸에 알맞은 말을 쓰시오.

1 Here _____ two stories _____ I _____ yesterday.

2 Do you want _____ _____ _____ them?

3 _____ Someone _____ _____.

4 New York _____ many _____ _____ on its streets.

5 _____, _____ really _____ them.

6 One day, a man _____ _____ _____ an idea.

7 He _____ _____ _____ one of the phones.

8 He also _____ _____ a sign _____ _____, " _____ Someone You _____."

9 Soon, _____ people _____ _____ the phone.

10 _____ they _____ _____ to someone _____ _____ _____, they _____ _____ _____.

11 His idea _____ _____ _____ _____.

12 _____ _____ _____, all the coins _____.

13 The man was very happy _____ his small idea _____ _____ _____ many people.

1 여기 내가 어제 읽은 이야기가 두 개 있어.

2 들어볼래?

3 당신이 사랑하는 누군가에게 전화하세요.

4 뉴욕에는 길거리에 공중전화가 많이 있었다.

5 그러나 아무도 그것들을 실제로 사용하지는 않았다.

6 어느 날, 한 남자에게 좋은 아이디어가 떠올랐다.

7 그는 공중전화 하나에 동전들을 붙였다.

8 그는 또한 "당신이 사랑하는 사람에게 전화하세요."라고 쓰인 표지판을 설치했다.

9 곧, 많은 사람들이 그 전화기를 사용하고 있었다.

10 그들이 사랑하는 누군가에게 전화하고 있을 때, 그들은 미소 짓기를 멈추지 않았다.

11 그의 아이디어는 커다란 성공이었다.

12 낮 동안, 모든 동전이 사라졌다.

13 그 남자는 자신의 작은 아이디어가 많은 사람에게 행복을 가져다 주었기 때문에 매우 행복했다.

14 The _____ _____ _____

15 _____ _____ _____ _____, the maps at bus stops in Seoul _____ very _____.

16 They _____ _____ _____ _____.

17 People had to _____ _____ _____ _____ the maps.

18 "_____ is this bus stop _____ _____ _____? Does this bus _____ _____ Gwanghwamun?"

19 Many people _____ _____ _____ _____ _____ and _____ their time.

20 One day, a young man _____ _____ this problem.

21 He bought _____ _____ _____ _____ _____.

22 _____ _____ he _____ his bicycle _____ the city and _____ the stickers _____ the bus maps.

23 Nobody _____ _____ _____ _____ this.

24 He just _____ _____ others.

25 _____ _____ _____ _____ _____, people _____ _____ the maps _____ and _____ _____.

14 빨간 화살표 청년

15 몇 년 전에, 서울의 버스 정류장의 지도는 매우 혼란스러웠다.

16 지도에는 충분한 정보가 없었다.

17 사람들은 다른 사람들에게 지도를 설명해 달라고 요청해야 했다.

18 "이 버스 정류장은 지도의 어디에 있는 건가요? 이 버스가 광화문으로 가나요?"

19 많은 사람이 종종 버스를 잘못타서 시간을 낭비하곤 했다.

20 어느 날, 한 젊은 청년이 이 문제를 해결해 보기로 했다.

21 그는 빨간 화살표 스티커를 많이 샀다.

22 매일 그는 자전거를 타고 서울 시내를 돌아다니며 버스 지도에 스티커를 붙였다.

23 아무도 그 청년에게 이 일을 하라고 요청하지 않았다.

24 그는 단지 다른 사람들을 돕고 싶었다.

25 그의 노력 덕분에, 사람들은 지도를 쉽게 이해하고 시간을 절약할 수 있었다.

※ 다음 문장을 우리말로 쓰시오.

1 Here are two stories which I read yesterday.

➡ _____

2 Do you want to hear about them?

➡ _____

3 Call Someone You Love

➡ _____

4 New York had many pay phones on its streets.

➡ _____

5 However, nobody really used them.

➡ _____

6 One day, a man came up with an idea.

➡ _____

7 He stuck coins to one of the phones.

➡ _____

8 He also put up a sign that said, "Call Someone You Love."

➡ _____

9 Soon, many people were using the phone.

➡ _____

10 When they were talking to someone whom they loved, they didn't stop smiling.

➡ _____

11 His idea became a big success.

➡ _____

12 During the day, all the coins disappeared.

➡ _____

13 The man was very happy because his small idea gave happiness to many people.

➡ _____

14 The Red Arrow Man

➡ _____

15 A few years ago, the maps at bus stops in Seoul were very confusing.

➡ _____

16 They didn't have enough information.

➡ _____

17 People had to ask others to explain the maps.

➡ _____

18 "Where is this bus stop on the map? Does this bus go to Gwanghwamun?"

➡ _____

19 Many people often took the wrong bus and wasted their time.

➡ _____

20 One day, a young man decided to solve this problem.

➡ _____

21 He bought lots of red arrow stickers.

➡ _____

22 Every day he rode his bicycle around the city and stuck the stickers on the bus maps.

➡ _____

23 Nobody asked him to do this.

➡ _____

24 He just wanted to help others.

➡ _____

25 Thanks to his effort, people could understand the maps easily and save time.

➡ _____

※ 다음 괄호 안의 단어들을 우리말에 맞도록 바르게 배열하시오.

1 (are / here / stories / two / I / which / yesterday. / read)

➡ _____

2 (you / do / to / want / them? / about / hear)

➡ _____

3 (You / Call / Love / Someone)

➡ _____

4 (York / New / many / had / phones / pay / streets. / its / on)

➡ _____

5 (nobody / however, / used / them. / really)

➡ _____

6 (day, / one / man / a / up / came / idea. / with / an)

➡ _____

7 (stuck / he / to / coins / of / one / phones. / the)

➡ _____

8 (also / he / up / put / sign / a / said, / that / "Call / You / Love." / Someone)

➡ _____

9 (many / soon, / people / using / were / phone. / the)

➡ _____

10 (were / they / when / talking / someone / to / whom / loved, / they / smiling. / stop / didn't / they)

➡ _____

11 (idea / his / became / success. / big / a)

➡ _____

12 (day, / the / during / the / all / disappeared. / coins)

➡ _____

13 (man / the / very / was / happy / because / small / his / idea / happiness / gave / people. / many / to)

➡ _____

1 여기 내가 어제 읽은 이야기가 두 개 있어.

2 들어볼래?

3 당신이 사랑하는 누군가에게 전화하세요.

4 뉴욕에는 길거리에 공중전화가 많이 있었다.

5 그러나 아무도 그것들을 실제로 사용하지는 않았다.

6 어느 날, 한 남자에게 좋은 아이디어가 떠올랐다.

7 그는 공중전화 하나에 동전들을 붙였다.

8 그는 또한 "당신이 사랑하는 사람에게 전화하세요."라고 쓰인 표지판을 설치했다.

9 곧, 많은 사람들이 그 전화기를 사용하고 있었다.

10 그들이 사랑하는 누군가에게 전화하고 있을 때, 그들은 미소 짓기를 멈추지 않았다.

11 그의 아이디어는 커다란 성공이었다.

12 낮 동안, 모든 동전이 사라졌다.

13 그 남자는 자신의 작은 아이디어가 많은 사람에게 행복을 가져다 주었기 때문에 매우 행복했다.

14 (Arrow / The / Man / Red)

➡ _____

16 (few / ago, / a / years / the / maps / bus / at / stops / Seoul / in / confusing. / very / was)

➡ _____

15 (didn't / they / have / information. / enough)

➡ _____

17 (had / people / ask / to / others / explain / to / maps. / the)

➡ _____

18 (is / "where / bus / this / stop / the / on / map? // this / go / does / bus / Gwanghwamun?" / to)

➡ _____

19 (people / many / took / often / wrong / the / bus / and / time / their / wasted)

➡ _____

20 (day, / one / young / a / man / to / decided / problem. / this / solve)

➡ _____

21 (bought / he / of / lots / red / stickers. / arrow)

➡ _____

22 (day / every / rode / he / bicycle / his / the / around / city / and / stuck / stickers / on / the / maps. / bus / the)

➡ _____

23 (asked / to / nobody / this. / do / him)

➡ _____

24 (just / wanted / he / others. / help / to)

➡ _____

25 (to / thanks / effort, / his / could / people / understand / maps / the / easily / time. / save / and)

➡ _____

14 빨간 화살표 청년

15 몇 년 전에, 서울의 버스 정류장의 지도는 매우 혼란스러웠다.

16 지도에는 충분한 정보가 없었다.

17 사람들은 다른 사람들에게 지도를 설명해 달라고 요청해야 했다.

18 "이 버스 정류장은 지도의 어디에 있는 건가요? 이 버스가 광화문으로 가나요?"

19 많은 사람이 종종 버스를 잘못 타서 시간을 낭비하곤 했다.

20 어느 날, 한 젊은 청년이 이 문제를 해결해 보기로 했다.

21 그는 빨간 화살표 스티커를 많이 샀다.

22 매일 그는 자전거를 타고 서울 시내를 돌아다니며 버스 지도에 스티커를 붙였다.

23 아무도 그 청년에게 이 일을 하라고 요청하지 않았다.

24 그는 단지 다른 사람들을 돕고 싶었다.

25 그의 노력 덕분에, 사람들은 지도를 쉽게 이해하고 시간을 절약할 수 있었다.

Step5

※ 다음 우리말을 영어로 쓰시오.

1 여기 내가 어제 읽은 이야기가 두 개 있어.

➡ _____

2 들어볼래?

➡ _____

3 당신이 사랑하는 누군가에게 전화하세요.

➡ _____

4 뉴욕에는 길거리에 공중전화가 많이 있었다.

➡ _____

5 그러나 아무도 그것들을 실제로 사용하지는 않았다.

➡ _____

6 어느 날, 한 남자에게 좋은 아이디어가 떠올랐다.

➡ _____

7 그는 공중전화 하나에 동전들을 붙였다.

➡ _____

8 그는 또한 "당신이 사랑하는 사람에게 전화하세요."라고 쓰인 표지판을 설치했다.

➡ _____

9 곧, 많은 사람들이 그 전화기를 사용하고 있었다.

➡ _____

10 그들이 사랑하는 누군가에게 전화하고 있을 때, 그들은 미소 짓기를 멈추지 않았다.

➡ _____

11 그의 아이디어는 커다란 성공이었다.

➡ _____

12 낮 동안, 모든 동전이 사라졌다.

➡ _____

13 그 남자는 자신의 작은 아이디어가 많은 사람에게 행복을 가져다 주었기 때문에 매우 행복했다.

➡ _____

14 빨간 화살표 청년

➡ _____

15 몇 년 전, 서울의 버스 정류장의 지도는 매우 혼란스러웠다.

➡ _____

16 지도에는 충분한 정보가 없었다.

➡ _____

17 사람들은 다른 사람들에게 지도를 설명해 달라고 요청해야 했다.

➡ _____

18 "이 버스 정류장은 지도의 어디에 있는 건가요? 이 버스가 광화문으로 가나요?"

➡ _____

19 많은 사람이 종종 버스를 잘못 타서 시간을 낭비하곤 했다.

➡ _____

20 어느 날, 한 젊은 청년이 이 문제를 해결해 보기로 했다.

➡ _____

21 그는 빨간 화살표 스티커를 많이 샀다.

➡ _____

22 매일 그는 자전거를 타고 서울 시내를 돌아다니며 버스 지도에 스티커를 붙였다.

➡ _____

23 아무도 그 청년에게 이 일을 하라고 요청하지 않았다.

➡ _____

24 그는 단지 다른 사람들을 돕고 싶었다.

➡ _____

25 그의 노력 덕분에, 사람들은 지도를 쉽게 이해하고 시간을 절약할 수 있었다.

➡ _____

※ 다음 우리말과 일치하도록 빈칸에 알맞은 말을 쓰시오.

Real Life Communication B

1. A: I'm _____ _____ _____ science. _____ can I do?
2. B: _____ _____ _____ you. _____ _____ you start with easier books?
3. A: Okay, I'll _____ _____ _____ _____. Thanks for the tip.
4. B: No _____. I'm _____ you like it.

Let's Write

1. _____ a Mentor!
2. My name is Semi and I'm _____ _____ _____ _____.
3. I _____ _____ _____ my mentee _____ her homework.
4. I _____ _____ my mentee _____ _____.
5. I'll _____ my mentee _____ _____ on time.
6. I _____ a good mentor _____ _____ a good friend.
7. So I want to become a good friend _____ _____ _____ _____ _____.

Culture & Life

1. Do you _____ toys _____ the bars of soap?
2. Children in South Africa _____ _____ _____ more often _____ _____ the toys.
3. _____ your hands _____ _____ many health problems.
4. _____ _____ this idea, _____ children are _____ _____.

※ 다음 우리말을 영어로 쓰시오.

Real Life Communication B

1. A: 나는 과학을 잘 못해. 어떻게 해야 할까?
   ➡ _____

2. B: 내가 도와줄게. 좀 더 쉬운 책으로 시작하는 게 어때?
   ➡ _____

3. A: 응, 한번 시도해 볼게. 조언 고마워.
   ➡ _____

4. B: 괜찮아. 네가 좋아하니 기뻐.
   ➡ _____

Let's Write

1. 멘토가 되세요!
   ➡ _____

2. 제 이름은 세미이고 저는 2학년입니다.
   ➡ _____

3. 저는 제 멘티의 숙제를 돕고 싶습니다.
   ➡ _____

4. 저는 방과 후에 제 멘티를 만날 수 있습니다.
   ➡ _____

5. 저는 제 멘티에게 시간을 지키라고 요청할 것입니다.
   ➡ _____

6. 저는 좋은 멘토는 좋은 친구가 될 수 있다고 생각합니다.
   ➡ _____

7. 그래서 저는 제 멘티가 믿을 수 있는 좋은 친구가 되고 싶습니다.
   ➡ _____

Culture & Life

1. 비누 안에 들어 있는 장난감이 보이나요?
   ➡ _____

2. 남아프리카의 어린이들은 장난감을 갖기 위해 더 자주 손을 씻습니다.
   ➡ _____

3. 손을 씻는 것은 많은 건강 문제를 막을 수 있습니다.
   ➡ _____

4. 이 아이디어 덕분에, 아픈 어린이들이 줄어들고 있습니다.
   ➡ _____

※ 다음 영어를 우리말로 쓰시오.

01 strange	22 worried
02 pointed	23 sunscreen
03 sweat	24 male
04 bug	25 advice
05 scratch	26 million
06 thirsty	27 tiny
07 miss	28 pack
08 protein	29 buzz
09 empty	30 reduce
10 sleeve	31 itchy
11 female	32 bump
12 prevent	33 trash
13 sense	34 useful
14 food poisoning	35 at that moment
15 mosquito	36 stay away from
16 stomach	37 feed on
17 blood	38 suffer from
18 happen	39 keep ~ in mind
19 sweaty	40 lose (~) by
20 itch	41 go for a walk
21 lay	42 for a while
	43 I'd love to

※ 다음 우리말을 영어로 쓰시오.

01 걱정[근심]하는

02 자외선 차단제

03 벌레

04 줄이다

05 쓰레기

06 100만, 다수

07 식중독

08 암컷의, 여성의

09 땀에 젖은

10 가렵다

11 수컷의, 남성의

12 (알을) 낳다

13 땀; 땀을 흘리다

14 햇볕에 탐, 그을림

15 날카로운

16 놓치다, 빼먹다

17 긁다

18 뾰족한

19 이상한

20 단백질

21 (옷의) 소매, 소맷자락

22 피

23 비우다

24 모기

25 위, 복부, 배

26 목마른

27 혹; 타박상

28 유용한

29 예방하다, 방지하다

30 아주 작은

31 충고, 조언

32 (가방을) 싸다

33 윙윙거리다

34 가려운

35 당분간

36 ~으로 고통받다

37 더 잘하다

38 ~을 먹고살다

39 ~을 명심하다

40 산책 가다

41 그때에

42 ~에서 떨어져 있다

43 ~을 …로 데려가다

※ 다음 영영풀이에 알맞은 단어를 <보기>에서 골라 쓴 후, 우리말 뜻을 쓰시오.

1 _____ : any small insect: _____

2 _____ : a wound made by biting: _____

3 _____ : to stop something from happening or existing: _____

4 _____ : to fail to do, take, make, or have something: _____

5 _____ : an area of skin that is raised because it was hit, bitten, etc.: _____

6 _____ : to rub your skin with something sharp: _____

7 _____ : to produce an egg outside the body: _____

8 _____ : a substance found in foods such as meat, milk, eggs, and beans:

_____

9 _____ : to make a low, continuous sound of a flying insect: _____

10 _____ : to take place especially without being planned: _____

11 _____ : to make something smaller in size, amount, number, etc.: _____

12 _____ : to have an unpleasant feeling on your skin that makes you want to

scratch: _____

13 _____ : to put something into a bag so that you can take it with you: _____

14 _____ : a condition in which your skin becomes sore and red from too much

sunshine: _____

15 _____ : a small flying insect that bites the skin of people and animals to suck

their blood: _____

16 _____ : to become aware of something even though you can't see it, hear it, etc.:

_____

보기			
pack	mosquito	prevent	protein
bump	buzz	scratch	bite
sense	itch	happen	reduce
miss	lay	sunburn	bug

※ 다음 우리말과 일치하도록 빈칸에 알맞은 말을 쓰시오.

 해석

Listen & Speak 1-A (1)

Brian: You _____ _____, Jimin. What's _____ ?

Jimin: I'm _____ because _____ _____ _____ _____ .

Brian: _____ _____ _____ _____ _____ . _____ _____ _____ _____ her to an animal doctor?

Jimin: Okay, _____ _____ .

Brian: 너 걱정 있어 보여, 지민아. 무슨 일이니?
Jimin: 내 고양이가 아파서 걱정돼.
Brian: 그것 참 안됐구나. 고양이를 수의사에게 데려가는 것이 어때?
Jimin: 응, 그럴게.

Listen & Speak 1-A (2)

Jane: _____ was the soccer game with Minsu's _____ , Alex?

Alex: We _____ _____ three goals.

Jane: _____ _____ _____ _____ _____ _____ . I hope _____ _____ _____ _____ _____ .

Alex: I _____ _____ , _____ .

Jane: 민수네 반과의 축구 시합은 어땠니, Alex?
Alex: 우리가 세 골 차로 졌어.
Jane: 그것 참 안됐구나. 다음번엔 네가 더 잘하길 바라.
Alex: 나도 그러길 바라.

Listen & Speak 1-B

Tom: _____ _____ _____ this weekend, Yujin.

Yujin: I'd _____ _____ , but _____ _____ .

Tom: _____ _____ ?

Yujin: I have an eye problem. The doctor told me _____ _____ _____ _____ _____ .

Tom: I'm _____ _____ _____ _____ . Maybe we _____ _____ _____ _____ .

Yujin: I really _____ _____ .

Tom: 이번 주말에 수영하러 가자, 유진아.
Yujin: 나도 그러고 싶지만, 그럴 수 없어.
Tom: 왜 그럴 수 없어?
Yujin: 내 눈에 문제가 있어. 의사 선생님이 내게 당분간 수영을 중단하라고 말씀하셨어.
Tom: 그것 참 안됐구나. 아마 우리는 다음 주말에나 갈 수 있겠구나.
Yujin: 나는 정말 그러길 바라.

Listen & Speak 2-A (1)

Emma: Tim, _____ _____ your face! You got _____ .

Tim: Yes, it _____ _____ _____ . I _____ _____ at the beach _____ _____ .

Emma: Oh dear! _____ _____ you _____ _____ next time.

Emma: Tim, 네 얼굴을 보렴! 햇볕에 심하게 탔구나.
Tim: 네, 매우 아파요. 저는 선크림을 바르지 않고 해변으로 수영하러 갔어요.
Emma: 이런 참! 다음번엔 꼭 선크림을 바르도록 해.

Listen & Speak 2-A (2)

Mom: Hojun, do you want to _____ _____ with me?

Hojun: Sorry, Mom. I'm _____ _____ _____ baseball with Alex this afternoon.

Mom: Okay. No problem. _____ _____ _____ _____ _____ _____ _____. It's _____ _____ _____ _____ this afternoon

Hojun: Okay, _____ _____.

Mom: 호준아, 나랑 장보러 갈래?
Hojun: 미안해요, 엄마. 저는 오후에 Alex와 야구할 거예요.
Mom: 알았어. 괜찮다. 모자를 꼭 쓰도록 해. 오후에 매우 더워질 거야.
Hojun: 네, 그럴게요.

Listen & Speak 2-B

Sujin: Dad, do we have _____ bug spray?

Dad: Yes, it's _____ _____ _____. Why?

Sujin: There are a lot of _____ _____ _____ the trash.

Dad: Oh no! What did you _____ in the _____?

Sujin: Some _____ _____.

Dad: Fruit flies love sweet things. _____ _____ _____ _____ _____ _____ _____ _____ _____ _____.

Sujin: I'll _____ that _____ _____. I think we _____ _____ _____ _____ _____ _____ more often.

Dad: That's a _____ _____.

Sujin: 아빠, 우리 벌레 퇴치 스프레이가 있나요?
Dad: 응, 그것은 싱크대 밑에 있단다. 왜?
Sujin: 쓰레기 주변에 많은 초파리가 있어요.
Dad: 오 안돼! 쓰레기에 무엇을 넣었니?
Sujin: 약간의 과일 쓰레기요.
Dad: 초파리는 달콤한 것들을 좋아해. 쓰레기통에 과일 쓰레기를 버리지 않도록 하렴.
Sujin: 명심할게요. 제 생각에 우리는 또한 쓰레기통을 더 자주 비워야 할 것 같아요.
Dad: 좋은 생각이구나.

Real Life Communication

Ms. Wheeler: Junsu, _____ _____ to your face?

Junsu: I got _____ _____ _____ _____ _____ _____.

Ms. Wheeler: _____ _____ _____ _____ _____ _____ _____. did it happen?

Junsu: It happened when I _____ _____ last weekend.

Ms. Wheeler: Oh dear. _____ _____ _____ _____!

Junsu: I know, but they're really _____.

Ms. Wheeler: Clean them _____ cool water. That'll help. Also, _____ _____ _____ _____ _____ _____ _____ _____ when you _____ _____.

Junsu: Okay, _____ _____.

Ms. Wheeler: 준수야, 얼굴이 왜 그러니?
Junsu: 모기에 많이 물렸어요.
Ms. Wheeler: 그것 참 안됐구나. 어쩌다 그랬니?
Junsu: 지난 주말에 캠핑 갔다가 그랬어요.
Ms. Wheeler: 이런 참. 물린 곳을 긁지 마라.
Junsu: 알아요, 하지만 정말 가려워요.
Ms. Wheeler: 물린 곳을 찬물로 닦으렴. 도움이 될 거야. 또한 캠핑 갈 때에는 긴 소매 옷을 입도록 해.
Junsu: 네, 감사합니다.

※ 다음 우리말에 맞도록 대화를 영어로 쓰시오.

Listen & Speak 1-A (1)

Brian: _____

Jimin: _____

Brian: _____

Jimin: _____

Brian: 너 걱정 있어 보여, 지민아. 무슨 일이니?
Jimin: 내 고양이가 아파서 걱정돼.
Brian: 그것 참 안됐구나. 고양이를 수의사에게 데려가는 것이 어때?
Jimin: 응, 그럴게.

Listen & Speak 1-A (2)

Jane: _____

Alex: _____

Jane: _____

Alex: _____

Jane: 민수네 반과의 축구 시합은 어땠니, Alex?
Alex: 우리가 세 골 차로 졌어.
Jane: 그것 참 안됐구나. 다음번엔 네가 더 잘하길 바라.
Alex: 나도 그러길 바라.

Listen & Speak 1-B

Tom: _____

Yujin: _____

Tom: _____

Yujin: _____

Tom: _____

Yujin: _____

Tom: 이번 주말에 수영하러 가자, 유진아.
Yujin: 나도 그러고 싶지만, 그럴 수 없어.
Tom: 왜 그럴 수 없어?
Yujin: 내 눈에 문제가 있어. 의사 선생님이 내게 당분간 수영을 중단하라고 말씀하셨어.
Tom: 그것 참 안됐구나. 아마 우리는 다음 주말에나 갈 수 있겠구나.
Yujin: 나는 정말 그러길 바라.

Listen & Speak 2-A (1)

Emma: _____

Tim: _____

Emma: _____

Emma: Tim, 네 얼굴을 보렴! 햇볕에 심하게 탔구나.
Tim: 네, 매우 아파요. 저는 선크림을 바르지 않고 해변으로 수영하러 갔어요.
Emma: 이런 참! 다음번엔 꼭 선크림을 바르도록 해.

Listen & Speak 2-A (2)

Mom: _____

Hojun: _____

Mom: _____

_____

Hojun: _____

Mom: 호준아, 나랑 장보러 갈래?
Hojun: 미안해요, 엄마. 저는 오후에 Alex와 야구할 거예요.
Mom: 알았어. 괜찮다. 모자를 꼭 쓰도록 해. 오후에 매우 더워질 거야.
Hojun: 네, 그럴게요.

Listen & Speak 2-B

Sujin: _____

Dad: _____

Sujin: _____

Dad: _____

Sujin: _____

Dad: _____

_____

Sujin: _____

Dad: _____

Sujin: 아빠, 우리 벌레 퇴치 스프레이가 있나요?
Dad: 응, 그것은 싱크대 밑에 있단다. 왜?
Sujin: 쓰레기 주변에 많은 초파리가 있어요.
Dad: 오 안돼! 쓰레기에 무엇을 넣었니?
Sujin: 약간의 과일 쓰레기요.
Dad: 초파리는 달콤한 것들을 좋아해. 쓰레기통에 과일 쓰레기를 버리지 않도록 하렴.
Sujin: 명심할게요. 제 생각에 우리는 또한 쓰레기통을 더 자주 비워야 할 것 같아요.
Dad: 좋은 생각이구나.

Real Life Communication

Ms. Wheeler: _____

Junsu: _____

Ms. Wheeler: _____

Junsu: _____

Ms. Wheeler: _____

Junsu: _____

Ms. Wheeler: _____

_____

Junsu: _____

Ms. Wheeler: 준수야, 얼굴이 왜 그러니?
Junsu: 모기에 많이 물렸어요.
Ms. Wheeler: 그것 참 안됐구나. 어쩌다 그랬니?
Junsu: 지난 주말에 캠핑 갔다가 그랬어요.
Ms. Wheeler: 이런 참. 물린 곳을 긁지 마라.
Junsu: 알아요, 하지만 정말 가려워요.
Ms. Wheeler: 물린 곳을 찬물로 닦으렴. 도움이 될 거야. 또한 캠핑 갈 때에는 긴 소매 옷을 입도록 해.
Junsu: 네, 감사합니다.

※ 다음 우리말과 일치하도록 빈칸에 알맞은 것을 골라 쓰시오.

1 _____ was a _____ summer _____ .
A. hot   B. it   C. evening

2 Seojun went _____ a _____ _____ the park.
A. for   B. in   C. walk

3 _____ , he was _____ .
A. sweating   B. soon

4 Seojun: I'm _____ . I want _____ _____ to _____ .
A. something   B. thirsty   C. cold   D. drink

5 _____ that moment, _____ flew at him and _____ his arm.
A. bit   B. tiny   C. something   D. at

6 Mrs. Mosquito: Hey, _____ me _____ you _____ .
A. catch   B. can   C. if

7 Seojun: Who are you? What _____ to me?
A. done   B. have   C. you

8 Mrs. Mosquito: I'm a mosquito. I've _____ _____ my dinner.
A. finished   B. just

9 Seojun: Where are you _____ ? _____ did you _____ me?
A. find   B. from   C. how

10 Mrs. Mosquito: I'm _____ a _____ river.
A. nearby   B. from

11 I was _____ _____ some blood _____ drink there.
A. looking   B. to   C. for

12 Then I smelled _____ _____ and _____ you here.
A. found   B. sweaty   C. something

13 Seojun: How _____ you _____ me _____ the river?
A. smell   B. from   C. could

14 Mrs. Mosquito: Mosquitoes can _____ and _____ very well.
A. smell   B. heat   C. sense

15 That's _____ we have _____ millions of years.
A. for   B. why   C. survived

16 Seojun: Do _____ mosquitoes drink blood _____ _____ ?
A. like   B. all   C. you

17 Mrs. Mosquito: No. Only _____ mosquitoes like me _____ _____ .
A. female   B. blood   C. drink

18 Male mosquitoes only _____ _____ fruit and _____ juice.
A. on   B. feed   C. plant

1 무더운 여름날의 저녁이었습니다.

2 서준이는 공원에 산책을 갔습니다.

3 곧, 그는 땀을 흘리고 있었습니다.

4 서준: 목말라. 뭔가 시원한 것을 마시고 싶어.

5 그때에, 뭔가 조그마한 것이 그에게로 날아와서 그의 팔을 물었습니다.

6 모기: 이봐, 나를 잡을 수 있으면 잡아 봐.

7 서준: 너는 누구니? 나한테 무슨 짓을 한 거지?

8 모기: 나는 모기야. 난 방금 저녁 식사를 마쳤어.

9 서준: 너는 어디에서 왔니? 너는 어떻게 나를 찾은 거야?

10 모기: 나는 근처 강에서 왔어.

11 나는 그곳에서 마실 피를 찾던 중이었지.

12 그러다가 땀 냄새를 맡았고, 여기서 너를 발견했어.

13 서준: 너는 어떻게 강에서부터 내 냄새를 맡을 수 있었지?

14 모기: 모기들은 열과 냄새를 매우 잘 감지해.

15 그래서 우리가 수백만 년 동안 살아남은 거야.

16 서준: 모든 모기가 너처럼 피를 마셔?

17 모기: 아니. 오직 나와 같은 암컷 모기만이 피를 마셔.

18 수컷 모기들은 과일과 식물의 즙만을 먹고 살아.

19 Seojun: That's _____ . So _____ do you _____ blood?
A. why　　　　　　B. interesting　　　C. drink

20 Mrs. Mosquito: I need the _____ in blood _____ _____ my eggs.
A. to　　　　　　　B. protein　　　　C. lay

21 Seojun: _____ do you drink blood? Do you have _____ _____ ?
A. teeth　　　　　B. how　　　　　C. sharp

22 Mrs. Mosquito: No, I _____ have _____ .
A. teeth　　　　　B. don't

23 But I have a _____ and _____ .
A. mouth　　　　B. pointed　　　C. long

24 _____ I can drink _____ blood _____ .
A. your　　　　　B. so　　　　　C. easily

25 Seojun: After you _____ me, I got a _____ . It _____ .
A. bit　　　　　　B. itches　　　　C. bump

26 Mrs. Mosquito: I'm _____ _____ _____ that.
A. hear　　　　　B. to　　　　　C. sorry

27 _____ _____ you _____ scratch it.
A. sure　　　　　B. make　　　　C. don't

28 Also, _____ it _____ alcohol _____ .
A. wipes　　　　B. clean　　　　C. with

29 Seojun: Alcohol wipes? I've _____ _____ that _____ .
A. tried　　　　　B. never　　　　C. before

30 Mrs. Mosquito: It will _____ the _____ .
A. itchiness　　　B. reduce

31 Seojun: Okay, I'll _____ that at _____ . Thanks.
A. home　　　　B. try

32 Mrs. Mosquito: I _____ _____ go. See you _____ .
A. have　　　　　B. soon　　　　C. to

33 Seojun: _____ are you _____ ?
A. going　　　　B. where

34 Mrs. Mosquito: I'm _____ _____ _____ the river.
A. back　　　　　B. going　　　　C. to

35 Seojun: Wait! A _____ of people _____ _____ from your bites.
A. suffered　　　B. lot　　　　　C. have

36 _____ _____ we _____ them?
A. can　　　　　B. how　　　　　C. prevent

37 Mrs. Mosquito: Stay _____ and _____ long _____ .
A. wear　　　　　B. sleeves　　　C. cool

38 Seojun: Thanks. I'll _____ your advice _____ .
A. mind　　　　　B. keep　　　　C. in

---

19 서준: 그거 재미있네. 그럼 너는 왜 피를 마시는 거야?

20 모기: 알을 낳으려면 핏속의 단백질이 필요해.

21 서준: 너는 피를 어떻게 마시는 거야? 날카로운 이빨이 있니?

22 모기: 아니. 나는 이빨이 없어.

23 하지만 길고 뾰족한 입이 있지.

24 그래서 나는 너의 피를 쉽게 마실 수 있는 거야.

25 서준: 네가 나를 문 다음, 부어오른 자국이 생겼어. 가려워.

26 모기: 그 말을 들으니 미안하군.

27 그것을 긁지 않도록 해.

28 또한, 그것을 알코올 솜으로 닦아.

29 서준: 알코올 솜? 나는 전에 그것을 한 번도 해 보지 않았어.

30 모기: 그것은 가려움을 줄여 줄 거야.

31 서준: 알았어. 집에서 해 볼게. 고마워.

32 모기: 나는 이제 가야겠어. 다음에 보자.

33 서준: 너는 어디로 가는데?

34 모기: 강으로 돌아가려고.

35 서준: 기다려! 많은 사람이 모기에 물려서 괴로워하고 있어.

36 어떻게 하면 모기에 물리는 것을 막을 수 있지?

37 모기: 시원하게 지내고 소매가 긴 옷을 입어.

38 서준: 고마워. 너의 충고를 명심할게.

※ 다음 우리말과 일치하도록 빈칸에 알맞은 말을 쓰시오.

1 _____ was a _____ _____ _____.

2 Seojun _____ _____ _____ _____ in the park.

3 Soon, he _____ _____.

4 Seojun: I'm _____. I want _____ _____ _____ _____.

5 At that moment, _____ _____ flew _____ him and _____ his arm.

6 Mrs. Mosquito: Hey, catch me _____ _____ _____.

7 Seojun: Who are you? What _____ _____ _____ to me?

8 Mrs. Mosquito: I'm a mosquito. I've _____ _____ my dinner.

9 Seojun: _____ are you _____? _____ did you _____ me?

10 Mrs. Mosquito: I'm _____ a _____ _____.

11 I _____ _____ _____ some blood _____ _____ there.

12 Then I _____ _____ _____ and found you here.

13 Seojun: _____ could you _____ _____ from the river?

14 Mrs. Mosquito: Mosquitoes can _____ _____ and _____ very well.

15 That's _____ we _____ _____ for _____ of years.

16 Seojun: Do all mosquitoes drink blood _____ _____?

17 Mrs. Mosquito: No. Only _____ mosquitoes _____ _____ _____ _____.

18 Male mosquitoes only _____ _____ fruit and plant juice.

1 무더운 여름날의 저녁이었습니다.

2 서준이는 공원에 산책을 갔습니다.

3 곧, 그는 땀을 흘리고 있었습니다.

4 서준: 목말라. 뭔가 시원한 것을 마시고 싶어.

5 그때에, 뭔가 조그마한 것이 그에게로 날아와서 그의 팔을 물었습니다.

6 모기: 이봐, 나를 잡을 수 있으면 잡아 봐.

7 서준: 너는 누구니? 나한테 무슨 짓을 한 거지?

8 모기: 나는 모기야. 난 방금 저녁 식사를 마쳤어.

9 서준: 너는 어디에서 왔니? 너는 어떻게 나를 찾은 거야?

10 모기: 나는 근처 강에서 왔어.

11 나는 그곳에서 마실 피를 찾던 중이었지.

12 그러다가 땀 냄새를 맡았고, 여기서 너를 발견했어.

13 서준: 너는 어떻게 강에서부터 내 냄새를 맡을 수 있었지?

14 모기: 모기들은 열과 냄새를 매우 잘 감지해.

15 그래서 우리가 수백만 년 동안 살아남은 거야.

16 서준: 모든 모기가 너처럼 피를 마셔?

17 모기: 아니. 오직 나와 같은 암컷 모기만이 피를 마셔.

18 수컷 모기들은 과일과 식물의 즙만을 먹고 살아.

19 Seojun: That's _____. So why do you drink _____?

20 Mrs. Mosquito: I need _____ _____ in blood _____ _____ my eggs.

21 Seojun: _____ do you _____ _____? Do you have _____ _____?

22 Mrs. Mosquito: No, I don't have _____.

23 But I have _____ _____ and _____ _____.

24 _____ I _____ _____ your blood _____.

25 Seojun: _____ you _____ me, I _____ _____ _____. It _____.

26 Mrs. Mosquito: I'm _____ _____ _____.

27 _____ _____ you don't _____ _____.

28 Also, _____ _____ _____ alcohol wipes.

29 Seojun: Alcohol wipes? I've _____ _____ _____ _____.

30 Mrs. Mosquito: It will _____ _____ _____.

31 Seojun: Okay, I'll _____ _____ at home. Thanks.

32 Mrs. Mosquito: I _____ _____ _____. See you soon.

33 Seojun: _____ are you _____?

34 Mrs. Mosquito: I'm _____ _____ to the river.

35 Seojun: Wait! _____ _____ _____ people _____ _____ from your bites.

36 _____ _____ we _____ _____?

37 Mrs. Mosquito: Stay _____ and _____ long _____.

38 Seojun: Thanks. I'll _____ your advice _____ _____.

---

19 서준: 그거 재미있네. 그럼 너는 왜 피를 마시는 거야?

20 모기: 알을 낳으려면 핏속의 단백질이 필요해.

21 서준: 너는 피를 어떻게 마시는 거야? 날카로운 이빨이 있니?

22 모기: 아니, 나는 이빨이 없어.

23 하지만 길고 뾰족한 입이 있지.

24 그래서 나는 너의 피를 쉽게 마실 수 있는 거야.

25 서준: 네가 나를 문 다음. 부어오른 자국이 생겼어. 가려워.

26 모기: 그 말을 들으니 미안하군.

27 그것을 긁지 않도록 해.

28 또한, 그것을 알코올 솜으로 닦아.

29 서준: 알코올 솜? 나는 전에 그것을 한 번도 해 보지 않았어.

30 모기: 그것은 가려움을 줄여 줄 거야.

31 서준: 알았어. 집에서 해 볼게. 고마워.

32 모기: 나는 이제 가야겠어. 다음에 보자.

33 서준: 너는 어디로 가는데?

34 모기: 강으로 돌아가려고.

35 서준: 기다려! 많은 사람이 모기에 물려서 괴로워하고 있어.

36 어떻게 하면 모기에 물리는 것을 막을 수 있지?

37 모기: 시원하게 지내고 소매가 긴 옷을 입어.

38 서준: 고마워. 너의 충고를 명심할게.

※ 다음 문장을 우리말로 쓰시오.

1 It was a hot summer evening.
➡ _____

2 Seojun went for a walk in the park.
➡ _____

3 Soon, he was sweating.
➡ _____

4 Seojun: I'm thirsty. I want something cold to drink.
➡ _____

5 At that moment, something tiny flew at him and bit his arm.
➡ _____

6 Mrs. Mosquito: Hey, catch me if you can.
➡ _____

7 Seojun: Who are you? What have you done to me?
➡ _____

8 Mrs. Mosquito: I'm a mosquito. I've just finished my dinner.
➡ _____

9 Seojun: Where are you from? How did you find me?
➡ _____

10 Mrs. Mosquito: I'm from a nearby river.
➡ _____

11 I was looking for some blood to drink there.
➡ _____

12 Then I smelled something sweaty and found you here.
➡ _____

13 Seojun: How could you smell me from the river?
➡ _____

14 Mrs. Mosquito: Mosquitoes can sense heat and smell very well.
➡ _____

15 That's why we have survived for millions of years.
➡ _____

16 Seojun: Do all mosquitoes drink blood like you?
➡ _____

17 Mrs. Mosquito: No. Only female mosquitoes like me drink blood.
➡ _____

18 Male mosquitoes only feed on fruit and plant juice.
➡ _____

19 Seojun: That's interesting. So why do you drink blood?
➡ _____

20 Mrs. Mosquito: I need the protein in blood to lay my eggs.
➡ _____

21 Seojun: How do you drink blood? Do you have sharp teeth?
➡ _____

22 Mrs. Mosquito: No, I don't have teeth.
➡ _____

23 But I have a long and pointed mouth.
➡ _____

24 So I can drink your blood easily.
➡ _____

25 Seojun: After you bit me, I got a bump. It itches.
➡ _____

26 Mrs. Mosquito: I'm sorry to hear that.
➡ _____

27 Make sure you don't scratch it.
➡ _____

28 Also, clean it with alcohol wipes.
➡ _____

29 Seojun: Alcohol wipes? I've never tried that before.
➡ _____

30 Mrs. Mosquito: It will reduce the itchiness.
➡ _____

31 Seojun: Okay, I'll try that at home. Thanks.
➡ _____

32 I have to go. See you soon.
➡ _____

33 Seojun: Where are you going?
➡ _____

34 Mrs. Mosquito: I'm going back to the river.
➡ _____

35 Seojun: Wait! A lot of people have suffered from your bites.
➡ _____

36 How can we prevent them?
➡ _____

37 Mrs. Mosquito: Stay cool and wear long sleeves.
➡ _____

38 Seojun: Thanks. I'll keep your advice in mind.
➡ _____

※ 다음 괄호 안의 단어들을 우리말에 맞도록 바르게 배열하시오.

1 ▶ (was / it / hot / a / evening. / summer)

➡ _____

2 ▶ (went / Seojun / a / for / walk / park. / the / in)

➡ _____

3 ▶ (he / soon, / sweating. / was)

➡ _____

4 ▶ (thirsty. / I'm // want / I / something / drink. / to / cold)

➡ Seojun: _____

5 ▶ (that / at / moment, / tiny / something / at / flew / him / and / arm. / his / bit)

➡ _____

6 ▶ (hey, / me / catch / can. / you / if)

➡ Mrs. Mosquito: _____

7 ▶ (are / who / you? // have / what / done / you / me? / to)

➡ Seojun: _____

8 ▶ (a / I'm / mosquito. // just / I've / dinner. / my / finished)

➡ Mrs. Mosquito: _____

9 ▶ (are / where / from? / you // did / how / find / me? / you)

➡ Seojun: _____

10 ▶ (from / I'm / river. / nearby / a)

➡ Mrs. Mosquito: _____

11 ▶ (was / I / looking / some / for / blood / there. / drink / to)

➡ _____

12 ▶ (I / then / smelled / sweaty / something / and / here. / you / found)

➡ _____

13 ▶ (could / how / smell / you / from / me / river? / the)

➡ Seojun: _____

14 ▶ (can / mosquitoes / sense / and / heat / smell / well. / very)

➡ Mrs. Mosquito: _____

15 ▶ (why / that's / have / we / for / survived / years. / of / millions)

➡ _____

16 ▶ (all / do / drink / mosquitoes / you? / like / blood)

➡ Seojun: _____

17 ▶ (no. // female / only / like / mosquitoes / me / blood. / drink)

➡ Mrs. Mosquito: _____

18 ▶ (mosquitoes / male / feed / only / fruit / on / and / juice. / plant)

➡ _____

---

1 무더운 여름날의 저녁이었습니다.

2 서준이는 공원에 산책을 갔습니다.

3 곧, 그는 땀을 흘리고 있었습니다.

4 서준: 목말라. 뭔가 시원한 것을 마시고 싶어.

5 그때에, 뭔가 조그마한 것이 그에게로 날아와서 그의 팔을 물었습니다.

6 모기: 이봐, 나를 잡을 수 있으면 잡아 봐.

7 서준: 너는 누구니? 나한테 무슨 짓을 한 거지?

8 모기: 나는 모기야. 난 방금 저녁 식사를 마쳤어.

9 서준: 너는 어디에서 왔니? 너는 어떻게 나를 찾은 거야?

10 모기: 나는 근처 강에서 왔어.

11 나는 그곳에서 마실 피를 찾던 중이었지.

12 그러다가 땀 냄새를 맡았고, 여기서 너를 발견했어.

13 서준: 너는 어떻게 강에서부터 내 냄새를 맡을 수 있었지?

14 모기: 모기들은 열과 냄새를 매우 잘 감지해.

15 그래서 우리가 수백만 년 동안 살아남은 거야.

16 서준: 모든 모기가 너처럼 피를 마셔?

17 모기: 아니. 오직 나와 같은 암컷 모기만이 피를 마셔.

18 수컷 모기들은 과일과 식물의 즙만을 먹고 살아.

19 (interesting. / that's // why / you / so / do / blood? / drink)

➡ Seojun: _____

20 (need / I / protein / the / blood / in / lay / to / eggs. / my)

➡ Mrs. Mosquito: _____

21 (do / how / you / blood? / drink // you / have / do / teeth? / sharp)

➡ Seojun: _____

22 (I / no, / have / teeth. / don't)

➡ Mrs. Mosquito: _____

23 (I / but / have / long / a / and / mouth. / pointed)

➡ _____

24 (I / so / drink / can / your / easily. / blood)

➡ _____

25 (you / me, / bit / after / got / I / bump. / a // itches. / it)

➡ Seojun: _____

26 (sorry / I'm / that. / hear / to)

➡ Mrs. Mosquito: _____

27 (sure / make / don't / you / it. / scratch)

➡ _____

28 (clean / also, / with / it / wipes. / alcohol)

➡ _____

29 (wipes? / alcohol // never / I've / before. / that / tried)

➡ Seojun: _____

30 (will / it / reduce / itchiness. / the)

➡ Mrs. Mosquito: _____

31 (I'll / okay, / that / try / home. / at // thanks.)

➡ Seojun: _____

32 (have / I / go. / to // soon. / you / see)

➡ Mrs. Mosquito: _____

33 (you / are / going? / where)

➡ Seojun: _____

34 (going / to / I'm / back / river. / the)

➡ Mrs. Mosquito: _____

35 (wait! // lot / a / of / have / people / from / suffered / bites. / your)

➡ Seojun: _____

36 (we / can / how / them? / prevent)

➡ _____

37 (cool / stay / wear / and / sleeves. / long)

➡ Mrs. Mosquito: _____

38 (thanks. // keep / I'll / advice / your / mind. / in)

➡ Seojun: _____

---

19 서준: 그거 재미있네. 그럼 너는 왜 피를 마시는 거야?

20 모기: 알을 낳으려면 핏속의 단백질이 필요해.

21 서준: 너는 피를 어떻게 마시는 거야? 날카로운 이빨이 있니?

22 모기: 아니, 나는 이빨이 없어.

23 하지만 길고 뾰족한 입이 있지.

24 그래서 나는 너의 피를 쉽게 마실 수 있는 거야.

25 서준: 네가 나를 문 다음, 부어오른 자국이 생겼어. 가려워.

26 모기: 그 말을 들으니 미안하군.

27 그것을 긁지 않도록 해.

28 또한, 그것을 알코올 솜으로 닦아.

29 서준: 알코올 솜? 나는 전에 그것을 한 번도 해 보지 않았어.

30 모기: 그것은 가려움을 줄여 줄 거야.

31 서준: 알았어, 집에서 해 볼게. 고마워.

32 모기: 나는 이제 가야겠어. 다음에 보자.

33 서준: 너는 어디로 가는데?

34 모기: 강으로 돌아가려고.

35 서준: 기다려! 많은 사람이 모기에 물려서 괴로워하고 있어.

36 어떻게 하면 모기에 물리는 것을 막을 수 있지?

37 모기: 시원하게 지내고 소매가 긴 옷을 입어.

38 서준: 고마워. 너의 충고를 명심할게.

※ 다음 우리말을 영어로 쓰시오.

1 무더운 여름날의 저녁이었습니다.

➡ _____

2 서준이는 공원에 산책을 갔습니다.

➡ _____

3 곧, 그는 땀을 흘리고 있었습니다.

➡ _____

4 서준: 목말라. 뭔가 시원한 것을 마시고 싶어.

➡ Seojun: _____

5 그때에, 뭔가 조그마한 것이 그에게로 날아와서 그의 팔을 물었습니다.

➡ _____

6 모기: 이봐, 나를 잡을 수 있으면 잡아 봐.

➡ Mrs. Mosquito: _____

7 서준: 너는 누구니? 나한테 무슨 짓을 한 거지?

➡ Seojun: _____

8 모기: 나는 모기야. 난 방금 저녁 식사를 마쳤어.

➡ Mrs. Mosquito _____

9 서준: 너는 어디에서 왔니? 너는 어떻게 나를 찾은 거야?

➡ Seojun: _____

10 모기: 나는 근처 강에서 왔어.

➡ Mrs. Mosquito: _____

11 나는 그곳에서 마실 피를 찾던 중이었지.

➡ _____

12 그러다가 땀 냄새를 맡았고, 여기서 너를 발견했어.

➡ _____

13 서준: 너는 어떻게 강에서부터 내 냄새를 맡을 수 있었지?

➡ Seojun: _____

14 모기: 모기들은 열과 냄새를 매우 잘 감지해.

➡ Mrs. Mosquito: _____

15 그래서 우리가 수백만 년 동안 살아남은 거야.

➡ _____

16 서준: 모든 모기가 너처럼 피를 마셔?

➡ Seojun: _____

17 모기: 아니. 오직 나와 같은 암컷 모기만이 피를 마셔.

➡ Mrs. Mosquito: _____

18 수컷 모기들은 과일과 식물의 즙만을 먹고 살아.

➡ _____

19 서준: 그거 재미있네. 그럼 너는 왜 피를 마시는 거야?

➡ Seojun: _____

20 모기: 알을 낳으려면 핏속의 단백질이 필요해.

➡ Mrs. Mosquito: _____

21 서준: 너는 피를 어떻게 마시는 거야? 날카로운 이빨이 있니?

➡ Seojun: _____

22 모기: 아니, 나는 이빨이 없어.

➡ Mrs. Mosquito: _____

23 하지만 길고 뾰족한 입이 있지.

➡ _____

24 그래서 나는 너의 피를 쉽게 마실 수 있는 거야.

➡ _____

25 서준: 네가 나를 문 다음, 부어오른 자국이 생겼어. 가려워.

➡ Seojun: _____

26 모기: 그 말을 들으니 미안하군.

➡ Mrs. Mosquito: _____

27 그것을 긁지 않도록 해.

➡ _____

28 또한, 그것을 알코올 솜으로 닦아.

➡ _____

29 서준: 알코올 솜? 나는 전에 그것을 한 번도 해 보지 않았어.

➡ Seojun: _____

30 모기: 그것은 가려움을 줄여 줄 거야.

➡ Mrs. Mosquito: _____

31 서준: 알았어, 집에서 해 볼게. 고마워.

➡ Seojun: _____

32 모기: 나는 이제 가야겠어. 다음에 보자.

➡ Mrs. Mosquito: _____

33 서준: 너는 어디로 가는데?

➡ Seojun: _____

34 모기: 강으로 돌아가려고.

➡ Mrs. Mosquito: _____

35 서준: 기다려! 많은 사람이 모기에 물려서 괴로워하고 있어.

➡ Seojun: _____

36 어떻게 하면 모기에 물리는 것을 막을 수 있지?

➡ _____

37 모기: 시원하게 지내고 소매가 긴 옷을 입어.

➡ Mrs. Mosquito: _____

38 서준: 고마워. 너의 충고를 명심할게.

➡ Seojun: _____

※ 다음 우리말과 일치하도록 빈칸에 알맞은 말을 쓰시오.

Let's check

1. Sora: You _____ _____, Minu. What's _____?

2. Minu: I _____ my hat. It was _____ _____.

3. Sora: I'm _____ _____ _____ _____.

4. _____ _____ you go to the _____ _____ _____ Center?

5. Minu: That's _____ _____ _____.

1. Sora: 속상해 보인다, 민우야. 무슨 일이니?
2. Minu: 내 모자를 잃어 버렸어. 내가 가장 좋아하는 거였는데.
3. Sora: 그것 참 안됐구나.
4. 분실물 센터에 가보는 게 어때?
5. Minu: 좋은 생각이다.

Let's Write

1. Summer _____ _____

2. _____

3. _____ you ever _____ _____ sunburn?

4. Here are some _____ _____ _____ _____ sunburn in summer.

5. 1. _____ sunscreen.

6. 2. _____ a hat.

7. _____ _____ and _____ the hot weather.

1. 여름철 건강관리 수칙
2. 햇볕 화상
3. 햇볕 화상으로 고통받은 적이 있나요?
4. 여기 여름에 햇볕 화상을 예방할 수 있는 유용한 팁이 있습니다.
5. 1. 선크림을 바르세요.
6. 2. 모자를 쓰세요.
7. 현명하게 무더운 날씨를 즐기세요.

Culture & Life

1. In summer, some people in Korea wear _____ and _____ pants _____ _____ _____.

2. They call them "_____ _____."

3. Refrigerator pants come in _____ _____.

4. Some of them _____ _____ _____.

1. 여름철 몇몇 한국 사람들은 시원함을 유지하기 위해 얇고 가벼운 바지를 입는다.
2. 그들은 그것을 '냉장고 바지'라고 부른다.
3. 화려한 무늬를 가진 냉장고 바지들이 나온다.
4. 어떤 것들은 매우 세련되어 보인다.

※ 다음 우리말을 영어로 쓰시오.

Let's check

1. Sora: 속상해 보인다, 민우야. 무슨 일이니?
   ➡ _____

2. Minu: 내 모자를 잃어 버렸어. 내가 가장 좋아하는 거였는데.
   ➡ _____

3. Sora: 그것 참 안됐구나.
   ➡ _____

4. 분실물 센터에 가보는 게 어때?
   ➡ _____

5. Minu: 좋은 생각이다.
   ➡ _____

Let's Write

1. 여름철 건강 관리 수칙
   ➡ _____

2. 햇볕 화상
   ➡ _____

3. 햇볕 화상으로 고통받은 적이 있나요?
   ➡ _____

4. 여기 여름에 햇볕 화상을 예방할 수 있는 유용한 팁이 있습니다.
   ➡ _____

5. 1. 선크림을 바르세요.
   ➡ _____

6. 2. 모자를 쓰세요.
   ➡ _____

7. 현명하게 무더운 날씨를 즐기세요.
   ➡ _____

Culture & Life

1. 여름철 몇몇 한국 사람들은 시원함을 유지하기 위해 얇고 가벼운 바지를 입는다.
   ➡ _____

2. 그들은 그것을 '냉장고 바지'라고 부른다.
   ➡ _____

3. 화려한 무늬를 가진 냉장고 바지들이 나온다.
   ➡ _____

4. 어떤 것들은 매우 세련되어 보인다.
   ➡ _____

※ 다음 영어를 우리말로 쓰시오.

01 block

02 half

03 delete

04 accident

05 throw

06 somewhere

07 dragon

08 bottom

09 suspect

10 lie

11 escape

12 outside

13 clue

14 hide

15 detective

16 luckily

17 bean

18 twice

19 space

20 inside

21 congratulation

22 scene

23 strange

24 thief

25 prize

26 safely

27 explain

28 straight

29 finally

30 disappear

31 fold

32 none

33 solve

34 riddle

35 button

36 help yourself

37 write down

38 turn over

39 catch a thief

40 fill A with B

41 for free

42 at the time of

43 make it to ~

※ 다음 우리말을 영어로 쓰시오.

01 단추 _____

02 장면 _____

03 단서, 실마리 _____

04 던지다 _____

05 맨 아래 (부분) _____

06 이상한 _____

07 설명하다 _____

08 접다 _____

09 건너다 _____

10 반, 절반 _____

11 어딘가에 _____

12 삭제하다 _____

13 두 번 _____

14 마침내 _____

15 숨기다, 숨다 _____

16 거짓말하다 _____

17 똑바로, 일직선으로 _____

18 사고 _____

19 해결하다 _____

20 사라지다 _____

21 콩 _____

22 용의자 _____

23 탈출하다 _____

24 다행히 _____

25 축하 _____

26 공간 _____

27 ~ 밖에, 밖으로 _____

28 상 _____

29 수수께끼 _____

30 안전하게 _____

31 탐정, 형사 _____

32 양초 _____

33 도둑 _____

34 우표 _____

35 용 _____

36 A를 B로 채우다 _____

37 뒤집다 _____

38 ~에 이르는데 성공하다 _____

39 공짜로 _____

40 ~이 일어나던 때에 _____

41 적다 _____

42 도둑을 잡다 _____

43 마음껏 드세요 _____

※ 다음 영영풀이에 알맞은 단어를 <보기>에서 골라 쓴 후, 우리말 뜻을 쓰시오.

1 _____ : to go or come into a place: _____

2 _____ : someone who is thought to be guilty of a crime: _____

3 _____ : a seed or a pod that comes from a climbing plant and is cooked as food: _____

4 _____ : the flat surface on the lowest side of an object: _____

5 _____ : someone who steals things from another person or place: _____

6 _____ : exactly or about 50% of an amount, time, distance, number etc.: _____

7 _____ : an object or piece of information that helps someone solve a crime or mystery: _____

8 _____ : to go from one side of something such as a road, river, room, etc. to the other: _____

9 _____ : to remove something that has been written down or stored in a computer: _____

10 _____ : a long wooden stick with a special shape that is used in some sports and games: _____

11 _____ : an event in which a car, train, plane, etc. is damaged and often someone is hurt: _____

12 _____ : someone who is paid to discover information about someone or something: _____

13 _____ : a question that is deliberately very confusing and has a humorous or clever answer: _____

14 _____ : to leave a place when someone is trying to catch you or stop you, or when there is a dangerous situation: _____

15 _____ : to put or keep someone or something in a place where they/it cannot be seen or found: _____

16 _____ : a small piece of paper with a design on it that you buy and stick on an envelope or a package before you post it: _____

보기			
riddle	suspect	detective	delete
bean	escape	hide	clue
accident	thief	bat	cross
enter	bottom	stamp	half

※ 다음 우리말과 일치하도록 빈칸에 알맞은 말을 쓰시오.

Listen & Speak 1-A

Jimin: Do you _____ _____ _____ the new game _____ I _____?

Brian: Sure, _____ is _____, Jimin?

Jimin: It's _____ a soccer game but the players are _____ and _____. You _____ _____ _____ these buttons _____ _____.

Brian: That _____ _____. _____ _____ _____ _____ _____ _____ the buttons?

Jimin: Sure.

Listen & Speak 1-B

Jack: Kelly, here's a _____. You can see this _____ _____ _____ _____, _____ in a year, but _____ _____ _____ _____. What is this?

Kelly: _____ _____ _____ _____.

Jack: It's the letter "E."

Kelly: I don't _____ _____. _____ _____ _____ _____ _____?

Jack: Well, there are two "E"s in the word "week," one "E" in the word "_____" but _____ "E"s in the word "_____."

Kelly: Aha! Now I _____ _____.

Listen & Speak 2-A

Tom: Yujin, _____ _____ my paper fox.

Yujin: That's cute. _____ _____ _____ _____ _____ _____?

Tom: _____, fold a paper _____ to _____ _____ _____. _____, _____ _____ _____ of the triangle to the _____ _____. _____, fold _____ _____ of the bottom line to the top _____ _____ _____. _____, _____ it _____ and draw a face.

Yujin: That _____ _____.

Listen & Speak 2-B

Jane: Minsu, do you know the TV show about the student _____?

Minsu: Yes. I love that show, but I _____ _____ it _____ _____. What was it _____?

Jane: Well, _____ _____ the bikes at school _____.

Minsu: So, what _____ he _____?

Jane: _____, he _____ _____ the school. _____, he met some _____ and asked questions. _____, he _____ the _____. The thief was ....

Minsu: No, _____ _____ me! I'll _____ it _____.

Jane: 민수야, 학생 탐정이 나오는 TV 쇼를 아니?
Minsu: 응, 나는 그 쇼를 아주 좋아하지만 이번 주에는 못 봤어. 무슨 내용이었어?
Jane: 음, 학교의 모든 자전거들이 사라졌어.
Minsu: 그래서 그가 무엇을 했어?
Jane: 첫째로, 그는 학교를 둘러 봤어. 그리고 나서, 몇몇의 용의자를 만나서 질문을 했지. 마침내, 그는 도둑을 찾았어. 도둑은....
Minsu: 안 돼, 말하지 마! 내가 나중에 볼 거야.

Real Life Communication

Emily: Junsu, do you want to _____ a riddle?

Junsu: Sure, what is it?

Emily: There is a farmer. _____, the farmer buys a fox, a duck, and _____ _____ _____ _____. Then, the farmer _____ _____ _____ _____ _____.

Junsu: What's the problem?

Emily: The boat _____ _____ _____ the farmer and _____ _____ thing.

Junsu: _____ _____ _____ that the farmer can _____ only one thing _____ _____ _____?

Emily: Yes. Also, the fox will eat the duck or the duck will eat the beans if the farmer isn't there. _____ _____ _____ _____ _____ _____ _____ _____ the river _____?

Junsu: Hmm ....

Emily: 준수야, 수수께끼 하나 풀어볼래?
Junsu: 물론이지, 뭔데?
Emily: 한 농부가 있어. 먼저 농부는 여우, 오리, 콩 자루를 하나씩 사. 그리고 나서, 농부는 강을 건너야 해.
Junsu: 뭐가 문제인데?
Emily: 보트는 단지 농부와 한 가지만 더 옮길 수 있어.
Junsu: 농부가 한 번에 오직 한 가지만 옮길 수 있다는 말이니?
Emily: 응. 또한 만약 농부가 없다면 여우가 오리를 먹거나, 오리가 콩을 먹을 거야. 전부를 강 건너로 안전하게 옮길 방법을 설명할 수 있겠니?
Junsu: 음....

Let's Check

Minjun: Wow! Something _____ really _____, Mom. What is it?

Mom: We're _____ _____ have tacos _____ _____. _____ _____.

Minjun: _____ _____ _____ _____ _____ _____ _____ a taco?

Mom: _____, _____ your tortilla _____ vegetables and meat. _____, _____ some sauce _____ _____ _____.

Minjun: Sounds _____!

Mom: _____ you _____ some cheese?

Minjun: No, _____.

Minjun: 와! 뭔가 정말 좋은 냄새가 나요, 엄마. 뭐예요?
Mom: 우리는 저녁 식사로 타코를 먹을 거야. 맘껏 먹으렴.
Minjun: 타코 만드는 법을 설명해 주실 수 있어요?
Mom: 먼저, 토르티야를 채소와 고기로 채워. 그 다음, 위에 약간의 소스를 추가하렴.
Minjun: 맛있을 것 같아요!
Mom: 치즈 좀 줄까?
Minjun: 아뇨, 괜찮아요.

※ 다음 우리말에 맞도록 대화를 영어로 쓰시오.

Listen & Speak 1-A

Jimin: _____

Brian: _____

Jimin: _____

_____

Brian: _____

Jimin: _____

Listen & Speak 1-B

Jack: _____

_____

Kelly: _____

Jack: _____

Kelly: _____

Jack: _____

_____

Kelly: _____

Listen & Speak 2-A

Tom: _____

Yujin: _____

Tom: _____

Yujin: _____

Listen & Speak 2-B

Jane: _____

Minsu: _____

Jane: _____

Minsu: _____

Jane: _____

_____

Minsu: _____

Real Life Communication

Emily: _____

Junsu: _____

Emily: _____

_____

Junsu: _____

Emily: _____

Junsu: _____

Emily: _____

_____

Junsu: _____

Let's Check

Minjun: _____

Mom: _____

Minjun: _____

Mom: _____

_____

Minjun: _____

Mom: _____

Minjun: _____

Jane: 민수야, 학생 탐정이 나오는 TV 쇼를 아니?

Minsu: 응, 나는 그 쇼를 아주 좋아하지만 이번 주에는 못 봤어. 무슨 내용이었어?

Jane: 음, 학교의 모든 자전거들이 사라졌어.

Minsu: 그래서 그가 무엇을 했어?

Jane: 첫째로, 그는 학교를 둘러 봤어. 그리고 나서, 몇몇의 용의자를 만나서 질문을 했지. 마침내, 그는 도둑을 찾았어. 도둑은....

Minsu: 안 돼, 말하지 마! 내가 나중에 볼 거야.

Emily: 준수야, 수수께끼 하나 풀어볼래?

Junsu: 물론이지, 뭔데?

Emily: 한 농부가 있어. 먼저 농부는 여우, 오리, 콩 자루를 하나씩 사. 그리고 나서, 농부는 강을 건너야 해.

Junsu: 뭐가 문제인데?

Emily: 보트는 단지 농부와 한 가지만 더 옮길 수 있어.

Junsu: 농부가 한 번에 오직 한 가지만 옮길 수 있다는 말이니?

Emily: 응. 또한 만약 농부가 없다면 여우가 오리를 먹거나, 오리가 콩을 먹을 거야. 전부를 강 건너로 안전하게 옮길 방법을 설명할 수 있겠니?

Junsu: 음....

Minjun: 와! 뭔가 정말 좋은 냄새가 나요, 엄마. 뭐예요?

Mom: 우리는 저녁 식사로 타코를 먹을 거야. 맘껏 먹으렴.

Minjun: 타코 만드는 법을 설명해 주실 수 있어요?

Mom: 먼저, 토르티야를 채소와 코기로 채워. 그 다음, 위에 약간의 소스를 추가하렴.

Minjun: 맛있을 것 같아요!

Mom: 치즈 좀 줄까?

Minjun: 아뇨, 괜찮아요.

Step1

※ 다음 우리말과 일치하도록 빈칸에 알맞은 것을 골라 쓰시오.

The Great Escape

1 _____ _____ the _____ Tower.

    A. Escape   B. to   C. Welcome

2 You will _____ the _____ room in _____ tower.

    A. first   B. our   C. enter

3 You need to _____ some _____ to _____ .

    A. riddles   B. solve   C. escape

4 Clues can _____ _____ somewhere _____ the room.

    A. inside   B. found   C. be

5 So, _____ you _____ to _____ like Sherlock Holmes?

    A. think   B. are   C. ready

Room # 1

6 Mr. Doodle was _____ _____ a car _____ Sunday afternoon.

    A. by   B. on   C. hit

7 _____, he wasn't _____ _____, but he didn't _____ the driver.

    A. see   B. badly   C. hurt   D. luckily

8 Three _____ were _____ _____ a police officer.

    A. by   B. suspects   C. questioned

9 Ms. A said she was _____ a book at the _____ of the _____ .

    A. accident   B. time   C. reading

10 Mr. B _____ he _____ _____ his dog.

    A. was   B. said   C. walking

11 Ms. C said she _____ _____ _____ .

    A. making   B. breakfast   C. was

12 _____ _____ Mr. Doodle? Can you _____ why?

    A. hit   B. explain   C. who

13 Do you _____ the answer? _____ it _____ .

    A. have   B. down   C. write

14 Then you can _____ _____ the _____ room.

    A. next   B. to   C. move

15 **Clue** The _____ _____ _____ the afternoon.

    A. in   B. happened   C. accident

16 Congratulations! You _____ _____ _____ the second room.

    A. to   B. made   C. it

대탈출

1 '탈출탑'에 오신 것을 환영합니다.

2 당신은 저희 탑의 첫 번째 방에 들어갈 것입니다.

3 당신은 탈출하기 위하여 몇 개의 수수께끼를 풀어야 합니다.

4 단서들은 방 어딘가에서 발견될 수 있습니다.

5 그러면 당신은 셜록 홈스처럼 생각할 준비가 되었나요?

방 # 1

6 Doodle씨는 일요일 오후에 차에 치였습니다.

7 다행히 그는 심하게 다치지 않았으나 그는 운전자를 보지 못했습니다.

8 세 명의 용의자들이 경찰에게 심문을 받았습니다.

9 A씨는 사고가 일어난 시간에 책을 읽고 있었다고 말했습니다.

10 B씨는 그의 개를 산책시키고 있었다고 말했습니다.

11 C씨는 아침을 만들고 있었다고 말했습니다.

12 누가 Doodle씨를 치었을까요? 왜 그런지 설명할 수 있나요?

13 답을 가지고 있나요? 적어 보세요.

14 그런 다음, 당신은 다음 방으로 갈 수 있습니다.

15 단서: 사건은 오후에 일어났습니다.

16 축하합니다! 당신은 두 번째 방에 오는 데 성공하셨습니다.

17 However, the second room is _____ _____ to _____ than the first one. Good luck!

A. escape　　　B. harder　　　C. much

Room #2

18 Jay _____ an email _____ his favorite _____ store.

A. clothing　　　B. from　　　C. gets

19 The title _____ "You _____ our Lucky Day _____!"

A. won　　　B. reads　　　C. event

20 Jay is _____. He _____ _____ it.

A. quickly　　　B. surprised　　　C. opens

21 JayJr@kmail.com

You _____ _____ 'Lucky Day' _____!

A. our　　　B. event　　　C. won

22 Congratulations! You _____ _____ a special _____.

A. prize　　　B. won　　　C. have

23 _____ our Lucky Day event, you can _____ any seven _____ from our store for _____!

A. free　　　B. choose　　　C. items　　　D. during

24 Come _____ our store _____ November 31.

A. on　　　B. to

25 We _____ _____ _____ see you.

A. wait　　　B. to　　　C. can't

26 _____ _____, Kay Brown

A. yours　　　B. truly

27 _____, Jay thinks that the event isn't _____ and _____ the email.

A. deletes　　　B. real　　　C. however

28 _____ you _____ _____?

A. explain　　　B. why　　　C. can

29 **Clue** _____ are _____ 30 or 31 _____ in a month.

A. usually　　　B. days　　　C. there

30 Do you _____ the _____?

A. answer　　　B. have

31 _____ it _____ and then you are _____ to go!

A. down　　　B. free　　　C. write

17 그러나 두 번째 방은 첫 번째 방보다 탈출하기 훨씬 더 어렵습니다. 행운을 빕니다!

방 # 2

18 Jay는 그가 가장 좋아하는 옷가게로부터 이메일을 받습니다.

19 제목은 "당신은 '행운의 날' 행사에 당첨되었습니다!"라고 적혀 있습니다.

20 Jay는 놀랍니다. 그는 재빨리 그것을 엽니다.

21 JayJr@kmail.com 당신은 우리의 '행운의 날' 행사에 당첨되었습니다!

22 축하합니다! 당신은 특별한 상품을 받게 되었습니다.

23 '행운의 날' 행사 동안, 당신은 우리 가게에서 일곱 가지 상품을 아무거나 무료로 선택할 수 있습니다!

24 11월 31일에 우리 가게로 오세요.

25 우리는 몹시 당신을 보기를 기대합니다.

26 안녕히 계십시오, Kay Brown

27 그러나 Jay는 그 행사가 사실이 아니라고 생각하고 이메일을 삭제합니다.

28 왜 그런지 설명할 수 있나요?

29 단서: 한 달은 주로 30일 또는 31일이 있습니다.

30 답을 가지고 계신가요?

31 그것을 적으면, 당신은 자유롭게 가실 수 있습니다!

※ 다음 우리말과 일치하도록 빈칸에 알맞은 말을 쓰시오.

The Great Escape

1 _____ _____ the Escape Tower.

2 You will _____ _____ _____ _____ in our tower.

3 You _____ _____ _____ _____ _____ to escape.

4 Clues can _____ _____ somewhere _____ the room.

5 So, _____ you _____ _____ _____ _____ Sherlock Holmes?

Room # 1

6 Mr. Doodle _____ _____ _____ a car _____ Sunday afternoon.

7 _____, he _____ _____ _____, but he _____ _____ the driver.

8 Three suspects _____ _____ _____ a police officer.

9 Ms. A said she was _____ _____ _____ _____ _____ _____ _____ _____ _____ .

10 Mr. B _____ he _____ _____ his dog.

11 Ms. C said she _____ _____ _____ .

12 _____ _____ Mr. Doodle? Can you _____ _____ ?

13 Do you have the answer? _____ _____ _____ .

14 Then you _____ _____ _____ the next room.

15 **Clue** The _____ _____ the afternoon.

16 Congratulations! You _____ _____ _____ the second room.

대탈출

1 '탈출탑'에 오신 것을 환영합니다.

2 당신은 저희 탑의 첫 번째 방에 들어갈 것입니다.

3 당신은 탈출하기 위하여 몇 개의 수수께끼를 풀어야 합니다.

4 단서들은 방 어딘가에서 발견될 수 있습니다.

5 그러면 당신은 셜록 홈스처럼 생각할 준비가 되었나요?

방 # 1

6 Doodle씨는 일요일 오후에 차에 치였습니다.

7 다행히 그는 심하게 다치지 않았으나 그는 운전자를 보지 못했습니다.

8 세 명의 용의자들이 경찰에게 심문을 받았습니다.

9 A씨는 사고가 일어난 시간에 책을 읽고 있었다고 말했습니다.

10 B씨는 그의 개를 산책시키고 있었다고 말했습니다.

11 C씨는 아침을 만들고 있었다고 말했습니다.

12 누가 Doodle씨를 치었을까요? 왜 그런지 설명할 수 있나요?

13 답을 가지고 있나요? 적어 보세요.

14 그런 다음, 당신은 다음 방으로 갈 수 있습니다.

15 단서: 사건은 오후에 일어났습니다.

16 축하합니다! 당신은 두 번째 방에 오는 데 성공하셨습니다.

17 _____, the second room is _____ _____ _____ _____ _____ the first one. Good luck!

Room #2

18 Jay _____ an email _____ his favorite _____ _____.

19 The title _____ "You _____ our Lucky Day event!"

20 Jay is _____. He _____ _____ it.

21 JayJr@kmail.com

You _____ _____ 'Lucky Day' event!

22 _____! You_____ _____ a special _____.

23 _____ our Lucky Day event, you can _____ any seven items _____ our store _____ _____!

24 _____ _____ our store _____ November 31.

25 We _____ _____ _____ _____ you.

26 _____ _____, Kay Brown

27 _____, Jay _____ _____ the event _____ _____ and _____ the email.

28 _____ you _____ _____?

29 **Clue** _____ _____ _____ 30 or 31 _____ in a month.

30 Do you _____ _____ _____?

31 _____ _____ _____ and then you _____ _____ _____ _____!

---

17 그러나 두 번째 방은 첫 번째 방보다 탈출하기 훨씬 더 어렵습니다. 행운을 빕니다!

방 # 2

18 Jay는 그가 가장 좋아하는 옷 가게로부터 이메일을 받습니다.

19 제목은 "당신은 '행운의 날' 행사에 당첨되었습니다!"라고 적혀 있습니다.

20 Jay는 놀랍니다. 그는 재빨리 그것을 엽니다.

21 JayJr@kmail.com
당신은 우리의 '행운의 날' 행사에 당첨되었습니다!

22 축하합니다! 당신은 특별한 상품을 받게 되었습니다.

23 '행운의 날' 행사 동안, 당신은 우리 가게에서 일곱 가지 상품을 아무거나 무료로 선택할 수 있습니다!

24 11월 31일에 우리 가게로 오세요.

25 우리는 몹시 당신을 보기를 기대합니다.

26 안녕히 계십시오, Kay Brown

27 그러나 Jay는 그 행사가 사실이 아니라고 생각하고 이메일을 삭제합니다.

28 왜 그런지 설명할 수 있나요?

29 단서: 한 달은 주로 30일 또는 31일이 있습니다.

30 답을 가지고 계신가요?

31 그것을 적으면, 당신은 자유롭게 가실 수 있습니다!

※ 다음 문장을 우리말로 쓰시오.

The Great Escape

1 Welcome to the Escape Tower.

➡ _____

2 You will enter the first room in our tower.

➡ _____

3 You need to solve some riddles to escape.

➡ _____

4 Clues can be found somewhere inside the room.

➡ _____

5 So, are you ready to think like Sherlock Holmes?

➡ _____

Room #1

6 Mr. Doodle was hit by a car on Sunday afternoon.

➡ _____

7 Luckily, he wasn't badly hurt, but he didn't see the driver.

➡ _____

8 Three suspects were questioned by a police officer.

➡ _____

9 Ms. A said she was reading a book at the time of the accident.

➡ _____

10 Mr. B said he was walking his dog.

➡ _____

11 Ms. C said she was making breakfast.

➡ _____

12 Who hit Mr. Doodle? Can you explain why?

➡ _____

13 Do you have the answer? Write it down.

➡ _____

14 Then you can move to the next room.

➡ _____

15 Clue The accident happened in the afternoon.

➡ _____

16 Congratulations! You made it to the second room.

➡ _____

17 However, the second room is much harder to escape than the first one. Good luck!

➡ _____

Room #2

18 Jay gets an email from his favorite clothing store.

➡ _____

19 The title reads "You won our Lucky Day event!"

➡ _____

20 Jay is surprised. He quickly opens it.

➡ _____

21 JayJr@kmail.com
You won our 'Lucky Day' event!

➡ _____

22 Congratulations! You have won a special prize.

➡ _____

23 During our Lucky Day event, you can choose any seven items from our store for free!

➡ _____

24 Come to our store on November 31.

➡ _____

25 We can't wait to see you.

➡ _____

26 Truly yours, Kay Brown

➡ _____

27 However, Jay thinks that the event isn't real and deletes the email.

➡ _____

28 Can you explain why?

➡ _____

29 Clue There are usually 30 or 31 days in a month.

➡ _____

30 Do you have the answer?

➡ _____

31 Write it down and then you are free to go!

➡ _____

※ 다음 괄호 안의 단어들을 우리말에 맞도록 바르게 배열하시오.

The Great Escape

1 (to / Welcome / Tower. / Escape / the)

➡ _____

2 (will / you / the / enter / room / first / tower. / our / in)

➡ _____

3 (need / you / solve / to / riddles / some / escape. / to)

➡ _____

4 (can / clues / found / be / inside / somewhere / room. / the)

➡ _____

5 (are / so, / ready / you / think / to / Sherlock / like / Holmes?)

➡ _____

Room #1

6 (Doodle / Mr. / hit / was / a / by / car / afternoon. / Sunday / on)

➡ _____

7 (he / luckily, / wasn't / hurt, / badly / but / didn't / he / driver. / the / see)

➡ _____

8 (suspects / three / questioned / were / a / by / officer. / police)

➡ _____

9 (A / Ms. / she / said / redaing / was / book / a / the / at / time / accident. / the / of)

➡ _____

10 (B / Mr. / he / said / walking / was / dog. / his)

➡ _____

11 (C / Ms. / she / said / making / was / breakfast.)

➡ _____

12 (hit / who / Doodle? / Mr. // you / can / why? / explain)

➡ _____

13 (you / do / have / answer? / the // down. / it / write)

➡ _____

14 (you / then / move / can / the / to / room. / next)

➡ _____

15 (clue // accident / the / in / happened / afternoon. / the)

➡ _____

16 (congratulations! // made / you / to / it / room. / second / the)

➡ _____

17 (however, / second / the / is / room / harder / much / escape / to / than / first / the / one. // luck! / good)

➡ _____

_____

Room #2

18 (gets / Jay / email / an / his / from / store. / clothing / favorite)

➡ _____

19 (title / the / reads / "you / our / won / Day / event!" / Lucky)

➡ _____

20 (is / Jay / surprised. // he / quickly / it. / opens)

➡ _____

21 JayJr@kmail.com

(won / you / event! / our / Day' / 'Lucky)

➡ JayJr@kmail.com _____

22 (congratulations! // have / you / a / prize. / special / won)

➡ _____

23 (our / during / event, / Day / Lucky / can / you / any / choose / items / seven / from / store / our / free! / for)

➡ _____

_____

24 (to / come / store / our / 31. / November / on)

➡ _____

25 (can't / we / see / wait / you. / to)

➡ _____

26 (yours, / truly / Brown / Kay)

➡ _____

27 (however, / thinks / Jay / the / that / isn't / event / deletes / and / real / email. / the)

➡ _____

28 (you / can / why? / explain)

➡ _____

29 (clue // are / there / 30 / usually / 31 / or / month. / a / in / days)

➡ _____

30 (you / do / have / answer? / the)

➡ _____

31 (down / it / write / then / and / are / you / go! / to / free)

➡ _____

17 그러나 두 번째 방은 첫 번째 방 보다 탈출하기 훨씬 더 어렵습 니다. 행운을 빕니다!

방 # 2

18 Jay는 그가 가장 좋아하는 옷 가게로부터 이메일을 받습니다.

19 제목은 "당신은 '행운의 날' 행 사에 당첨되었습니다!"라고 적 혀 있습니다.

20 Jay는 놀랍니다. 그는 재빨리 그것을 엽니다.

21 JayJr@kmail.com 당신은 우리의 '행운의 날' 행사 에 당첨되었습니다!

22 축하합니다! 당신은 특별한 상 품을 받게 되었습니다.

23 '행운의 날' 행사 동안, 당신은 우리 가게에서 일곱 가지 상품 을 아무거나 무료로 선택할 수 있습니다!

24 11월 31일에 우리 가게로 오 세요.

25 우리는 몹시 당신을 보기를 기 대합니다.

26 안녕히 계십시오, Kay Brown

27 그러나 Jay는 그 행사가 사실이 아니라고 생각하고 이메일을 삭 제합니다.

28 왜 그런지 설명할 수 있나요?

29 단서: 한 달은 주로 30일 또는 31일이 있습니다.

30 답을 가지고 계신가요?

31 그것을 적으면, 당신은 자유롭 게 가실 수 있습니다!

※ 다음 우리말을 영어로 쓰시오.

The Great Escape

1 '탈출 탑'에 오신 것을 환영합니다.

➡ _____

2 당신은 저희 탑의 첫 번째 방에 들어갈 것입니다.

➡ _____

3 당신은 탈출하기 위하여 몇 개의 수수께끼를 풀어야 합니다.

➡ _____

4 단서들은 방 어딘가에서 발견될 수 있습니다.

➡ _____

5 그러면 당신은 셜록 홈스처럼 생각할 준비가 되었나요?

➡ _____

Room #1

6 Doodle씨는 일요일 오후에 차에 치였습니다.

➡ _____

7 다행히 그는 심하게 다치지 않았으나 그는 운전자를 보지 못했습니다.

➡ _____

8 세 명의 용의자들이 경찰에게 심문을 받았습니다.

➡ _____

9 A씨는 사고가 일어난 시간에 책을 읽고 있었다고 말했습니다.

➡ _____

10 B씨는 그의 개를 산책시키고 있었다고 말했습니다.

➡ _____

11 C씨는 아침을 만들고 있었다고 말했습니다.

➡ _____

12 누가 Doodle씨를 치었을까요? 왜 그런지 설명할 수 있나요?

➡ _____

13 답을 가지고 있나요? 적어 보세요.

➡ _____

14 그런 다음, 당신은 다음 방으로 갈 수 있습니다.

➡ _____

15 단서: 사건은 오후에 일어났습니다.

➡ _____

16 축하합니다! 당신은 두 번째 방에 오는 데 성공하셨습니다.

➡ _____

17 그러나 두 번째 방은 첫 번째 방보다 탈출하기 훨씬 더 어렵습니다. 행운을 빕니다!

➡ _____

Room #2

18 Jay는 그가 가장 좋아하는 옷 가게로부터 이메일을 받습니다.

➡ _____

19 제목은 "당신은 '행운의 날' 행사에 당첨되었습니다!"라고 적혀 있습니다.

➡ _____

20 Jay는 놀랍니다. 그는 재빨리 그것을 엽니다.

➡ _____

21 JayJr@kmail.com
당신은 우리의 '행운의 날' 행사에 당첨되었습니다!

➡ JayJr@kmail.com _____

22 축하합니다! 당신은 특별한 상품을 받게 되었습니다.

➡ _____

23 '행운의 날' 행사 동안, 당신은 우리 가게에서 일곱 가지 상품을 아무거나 공짜로 선택할 수 있습니다!

➡ _____

24 11월 31일에 우리 가게로 오세요.

➡ _____

25 우리는 몹시 당신을 보기를 기대합니다.

➡ _____

26 안녕히 계십시오, Kay Brown

➡ _____

27 그러나 Jay는 그 행사가 사실이 아니라고 생각하고 이메일을 삭제합니다.

➡ _____

28 왜 그런지 설명할 수 있나요?

➡ _____

29 단서: 한 달은 주로 30일 또는 31일이 있습니다.

➡ _____

30 답을 가지고 계신가요?

➡ _____

31 그것을 적으면, 당신은 자유롭게 가실 수 있습니다!

➡ _____

※ 다음 우리말과 일치하도록 빈칸에 알맞은 말을 쓰시오.

Listen and Speak 1-C

1. A: _____ _____ _____ this riddle.

2. B: Sure.

3. A: Four people _____ _____ one umbrella, but nobody _____ _____ . Can you _____ _____ ?

4. B: Yes! It's _____ it's _____ _____ _____ !

1. A: 이 수수께끼를 풀어봐.
2. B: 그래.
3. A: 4명의 사람들이 하나의 우산 아래 있는데 아무도 젖지 않아. 이유를 설명할 수 있겠니?
4. B: 응! 왜냐하면 맑은 날이기 때문이야.

Let's Write

1. _____ was _____ Sunday.

2. Dohun was _____ _____ .

3. _____ , he _____ _____ _____ in the next room.

4. When he _____ _____ the room, the window _____ _____ .

5. When he _____ _____ , Sujin _____ _____ a baseball bat and Ted _____ _____ a ball to his dog.

6. Who _____ the window?

7. How _____ it be _____ ?

1. 지난 일요일이었다.
2. 도훈이는 집에 있었다.
3. 갑자기, 그는 옆방에서 나는 어떤 소리를 들었다.
4. 그가 그 방으로 갔을 때, 창문이 깨져 있었다.
5. 도훈이가 밖을 보았을 때, 수진이는 야구 방망이를 들고 있었고 Ted는 그의 개에게 공을 던지고 있었다.
6. 누가 창문을 깼을까?
7. 그것은 어떻게 설명될 수 있을까?

Culture & Life

1. This is the _____ _____ of the Sphinx.

2. Oedipus _____ _____ it to _____ _____ Thebes.

3. This is the question _____ the Sphinx _____ _____ .

4. _____ creature _____ _____ _____ _____ in the morning, two legs in the afternoon, and three legs in the evening?

1. 이것은 스핑크스의 유명한 수수께끼이다.
2. 오이디푸스는 Thebes에 들어가기 위해 그것을 풀어야 한다.
3. 이것은 스핑크스가 그에게 묻는 질문이다.
4. 어느 생명체가 아침에는 네 다리로 걷고, 오후에는 두 다리로 걷고, 저녁에는 세 다리로 걷는가?

※ 다음 우리말을 영어로 쓰시오.

Listen and Speak 1-C

1. A: 이 수수께끼를 풀어봐.

➡ _____

2. B: 그래.

➡ _____

3. A: 4명의 사람들이 하나의 우산 아래 있는데 아무도 젖지 않아. 이유를 설명할 수 있겠니?

➡ _____

4. B: 응! 왜냐하면 맑은 날이기 때문이야.

➡ _____

Let's Write

1. 지난 일요일이었다.

➡ _____

2. 도훈이는 집에 있었다.

➡ _____

3. 갑자기, 그는 옆방에서 나는 어떤 소리를 들었다.

➡ _____

4. 그가 그 방으로 갔을 때, 창문이 깨져 있었다.

➡ _____

5. 도훈가 밖을 보았을 때, 수진이는 야구 방망이를 들고 있었고 Ted는 그의 개에게 공을 던지고 있었다.

➡ _____

6. 누가 창문을 깼을까?

➡ _____

7. 그것은 어떻게 설명될 수 있을까?

➡ _____

Culture & Life

1. 이것은 스핑크스의 유명한 수수께끼이다.

➡ _____

2. 오이디푸스는 Thebes에 들어가기 위해 그것을 풀어야 한다.

➡ _____

3. 이것은 스핑크스가 그에게 묻는 질문이다.

➡ _____

4. 어느 생명체가 아침에는 네 다리로 걷고, 오후에는 두 다리로 걷고, 저녁에는 세 다리로 걷는가?

➡ _____

_____

MEMO

MEMO

영어 기출 문제집

적중'100

1학기

정답 및 해설

지학 | 민찬규

중 2

Happy Others, Happier Me

시험대비 실력평가 p.08

01 ②	02 ③	03 ①	04 danger
05 ①	06 (1) confusing	(2) decide	(3) soap
(4) secret			

01 국가, 마을, 강 등을 보여주는 지구의 표면 또는 그것의 일부의 그림이나 도면을 나타내는 것은 map(지도)이다.

02 say: (글이) 쓰이다, 말하다

03 sign: 표지판

04 주어진 단어의 관계는 반의어 관계이다. danger: 위험, safety: 안전

05 주어진 문장에서 'free'는 '무료의'를 의미한다. 이와 같이 쓰인 문장은 ①번이다. 나머지는 '자유로운'을 의미한다.

06 confusing: 혼란스러운, secret: 비결, soap: 비누, decide: 결정하다, 결심하다

서술형 시험대비 p.09

01 impossible

02 (A)good (B)help (C)try (D)tip (E)glad

03 (1) He put up a 'For Sale' sign in front of his house.
   (2) I finished this work earlier thanks to his help.
   (3) We have to do our homework on our own.

04 (1) Thanks to (2) the other day (3) give out

05 (1) give out (2) come up with (3) put up (4) One day

06 sign

01 주어진 단어의 관계는 반의어 관계이다. possible: 가능한, impossible: 불가능한

03 (1) put up: ~을 세우다 in front of: ~ 앞에 (2) thanks to: ~ 덕택에 (3) on one's own: 자기 스스로

04 thanks to: ~ 덕분에, the other day: 며칠 전에, give out: ~ 을 나누어 주다

05 give out: 나누어 주다, come up with: 제시하다, put up: 세우다, 설치하다, one day: 어느 날

06 어떤 것에 관한 정보를 제공하는 글귀나 사진들이 위에 있는 종이나 나무 등을 가리키는 말은 sign(표지판)이다.

교과서 Conversation

핵심 Check p.10~11

1 me help you 2 Do you need any help
3 deep / Don't worry, help you
4 glad you like it   5 My pleasure
6 for saying so

교과서 대화문 익히기

Check(√) True or False p.12

(1) T   (2) F   (3) T   (4) F

교과서 확인학습 p.14~15

Listen & Speak 1 A

give out / Let me help you then / volunteer club activity / mean / It means that, each other, better place

Listen & Speak 1 B

my mentee / Do you teach her every weekend / You are a good mentor

Listen & Speak 2 A

this is for you / How did you know that / the other day / How nice / I'm glad you like it

Listen & Talk 2 B

I read a story about a special boy in India / Why is he special / had to work / I'm glad you like it

Real Life Communication

Are you feeling better / on my own / Let me help you, join my study group / we can learn better when we teach each other / Thanks for helping me

Let's Check 1

looks heavy. Let me help you / Where is the bus stop around here / No problem

01 ②   02 ④   03 ⓒ which → that

04 ④

01 'Let me help you.'는 '내가 도와줄게.'라고 도움을 제안하는 표현이다.

02 Henry는 Sujin과 같이 버스 정류장으로 가고 있다.

03 명사절을 이끄는 접속사 that이 적절하다.

01 ②   02 Let me help you.   03 ④

04 smile   05 ③   06 ⑤   07 (A) her mentee (B) her old books (C) she felt happy (D) she was a good mentor   08 She suggested joining her study group to him.

09 Because she thought that they can learn better when they teach each other.

10 (B) → (D) → (A) → (C)   11 a massage

12 He gave Aram a massage.

03 ④번은 유감을 나타낸다.

04 스티커는 웃음의 중요성을 강조한다.

05 주어진 문장의 앞에서 그가 많은 학생들을 집에서 가르치는 이유를 설명하고 있으므로 (C)번이 알맞다.

06 Yujin이 인도에 있는 많은 학생들을 돕기 위해 무엇을 했는지는 알 수 없다.

07 오늘 나는 지민이 인상 깊었다. 그녀는 매주 아동 센터에서 그녀의 멘티를 가르친다. 게다가 그녀는 그녀의 멘티에게 그녀가 보던 책을 주려고 하였다. 그녀는 멘티를 가르칠 때 행복을 느낀다고 말했다. 나는 그녀가 좋은 멘토라고 생각했다. 상자가 무거워 보여서 나는 그녀를 도와주었다. 나는 타인을 돕는 것이 세상을 더 나은 곳으로 만들어 준다고 생각한다.

08 Emily는 Brian에게 그녀의 공부 모임에 함께 할 것을 제안했다.

09 Emily가 공부 모임을 시작한 것은 서로 가르칠 때 더 잘 학습할 수 있다고 생각했기 때문이다.

10 (B) 고민 이야기 및 조언 구함 → (D) 도움 및 방법 제안 → (A) 시도할 계획 나타내기 및 고마움 표현 → (C) 칭찬에 대해 응답하기

12 Jack은 Aram의 기분이 나아지도록 마사지를 해 주었다.

01 I feel happy when I teach her.

02 (m)entor

03 many children in his town

04 (A) a special boy in India

    (B) he was special

    (C) couldn't go to school and had to work

05 She is going to give out free stickers.

06 서로에게 미소 지을 때 세상은 더 좋은 곳이 될 것이다.

02 경험이 별로 없거나 종종 어린 사람에게 도움이나 조언을 주거나 가르치는 사람을 가리키는 말은 mentor(멘토)이다.

04 오늘 Yujin은 나에게 인도의 어느 특별한 소년에 관한 이야기를 해주었다. 나는 왜 그녀가 그가 특별하다고 하는지 궁금했다. Yujin은 그 소년이 그의 마을에서 학교에 갈 수 없고 일을 해야 하는 많은 아이들을 자기 집에서 매일 가르친다고 이야기했다. 그것은 정말 좋은 이야기였다.

05 Sora는 Tom을 돕기 위해 무료 스티커를 나누어 줄 것이다.

[교과서]

Grammar

(1) which(또는 that)   (2) who(m)(또는 that)

(1) persuaded, to shake   (2) expect, to eat   (3) told, not to be

01 (1) who → which 또는 that   (2) were → was

    (3) continue → to continue   (4) to passing → to pass

02 (1) lives   (2) which   (3) to stay   (4) to start

03 (1) This is the table that[which] they needed.

    (2) She came to a meeting that[which] I ran.

    (3) We can't force them to work hard.

    (4) What made you think so?

01 (1) 사물이 선행사이므로 which 또는 that, (2) The building이 주어이므로 단수동사 was, (3), (4) enable과 allow는 to부정사(to+동사원형)를 목적격보어로 취하는 동사이다.

02 (1) 주어가 The man이므로 단수동사 lives를 쓴다. (2) 사물을 선행사로 취하는 목적격 관계대명사 which를 쓰면 된다.

3

(3), (4) tell과 encourage는 5형식으로 쓰일 때 to부정사를 목적격보어로 사용한다.

03 (1) 'They needed the table.'을 관계절로 만든다. (2) 'I ran a meeting.'을 관계사절로 만든다. (3) force는 to부정사를 목적격보어로 취하는 동사이다. (4) '네가 생각하게 만들다'이므로 make를 사역동사로 사용한다.

시험대비 실력평가   p.23~25

01 ③, ④   02 ④   03 ④   04 He didn't allow me to use all the money that I have.
05 ⑤   06 ③   07 ⑤   08 which you should do, to boil   09 ③   10 ②
11 ⑤   12 Do you remember those people who(m) you met on holiday?   13 ⑤
14 ④   15 ③   16 to help me with math
17 ⑤   18 which I did yesterday
19 we will force you to
20 The only thing that you should not do is to cut in while others are talking.   21 ⑤   22 ④
23 taught us to love

---

01 사물을 선행사로 받아주면서, 이끄는 문장에 동사의 목적어가 비어 있으므로 목적격 관계대명사 which가 들어간다. which를 대신하여 that을 쓸 수 있다.

02 'My mom bought the shoes for me.'를 관계절로 만든 것이다. 따라서 ④번이 옳다.

03 사역동사 make는 원형부정사를 목적격보어로 취한다.

04 '내가 가진 모든 돈'이므로 I have가 all the money를 수식하도록 문장을 만든다. 관계대명사 which를 써도 좋다.

05 목적격 관계대명사를 생략할 수 있다. ⑤번은 명사절을 이끄는 접속사로 생각할 수 없다. go bad: 상하다

06 '작은 가게들'이 주어이므로 복수동사 are를 쓴다. be crowded with: ~으로 붐비다

07 allow, encourage는 to부정사를 목적격보어로 취하는 동사이며, decide와 refuse는 to부정사를 목적어로 취하는 동사이다. ⑤번은 전치사 in의 목적어로 동명사가 들어간다.

08 목적격 관계대명사 which를 대신하여 that을 써도 무방하다.

09 cause는 to부정사를 목적격보어로 취하는 동사이다. 따라서 to stop이 옳다.

10 ⓐ The toys가 주어이므로 동사는 are를 쓴다.
ⓑ, ⓔ want, require는 to부정사를 목적격보어로 취하는 동사이므로 각각 to do the job, to hand in the reports라고 쓰는 것이 옳다.
ⓒ look for~ : ~을 찾다

11 빈칸에는 to부정사를 목적격보어로 취하는 동사가 들어가야 한다

12 who(m)을 대신하여 that을 써도 무방하며 목적격 관계대명사이므로 생략해도 좋다.

13 <보기>의 that은 관계대명사로 동사의 목적어가 빠져 있는 불완전한 문장을 이끈다. 따라서 ⑤번이 관계대명사이다. 나머지는 모두 명사절을 이끄는 접속사 that으로 완전한 문장을 이끈다.

14 선행사가 사람이 아니므로 관계대명사 which를 쓰고, persuade는 to부정사를 목적격보어로 취하는 동사이므로 to tell, '내가 돈을 지불하게 만들었다'는 사역동사로 쓰인 make이므로 원형부정사 pay를 쓰는 것이 적절하다.

15 불완전한 문장을 이끄는 관계대명사와 완전한 문장을 이끄는 명사절 접속사로 모두 쓰일 수 있는 것은 that이다.

16 수학을 도와줄 멘토가 필요하다고 하였으므로 help me with math를 어법에 맞게 to help me with math로 쓰면 된다.

17 모두 목적격 관계대명사가 들어가지만 ⑤번에는 주격 관계대명사가 들어간다.

18 목적격 관계대명사 which 대신 that을 써도 좋다.

19 force는 to부정사를 목적격보어로 취하여 '목적어가 V하게 강요하다'라는 의미로 쓰인다.

20 'The only thing is to cut in while others are talking. You should not do it.'을 목적격 관계대명사를 이용하여 하나로 합친 문장이다.

21 need는 5형식으로 쓰일 때 to부정사를 목적격보어로 취한다. 따라서 to do라고 쓰는 것이 옳다.

22 would like는 5형식으로 쓰일 때 to부정사를 목적격보어로 취한다. to부정사는 'to+동사원형' 형태이다.

23 '우리가 삶을 사랑하도록'이므로 teach를 5형식으로 사용하며, 목적격보어로 to부정사를 쓴다. 시제에 유의한다.

서술형 시험대비   p.26~27

01 are, know, to believe, to clean, to focus
02 Hannah's cousin taught her how to play the piano.
03 What do you want me to do
04 the girl to turn down the music.
05 (1) Kyle has the money.
     He found it on the street.
  (2) Is this the book?
     You are looking for it.
06 James advises Olivia to see a doctor.
07 I want to get the job that I applied for.

08 allows him to go shopping with Ann on Monday.
09 to play the guitar for her.
10 The technology that they have developed enables us to drive a car safely.
11 I like the cat that John found at the park.
12 cause people to have headaches.
13 (1) Osaka is the city which my sister visited last week.
    (2) Robert is an actor whom we like very much.
    (3) My dad gave me the wallet which I really wanted to have.
14 that I can do is to be quiet
15 told me to have

01 관계사절의 수의 일치는 선행사에 달려 있다. people이 선행사이므로 be동사는 are를 쓴다. let은 목적격보어로 원형부정사를 취하는 사역동사이며, expect, get, order는 to부정사를 목적격보어로 취하는 5형식 동사이다.

02 teach+목적어+how 'to부정사'의 형을 취한다.

03 want는 to부정사를 목적격보어로 취하는 동사이다.

04 ask는 to부정사를 목적격보어로 취하는 동사이다.

05 동사와 전치사의 목적어를 목적격 관계대명사로 만들었으므로 the money, the book을 동사와 전치사의 목적어로 하여 문장을 둘로 나눈다.

06 James는 Olivia에게 병원으로 가서 진찰 받을 것을 권하고 있다.

07 apply for: ~에 지원하다

08 allow는 to부정사를 목적격보어로 취하는 동사이다.

09 Emma가 자신을 위해 기타를 연주해 줄 수 있는지 내게 묻고 있다. to부정사를 목적격보어로 취하는 동사 ask를 이용하여 빈칸을 채운다.

10 enable은 to부정사를 목적격보어로 취하는 동사이며, the technology가 주어이므로 enable을 단수동사로 만드는 것에 유의한다.

11 'John이 공원에서 발견했던 고양이'이므로 목적격 관계대명사가 이끄는 문장 'John found at the park'가 the cat을 수식하도록 문장을 만드는 것이 옳다.

12 cause는 목적격보어로 to부정사를 취하는 동사이다. '사람들에게 두통을 일으키는 것'이므로 목적어 people, 목적격보어로 to have를 사용하여 문장을 만든다.

13 (1), (3) which를 대신하여 that을 쓸 수 있다.
    (2) whom을 대신하여 who, that을 쓸 수 있으며, 모두 목적격 관계대명사이므로 생략이 가능하다.

14 The only thing이 주어이므로 단수 동사를 쓰는 것에 유의한다.

15 tell은 5형식으로 쓰일 때 to부정사를 목적격보어로 취한다.

Reading

확인문제   p.28

1 T   2 T   3 F   4 F   5 F

확인문제   p.29

1 T   2 F   3 F   4 T   5 F

교과서 확인학습 A   p.30~31

01 are, which   02 to hear, them   03 You Love
04 had   05 However, nobody
06 came up with   07 stuck, to   08 put up, that
said   09 were using   10 When, whom
they loved, smiling   11 a big success
12 During, disappeared   13 because,
happiness to   14 Arrow Man   15 A few years
ago, were, confusing   16 enough
information   17 ask others to explain
18 Where, on, go to   19 often took,
wasted   20 decided to solve
21 lots of red arrow stickers   22 rode, around,
stuck, on   23 asked him to do
24 wanted to help
25 Thanks to, easily, save time

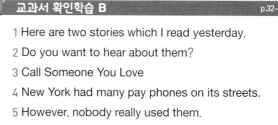

교과서 확인학습 B   p.32~33

1 Here are two stories which I read yesterday.
2 Do you want to hear about them?
3 Call Someone You Love
4 New York had many pay phones on its streets.
5 However, nobody really used them.
6 One day, a man came up with an idea.
7 He stuck coins to one of the phones.
8 He also put up a sign that said, "Call Someone You Love."
9 Soon, many people were using the phone.
10 When they were talking to someone whom they loved, they didn't stop smiling.
11 His idea became a big success.
12 During the day, all the coins disappeared.
13 The man was very happy because his small idea

gave happiness to many people.

14 The Red Arrow Man

15 A few years ago, the maps at bus stops in Seoul were very confusing.

16 They didn't have enough information.

17 People had to ask others to explain the maps.

18 "Where is this bus stop on the map? Does this bus go to Gwanghwamun?"

19 Many people often took the wrong bus and wasted their time.

20 One day, a young man decided to solve this problem.

21 He bought lots of red arrow stickers.

22 Every day he rode his bicycle around the city and stuck the stickers on the bus maps.

23 Nobody asked him to do this.

24 He just wanted to help others.

25 Thanks to his effort, people could understand the maps easily and save time.

시험대비 실력평가
p.34~37

01 two stories which I read yesterday
02 ⑤　　　03 who, whom, that　　　04 ②
05 ③　　　06 ④　　　07 ③
08 It said, "Call Someone You Love."　　　09 ②
10 wasted
11 화살표 모양의 스티커를 사서 서울 시내를 돌아다니며 버스 지도에 스티커를 붙이는 것
12 ③　　　13 ③　　　14 Because there wasn't enough information on the maps.　　　15 ④
16 ⓐ to hear ⓒ talking　　　17 ⑤
18 disappear　19 ④　　　20 ②　　　21 which, stuck coins to　　　22 ③
23 (B)-(A)-(C) 24 ②　　　25 explain → to explain
26 ③　　　27 ⑤　　　28 They didn't have enough information.　　　29 ③　　　30 Seoul, right, save their time

01 어제 내가 읽은 두 개의 이야기를 가리키는 대명사이다.

02 길거리에 공중전화가 많이 있었지만 아무도 사용하지 않았다는 의미이므로 However를 쓰는 것이 옳다.

03 사람을 선행사로 받아주는 목적격 관계대명사 whom이 들어가야 한다. whom을 대신하여 who 혹은 that을 써도 좋다.

04 4형식 동사를 3형식으로 전환할 때 동사 give는 간접목적어 앞에 전치사 to를 붙인다.

05 한 남자가 표지판을 설치하자 곧 많은 사람들이 전화기를 사용하기 시작했다고 이어지는 것이 옳으며, ③번 뒤 문장의 they가 가리키는 것은 주어진 문장의 many people이다.

06 (A) hear about: ~에 관하여 듣다, hear from: ~로부터 소식을 듣다 (B) pay phones를 가리키고 있으므로 복수명사를 지칭하는 them (C) 명사를 이끌고 있으므로 전치사 During, While은 접속사로 부사절을 이끈다.

07 어떤 남자가 공중전화 하나에 동전들을 붙였다고 하였다.

08 표지판에는 '당신이 사랑하는 사람에게 전화 하세요.'라고 쓰여 있었다.

09 빈칸 ⓐ에는 좁은 장소 앞에 쓰이는 전치사 at이 들어간다. ① turn off: ~을 끄다 turn on: ~을 켜다 ② be surprised at: ~에 놀라다 ③ pick somebody up: ~을 (차에) 태우러 가다 ④ take care of: ~을 돌보다 ⑤ wait for: ~을 기다리다

10 시간을 낭비했다는 의미이다.

11 간단하게 '버스 지도에 스티커를 붙이는 것'이라고 써도 좋다.

12 청년의 노력 덕분에 사람들이 지도를 쉽게 이해할 수 있게 되었다는 의미이다. Depending on: ~에 따라

13 (A) 셀 수 있는 명사를 수식하는 것은 a few, (B) 지도가 혼란을 유발하는 것이므로 confusing, (C) 사람들의 시간을 가리키는 것이므로 복수 명사를 지칭하는 their를 쓰는 것이 옳다.

14 사람들이 서울에서 버스를 잘못 탔던 이유는 지도에 충분한 정보가 없었기 때문이었다.

15 아무도 이 청년에게 이 일을 하라고 요청하지 않았다고 하였다.

16 ⓐ want는 to부정사를 목적어로 취한다. ⓒ '누군가에게 전화하고 있을 때'라는 의미이므로 진행형을 만들어 주는 것이 옳다.

17 ⓑ 길거리 위에 공중전화가 있다는 의미이므로 전치사 on을 쓴다. ① be interested in: ~에 흥미가 있다 ② be satisfied with: ~에 만족하다 ③ pay attention to: ~에 주목하다 ④ take care of: ~을 돌보다 ⑤ depend on: ~에 의지하다

18 '보여지는 것을 멈추다' '사라지다'이다.

19 (A)는 관계대명사 that이다. ④번은 명사절을 이끄는 접속사 that이다.

20 Soon은 '곧'이란 의미로 before long과 같다. For a long time: 오랫동안 Hardly: 거의 ~하지 않는 Still: 그럼에도 불구하고 Lately: 최근에

21 which를 대신하여 that을 써도 무방하다.

22 'nobody really used them'은 아무도 실제로 그것을 사용하지 않았다는 의미로 'not everyone used the pay phone'과는 의미가 다르다. 후자는 모두가 공중전화를 사용한 것은 아니었다는 의미로 누군가는 사용했다는 뜻이다.

23 공중전화(pay phones)가 있지만 → (B) 누구도 그것들(them)을 사용하지 않아 한 남자가 좋은 아이디어를 떠올리고 동전을 붙여 둠 → (A) 또한(also) 표지판을 설치하자 곧 많은 사람들이 전화기를 사용함 → (C) 그들이(they) 통화할 때 계속 미소를

지음

24 지도에 정보가 부족하다고 하였고, 사람들이 다른 사람들에게 지도를 설명해 달라고 요청해야 하므로 '혼란스러운 (confusing)'이 들어가는 것이 옳다.

25 ask가 5형식으로 쓰일 때는 to부정사를 목적격보어로 취한다.

26 지도상에서 정류장을 확인하고 지도 위에 스티커를 붙이는 것이다. 전치사 on은 '~(위)에'라는 의미로 어떤 것의 표면에 닿거나 그 표면을 형성하는 것을 나타낼 때 쓰인다.

27 내용상 청년은 다른 사람을 돕기 위해 스티커를 붙였다고 볼 수 있으며, 또한 청년의 노력 덕분에 사람들이 지도를 쉽게 이해할 수 있게 되었다고 하였으므로 bother는 help를 쓰는 것이 옳다.

28 서울의 버스 지도가 가진 문제는 충분한 정보가 없다는 것이다.

29 광화문으로 가는 버스 번호는 위 글에 나와 있지 않다.

30 버스를 잘못 타서 시간을 낭비했다고 했으므로, 청년의 노력 덕분에 서울 사람들은 버스를 제대로 타서 시간을 절약할 수 있었다고 말할 수 있다.

서술형 시험대비   p.38~39

01 (A) happy (B) happiness
02 Here are two stories. / I read them yesterday.
03 Call Someone Who(m) You Love
04 pay phones (on its streets)
05 they kept smiling
06 coins, which(또는 that) nobody really used
07 who, coins
08 A: stick, B: stuck coins, to use, someone whom
09 put up a sign
10 The maps at bus stops in Seoul
11 who asked him to do this
12 they(또는 the maps) didn't have enough information.
13 He stuck red arrow stickers on them.
14 His effort enabled people to understand the maps easily.
15 which, was red
16 confusing, them, waste
17 wanted the maps at bus stops to have enough information.
18 It's because he just wanted to help others.

01 (A) be동사의 보어가 들어가야 하므로 형용사 happy (B) 목적어가 들어가야 하므로 happiness로 쓰는 것이 옳다.

02 목적격 관계대명사를 이용하여 하나로 만들어진 문장이다. two stories가 선행사이므로 복수명사 them을 이용하여 문장을 둘로 나눈다.

---

03 목적격 관계대명사 whom이 생략되어 있다. whom을 대신하여 who 혹은 that을 써도 좋다.

04 길거리에 있는 공중전화를 가리키는 대명사이다.

05 didn't stop Ving는 'V하는 것을 멈추지 않았다'는 의미이므로 keep Ving를 써서 '계속 V하다'로 쓸 수 있다.

06 누구도 사용하지 않았던 공중전화기 중 하나에 동전들을 붙여 놓은 것을 의미한다.

07 who를 대신하여 that을 써도 좋다.

08 whom을 대신하여 who 또는 that을 써도 무방하다.

09 B as well as A: A 뿐만 아니라 B도

10 서울의 버스 정류장에 있는 지도들을 가리키는 말이다.

11 who를 대신하여 that을 써도 좋다.

12 사람들이 다른 사람들에게 지도를 설명해 달라고 요청해야 했던 이유는 지도에 충분한 정보가 없었기 때문이었다.

13 청년은 버스 지도에 스티커를 붙였다.

14 enable은 목적격보어로 to부정사를 취하는 동사이다.

15 청년이 산 스티커의 색깔은 빨간색이었다. 관계대명사 which를 대신하여 that을 써도 무방하다.

16 don't have to V: V할 필요가 없다

17 want는 to부정사를 목적격보어로 취하는 동사이다. '정류장의 지도가 정보를 갖는 것'이므로 목적어로 the maps at bus stops를 쓰고 목적격보어로 to have ~를 쓴다.

18 남자가 매일 스티커를 지도에 붙인 이유는 다른 사람들을 돕고 싶어서였다.

영역별 핵심문제   p.41~45

01 ②   02 ②   03 (1) waste your time (2) on your own (3) stopped playing
04 mentee   05 (1) come up with (2) The other day (3) on your own   06 ⑤   07 ②
08 volunteer   09 ⑤   10 ①   11 ④, ⑤
12 ⑤   13 ②   14 He made a basket with plastic bags for his mom.
15 She talked about it when they were having dinner the other day.
16 (D) → (C) → (E) → (B) → (A)
17 ④   18 ⓐ which 또는 that ⓑ to save
19 ③   20 ①   21 ④   22 ask her to copy   23 ⑤   24 ⑤   25 ⑤
26 whom(또는 that) they loved   27 ②
28 ④번 used → using   29 ⑤
30 (A) to explain (B) to solve (C) to do   31 ①
32 ④   33 ③   34 People often took the wrong bus and wasted their time.

01 사물들을 차갑게 유지하기 위해 사용되는 장치나 공간을 가리키는 말은 refrigerator(냉장고)이다.

02 ② effort: 노력

03 waste one's time: ~자신의 시간을 낭비하다, on one's own: 자기 스스로, stop ~ing: ~하기를 멈추다

04 주어진 단어의 관계는 상대어 관계이다. mentor: 멘토, mentee: 멘티

05 come up with: ~을 생각해 내다, the other day: 며칠 전에, 지난번, come across: ~을 우연히 만나다 on one's own: 자기 스스로

06 주어진 문장을 포함한 나머지는 모두 '휴식'을 의미하지만 ⑤번은 '나머지'를 의미한다.

07 ②번은 '그러면 내가 도와줄게.'라는 의미로 도움을 제안할 때 쓴다. 나머지는 도와달라는 의미로 쓴다.

08 보수를 받지 않고 무언가를 해주는 사람을 가리키는 말은 volunteer(자원봉사자)이다.

10 주어진 문장은 상자에 든 것이 무엇인지 묻는 질문에 대한 대답이므로 (A)가 알맞다.

11 amazing: 놀라운 discouraged: 낙심한

12 Mike는 지역 아동 센터에서 책을 읽을 것이라는 설명은 대화 내용과 일치하지 않는다.

13 이어지는 대답으로 어떻게 새 바구니를 필요로 하는지 알게 된 것을 설명하는 내용이 이어져야 하므로 ⓑ가 적절하다.

14 Alex는 엄마를 위해 비닐봉지로 바구니를 만들었다.

15 Alex와 엄마는 며칠 전 저녁을 먹으며 새 바구니에 대해 이야기했었다.

16 (D) 이야기 주제 언급 → (C) 주인공이 특별한 이유 질문 → (E) 이야기 내용 설명 → (B) 반응 → (A) 칭찬에 답하기

17 warn은 '~하지 말라고 경고하다'라는 의미로 쓰일 때 to부정사를 목적격보어로 취한다. leak: (물 따위가) 새다

18 ⓐ에는 두 개의 문장을 이어주는 주격 관계대명사를 써야 하며, ⓑ에는 내용상 '물을 절약하도록 조언한다'는 내용이 들어가는 것이 옳다. advise는 to부정사를 목적격보어로 취하므로 to save를 쓴다.

19 want는 to부정사를 목적격보어로 취하는 동사이며, 두 번째 빈칸에는 목적격 관계대명사 which 혹은 that이 들어가는 것이 옳다.

20 목적격 관계대명사로 쓰이면서 동시에 '어느, 어떤'이라고 해석되는 의문사는 which이다.

21 ④ would like는 5형식으로 쓰일 때 to부정사를 목적격보어로 취한다. 따라서 to accept라고 쓰는 것이 옳다.

22 ask가 5형식으로 쓰일 때는 목적격보어로 to부정사를 취한다. '그녀가 복사하는 것'이므로 목적어로 her, 목적격보어로 to copy를 쓴다.

23 주어가 The bananas이므로 복수 동사를 쓰는 것이 옳다.

24 주격 관계대명사는 생략할 수 없다.

25 say는 to부정사를 목적격보어로 취할 수 없다.

26 글의 내용상 그들이 사랑하는 사람에게 전화하고 있다고 보는 것이 옳다.

27 (A) 공중전화기가 많지만 아무도 쓰지 않는다는 것이 옳으므로 nobody, (B) come up with: (생각을) 떠올리다, come down with: (병으로) 앓아눕다 (C) 낮 동안에 모든 동전이 사라졌다는 것이 내용상 적절하다.

28 사람들이 그 전화기를 사용했다는 것이므로 현재분사를 써서 수동태가 아닌 진행형으로 표현하는 것이 옳다.

29 사람들이 몇 통의 전화를 했는지는 글을 읽고 알 수 없다.

30 ask는 5형식으로 쓰일 때 to부정사를 목적격보어로 취한다. decide는 to부정사를 목적어로 취하는 동사이다.

31 ①번에 이어지는 문장에서 the stickers는 청년이 산 lots of red arrow stickers를 의미한다.

32 ⓐ는 (교통수단 등을) 타다[이용하다]는 의미로 쓰였다. ① 넣다, ② 선택하다, 사다, ③ 가지고 가다, ④ 타다, ⑤ 잡다

33 사람들이 버스를 잘못 타는 일이 종종 있었다고 했을 뿐 사람들이 항상 버스를 잘못 탔다는 것은 글의 내용과 맞지 않는다.

34 버스 정류장 지도로 인해서 사람들은 종종 버스를 잘못 타서 시간을 낭비하였다.

단원별 예상문제 p.46~49

01 ①   02 ⑤   03 ⑤

04 ①, ⑤   05 I'm glad (that) you like it. 06 ⑤

07 (A)many children in his town   (B)couldn't go to school and had to work

08 How about joining my study group?

09 ⓓ disagree → agree   10 ⑤   11 ④

12 ②   13 ③   14 The car that I want to buy is minivan.

15 (1) He gave some candies to the little kids who(m) he saw.

(2) There was a festival which many people took part in.

(3) The dish which you broke was not that expensive.

16 to close the window   17 ③

18 that, which 19 ②   20 ④

21 the man was very happy 22 (D)–(A)–(C)–(B)

23 빨간 화살표 스티커를 버스 지도에 붙이다.   24 ⑤

25 People could understand the maps easily and save time.

01 주어진 문장은 도움을 제공하고자 하는 표현으로 Tom의 고민에 대한 대답으로 적절하므로 (A)번이 적절하다.

02 ⓐ는 '무료의'라는 의미로 이와 같은 의미로 쓰인 것은 ⑤번이다.

03 왜 Hojun이 봉사활동을 하러 나오지 않았는지는 알 수 없다.

04 (A)는 '정말 멋있구나!'라는 표현으로 ①, ⑤번과 바꾸어 쓸 수 있다.

07 인도의 소년이 특별한 이유는 그의 마을에서 학교에 갈 수 없고 일을 해야 하는 많은 아이들을 매일 그의 집에서 가르쳤기 때문이다.

08 'Why don't you ~?'는 '~하는 게 어때?'라고 제안하는 표현으로 'how about ~?'으로 바꾸어 쓸 수 있다.

09 이어지는 대화에서 좋은 구성원이 되기 위해 열심히 노력한다고 하였으므로 상대방의 의견에 동의하는 'I agree.'가 적절하다.

10 ⑤ Brian은 혼자서 병원에서 공부하려고 노력했었다.

11 ask는 to부정사를 목적격보어로 취하는 동사이다. 목적격 관계대명사 which 혹은 that과 to부정사가 짝지어지는 것이 옳다.

12 '내가 답변하는 것'이므로 목적어로 me, 목적격보어로 to answer를 써서 문장을 만든 ②번이 가장 적절하다.

13 주어가 복수 명사 men이므로 수의 일치는 복수 동사로 하는 것이 옳으므로 are를 쓴다.

14 'The car is minivan. I want to buy it.'을 하나로 합친 문장이다. 목적격 관계대명사를 이용하여 문장을 쓴다.

15 관계대명사 who(m), which를 대신하여 that을 쓸 수 있으며 목적격 관계대명사이므로 생략해도 좋다.

16 창문이 열려 있어 추웠다고 하였다. 창문 옆에 앉아 있던 Jimmy에게 창문을 닫아 달라고 요청하는 말을 쓰는 것이 옳다.

17 <보기>의 that은 동격의 명사절을 이끄는 접속사이다.

18 사물을 선행사로 받아주는 주격 관계대명사가 쓰인다.

19 ⓐ와 ⓓ가 글의 내용과 일치한다.

20 두 가지 이야기를 읽었다고 하였으므로 다른 한 가지 이야기가 이어질 것이라고 보는 것이 옳다.

21 그 남자가 행복한 이유는 많은 사람들에게 행복을 주었기 때문이라고 하였다. so는 결과를 이끄는 접속사이다.

22 (D)에서 They는 주어진 문장의 the maps를 가리키고, (A)는 사람들이 지도에 대한 설명을 요구하는 글이며, (C)는 이에 대한 해결책을 한 남자가 떠올려 스티커를 사서 (B) 그 스티커를 붙이고 다녔다는 순서가 가장 적절하다.

23 do this=stick the stickers on the bus maps

24 매일 스티커를 붙였다고 하였다. 따라서 주말마다 붙였다는 것은 글의 내용과 일치하지 않는다.

25 남자의 노력이 있은 후 사람들은 지도를 쉽게 이해하고 시간을 절약할 수 있었다.

서술형 실전문제
p.50~51

01 She is going to give her old books to her.

02 Jimin feels happy when she teaches her mentee.

03 He is going to carry the box.

04 to open

05 Do you have the book which we checked out from the library?

06 My mom allowed me to stay out late.

07 asks Jimmy to get in line

08 Is the book which you are reading interesting?

09 you were talking to[with]

10 ④번 to smile → smiling

11 sticking coins / to call, they love

12 his small idea gave happiness to many people

13 that he bought to solve the problem

14 They had to ask others to explain the maps.

01 지민은 오늘 멘티에게 그녀가 보던 책을 줄 것이다.

02 지민은 멘티를 가르칠 때 행복을 느낀다.

03 Mike는 지민을 도와주기 위해 상자를 날라 줄 것이다.

04 입을 벌리라고 했지만 너무 무서워서 벌릴 수 없었다는 의미가 되므로 tell의 목적격보어로 to부정사를 사용하여 답을 쓴다.

05 check out: (도서관에서 책을) 대출하다

06 3인칭 단수 주어에 let을 썼으므로 과거 시제임을 알 수 있다. 따라서 allowed를 쓴다. let+목적어+V: 목적어가 V하게 허락하다

07 Paul은 Jimmy에게 줄을 서라고 요청하였다. ask는 to부정사를 목적격보어로 취하는 동사이다.

08 which를 대신하여 that을 써도 무방하다.

09 목적격 관계대명사를 생략해야 빈칸에 맞게 답을 쓸 수 있다. talk to[with]: ~와 이야기하다

10 stop to V: ~하기 위해 멈추다, stop Ving: ~하던 것을 멈추다

11 뉴욕 사람들 누구도 공중전화를 사용하지 않는 것에 대하여 좋은 생각을 떠올린 한 남자와의 대화이다. enable은 목적격보어로 to부정사를 취한다.

12 그의 생각이 많은 사람들에게 행복을 주었기 때문에 남자는 행복했다.

13 that을 대신하여 which를 써도 무방하다.

14 사람들은 올바른 버스를 타기 위해서 다른 사람들에게 지도를 설명해 달라고 요청해야 했다

창의사고력 서술형 문제
p.52

|모범답안|

01 (A)on my own   (B)joining her study group.
(C)we can learn better when we teach each other   (D)be a good member

02 (1) A painter is an artist who paints pictures.
(2) A purse is a small bag which people keep their money in.
(3) A baker is a person whose job is to bake and

sell bread.

　　(4) A chair is a piece of furniture which people sit on.

03 (1) She asked me to go there with her.

　　(2) The teacher encourages me to try again.

　　(3) They forced him to tell the truth.

　　(4) Computers enables us to live convenient lives.

　　(5) I allowed my friend to use my pen. / We told them to stay calm.

01 나는 학교에 다시 돌아오게 되어 행복했다. Emily는 나를 매우 따뜻하게 반겨주었다. 우리는 공부를 포함한 많은 것들에 대해 이야기했다. 내가 병원에 있는 동안 나는 혼자 공부하려고 노력했지만 어려웠다. 내가 이것에 관해 Emily에게 이야기했을 때 그녀는 나를 도와주었다. 그녀는 내게 그녀의 스터디 모임에 가입할 것을 제안했다. 그녀는 우리가 서로 가르칠 때 더욱 잘 배울 수 있다고 생각했기 때문에 스터디 모임을 시작했다. 나는 그녀의 생각에 동의했다. 나는 좋은 구성원이 되기로 결심했다. 나는 정말로 그녀에게 고마웠다.

단원별 모의고사
p.53~56

01 outside　　02 ①

03 (1) Bats mostly sleep during the day.

　　(2) I used a pay phone to call my mom.

　　(3) He came up with a great idea at the meeting.

04 ②　　　　05 ②　　　　06 ⑤

07 (A)on　(B)that　(C)like　08 ⑤　　　09 ⑤

10 She was looking for the bus stop.

11 He helped Sujin by carrying her bag to the bus stop.

12 ⑤　　　13 ①　　　14 to eat　15 ⑤

16 I want to make a movie which many people will love.

17 The teacher told us to be on time.　　18 ④

19 ③, ⑤　　　20 ②　　　21 Thanks to a man's idea, many people in New York became happy when they called someone they loved.　　22 ⑤

23 ②　　　24 ③　　　25 people to understand

01 주어진 단어의 관계는 반의어 관계이다. inside: 안쪽에, outside: 바깥에

02 더 경험이 있는 사람에 의해 조언을 받거나 도움을 받는 사람을 가리키는 말은 mentee(멘티)이다.

04 'How+형용사(+주어+동사)!'의 감탄문이다.

05 엄마는 Alex의 선물을 받고 기뻐하였으므로 happy(행복한)가 적절하다.

06 대화를 통해 Alex가 어디에서 바구니 만드는 법을 배웠는지는 알 수 없다.

07 (A) on own's own: 혼자서, (B) 명사절을 이끄는 접속사 that이 알맞다. (C) 명사절의 주어 you 다음이므로 동사 like가 알맞다.

08 나머지는 모두 감사함에 대한 대답을 나타내며 ⑤번은 비난을 거부하는 표현이다.

09 Emily와 Brian이 공부 모임에서 무엇을 배웠는지는 알 수 없다.

10 Sujin은 버스 정류장을 찾고 있었다.

11 Henry는 버스 정류장까지 Sujin의 가방을 들어주며 그녀를 도왔다.

12 ⑤ 그 말을 들으니 기쁘다는 대답이 자연스럽다.

13 사람과 사물을 모두 선행사로 받아줄 수 있는 관계대명사는 that이다.

14 엄마는 내가 야채를 먹기를 원한다는 말이 들어가는 것이 적절하다. want는 to부정사를 목적격보어로 취한다.

15 make는 목적격보어로 원형부정사를 취하는 사역동사이다.

16 which를 대신하여 that을 써도 좋다.

17 tell은 to부정사를 목적격보어로 취하는 동사이다.

18 (A)는 동명사이다. 모두 동명사이지만 ④번은 현재진행형을 만드는 현재분사이다.

19 이유를 나타내는 접속사가 들어가는 것이 적절하다.

20 한 남자가 뉴욕에서 사용되지 않는 공중전화기에 동전을 붙여두었다고 하였다.

21 한 남자의 아이디어 덕분에, 뉴욕에 있는 많은 사람들이 그들이 사랑하는 사람들에게 전화했을 때 행복해졌다.

22 much는 셀 수 없는 명사를 수식하는 수량형용사이다.

23 (A) 주어가 the maps이므로 복수 동사 were, (B) 빈도부사는 일반동사 앞에 위치하므로 often took, (C) 스티커들을 지도들에 붙였다는 의미이므로 them이 옳다.

24 ⓐ 서울 버스 정류장의 지도에 정보가 부족한 것이 문제였고, ⓓ 청년은 문제를 해결하기 위히어 회살표 스티커를 붙이고 다녔으며, ⓔ 사람들이 종종 버스를 잘못 탔던 이유는 지도에 정보가 부족했기 때문이었다.

25 help는 원형부정사나 to부정사를 모두 목적격보어로 취할 수 있다. 따라서 other people understand를 답으로 써도 좋다.

For a Healthy Summer

시험대비 실력평가
p.60

01 female   02 ①   03 ③

04 (1) bump   (2) itches   (3) scratch

05 (1) At that moment   (2) went for a walk   (3) feed on

06 (1) sweaty   (2) pointed   (3) protein   (4) tiny   (5) standing

07 ④

01 주어진 관계는 반의어 관계를 나타낸다. male: 수컷의, 남성의, female: 암컷의, 여성의

02 날카로운 무언가로 당신의 피부를 문지르는 것을 나타내는 말은 scratch(긁다)이다.

03 sweat: 땀

06 tiny: 아주 작은 sweaty: 땀을 흘리는 protein: 단백질 standing: 괴어 있는 pointed: 뽀족한

07 주어진 문장에서 pointed는 '뽀족한'을 의미하며 이와 같은 의미로 쓰인 것은 ④번이다.

서술형 시험대비
p.61

01 empty   02 mosquito

03 (1) buzzing   (2) prevent   (3) lay   (4) strange

04 (1) do better   (2) keep, in mind   (3) suffering from

05 (1) Why don't we stay here for a while?

(2) I'd love to go back to Korea.

(3) Many people suffered from food poisoning.

06 (1) If you take the bone from the dog, he will bite you.

(2) I don't like summer because I get too hot and sweaty.

(3) To prevent an eye disease, always wash your hands with soap.

01 주어진 관계는 반의어 관계를 나타낸다. empty: 텅 빈, full: 가득 찬

02 사람이나 동물의 피부를 물어 그들의 피를 빠는 작은 날아다니는 곤충을 가리키는 말은 mosquito(모기)이다.

03 whether: ~인지 아닌지 frog: 개구리

04 suffer from: ~으로 고통 받다

교과서 Conversation

핵심 Check
p.62~63

1 (1) sorry to hear   (2) too bad   (3) That's terrible

2 (1) Make sure   (2) Don't forget   (3) I'll keep that in mind

교과서 대화문 익히기

Check(√) True or False
p.64

(1) T   (2) F   (3) T   (4) T

교과서 확인학습
p.66~67

Listen & Speak 1-A (1)

worried / worried, my cat is sick / I'm sorry to hear that / I will

Listen & Speak 1-A (2)

How / lost by / I'm sorry to hear that, you do better next time

Listen & Speak 1-B

I can't / Why not / to stop swimming for a while / hear that, next weekend / hope so

Listen & Speak 2-A (1)

sunburn / a lot, without sunscreen / Make sure

Listen & Speak 2-A (2)

Just make sure you, wear a hat / I will

Listen & Speak 2-B

any / the sink / fruit flies / put, trash / Make sure you don't put fruit waste in the trash can / keep, in mind, empty our trash can

Real Life Communication

what happened / mosquito bites / I'm sorry to hear that, How / went camping / Don't scratch them / itchy / with, make sure you wear long sleeves

11

01 ②   02 (B) → (C) → (D) → (A)   03 ④

04 ⑤

01 이어지는 대화로 유감을 표현하고 있으므로 ②번이 적절하다.

02 (B) 쇼핑가고 싶은지 질문 → (C) 거절 및 이유 설명 → (D) 당부하기 → (A) 대답

03 ④번은 안도감을 나타낸다.

04 Brian이 Jimin을 의사에게 데려가려 했다는 설명은 대화의 내용과 일치하지 않는다.

01 ⑤

02 The doctor told me to stop swimming for a while.

03 ①, ③

04 How about taking her to an animal doctor?

05 ②

06 Just keep in mind that you should wear a hat.

07 ⑤   08 ⑤   09 empty

10 (A)fruit waste   (B)Empty your trash can

11 ②   12 I'm sorry to hear that.

01 don't have to: ~할 필요가 없다

02 tell은 목적격보어로 to부정사가 나오며 'stop+~ing'는 '~하기를 멈추다'라는 뜻이다.

03 제안을 나타내는 표현으로는 Let's+동사원형 ~. / Why don't we+동사원형 ~? / How about -ing ~? 등이 있다.

04 Why don't you~? = How about -ing ~? = ~하는 게 어때?

05 Jimin의 고양이가 아프기 때문에 걱정스러운(anxious)이 적절하다. ① pleased: 즐거운 ③ nervous: 긴장된, ④ excited: 흥분된, 신난 ⑤ encouraged: 격려 받은

07 Hojun이 Alex와 야구 경기할 때 모자를 쓸 것이라는 것은 대화의 마지막에 나타난다.

08 주어진 문장은 상대방의 당부의 말에 대한 대답으로 적절하므로 (E)가 적절하다.

09 용기 등에 있는 모든 것을 없애는 것을 가리키는 말은 empty (비우다)이다.

10 초파리를 막기 위해 쓰레기통에 과일 쓰레기를 버리지 말아야 하며 쓰레기통을 더 자주 비워야 한다.

11 축구 경기에서 졌다는 것으로 보아 낙담한(discouraged)이 적절하다.

01 I'm sorry to hear that.

02 Make sure you wear sunscreen next time.

03 Because he went swimming at the beach without sunscreen.

04 He got the mosquito bites at the camp.

05 you clean the mosquito bites with cool water

06 (B) → (D) → (C) → (A) → (E)

02 make sure: 반드시 ~해라

05 모기에 물렸을 때는 찬물로 모기 물린 곳을 닦아 주어야 한다.

06 (B) 찾고 있는 물건 위치 설명 및 이유 질문 → (D) 이유로 쓰레기통에 초파리가 많다고 설명 → (C) 쓰레기통에 무엇을 버렸는지 질문 → (A) 대답 → (E) 당부하기

교과서

Grammar

1 (1) something strange   (2) something, to play with

  (3) cold to drink

2 (1) Have, made   (2) have been   (3) has been

  (4) have travel(l)ed

01 (1) wrong anything → anything wrong

  (2) to eat healthy → healthy to eat

  (3) have talked → talked

  (4) played → has played

02 (1) has not[hasn't] polished (2) I ave, seen

  (3) have not[haven't] told (4) has just read

  (5) has worn

03 (1) I need something cold to drink.

  (2) We have been to France twice.

  (3) Do you have anything fun to read?

  (4) Have you ever played this game?

01 (1), (2) -thing으로 끝나는 대명사는 형용사의 수식을 뒤에서 받으며, to부정사와 동시에 수식을 받을 때는 '-thing+형용사+to부정사'의 어순으로 수식받는다. (3) 과거를 나타내는 부사구 last month가 있으므로 현재완료를 쓸 수 없다. (4) 아이였을 때부터 연주해 온 것이므로 현재완료 시제를 써야 한다.

02 (1), (3), (4), (5)에서 쓰인 already, yet, just, many times

는 모두 현재완료 시제와 함께 쓰이는 어구이다. (2) 오늘 그녀를 본 적이 있는지 묻는 말이므로 현재완료를 쓰는 것이 옳다.

03 (1) -thing으로 끝나는 대명사는 형용사의 수식을 뒤에서 받는다. to부정사의 to를 추가해야 한다. (2) '가 본 적이 있다'는 have been to이다. (3) '-thing+형용사+to부정사' 순서로 수식한다. (4) 경험을 물을 때에는 현재완료 시제를 사용한다.

시험대비 실력평가   p.75~77

01 ②   02 ③   03 ④

04 She told me something important.   05 ③

06 ④   07 ③

08 They have already arrived.   09 ③

10 ⑤   11 ③   12 dangerous to do

13 ②   14 ④   15 ⑤

16 I need someone diligent to work with.   17 ④

18 ⑤   19 ③

20 I want to do something different.   21 ④

22 ②   23 ③

24 I need something new to play with.

01 지난해 이래로 만난 적이 없다는 계속 용법의 현재완료가 들어가는 것이 가장 적절하다.

02 has been to: ~에 가 본 적이 있다

03 Ron이 현재 휴가를 갔다는 말에 어디에 가서 없느냐고 물을 수 있다. has gone to: ~에 가서 (지금) 없다

04 -thing으로 끝나는 대명사는 형용사의 수식을 뒤에서 받는다.

05 너에게 소개할 사람이므로 someone to introduce to you라고 쓰는 것이 옳으며 형용사는 someone 바로 뒤에 놓는다. introduce A to B: A를 B에게 소개하다

06 주어진 문장은 현재완료의 '경험' ①, ② 완료 ③, ⑤ 계속 ④ 경험

07 ① nothing interesting ② been to ④ Did you see ⑤ something to talk about이라고 쓰는 것이 옳다.

08 김씨 가족이 몇 시에 오느냐는 질문에 이미 도착했다고 하였으므로 현재완료와 already를 사용하여 문장을 만든다.

09 '한 시간 전'이라는 과거를 나타내는 부사어구가 있으므로 과거동사, '오랜 시간'이라는 기간이 나오므로 전치사 for, '여러 번'이라고 하였으므로 읽은 경험을 나타내는 현재완료 시제가 가장 적절하다.

10 ⑤ something warm to eat이 옳다.

11 ③ 어제 새 차를 샀다고 하였으므로 'She bought a new car yesterday.'라고 쓰는 것이 옳다. 현재완료는 과거를 나타내는 어구와 함께 쓸 수 없다.

12 -thing으로 끝나는 대명사는 형용사의 수식을 뒤에서 받으며, to부정사와 동시에 수식을 받을 때에는 '-thing+형용사+to부정사' 어순으로 수식받는다.

13 벌써 끝냈느냐는 질문에 아직 끝내지 못했다고 답하는 것이 가장 자연스럽다.

14 피아노를 배운 것은 과거의 일이므로 learned를 쓴다.

15 의문문이므로 anyone을 쓰고, -one으로 끝나는 대명사이므로 뒤에서 형용사의 수식을 받는다. '아직 아무도 못 만났다'는 의미이므로 현재완료를 쓰는 것이 적절하다.

16 -one으로 끝나는 대명사이므로 '형용사+to부정사' 어순으로 수식한다.

17 12살 이래로 쭉 알아왔다는 의미이므로 현재완료 시제를 쓰고, Julia가 Grace를 잘 아는 것은 현재 상태를 나타내는 것이므로 knows를 쓴다.

18 형용사가 -thing, -one, -body로 끝나는 단어를 수식할 때는 형용사가 뒤에 위치한다. ⑤ special everything → everything special

19 그녀는 나가고 없다는 의미의 결과 용법의 현재완료 문장으로 만들 수 있다.

20 -thing으로 끝나는 대명사는 형용사의 수식을 뒤에서 받는다.

21 의문문이므로 anyone을 써야 한다. ~을 돌보다: take care of / look after

22 since+특정한 때, for+기간, 부정문과 함께 쓰이는 것은 yet이다.

23 지금까지 '10년 동안'이라고 하였으므로 현재완료 시제를 써서 '계속'을 나타내는 것이 옳다.

24 -thing으로 끝나는 대명사이므로 '형용사+to부정사'의 어순으로 수식하는 것에 유의한다.

서술형 시험대비   p.78~79

01 It has rained since last night.

02 have you had, have had

03 nothing to eat

04 Have you ever been, did you go

05 Have you ever met anyone famous?

06 (1) has had (2) has gone (3) happened (4) has been (5) taught

07 I don't want to do anything to hurt her feelings.

08 interesting to see

09 ⓐ Is there anything warm to drink? ⓑ I have just made some coffee.

10 Amelia has been[lived] in this city for 5 years. / Amelia has been[lived] in this city since 2016.

11 she arrived in / has been

12 Have you ever been to the museum?

13 There is nothing important to read in the magazine.

14 Is there anything comfortable to sit on?

15 warm to wear

16 How long have you learned English? / I have learned English for eight months.

01 어젯밤 이후로 계속 비가 오고 있다는 문장을 쓰면 된다.

02 'since March'로 미루어 보아, 자동차를 얼마나 오랫동안 소유 해 왔는지를 물었고 이에 3월부터 소유하고 있다고 답할 수 있다.

03 집에 음식이 하나도 없으므로 '먹을 것이 아무것도 없다'는 표현을 쓸 수 있다.

04 베트남에 가 본 적이 있느냐는 질문에 가봤다고 답하자, 언제 갔었 느냐는 질문이 이어지고 있다. '가 본 적이 있느냐'는 질문은 현재완 료를 써서 답할 수 있고, '언제 갔었느냐'는 질문은 과거시제로 표현 한다.

05 경험을 묻고 있으므로 현재완료 시제를 쓰고 –one으로 끝나는 대명사이므로 형용사가 뒤에서 수식을 하도록 문장을 만든다.

06 과거를 나타내는 어구인 '~ ago', 'in+년도'는 현재완료와 함께 쓸 수 없음에 유의한다.

07 -thing으로 끝나는 대명사이므로 to부정사가 뒤에서 수식하도 록 문장을 만들 수 있다.

08 글의 흐름상 흥미로운 볼거리를 찾고 있다고 볼 수 있다. -thing 으로 끝나는 대명사는 '형용사+to부정사' 어순으로 뒤에서 수식 받는다.

09 -thing으로 끝나는 대명사이므로 '형용사+to부정사' 어순으로 뒤에서 수식하며, '지금 막 커피를 끓였다'고 하였으므로 현재완 료를 써서 나타낸다.

10 for+기간, since+특정 시점

11 도착한 것은 과거 시제로 표현하고, 이틀간 머문 것은 현재완료 시제로 표현할 수 있다.

12 경험을 묻고 있으므로 현재완료 시제를 쓴다.

13 -thing으로 끝나는 대명사이므로 to부정사가 뒤에서 수식하도 록 문장을 만들 수 있다.

14 의문문이므로 anything을 쓰며, -thing으로 끝나는 대명사이 므로 '형용사+to부정사'의 어순으로 수식하는 것에 유의한다.

15 답변으로 미루어 보아 '따뜻한 입을 무언가'가 필요하다고 말했 음을 유추할 수 있다.

16 현재완료의 '계속' 용법을 이용하여 묻고 답하는 문제이다. 8개 월째 영어를 배우고 있다고 하였으므로 기간을 나타내는 전치사 for를 써서 문장을 쓰는 것이 옳다

교과서
Reading

확인문제 p.80

1 T 2 T 3 F

확인문제 p.81

1 T 2 F 3 F 4 T 5 F

교과서 확인학습 A p.82~83

01 It, evening 02 went for a walk

03 sweating 04 thirsty, cold to drink

05 something tiny, at, bit

06 if you can 07 have you done

08 just finished 09 from, How, find

10 from, nearby 11 was looking for, to drink

12 something sweaty 13 smell me

14 sense heat, smell

15 why, have survived 16 like you

17 female, drink blood 18 feed on

19 interesting 20 the protein, to lay

21 How, sharp teeth 22 teeth.

23 a long, pointed mouth 24 So, easily

25 bit, got a bump, itches 26 to hear that

27 Make sure, it 28 clean it

29 never tried that before 30 the itchiness

31 try that 32 have to go 33 Where, going

34 going back 35 have suffered 36 prevent them

37 cool, wear, sleeves

38 keep, in mind

교과서 확인학습 B p.84~85

1 It was a hot summer evening.

2 Seojun went for a walk in the park.

3 Soon, he was sweating.

4 I'm thirsty. I want something cold to drink.

5 At that moment, something tiny flew at him and bit his arm.

6 Hey, catch me if you can.

7 Who are you? What have you done to me?

8 I'm a mosquito. I've just finished my dinner.

9 Where are you from? How did you find me?

10 I'm from a nearby river.

11 I was looking for some blood to drink there.

12 Then I smelled something sweaty and found you here.

13 How could you smell me from the river?

14 Mosquitoes can sense heat and smell very well.

15 That's why we have survived for millions of years.

16 Do all mosquitoes drink blood like you?

17 No. Only female mosquitoes like me drink blood.

18 Male mosquitoes only feed on fruit and plant juice.

19 That's interesting. So why do you drink blood?

20 I need the protein in blood to lay my eggs

21 How do you drink blood? Do you have sharp teeth?

22 No, I don't have teeth.

23 But I have a long and pointed mouth.

24 So I can drink your blood easily.

25 After you bit me, I got a bump. It itches.

26 I'm sorry to hear that.

27 Make sure you don't scratch it.

28 Also, clean it with alcohol wipes.

29 Alcohol wipes? I've never tried that before.

30 It will reduce the itchiness.

31 Okay, I'll try that at home. Thanks.

32 I have to go. See you soon.

33 Where are you going?

34 I'm going back to the river.

35 Wait! A lot of people have suffered from your bites.

36 How can we prevent them?

37 Stay cool and wear long sleeves.

38 Thanks. I'll keep your advice in mind.

시험대비 실력평가　p.86~89

01 sweating　02 ③　03 ③　04 ⑤

05 She was looking for some blood to drink there.

06 ③

07 It happened in a park on a hot summer evening.

08 ③　　09 drink blood　　10 ③

11 ⑤　　12 ④

13 they need the protein in blood to lay their eggs.

14 ②　　15 ⑤

16 Cleaning the bump with alcohol wipes

17 ⑤　　18 ③　　19 ⑤　　20 ⑤

21 your bites　22 I will keep your advice in mind.

23 ⑤　　　24 how to prevent

25 We have lived in Korea for six years.　26 ③

27 ④　　　28 She is going to visit Jeju.

01 덥거나 긴장할 때 피부에서 투명한 액체를 만들어 내는 것은 '땀을 흘리다(sweat)'이고, 빈칸에는 '땀을 흘리고 있었다'는 과거진행형으로 쓰는 것이 옳다.

02 ⓑ는 조건의 부사절 접속사이다. '~라면'이라고 해석되며, ③번은 '~인지 아닌지'라고 해석되는 명사절 접속사이다.

03 모기의 답변으로 보아 서준이가 모기에게 어디에서 왔는지를 묻는 것이 가장 적절하다.

04 서준이와 함께 저녁식사를 한 것은 아니다.

05 모기는 강에서 마실 피를 찾던 중이었다고 하였다.

06 (A), (C) -thing으로 끝나는 부정대명사는 형용사의 수식을 뒤에서 받으며 '형용사+to부정사' 순서로 수식받는다. (B) fly at: ~을 향해 날아가다

07 무더운 여름날 저녁 공원에서 발생한 이야기이다.

08 '~에서, ~에서부터'라는 의미를 동시에 지니는 전치사는 from이다.

09 모기의 답변에서 암컷 모기만이 피를 마신다고 하였으므로 '모든 모기가 너처럼 피를 마셔?'라고 물었음을 알 수 있다.

10 ⓓ는 부사적 용법 중 '목적'에 해당한다. ① 형용사 ② 명사 - 진주어 ③ 부사적 용법 중 '목적' ④ 명사 - hope의 목적어 ⑤ 명사 – 주어

11 수컷 모기가 식물 즙을 먹고 산다고 나와 있을 뿐, 암컷 모기도 식물 즙을 먹을 수 있는지는 알 수 없다.

12 ① feed on ② lay ③ sweaty ④ buzz ⑤ protein을 풀이한 말이다.

13 암컷 모기는 알을 낳기 위해 핏속에 있는 단백질이 필요해서 피를 마신다고 하였다.

14 길고 뾰족한 입을 가지고 있기 때문에 피를 쉽게 마실 수 있다는 의미가 적절하다. ② since: ~이기 때문에

15 ⓐ에서 쓰인 현재완료는 '경험'을 나타낸다. 경험적 용법으로 쓰인 것은 ⑤번이다.

16 알코올 솜으로 부어오른 자국을 닦는 것을 가리키는 대명사이다.

17 모기가 서준이를 문 것은 과거의 일이므로 bit이라고 쓰는 것이 옳다.

18 ③ 모기가 서준이를 어디에서 물었는지는 알 수 없다.

19 ⓐ에 쓰인 현재완료 용법은 '경험'이다. ⑤번은 '경험'을 나타내는 현재완료이다.

20 suffer from: ~로부터 고통받다, pick up: ~을 줍다, give up: 포기하다, be surprised at: ~에 놀라다, look forward to: ~을 고대하다 come from: ~에서 오다

21 모기에 물린 것을 의미한다.

22 keep ~ in mind: ~을 명심하다

23 'Thanks'라고 하였으므로 ⑤번은 옳지 않다.

24 모기는 서준이에게 모기 물리는 것을 예방하는 방법에 관하여 조언하고 있다.

25 우리가 6년 전에 한국으로 이사 와서 여전히 한국에 살고 있다고 하였으므로 '한국에서 6년 동안 살고 있다'는 현재완료 문장을 쓸 수 있다.

26 ③ 내일 제주로 간다고 하였다.

27 (B) '~에 가 본 적이 있다'는 경험을 나타내는 표현은 been to, (C) 감정을 느낄 때에는 과거분사형 형용사, (D) finish는 동명사를 목적어로 취하는 동사이다.

28 여름 방학 첫날 이 글을 쓴 Kate는 다음 날 제주로 간다고 하였다. 따라서 여름 방학 둘째 날에 제주로 갈 예정이라고 할 수 있다.

01 I want something cold to drink.

02 if you can catch me

03 She has bitten his arm.

04 sweat

05 reducing the itchiness

06 I have never tried that before.

07 to scratch it / to clean it with alcohol wipes

08 pointed

09 interesting

10 feed on, why

11 She needs the protein in blood.

12 fruit and plant juice, blood

13 A lot of people have suffered from your bites.

14 Staying cool and wearing long sleeves

15 She is from the river.

16 ⑤번 → advice

01 -thing으로 끝나는 부정대명사는 '형용사+to부정사' 순서로 후치 수식받는다.

02 자신을 잡을 수 있으면 잡아 보라는 의미이다.

03 글에 따르면 모기는 서준이의 팔을 물었다.

04 무더운 여름에 걷는 것은 서준이가 땀을 흘리게 만들었다.

05 알코올 솜으로 부어오른 자국을 닦는 것은 가려움을 줄이는 데 도움이 될 것이다.

06 try는 '한 번 해보다'라는 의미이다.

07 서준이의 이야기를 듣고서, 모기는 그것을 긁지 말라고 말했다. 또한 서준이에게 그것을 알코올 솜으로 닦으라고 조언해 주었다. tell과 advise는 모두 to부정사를 목적보어로 취하는 동사임에 유의한다.

08 모기의 입은 길고 뾰족하다고 하였다.

09 흥미를 '유발'할 때에는 interesting을 쓴다.

10 모기들이 무엇을 먹는지, 그리고 암컷 모기들이 왜 피를 마시는지에 관하여 이야기하고 있다.

11 알을 낳기 위해 암컷 모기는 핏속의 단백질이 필요하다고 하였다.

12 수컷 모기는 과일과 식물의 즙을 먹지만 암컷 모기는 피를 먹으며 산다고 하였다.

13 많은 사람들이 모기에 물려 괴로워하는 것은 과거부터 현재까지 이어지는 일이므로 현재완료 시제를 쓰는 것에 유의한다.

14 시원하게 지내고 소매가 긴 옷을 입는 것이 사람들이 모기에 물리지 않게 예방할 수 있다. 주어 자리이므로 동명사나 to부정사를 이용하여 답을 쓰는 것이 옳으며 빈칸 개수에 맞게 동명사를 쓸 수 있다. prevent A from B: A가 B하지 않도록 예방하다 [막다]

15 강으로 돌아간다고 말하고 있으므로 모기는 강에서 왔음을 알 수 있다.

16 명사를 쓰는 것이 옳다.

01 thin   02 ④

03 (1) stay away from   (2) took, to   (3) lost, by

04 (1) Birds feed on insects.

　(2) The queen ant's job is to lay eggs.

　(3) I sensed danger.

05 ②   06 ①   07 ③   08 happen

09 mosquito bites   10 ④

11 ⓒ → Make 12 ⑤   13 sunburn

14 She told him to wear sunscreen next time.

15 (A)going swimming this weekend

　(B)her eye problem   (C)stop swimming for a while

16 His class played soccer with Minsu's class.

17 He hoped to do better next time.   18 ⑤

19 ③   20 ⑤   21 ⑤

22 Did you find anything strange?   23 ①, ④

24 ④   25 has died → died   26 ④

27 The movie hasn't started yet.   28 ④

29 ③   30 ④

31 She smelled something sweaty from a nearby river.

32 ④   33 ④

34 a long and pointed mouth   35 bump

36 He will clean the bump with alcohol wipes.

01 주어진 관계는 반의어 관계를 나타낸다. thick: 두꺼운, thin: 얇은

02 맞거나 물려서 부푼 피부의 한 부분을 나타내는 말은 bump(혹, 타박상)이다.

03 stay away from: ~로부터 떨어져 있다 lose (~) by …(점, 골 등) 차로 (경기에서) 지다

04 feed on: …을 먹고살다 queen ant: 여왕개미

05 sleeve: 소매

06 주어진 문장에서 lay는 '(알을) 낳다'라는 의미로 이와 같이 쓰인 것은 ①번이다. ②, ③번은 '놓다', ④, ⑤번은 '누워 있었다'를 나타낸다. (lie의 과거)

07 suffer from: ~로 고통 받다, stay away from: ~로부터 떨어져 있다

08 특히 계획됨 없이 발생하다를 가리키는 것은 happen(발생하다)이다.

10 준수는 모기에 물리지 않기 위해 찬물로 샤워를 해야 한다는 설명은 대화의 내용과 일치하지 않는다.

11 ⓒ는 명령문이므로 동사원형 Make가 적절하다.

12 위 대화를 읽고 수진이가 쓰레기를 줄이기 위해 무엇을 해야 하

느지는 알 수 없다.

13 너무 많은 햇빛으로 당신의 피부가 쓰리고 붉어진 상태를 가리키는 말은 sunburn(햇볕에 탐, 그을림)이다.

14 Emma는 Tim에게 다음에는 자외선 차단제를 바르라고 말하였다.

15 오늘 나는 유진에게 이번 주에 수영을 가자고 제안했다. 불행하게도, 그녀는 눈에 문제가 있기 때문에 나와 함께 갈 수 없었다. 그녀는 당분간 수영을 그만해야 한다고 말했다. 나는 그 이야기를 듣고 유감이었다. 나는 우리가 다음 주말에 함께 갈 수 있기를 바랐다.

18 '~에 관하여 생각하다'는 think about이다.

19 over a week는 기간이므로 for를 쓰는 것이 옳다. go see a doctor: 병원에 가다, 진찰을 받다

20 Jessica has been sick since last week.이라고 쓰는 것이 옳다.

21 과거를 나타내는 어구는 현재완료 시제와 함께 쓰일 수 없다.

22 의문문이므로 anything을 쓰고, -thing으로 끝나는 대명사이므로 형용사가 뒤에서 수식하도록 문장을 만드는 것에 유의한다.

23 주어진 문장은 Grace가 병원을 벌써 퇴원했다는 뜻이다. 과거에 병원에 있었으나 지금은 병원에 없다는 의미이다.

24 주어진 문장의 현재완료는 '완료' 용법으로 쓰였다. ④번은 '계속' 용법이다.

25 2년 전이라는 과거를 나타내는 부사어구가 있으므로 현재완료 시제를 쓸 수 없다.

26 과거를 나타내는 부사어구인 the other day(지난번)와 현재완료 시제는 함께 쓸 수 없다.

27 '아직 시작하지 않았다'고 하였으므로 현재완료 시제와 yet을 사용하여 문장을 만든다.

28 ⓐ는 비인칭 주어로 날씨, 날짜, 요일, 거리, 명암 등을 나타낼 때 쓰이며 해석되지 않는다. ④번은 인칭대명사 it으로 '그것'이라고 해석된다

29 ⓑ는 완료 용법으로 쓰였다. ③번은 경험을 나타내는 현재완료이다.

30 ④ 서준이가 어디 출신인지는 알 수 없다.

31 모기는 근처 강에서 마실 피를 찾던 중 땀 냄새를 맡았다고 하였다.

32 it이 가리키는 것은 a bump이다.

33 ④ 서준이는 알코올 솜을 쓰는 방법을 궁금해 하지는 않는다.

34 길고 뾰족한 입 덕분에 피를 쉽게 마실 수 있다.

35 맞거나 물려서 볼록하게 올라온 피부의 일부분은 혹이나 타박상이라고 한다.

36 서준이는 집에 가서 알코올 솜으로 부어오른 곳을 닦을 것이다.

단원별 예상문제
p.98~101

01 ③

02 과일 쓰레기를 쓰레기통에 넣지 말아야 한다는 것

03 ⑤   04 ⑤

05 lost by three goals, do better

06 ⓒ → because   07 Her cat is sick.

08 She is going to take her cat to an animal doctor.

09 He suggested going swimming this weekend.

10 Because she had an eye problem.

11 She needs someone strong to help her.   12 ③

13 ④   14 ③

15 has won / Have you seen / saw

16 ⑤   17 cold to drink   18 ④

19 ③   20 sensing heat and smell

21 ③   22 ③   23 ⑤   24 ④

25 Cleaning the area with alcohol wipes can reduce the itchiness.

01 for a while: 당분간, go for a walk: 산책하러 가다

03 ⑤ Sujin이는 쓰레기통에 과일 쓰레기를 버리면 안 된다.

04 축구 경기가 어땠는지 묻는 질문으로 'How', lose by: ~ 차이로 (경기에서) 지다, do better: 더 잘하다

06 'because+주어+동사', 'because of+명사구'

07 Jimin의 고양이가 아프다.

08 Jimin은 고양이를 수의사에게 데려갈 것이다.

09 Tom은 Yujin에게 이번 주말에 수영하러 갈 것을 제안하였다.

10 Yujin은 눈에 문제가 있기 때문에 수영을 갈 수 없었다.

11 -one으로 끝나는 부정대명사이므로 '형용사+to부정사' 어순으로 뒤에서 수식하는 것에 유의한다.

12 주어진 문장과 ③의 빈칸에는 since가 들어간다. 나머지는 모두 for가 들어간다.

13 경험을 나타내는 현재완료로 표현할 수 있다. have gone to는 '~에 가고 없다'는 의미의 결과 용법이다.

14 ⓑ, ⓓ, ⓔ가 옳은 문장이다. ⓐ anyone strange, ⓒ Where were you last night?

15 현재도 조각가로 활동하고 있으므로 작품으로 상을 받은 것은 현재완료 시제를 써서 나타내는 것이 옳다.

16 ⑤번은 현재완료의 용법 중 '경험'에 해당한다. 나머지는 모두 '계속' 용법이다.

17 차가운 우유가 있다고 답하는 것으로 보아 '마실 시원한 것'을 원한다고 했음을 짐작할 수 있다.

18 (A) '그래서'라는 의미로 결과를 나타내는 것은 That's why (B) 기간을 나타내는 어구를 이끄는 것은 전치사 for (C) '(알을) 낳다'는 lay이다.

19 오직 암컷 모기만 피를 마신다고 하였다.

20 모기들은 열과 냄새를 감지하는

21 길고 뾰족한 입이 있어서 그 결과 피를 쉽게 마실 수 있다는 의미가 가장 자연스럽다.

22 ⓐ에서 쓰인 현재완료의 용법은 '경험'이다. have gone to는 '~에 가고 없다'는 의미로 결과를 나타낸다.

23 모두 부어오른 자국을 가리키는 말이지만 ⑤번은 알코올 솜으로 닦는 것을 가리킨다.

24 ④ 모기의 입이 얼마나 긴지는 알 수 없다.

25 알코올 솜으로 닦는 것이 가려움을 줄여줄 수 있다고 하였다. 주어 자리이므로 동명사 혹은 to부정사를 써서 문장을 만들 수 있다.

01 It's under the sink.

02 Because there are a lot of fruit flies around the trash.

03 She should not put fruit waste in the trash and should empty the trash can more often.

04 I have nothing special to do.

05 (E) → (B) → (A) → (C) → (D)

06 have seen, have never spoken, Have you ever spoken / met

07 I need someone funny to talk with.

08 I have never lied to you.

09 for, since

10 anything dangerous

11 something sweaty

12 She smelled him from the river.

13 They can sense heat and smell very well.

14 female, male

15 ⑤번 → drink

16 Unlike male mosquitoes, female mosquitoes feed on blood.

01 under the sink라고 아버지가 답하고 있다.

02 Why?라는 아버지의 질문에 답하는 Sujin의 말을 쓴다.

03 대화의 마지막 부분에 두 가지가 나와 있다.

04 오늘을 위한 특별한 계획이 있느냐는 질문이다. '특별히 할 일은 없어.'라고 답할 수 있다.

05 (E) 수영하러 가자는 제안에 → (B) 그리고 싶지만 갈 수 없다고 대답하고 → (A) 이유를 묻고 → (C) 이유 설명하며 → (D) 유감을 나타내는 순서가 적절하다.

06 '몇 번 만난 적이 있다'거나 '말해 본 적 있다'는 현재완료 시제를 이용하여 '경험'을 나타내는 문장으로 쓸 수 있다. '지난달에 파티에서 만났다'는 것은 과거의 일이므로 과거 시제를 쓴다.

07 talk with: ~와 함께 이야기하다

08 lie to ~: ~에게 거짓말을 하다

09 for+기간, since+특정 시점

10 부정문이므로 anything을 쓰고 –thing으로 끝나는 대명사이므로 형용사의 수식을 뒤에서 받는다.

11 -thing으로 끝나는 부정대명사는 형용사의 수식을 뒤에서 받는다.

12 모기는 강에서 서준이의 냄새를 맡았다고 하였다.

13 모기들은 열과 냄새를 매우 잘 감지하기 때문에 수백만 년 동안 살아남은 것이라고 하였다.

14 사람을 물어 피를 마시는 것은 암컷 모기라고 하였다.

15 주어가 복수명사 female mosquitoes이므로 복수 동사를 쓰는 것이 옳다.

16 해석: 수컷 모기와는 달리 암컷 모기는 피를 먹고 산다.

|모범답안|

01 (A) packing for the school trip tomorrow
  (B) take an umbrella.

02 (1) I have already sent an e-mail to my friend.
  (2) I have played the violin since I was five.
  (3) I have been to Alaska once.
  (4) I have found the solution to the problem.

03 (1) I want something cold to drink.
  (2) I need something cool to wear.
  (3) I want someone funny to play with in a pool.
  (4) I want something scary to watch at night in the summer.

01 Sue는 내일 수학여행을 위해 가방을 싼 후 그녀의 목록을 다시 확인하고 있었다. 왜냐하면 그녀는 아무것도 놓치고 싶지 않았기 때문이다. 그때, Mike가 내일 비가 올지도 모르기 때문에 그녀에게 우산을 가져가도록 상기시켜 주었다.

01 (1) go for a walk (2) At that moment
  (3) lose by (4) Keep in mind   02 ③

03 ⑤   04 ⑤

05 Make sure you take an umbrella with you.

06 ⑤   07 (A) To prevent, (B) sweating

08 She can hold a green tea bag on the itchy area.

09 ②   10 (A) mosquito bites, (B) itchy, (C) clean them with cool water, (D) I wear long sleeves

11 (C) → (B) → (D) → (A)

12 (that) you don't watch TV   13 ②

14 Claire has studied medicine at the university for two years.

15 ③   16 ②

17 I have something more important to do.

18 something tiny flew at him   19 ③

20 ③   21 some blood to drink   22 ②

23 ⑤   24 She is fourteen years old now.

25 since

02 주어진 문장은 수영하러 갈 수 없는 이유를 설명하고 있으므로 (C)가 적절하다.

03 ⑤ Yujin은 다음 주말에 수영을 가길 원하지만 계획을 세운 것은 아니므로 대화의 내용과 일치하지 않는다.

04 worried: 걱정하는, worrying: 걱정시키는, 'because+주어+동사', 'because of+명사구', 감정의 이유를 나타내는 to부정사가 알맞다.

06 위 대화를 통해 Sue가 무엇을 빼먹었는지 알 수 없다.

07 (A)에는 문맥상 '~을 예방하기 위해'라는 의미가 되어야 하므로 To prevent, (B)에는 avoid가 동명사를 목적어로 취하므로 sweating이 적절하다.

09 주어진 문장은 유감을 표현하므로 모기에 많이 물렸다는 Junsu의 말에 이어지는 대답으로 적합하므로 (B)가 알맞다.

10 나는 얼굴에 모기에 물린 상처로 고통 받고 있다. 나는 지난 주말 캠핑 가서 이 상처를 얻었다. 그것들은 정말로 가렵다. Ms. Wheeler는 내게 차가운 물로 물린 곳을 닦으라고 조언해 주었다. 더욱이, 나는 내가 캠핑 갈 때 긴 소매를 입어야 한다는 것을 명심하고 있다.

11 (C) 축구 경기에 대해 질문 → (B) 경기 결과 설명 → (D) 유감 표현 및 격려 → (A) 희망 표현

12 Make sure (that)~. : 꼭 ~하도록 해라.

13 ② since last Friday라고 해야 올바르다.

14 2년 전에 의학 공부를 시작하여 현재도 하고 있으므로 '2년 동안 공부하고 있다'는 현재완료 문장으로 쓸 수 있다.

15 오후 내내 찾았으나 지금에서야 발견하여 '어디에 있었느냐'고 묻고 있다. 따라서 ③번이 가장 적절하다.

16 -thing으로 끝나는 대명사를 to부정사가 뒤에서 수식하고, '방금 점심을 먹었다'는 표현이 가장 적절하다.

17 -thing으로 끝나는 대명사이므로 '형용사+to부정사' 어순으로 뒤에서 수식하는 것에 유의한다.

18 -thing으로 끝나는 부정대명사는 형용사의 수식을 뒤에서 받는다.

19 ③ 모기는 서준이의 다리가 아닌 팔을 물었다.

20 모기는 강 근처에서 마실 피를 찾고 있었다.

21 모기는 마실 피가 필요하다고 하였다.

22 많은 훌륭한 곳을 방문한 적이 있다는 경험을 나타내는 문장이다.

23 ⑤ 짐 싸는 것을 끝냈다고 하였다.

24 8살에 이사 와서 6년 동안 살고 있다고 하였으므로 현재 Kate는 14살이다.

25 8살에 이사 왔다고 하였으므로 8살 이래로 쭉 살아왔다고 쓸 수 있다.

Lesson 5

I Don't Have a Clue

시험대비 실력평가   p.112

01 disappear   02 ②   03 ④

04 (1) detectives (2) Fold, half (3) solved

05 (1) made it to (2) for free (3) turn over (4) Help yourself

06 ②   07 ⑤

01 주어진 단어의 관계는 반의어 관계이다. appear: 나타나다, disappear: 사라지다

02 '적어 놓았거나 컴퓨터에 저장해 놓은 무언가를 제거하다'를 나타내는 것은 delete(삭제하다)이다.

03 hide는 '숨기다'를 뜻한다.

04 detective: 탐정, fold: 접다, solve: 해결하다

05 make it to: ~에 이르는 데 성공하다, for free: 무료로, turn over: 뒤집다, help yourself: 마음껏 드세요

06 주어진 문장에서 suspect는 '용의자'를 뜻하며 이와 같은 의미로 쓰인 것은 ②번이다. 나머지는 모두 '의심하다'라는 의미로 사용되었다. food poisoning: 식중독

07 첫 번째 문장에서 lie는 '눕다'를 뜻하지만 두 번째, 세 번째 문장에서는 '거짓말하다'를 의미한다.

서술형 시험대비   p.113

01 outside

02 (1) twice (2) at the time (3) for free

03 (1) Can you explain the story to me?

   (2) You should take the pills twice a day.

   (3) I cut the bread into triangles.

04 (1) accident (2) hurt (3) question (4) delete

05 (1) The police were sure (that) they could catch the thief.

   (2) Turn over the page and look at the picture.

   (3) Would you fill this bottle with water?

06 table

01 주어진 단어의 관계는 반의어 관계이다. inside: ~ 안에, outside: ~ 밖에

02 twice: 두 번, at the time of: ~이 일어나던 때에, for free: 무료로

03 explain A to B: A를 B에게 설명하다 ('explain A B'의 형식으로 쓰이지 않음에 유의한다.) pill: 환약, 알약 triangle: 삼각형

06 세 개 또는 네 개의 다리가 있지만 걸을 수 없는 것은 table을 가리킨다.

교과서
Conversation

핵심 Check   p.114~115

1 (1) explain

  (2) Let me know

  (3) Can you tell me what happened yesterday

2 (1) First / Then (2) First / Then (3) First / Second / Third / Then

교과서 대화문 익히기

Check(√) True or False   p.116

1 T   2 T   3 T   4 F

교과서 확인학습   p.118~119

Listen & Speak 1 - A

that, bought / like, dragons, seahorses / need to use, to play / sounds, Can you explain how to use

Listen & Speak 1 - B

riddle, twice, once, never in a day / I have no idea / get it, Can you explain why / get it

Listen & Speak 2 - A

look at / How did you make it / First, in half / Second, bottom line / Third, both ends / Then, turn, over / easy

Listen & Talk 2 - B

detective / didn't see, this week, about / all of, disappeared / did, do / First, looked around / Then, suspects / Finally, thief / don't tell, watch, later

Real Life Communication

solve / First, a bag of beans / needs to cross a river / hold, one more / take, at a time / Can you explain how to move everything across

Let's Check

smells, good / going to, for dinner / Help yourself /

Can you explain how to make / First, fill, with / Then, on the top / delicious / Would, like / thanks

 시험대비 기본평가   p.120

01 (D) → (A) → (C) → (B)   02 triangle

03 (A) Second (B) Third   04 ③

01 (D) 제안 → (A) 수용 및 질문 → (C) 게임 설명 → (B) 반응

02 3개의 선과 3개의 각으로 구성된 모양을 가리키는 말은 triangle(삼각형)이다.

04 ③ 두 번째 단계에서 세모의 꼭대기를 맨 아랫선 쪽으로 접어야 한다.

 시험대비 실력평가   p.121~122

01 ②, ⑤   02 ②   03 E   04 ②

05 the paper fox   06 She should fold the top of the triangle to the bottom line.

07 She should make the ears first.   08 ④

09 ③   10 맘껏 먹으렴.

11 Can you explain how to make a taco? 12 ①

13 (a) with (b) delicious

01 (A)는 설명을 요청하는 표현이다. ②번은 상대방의 이해를 점검하는 표현이며 ⑤번은 제안을 나타낸다.

02 ② Brian이 Jimin과 운동장에서 축구하고 싶어한다는 설명은 대화의 내용과 일치하지 않는다.

03 'week'이라는 단어에는 'E'가 2번, 'year'라는 단어에는 한 번 나오지만 'day'라는 단어에는 한 번도 나오지 않는다.

06 유진은 종이를 반으로 접어 삼각형을 만든 후에 세모의 꼭대기를 맨 아랫선 쪽으로 접어야 한다.

07 유진은 얼굴을 그리기 전에 귀를 먼저 만들어야 한다.

08 이어지는 대화에서 Then ~ 그리고 Finally로 절차를 열거하고 있으므로 (D)가 적절하다.

09 대화를 통해 학교에서 모든 자전거를 훔친 도둑이 누구인지는 알 수 없다.

10 Help yourself.: 마음껏 드세요.

11 explain: 설명하다

12 (C)는 음식을 권유하는 표현으로 ①번과 바꾸어 쓸 수 있다.

13 (a) fill A with B: A를 B로 채우다, (b) sound+형용사 보어: ~일 것 같다

 서술형 시험대비   p.123

01 He bought a fox, a duck, and a bag of beans.

02 He could load only one thing at a time.

03 The fox will eat the duck.

04 how to move

05 (D) → (B) → (A) → (C)

06 (A) Fold the top of the triangle to the bottom line.

(B) Fold both ends of the bottom line to the top to make ears.

(C) Turn it over and draw a face.

01 농부는 강을 건너기 전에 여우, 오리, 한 자루의 콩을 샀다.

02 농부는 한 번에 하나씩만 배에 실을 수 있다.

03 농부가 없다면 여우가 오리를 먹을 것이다.

04 how to+동사원형: ~하는 방법

05 (D) 좋은 냄새가 무엇인지 질문 → (B) 저녁 메뉴 설명 → (A) 만드는 법 질문 → (C) 만드는 과정 설명

교과서

 Grammar

핵심 Check   p.124~125

1 (1) was painted by   (2) was taught

2 (1) will clean the room / will be cleaned by me

(2) must do our homework / must be done by us

(3) will help her / will be helped by him

시험대비 기본평가   p.126

01 (1) made → was made

(2) will complete → will be completed

(3) is caused → causes

(4) can't open → can't be opened

02 (1) was stolen (2) be sent (3) visit (4) are held

(5) is looked up to (6) play (7) be played

03 (1) The classroom is cleaned every day.

(2) When was this building built?

(3) We were not given tickets by him.

(4) This must be done before tonight.

(5) The door will be closed in 10 minutes.

01 (1), (2) 스웨터는 만들어지는 것이고, 건물 역시 완공되어지는 것이므로 수동태를 쓰는 것이 옳다. (3) 부주의한 운전이 사고를 유발하는 것이므로 능동태를 써야 한다. (4) 창문은 스스로 여는 것이 아니므로 수동태를 쓰는 것이 옳다.

02 주어가 동사의 행위의 주체가 될 수 있으면 능동태를, 동사의 행위의 대상이 될 경우 수동태를 쓴다.

03 동사의 행위의 주체가 될 수 없는 주어들이므로 수동태를 쓰는 것이 옳다. 수동태의 형태는 'be 동사+p.p.' 형태임에 유의한다.

시험대비 실력평가
p.127~129

01 ⑤　　　　02 ④　　　　03 ③

04 was not woken up　　05 ④　　　　06 ③

07 ⑤　　　　08 The fish will be cooked by her.

09 ③

10 Will the letter be sent to the right address?

11 ②

12 You will be punished by the teacher.　13 ④

14 ③　　　　15 ⑤　　　　16 ③

17 are taken care of by　　18 ⑤

19 Stamps are sold in a post office (by them).

20 seen　　　21 (1) He was seen dancing by me.

　(2) The cake will be bought by Jack.

　(3) Was the juice drunk by you?　　22 ②

23 ⑤　　　　24 ①

25 will be taken care of by me

26 This bridge must be repaired.

01 사고 발생이 과거이며 주어가 복수이므로 ⑤번이 옳다.

02 고기는 '보관되는 것'이므로 수동태를 쓰는 것이 옳다.

03 목적어가 these books이므로 이를 주어로 하고 동사 should return을 수동태로 만든 ③번이 같은 의미의 문장이다.

04 능동태에서 일반동사의 부정형이 쓰였으므로 수동태 역시 부정문으로 쓰는 것에 유의한다.

05 ④ '노래'가 주어이므로 수동태를 써서 was sung이라고 쓰는 것이 옳다.

06 모든 시점이 과거이며 주어가 동사의 행위의 대상이므로 수동태를 쓰는 것이 옳다. find(찾다)-found-found

07 동작의 주체가 일반인이거나 막연한 사람일 때, 그리고 명확하지 않을 때 'by+행위자'를 생략한다.

08 목적어가 the fish이므로 이를 주어로 하고 조동사의 수동태는 '조동사+be+p.p.'를 쓰는 것에 유의하여 문장을 만든다.

09 shut은 3단 변화가 동일한 형태인 shut-shut-shut임에 유의한다. shut down: 문을 닫다

10 편지는 '보내지는' 것이므로 will be sent를 쓰되 의문문임에 유의하여 will the letter be sent의 어순으로 쓴다.

11 모두 동사의 행위의 대상이 되어 played가 들어가지만 ②번은 행위의 주체이므로 playing이 들어간다.

12 너희들이 벌을 받는 대상이 되므로 수동태를 쓰는 것이 옳다.

13 speak well of: ~에 대해 좋게 말하다

14 바깥이 추웠으므로 히터를 틀었다고 보는 것이 옳으며, 'by+행위자'를 써야 한다. 구동사의 수동태의 경우 동사만 p.p형으로 변화시켜 수동태를 만들 수 있다.

15 by 이외의 다른 전치사를 쓰는 수동태에 유의하자. be interested in: ~에 흥미가 있다

16 run의 3단 변화는 run-ran-run이다.

17 take care of의 수동태는 be taken care of를 써야 하며 주어가 복수 명사이므로 are taken care of를 쓴다. 'by+행위자'를 쓰는 것을 잊지 않는다.

18 be crowded with: ~으로 붐비다, be satisfied with: ~에 만족하다

19 sell–sold–sold: ~을 팔다, 팔리다

20 주어진 우리말을 수동태를 활용하여 영어로 쓰면 'This performance will be seen by many people.'이다.

21 (1) 5형식 동사의 수동태에서 목적격 보어가 원형부정사가 아닌 경우 그대로 쓸 수 있다. (2) 조동사가 있는 수동태는 '조동사+be+p.p.'를 쓴다. (3) 의문문이므로 수동태 의문문을 쓴다.

22 ② happen은 자동사이므로 수동태로 쓸 수 없다.

23 'Your brothers help you.'를 수동태로 고쳐 'You are helped by your brothers.'를 쓰고 의문문을 만들기 위하여 주어와 동사 자리를 바꾸면 된다.

24 buy와 make는 4형식 동사로, 직접목적어를 주어로 한 수동태에서 간접목적어에 전치사 for를 쓴다.

25 조동사의 수동태는 '조동사+be+p.p.' 형태임에 유의한다.

26 의무를 나타내는 조동사 must를 대신하여 should를 써도 무방하다. 다리는 수리되는 대상이므로 수동태를 쓰는 것에 유의하자.

서술형 시험대비
p.130~131

01 The project will not be given up by us.

02 My parents will use the treadmill.

03 will be offered　　　　04 were put on by David

05 be made, be bought, be invited

06 (1) was laughed at (2) be arrested (3) ate (4) be cut

　(5) serves

07 will be written

08 When was this house built?

09 should be told the news

10 (1) Chris may be offered a job by the company. / A job may be offered to Chris by the company.

　(2) This letter must be sent by you before June 1.

　(3) Thomas Edison invented the electric light bulb in 1879.

　(4) The class will be divided into two sections by me.

　(5) People grow rice in many countries.

11 must be worn

12 should be finished

13 is married

14 originated, are grown, were introduced

15 are required to wear uniforms

16 was dropped by Timmy after dinner last night

17 (1) Food must not be brought into the lab (by you).

(2) Cell phones should be turned off (by you).

(3) UFO sightings cannot be explained (by us).

01 조동사가 있는 문장의 수동태는 '조동사+be+p.p.' 형태를 쓰며 부정어는 조동사 뒤에 위치시킨다.

02 주어가 동사의 행위의 주체가 되므로 능동태를 쓰는 것이 옳다. The treadmill will be used by my parents.로 고칠 수도 있다. treadmill: 러닝머신

03 주어가 행위의 대상이 되는 사물이므로 수동태를 쓰는 것이 옳다.

04 3인칭 단수 주어에서 동사 put이 쓰인 것으로 보아 과거시제임을 알 수 있다. 따라서 수동태로 바꿀 경우 복수 주어 The pants에 맞추어 were put on을 쓴다.

05 케이크가 만들어지고, 풍선이 구매되며, 친구들이 초대되는 것이므로 모두 수동태를 쓰는 것이 옳다.

06 (1) Julia는 반 친구들에 의해 웃음거리가 되었다. 그녀는 매우 당황했다. (2) 걱정 마. 그 용의자는 경찰에 의해 반드시 체포될 거야. (3) 내 개가 어젯밤에 탁자 위에 있던 모든 피자를 먹었다. (4) 등록금이 절반으로 삭감될 것이라는 소식은 나를 행복하게 한다. (5) 주방장은 직접 고객을 응대한다. 그래서 고객들은 만족을 느낀다.

07 주어인 '대본(a script)'은 행위의 대상이므로 수동태를 쓰는 것이 옳다.

08 집이 지어지는 것이므로 수동태를 쓰고, 시점은 과거이므로 was를 쓰는 것이 옳다.

09 4형식 동사의 간접목적어가 주어로 쓰인 수동태에서, 직접목적어에는 전치사를 쓰지 않는다.

10 (1) 4형식 동사는 목적어가 두 개이므로 두 개의 수동태를 만들 수 있다. 직접목적어가 주어로 쓰인 경우 간접목적어에 전치사를 붙이는 것에 유의하자. (2), (4) 조동사의 수동태는 '조동사+be+p.p.' 형태이다. (3) 과거에 발생한 일이므로 과거시제를 쓰는 것에 유의한다. (5) 능동태의 주어가 복수이므로 동사의 수를 일치시키는 것에 유의한다.

11 능동태의 목적어가 주어 자리에 있으므로 수동태로 쓰인 문장임을 알 수 있다.

12 주어가 동사의 행위의 대상이 되므로 수동태를 쓰는 것이 옳다. chore: 허드렛일, 하기 싫은 일

13 결혼한 상태를 말할 때에는 'be married'를 쓴다.

14 바나나는 아시아에서 유래했지만 지금은 전 세계 사람들에 의해 재배되고 있다. 바나나는 1516년에 미국에 소개되었다.

originate은 '비롯되다, 유래하다'는 의미로 쓰일 경우 자동사로 수동태로 쓰이지 않는다.

15 교복을 입도록 요구받는다는 의미가 자연스럽다. 따라서 수동태를 활용하여 문장을 완성할 수 있다.

16 능동태의 목적어가 주어로 쓰이고 있으므로 수동태를 쓰는 것이 옳다.

17 조동사가 있는 수동태는 '조동사+be+p.p.'이다.

교과서
Reading

확인문제 p.132

1 T 2 F 3 T 4 F

확인문제 p.133

1 F 2 T 3 F 4 F 5 T 6 F

교과서 확인학습 A p.134~135

01 to 02 enter the first room

03 to solve some riddles

04 be found, inside 05 are, to think

06 was hit by, on

07 Luckily, badly hurt, see

08 were questioned by

09 reading a book, the accident 10 was walking

11 was making breakfast

12 Who hit, explain 13 Write it down

14 move to 15 happened in

16 made it to

17 much harder to escape than

18 gets, from 19 reads, won 20 surprised

21 won 22 Congratulations, have won

23 During, choose, from, for free

24 to, on 25 wait to see 26 Truly yours

27 However, isn't real, deletes

28 Can, why 29 There are usually, days

30 have the answer

31 it, are free to go

1 Welcome to the Escape Tower.

2 You will enter the first room in our tower.

3 You need to solve some riddles to escape.

4 Clues can be found somewhere inside the room.

5 So, are you ready to think like Sherlock Holmes?

6 Mr. Doodle was hit by a car on Sunday afternoon.

7 Luckily, he wasn't badly hurt, but he didn't see the driver.

8 Three suspects were questioned by a police officer.

9 Ms. A said she was reading a book at the time of the accident.

10 Mr. B said he was walking his dog.

11 Ms. C said she was making breakfast.

12 Who hit Mr. Doodle? Can you explain why?

13 Do you have the answer? Write it down.

14 Then you can move to the next room.

15 Clue The accident happened in the afternoon.

16 Congratulations! You made it to the second room.

17 However, the second room is much harder to escape than the first one. Good luck!

18 Jay gets an email from his favorite clothing store.

19 The title reads "You won our Lucky Day event!"

20 Jay is surprised. He quickly opens it.

21 You won our 'Lucky Day' event!

22 Congratulations! You have won a special prize.

23 During our Lucky Day event, you can choose any seven items from our store for free!

24 Come to our store on November 31.

25 We can't wait to see you.

26 Truly yours, Kay Brown

27 However, Jay thinks that the event isn't real and deletes the email.

28 Can you explain why?

29 Clue There are usually 30 or 31 days in a month.

30 Do you have the answer?

31 Write it down and then you are free to go!

01 clue   02 ⑤   03 ②   04 ④

05 ②   06 ①

07 There are three suspects.

08 We have to go to the second room.

09 is surprised   10 the email   11 ③

12 ④

13 He can choose any seven items from their store for free.   14 ②

15 can find clues somewhere inside the room

16 ②   17 ①   18 was not seen by

19 She was reading a book (when Mr. Doodle was hit by a car).   20 ③

21 is written down   22 accident   23 ③

24 ④   25 ③   26 you are free to go

27 is deleted by Jay   28 ⑤

29 on November 31, 30 days

30 easy to escape

01 무언가를 발견하고, 이해하고 또는 미스터리나 수수께끼를 풀도록 돕는 것은 '단서(clue)'이다.

02 ⑤ 셜록 홈즈처럼 생각할 준비가 되었느냐고 물었을 뿐 그가 이 타워에서 많은 것을 생각하곤 했다는 말은 없다.

03 밑줄 친 (A)는 동사 need의 목적어로 쓰인 to부정사이다. ① anything을 수식하는 형용사 ② hopes의 목적어 ③ 부사적 용법 중 목적 ④ 부사적 용법 중 감정의 원인 ⑤ 부사적 용법 중 판단의 근거

04 과거에 발생한 일이며 차에 치였다는 의미이므로 ④번이 옳다.

05 ② Mr. Doodle이 운전자를 보지 못한 이유는 위 글에 나와 있지 않다.

06 심하게 다치지 않았다고 하였으므로 Luckily라고 쓰는 것이 옳다.

07 용의자는 세 명이라고 하였다.

08 첫 번째 방에서 탈출하고 나면 두 번째 방으로 가야 한다.

09 시점은 현재이며, 이메일 제목이 Jay를 놀라게 한 것이다. Jay가 주어로 쓰였으므로 수동태로 빈칸을 채워야 한다.

10 옷 가게에서 온 이메일을 가리키는 인칭대명사이다.

11 특정 날짜 앞에는 전치사 on을 쓴다.

12 밑줄 친 (D)는 명사절 접속사로 완전한 문장을 이끈다. ④번은 불완전한 문장을 이끄는 관계대명사이다.

13 행운의 날 행사 동안 그들의 가게에서 아무거나 일곱 가지 상품을 공짜로 선택할 수 있다고 하였다.

14 이메일의 제목은 'You won our Lucky Day event!'였다.

15 수동태를 능동태로 바꾸는 문제이다. 수동태에 쓰인 주어를 능동태의 목적어로 만든다.

16 특정한 순간이나 시각 앞에 쓰이는 전치사는 at이다.

17 (A) 주어가 동사의 행위의 주체가 되므로 수동태를 쓸 수 없다. (B) 지칭하는 것이 the answer이므로 단수 명사를 지칭하는 it이 알맞다. (C) happen은 자동사이므로 수동태로 쓰일 수 없다.

18 Mr. Doodle은 운전자를 보지 못했다고 하였다. 운전자가 주어이므로 수동태를 쓰는 것이 옳다.

19 Ms. A는 Mr. Doodle이 차에 치였을 때 책을 읽고 있었다고

하였다.

20 hardly는 '거의 ~하지 않은'이란 의미의 부사이다. Mr. Doodle이 거의 다치지 않았다는 것은 글의 내용과 일치하지 않는다.

21 답을 쓰면 다음 방으로 갈 수 있다고 하였다. 사물이 주어이므로 수동태를 쓰는 것이 옳다.

22 예고되지 않고 피해나 부상을 유발하는 갑작스러운 사건은 '사고(accident)'이다.

23 두 번째 방으로 온 것을 축하하지만 두 번째 방은 첫 번째 방보다 탈출하기 더 어렵다고 하였으므로 '그러나'가 가장 적절하다.

24 '~로부터'라는 의미의 전치사 from이 들어가는 것이 옳다.

25 for free는 '무료로'라는 의미이다. 따라서 ③번이 옳다.

26 free: 자유로운, 자유의

27 Jay가 이메일을 지운다고 하였다. 주어가 사물이며 시점은 현재이므로 is deleted를 쓴다.

28 Jay가 이메일을 언제 받았는지는 위 글을 읽고 알 수 없다.

29 Jay가 이메일을 믿지 않은 이유는, 11월은 30일까지 있는데 행사 날짜가 11월 31일이라고 표기되어 있었기 때문이다.

30 두 번째 방은 첫 번째 방보다 탈출하기 훨씬 더 어렵다고 하였으므로, 두 번째 방은 첫 번째 방만큼 탈출하기 쉽지 않다는 말을 쓸 수 있다.

서술형 시험대비   p.142~143

01 We need to solve some riddles.

02 You will enter the first room in our tower.

03 escape, like Sherlock Holmes

04 A car hit Mr. Doodle on Sunday afternoon.

05 wasn't seen by him

06 He was walking his dog.

07 He was hit by a car (on Sunday afternoon).

08 The second room is much harder to escape than the first one.

09 is opened quickly by Jay

10 There are usually 30 or 31 days in a month.

11 He won their 'Lucky Day' event.

12 He thinks that the event isn't real and deletes the email.

13 is surprised at[by]

14 a sound in the next room was heard by him.

15 It was broken last Sunday.

16 was the window broken

17 Sujin was holding a baseball bat.

01 방을 탈출하기 위하여 몇 개의 수수께끼를 풀어야 한다고 하였다.

02 enter는 타동사이므로 목적어 앞에 전치사 into가 불필요하다.

03 해석: 방을 탈출하기 위해서는 셜록 홈즈처럼 생각해야 한다.

04 by a car가 쓰인 것으로 보아 행위의 주체가 a car임을 알 수 있다. 과거시제이므로 hit을 쓴다.

05 목적어가 주어로 쓰였으므로 능동태를 수동태로 전환하는 문제이다.

06 두 번째 용의자인 Mr. B는 개를 산책시키던 중이라고 하였다.

07 Mr. Doodle은 일요일 오후에 차에 치었다고 하였다.

08 much는 비교급을 강조하는 부사로 '훨씬'이라고 해석된다.

09 목적어를 주어 자리에 배치하였으므로 능동태를 수동태로 전환하는 문제임을 알 수 있다.

10 '~이 있다'는 표현은 There is/are로 쓴다. 빈도부사 usually의 위치는 be동사 뒤이다.

11 이메일에 따르면 Jay는 옷가게의 '행운의 날' 행사에 당첨되었다고 하였다.

12 이메일을 읽은 후 Jay는 그 행사가 사실이 아니라고 생각하고 이메일을 삭제한다고 하였다.

13 Jay는 이메일 제목을 읽고 놀란다고 하였다. surprise는 수동태로 쓰일 때 by 대신에 at을 주로 쓴다. by를 써도 좋다.

14 과거동사이므로 수동태로 전환할 때 was heard로 쓴다.

15 지난 일요일에 창문이 깨졌다고 하였다.

16 의문문이 있는 문장의 수동태이다. 우선 'The window was broken by whom.'을 쓴 후 전치사와 의문사를 문두에 배치하면 된다.

17 수진이는 야구 방망이를 들고 있었다고 하였다.

영역별 핵심문제   p.145~149

01 ③   02 ⑤

03 (1) Frist, draw a circle.

(2) Second, put a star inside the circle.

(3) Then, put a triangle on top of the circle.

04 (1) escaped (2) suspect (3) clues (4) Delete

05 (1) ready to (2) at the time of (3) Write down

06 ①   07 ⓐ → that (또는 which)   08 ⑤

09 riddle   10 ③   11 ⓔ → draw 12 ①

13 ③   14 ⑤   15 ④   16 ⑤

17 ⑤   18 When will the food be delivered?

19 ③   20 ④   21 ②

22 We are interested in studying English. 23 ②, ④

24 ②   25 ④

26 (1) Trash must be picked up by us.

(2) Peter looks down on Kelly.   27 ①

28 ②   29 It happened in the afternoon.

30 a bike → a car / dinner → breakfast   31 title

32 Our Lucky Day event was won by you.

33 ⑤   34 ③

25

01 '다른 사람이나 장소로부터 물건들을 훔치는 사람'을 가리키는 말은 thief(도둑)이다.

02 hold: 잡다, 쥐다, by oneself: 도움을 받지 않고, 혼자서, detective: 탐정

03 circle: 원, inside: ~의 안에, on top of: ~의 위에, triangle: 삼각형

04 escape: 탈출하다, suspect: 용의자, clue: 단서, delete: 삭제하다

06 주어진 문장에서 cross는 '건너다'를 뜻하며 이와 같은 의미로 쓰인 것은 ①번이다. 나머지는 모두 '십자가, X표'를 의미한다.

07 the new game을 수식하는 목적격 관계대명사 that이나 which가 적절하다.

09 '게임으로 질문하고 놀랍거나 재미있는 대답을 갖는 질문'을 가리키는 말은 riddle(수수께끼)이다.

10 이어지는 문장에서 이해되지 않은 답에 대해 설명을 요청하고 있으므로 (C)가 적절하다.

11 명령문의 동사 turn과 병렬 구조로 draw가 적절하다.

12 열거를 나타내고 있으므로 next 등으로 열거를 이어나갈 수 있다.

13 주어진 문장은 타코를 만드는 과정의 일부를 Then으로 이어서 설명하고 있으므로 (C)가 적절하다.

15 by 이외에 다른 전치사를 쓰는 수동태 문제이다. 모두 전치사 with를 쓰지만 surprised는 전치사 at을 쓴다.

16 die는 자동사이므로 수동태로 쓸 수 없다.

17 make를 p.p.로 바꾸고 나머지는 그대로 쓴다. 행위자 앞에 전치사 by를 쓰는 것을 기억하자.

18 음식이 배달되는 것이므로 수동태를 쓴다. 미래의 일이므로 will을 쓰고 의문사는 문장 맨 앞에 놓는다.

19 ③ 4형식 동사 ask가 직접목적어를 수동태의 주어로 사용할 경우 간접목적어에 전치사 of를 쓴다.

20 be located: ~에 위치해 있다, '존재하다'는 의미의 exist는 자동사로 수동태가 불가능하다.

21 작문이 쓰여지는 것이므로 should be written이라고 써야 한다. composition: 작문, 작곡

22 interest는 by 이외의 전치사를 쓰는 수동태이다.

23 4형식 동사의 수동태에서 직접목적어가 주어로 쓰인 경우 간접목적어에 특정 전치사를 부여한다. teach는 to를 쓰는 동사이다.

24 ⓐ will be sharpened ⓑ Were the flowers picked up? ⓔ is played

25 *Romeo and Juliet*은 책 이름으로 단수 취급하며 시점이 과거이므로 was written by를 쓰는 것이 옳다.

26 (1) 조동사의 수동태는 '조동사+be+p.p.' 형태이다. (2) look down on: 무시하다, 경멸하다

27 많이 다치지는 않았지만 운전자를 보지 못했다는 내용이 가장

자연스럽다. 따라서 ①번에 들어가는 것이 옳다.

28 (A)는 to부정사의 부사적 용법 중 '목적'으로 쓰였다. ① 명사적 용법(목적격 보어) ② 부사적 용법 '목적' ③ 형용사적 용법 ④ 명사적 용법(진주어) ⑤ 부사적 용법 '감정의 원인'

29 그 사건은 오후에 발생하였다.

30 Mr. Doodle은 자전거가 아닌 차에 치였으며, Ms. C는 아침을 만들고 있었다고 하였다.

31 책, 노래, 혹은 영화 같은 것에 식별하거나 묘사하기 위해서 주어지는 이름은 '제목'이다.

32 능동태의 목적어인 our Lucky Day event가 주어가 되고 시제는 과거이므로 was won으로 쓰는 것에 유의한다.

33 답을 알면 적으라고 하였다. 따라서 ⑤번은 답할 수 있다.

34 ③ Jay가 이메일을 지운 이유는 행사가 사실이 아니라고 생각해서이다.

단원별 예상문제 p.150~153

01 ① 02 ④ 03 ② 04 ②, ④

05 Can you explain why? 06 ③

07 Help yourself. 08 (A) tacos (B) I should fill my tortilla with vegetables and meat (C) add some sauce on the top

09 (B) → (C) → (D) → (A)

10 E'는 'week'이라는 단어에는 2번, 'year'라는 단어에는 한 번 나오지만, 'day'라는 단어에는 한 번도 나오지 않기 때문이다.

11 ③ 12 ④

13 The table was set and the candles were lit.

14 ⑤ 15 ①, ⑤ 16 will be delivered

17 (1) The kids were told to leave.
   (2) I was heard singing in my room by Thomas.

18 ⑤ 19 ③

20 You made it to the second room.

21 three suspects / questioned them

22 ⑤ 23 ⑤

24 He was throwing a ball to his dog. 25 ③

01 (A)는 자신의 이해를 점검하는 표현이므로 이해를 점검하는 ①번과 바꾸어 쓸 수 있다.

03 '어떤 범죄의 죄가 있다고 생각되는 사람'을 가리키는 말은 suspect(용의자)이다.

04 Finally는 '마침내'를 뜻하며 이와 바꾸어 쓸 수 있는 표현은 'Eventually(결국), At last(마침내)'이다. Though: 비록 ~일지라도, Nevertheless: 그럼에도 불구하고, Initially: 처음에는

06 Kelly는 처음에 답을 이해하지 못했다는 설명이 대화의 내용과 일치한다.

08 나는 엄마와 저녁식사로 타코를 먹었다. 매우 맛있었다. 나는 타코를 어떻게 만드는지 궁금했다. 엄마는 내게 먼저 토르티야에 야채와 고기를 넣고 그 다음에 위에 소스를 추가해야 한다고 말해 주셨다. 다음에 나는 그것을 혼자 만들어볼 것이다.

09 (B) 관심 끌기 → (C) 만드는 방법 질문 → (D) 만드는 방법 설명 → (A) 반응

11 행위자가 불분명하거나 일반 사람들일 때 'by+행위자'를 생략할 수 있다.

12 disappoint는 수동태로 쓰일 때 by 대신에 전치사 with를 쓰는 동사이다.

13 식탁이 차려지고 양초들에 불이 켜지는 것은 모두 수동태를 쓰는 것이 옳다.

14 건물은 손상을 입는 것이므로 수동태로 쓰는 것이 옳으며, disappear는 자동사이므로 수동태로 쓰일 수 없다.

15 그 소녀가 공에 맞았다는 것은 공이 그 소녀를 쳤다는 의미이다. 따라서 ①, ⑤번이 옳다.

16 조동사가 있는 수동태의 형태는 '조동사+be+p.p.'이다.

17 5형식 동사의 수동태에서 목적격 보어가 원형부정사가 아닌 경우는 그대로 쓰일 수 있다.

18 Mr. Doodle이 일요일 오후에 차에 치임 - (C) 다행히도 많이 다치지 않았지만 운전자를 보지 못하고 경찰은 용의자 세 명을 심문함 - (B) 용의자 셋을 심문한 이야기가 나오고 - (A) 누가 범인인지 답을 쓰면 다음 방으로 갈 수 있다는 순서가 가장 자연스럽다.

19 (A)는 '다행히도'라는 의미이다. 따라서 ③번이 옳다. ① 특히 ② 최근에 ④ 갑자기 ⑤ 특히

20 make it to: ~에 이르다

21 용의자는 세 명이라고 하였으며, 경찰이 그들을 심문했다고 하였다. 경찰이 주어로 있으므로 능동태를 써서 표현한다.

22 두 번째 방은 첫 번째 방보다 탈출하기 훨씬 더 어렵다고 하였다. 따라서 ⑤번은 옳지 않다.

23 주어가 동사의 행위의 주체가 되는지 유무를 판단하여 답을 고를 수 있다.

24 도훈이 창밖을 보았을 때 Ted는 개에게 공을 던지는 중이었다.

25 ③ 도훈이가 있던 옆방의 창문이 깨졌다.

🦉 서술형 실전문제　　　　　　　　p.154~155

01 Can you explain how to use the buttons?

02 They are going to play the new game that Jimin bought.

03 They can play the game by using the buttons.

04 all of the bikes at school disappeared

05 He looked around the school. Then, he met some suspects and asked questions.

06 (1) The coffee was already made.
　(2) Was the book returned by you?
　(3) My friends will be invited by me.

07 were attacked by

08 will be made by

09 The missing girl was found by the police yesterday.

10 is expected

11 Luckily

12 were questioned by a police officer

13 I[We] can find them inside the room.

14 broke the window

15 He was at home last Sunday.

16 explain

01 how to+동사원형: ~하는 방법

02 Jimin과 Brain은 Jimin이 산 새로운 게임을 함께 할 것이다.

03 Jimin과 Brian은 버튼을 사용해서 게임을 할 수 있다.

04 민수가 놓친 TV쇼는 학교에 있던 모든 자전거가 사라진 사건에 대한 것이다. case: 사건

05 학생 탐정은 도둑을 찾기 위해 학교를 둘러보았다. 그리고 나서 그는 몇 명의 용의자들을 만나 질문을 하였다.

06 (1) 행위의 주체가 불분명할 때에는 'by+행위자'를 생략할 수 있다. (3) 조동사가 있는 문장의 수동태는 '조동사+be+p.p.' 형태를 쓰는 것에 유의한다.

07 attack: ~을 공격하다

08 사물이 주어이므로 수동태를 써서 문장을 완성할 수 있다.

09 발견된 것이므로 수동태를 써야 하며, 어제 일어난 일이므로 과거 시제를 쓴다.

10 정시에 올 것으로 예상된다는 의미가 적절하므로 수동태를 써야 한다.

11 문맥상 문장을 수식하는 부사로 바꾼다.

12 목적어 three suspects가 주어로 쓰이고 있으므로 수동태 문장을 완성하는 문제임을 알 수 있다.

14 행위의 주체가 불분명할 때에는 'by+행위자'를 생략하여 수동태를 만들며 문장 (A)는 이에 해당한다. 불분명한 주어로 시작하는 문장이므로 능동태를 쓰는 것이 옳다.

15 도훈이는 지난주 일요일에 집에 있었다.

16 수동태 문장을 능동태로 전환한 것이다. 주어가 동사의 행위의 주체가 될 수 있으므로 explain을 쓰는 것이 옳다.

01 (A) all of the bikes at school disappeared

　　(B) had missed[hadn't seen]

　　(C) the student detective

　　(D) the thief

02 (A) was the book read

　　(B) were not[weren't] seen

　　(C) was made by

|모범답안|

03 (1) The flowers will be sent to her on Monday

　　(2) The mountain can be seen from here.

　　(3) The performance was shown last month.

　　(4) The food can't be eaten inside the building.

　　(5) Only three books can be borrowed by a person
　　　at a time.

01 나는 학생 탐정이 나오는 TV 쇼에 매료되었다. 나는 민수 또한 그 TV 쇼를 아주 좋아한다는 이야기를 듣고 기뻤다. 이번 주, 방송분은 매우 흥미로웠다. 쇼는 학교의 모든 자전거들이 사라진 범죄에 관한 것이었다. 나 또한 자전거를 잃어버린 경험이 있었기 때문에 그것은 더 재미있었다. 내가 이것에 대해 민수에게 이야기했을 때, 그는 이 방송분을 보지 못했다고 이야기했다. 나는 그에게 범인을 잡기 위해 학생 탐정이 한 것에 대해 이야기했다. 나는 누가 범인인지 알지만 민수는 알고 싶어 하지 않았다. 그는 나중에 그것을 볼 것이라고 말했다.

02 경찰이 용의자 A에게 책을 어디에서 읽었느냐고 묻는 말이다. by you가 있으므로 수동태를 쓸 수 있다. (B) 누구도 용의자 B가 개를 산책시키는 것을 보지 못했다고 하였고, 이것은 누구에 의해서도 목격되지 않았다는 의미이므로 마찬가지로 수동태를 쓸 수 있다. (C) 대답으로 미루어 보아 무엇이 만들어졌는지를 묻는 말이 들어가는 것이 옳다.

01 (s)afe   02 ①

03 (1) hide   (2) case   (3) candle   (4) triangle

04 ②   05 detective   06 ⑤   07 ⑤

08 Can you explain how to move everything across
　　the river safely?

09 ③

10 (A) the fox (B) the duck (C) the beans (D) the duck

11 (E) → (B) → (A) → (C) → (D)   12 ⑤

13 ⑤   14 ②

15 The rock star was surrounded by hundreds of fans
　　outside the theater.

16 ④   17 was caused by lightning

18 당신은 우리 가게에서 일곱 가지 상품을 아무거나 무료로

선택할 수 있습니다.   19 ④   20 ④

21 November 31 / deleted his email

22 Seven items are free during the event.   23 ③

24 ③   25 How can it be explained?

01 주어진 단어의 관계는 반의어 관계이다. safe: 안전한, dangerous: 위험한

02 '누군가가 범죄나 미스터리를 풀도록 도와주는 물체나 정보'를 가리키는 말은 clue(단서)이다.

03 case: 사건 opposite: 맞은편의, 반대쪽의

04 scene은 '현장, 장면, 풍경' 등을 뜻한다.

05 범죄를 조사하고 범죄자를 잡는 경찰을 가리키는 말은 detective(형사)이다. detective: 탐정, 형사

06 appear: 나타나다, disappear: 사라지다, suspect: 용의자, suspend: 매달다, thief: 도둑, chief: 장(長), 우두머리

07 Minsu는 Jane에게 도둑이 누구인지 이야기하지 말라고 했으므로 ⑤번 설명은 대화의 내용과 일치하지 않는다. deal with: 다루다 investigate: 조사하다

09 ③ 농부가 왜 강을 건너야 하는지는 알 수 없다.

11 (E) 수수께끼 제시 → (B) 모르겠다고 말함 → (A) 정답 제시 → (C) 설명 요청 → (D) 정답에 대한 이유 설명

13 조동사 부정형의 수동태이므로 '조동사+not+be+p.p.' 형태를 써야 한다.

14 belong to는 상태를 나타내는 동사이므로 수동태로 쓰일 수 없다. symptom: 증상

15 목적어가 the rock star이므로 이를 주어로 하여 수동태를 만들 수 있다.

16 annoy는 수동태로 쓰일 경우 전치사 with, about, at과 주로 함께 쓰인다.

17 '불은 번개에 의해 야기되었다'는 문장을 완성하는 것이 적절하다.

18 any는 긍정문에서 '무엇이든, 아무것이든'의 뜻이다.

19 thinks와 병렬 관계에 있으므로 deletes라고 쓰는 것이 옳다.

20 Jay는 이메일 제목을 보고 놀라 빠르게 그것을 열어보았다고 하였으므로 ④번이 글의 내용과 일치한다.

21 행사 날짜는 11월 31일이라고 하였고, Jay는 이메일 내용이 사실이 아니라고 생각하여 메일을 지운다고 하였다.

22 행사 동안 일곱 가지 상품을 무료로 선택할 수 있다고 하였다.

23 Jay 외에 몇 명의 사람들이 이메일을 받았는지는 위 글을 읽고 알 수 없다.

24 도훈이네 집으로 던져진 공은 위 글에서 찾아볼 수 없다.

25 주어로 쓸 수 있는 것은 it밖에 없으므로 행위의 대상으로 보아 수동태를 써서 나타내는 것이 옳다.

교과서 파헤치기

Lesson 3

01 쉬다, 휴식하다	02 피하다	03 공중전화
04 활동	05 화살, 화살표	06 위험
07 (글·글씨 등이) 쓰이다		08 노력
09 성공	10 가능한	11 자원 봉사 동아리
12 ~하려고 계획하다		13 해결책
14 멘티	15 훌륭한, 굉장한	16 거리
17 설명하다	18 혼란스러운	19 냉장고
20 필요로 하다	21 잊어버리다	22 쓰레기
23 비밀, 비결; 비밀의		24 사라지다
25 다른	26 틀, 테	27 바깥의, 외부의
28 아동 센터	29 동전	30 해결하다
31 지도	32 무료의	33 비닐봉지
34 표지판	35 (생각을) 찾아내다, 제시하다	
36 낮 동안	37 자기 스스로	
38 시도하다, 한번 해 보다		39 설치하다, 세우다
40 ~하는 것을 멈추다		41 ~ 덕분에
42 ~해야 한다	43 (과거의) 어느 날	

01 sticker	02 basket	03 coin
04 sign	05 confusing	06 secret
07 solve	08 few	09 bus stop
10 children's center		11 disappear
12 frame	13 free	14 soap
15 glad	16 hear	17 map
18 different	19 mentor	20 outside
21 plastic bag	22 trash	23 refrigerator
24 explain	25 effort	26 decide
27 avoid	28 trash	29 danger
30 rest	31 success	32 pay phone
33 solution	34 forget	35 the other day
36 give out	37 come up with	38 during the day
39 stop -ing	40 on one's own	41 put up
42 thanks to	43 give it a try	

1 few, 몇몇의   2 confusing, 혼란스러운   3 start, 시작하다
4 disappear, 사라지다   5 free, 무료의   6 secret, 비밀의
7 activity, 활동   8 hear, 듣다   9 success, 성공
10 refrigerator, 냉장고   11 arrow, 화살표
12 mentee, 멘티   13 sign, 표지판
14 rest, 쉬다, 휴식하다   15 map, 지도   16 mentor, 멘토

Listen & Speak 1 A

planned to give out / think, forgot / Let me help you then, going, give out / part, volunteer club activity / mean / It means that, smile at each other, become a better place / wonderful idea

Listen & Speak 1 B

in the box / my mentee, going to give / Do you teach her every weekend / feel happy, teach / You are a good mentor, looks heavy, Let, help

Listen & Speak 2 A

this is for you, made, with / How did you know that, needed / talked about, the other day / How nice, many different colors / I'm glad you like it

Listen & Speak 2 B

I read a story about a special boy in India, hear about / Why is he special / couldn't go, had to work, taught, every day / great story / I'm glad you like it

Real Life Communication

Are you feeling better / tried to, on my own, but / Let me help you, join my study group / study group / we can learn better when we teach each other / try hard, Thanks for helping me / welcome, glad, like

Let's Check 1

looks heavy, Let me help you / Where is the bus stop around here / over there, carry / very kind / No problem, going, too

Listen & Speak 1 A

Tom: Hojun and I planned to give out free stickers today, but I think he forgot.

Sora: Really? Let me help you then. Why are you going to give out stickers?

Tom: It's part of our volunteer club activity.

Sora: I see. What does this sticker mean?

Tom: It means that when we smile at each other, the world will become a better place.

Sora: That's a wonderful idea.

Mike: Jimin, what are all these things in the box?

Jimin: They're for my mentee at the children's center. I'm going to give her my old books today.

Mike: Do you teach her every weekend?

Jimin: Yes. I feel happy when I teach her.

Mike: You are a good mentor. Oh, the box looks heavy. Let me help you.

Jimin: Thanks.

Listen & Speak 2 A

Alex: Mom, this is for you. I made it with plastic bags

Mom: That's very cute, Alex. How did you know that I needed a new basket?

Alex: You talked about it when we were having dinner the other day.

Mom: How nice! I really like this basket. It has many different colors.

Alex: I'm glad you like it.

Listen & Speak 2 B

Yujin: I read a story about a special boy in India. Do you want to hear about it?

Jack: Sure. Why is he special, Yujin?

Yujin: Many children in his town couldn't go to school and had to work . So he taught them in his house every day.

Jack: That's a great story

Yujin: I'm glad you like it.

Real Life Communication

Emily: Welcome back, Brian. Are you feeling better?

Brian: Yes, thanks. I tried to study on my own in the hospital, but it was hard.

Emily: Let me help you. Why don't you join my study group?

Brian: Did you start a study group? That's wonderful

Emily: Thanks. I think that we can learn better when we teach each other.

Brian: I agree. I'll try hard to be a good member. Thanks for helping me.

Emily: You're welcome. I'm glad you like my idea.

Let's Check 1

Henry: Your bag looks heavy. Let me help you.

Sujin: Thanks. Where is the bus stop around here?

Henry: It's over there. I'll carry your bag to the bus stop for you.

Sujin: You're very kind.

Henry: No problem. I am going that way, too.

본문 TEST Step 1 p.09~10

01 are, which, read

02 want, hear about 03 Call, You Love

04 had, pay, on, streets

05 However, nobody, used 06 One, up with

07 stuck, to, of 08 put up, that

09 many, were using

10 When, talking, whom, smiling

11 His, became, success

12 During, all, disappeared

13 because, gave happiness 14 Arrow Man

15 few, ago, were, confusing

16 didn't, enough information

17 had, others, explain

18 Where, on, go to

19 often took, wasted

20 One, decided to solve

21 bought lots, arrow

22 rode, around, stuck, on 23 asked, to do

24 just, help others

25 Thanks, could, easily, save

본문 TEST Step 2 p.11~12

01 are, which, read

02 to hear about 03 Call, You Love

04 had, pay, phones

05 However, nobody, used 06 came up with

07 stuck coins to 08 put up, that said, Call, Love

09 many, were using

10 When, were talking, whom they loved, didn't stop smiling 11 became a big success

12 During the day, disappeared

13 because, gave happiness to

14 Red Arrow Man

15 A few years ago, were, confusing

16 didn't have enough information

17 ask others to explain

18 Where, on the map, go to

19 often took the wrong bus, wasted

20 decided to solve

21 lots of red arrow stickers

22 Every day, rode, around, stuck, on

23 asked him to do 24 wanted to help

25 Thanks to his effort, could understand, easily, save time

1 여기 내가 어제 읽은 이야기가 두 개 있어.

2 들어볼래?

3 당신이 사랑하는 누군가에게 전화하세요.

4 뉴욕에는 길거리에 공중전화가 많이 있었다.

5 그러나 아무도 그것들을 실제로 사용하지는 않았다.

6 어느 날, 한 남자에게 좋은 아이디어가 떠올랐다.

7 그는 공중전화 하나에 동전들을 붙였다.

8 그는 또한 "당신이 사랑하는 사람에게 전화하세요."라고 쓰인 표지판을 설치했다.

9 곧, 많은 사람들이 그 전화기를 사용하고 있었다.

10 그들이 사랑하는 누군가에게 전화하고 있을 때, 그들은 미소 짓기를 멈추지 않았다.

11 그의 아이디어는 커다란 성공이었다.

12 낮 동안, 모든 동전이 사라졌다.

13 그 남자는 자신의 작은 아이디어가 많은 사람에게 행복을 가져다 주었기 때문에 매우 행복했다.

14 빨간 화살표 청년

15 몇 년 전, 서울의 버스 정류장의 지도는 매우 혼란스러웠다.

16 지도에는 충분한 정보가 없었다.

17 사람들은 다른 사람들에게 지도를 설명해 달라고 요청해야 했다.

18 "이 버스 정류장은 지도의 어디에 있는 건가요? 이 버스가 광화문으로 가나요?"

19 많은 사람이 종종 버스를 잘못 타서 시간을 낭비하곤 했다.

20 어느 날, 한 젊은 청년이 이 문제를 해결해 보기로 했다.

21 그는 빨간 화살표 스티커를 많이 샀다.

22 매일 그는 자전거를 타고 서울 시내를 돌아다니며 버스 지도에 스티커를 붙였다.

23 아무도 그 청년에게 이 일을 하라고 요청하지 않았다.

24 그는 단지 다른 사람들을 돕고 싶었다.

25 그의 노력 덕분에, 사람들은 지도를 쉽게 이해하고 시간을 절약할 수 있었다.

1 Here are two stories which I read yesterday.

2 Do you want to hear about them?

3 Call Someone You Love

4 New York had many pay phones on its streets.

5 However, nobody really used them.

6 One day, a man came up with an idea.

7 He stuck coins to one of the phones.

8 He also put up a sign that said, "Call Someone You Love."

9 Soon, many people were using the phone.

10 When they were talking to someone whom they loved, they didn't stop smiling.

11 His idea became a big success.

12 During the day, all the coins disappeared.

13 The man was very happy because his small idea gave happiness to many people.

14 The Red Arrow Man

15 A few years ago, the maps at bus stops in Seoul were very confusing.

16 They didn't have enough information.

17 People had to ask others to explain the maps.

18 "Where is this bus stop on the map? Does this bus go to Gwanghwamun?"

19 Many people often took the wrong bus and wasted their time.

20 One day, a young man decided to solve this problem.

21 He bought lots of red arrow stickers.

22 Every day he rode his bicycle around the city and stuck the stickers on the bus maps.

23 Nobody asked him to do this.

24 He just wanted to help others.

25 Thanks to his effort, people could understand the maps easily and save time.

Real Life Communication B

1. not good at, What

2. Let me help, Why don't

3. give it a try

4. problem, glad

Let's Write

1. Be

2. in the second grade

3. want to help, with

4. can meet, after school

5. ask, to be

6. think, can be

7. whom my mentee can trust

Culture & Life

1. see, inside

2. wash their hands, to get

3. Washing, can prevent

4. Thanks to, fewer, getting sick

Real Life Communication B

1. A: I'm not good at science. What can I do?

2. B: Let me help you. Why don't you start with easier books?

3. A: Okay, I'll give it a try. Thanks for the tip.

4. B: No problem. I'm glad you like it.

Let's Write

1. Be a Mentor!

2. My name is Semi and I'm in the second grade.

3. I want to help my mentee with her homework.

4. I can meet my mentee after school.

5. I'll ask my mentee to be on time.

6. I think a good mentor can be a good friend.

7. So I want to become a good friend whom my mentee can trust.

Culture & Life

1. Do you see toys inside the bars of soap?

2. Children in South Africa wash their hands more often to get the toys.

3. Washing your hands can prevent many health problems.

4. Thanks to this idea, fewer children are getting sick.

11 reduce, 줄이다   12 itch, 가렵다   13 pack, (가방을) 싸다

14 sunburn, 햇볕에 탐, 그을림   15 mosquito, 모기

16 sense, 느끼다, 감지하다

단어 TEST Step 1　　　　p.21

01 이상한	02 뾰족한	03 땀; 땀을 흘리다
04 벌레	05 긁다	06 목마른
07 놓치다, 빼먹다	08 단백질	09 비우다
10 (옷의) 소매, 소맷자락		11 암컷의, 여성의
12 예방하다, 방지하다		13 느끼다, 감지하다
14 식중독	15 모기	16 위, 복부, 배
17 피	18 일어나다, 발생하다	
19 땀에 젖은	20 가렵다	21 (알을) 낳다
22 걱정[근심]하는	23 자외선 차단제	24 수컷의, 남성의
25 충고, 조언	26 100만, 다수	27 아주 작은
28 (가방을) 싸다	29 윙윙거리다	30 줄이다
31 가려운	32 혹, 타박상	33 쓰레기
34 유용한	35 그때에	
36 ~에서 떨어져 있다, 멀리하다		37 ~을 먹고살다
38 ~으로 고통받다	39 ~을 명심하다	
40 ~(점, 골 등) 차로 (경기에서) 지다		41 산책 가다
42 당분간	43 ~하고 싶다	

단어 TEST Step 2　　　　p.22

01 worried	02 sunscreen	03 bug
04 reduce	05 trash	06 million
07 food poisoning		08 female
09 sweaty	10 itch	11 male
12 lay	13 sweat	14 sunburn
15 sharp	16 miss	17 scratch
18 pointed	19 strange	20 protein
21 sleeve	22 blood	23 empty
24 mosquito	25 stomach	26 thirsty
27 bump	28 useful	29 prevent
30 tiny	31 advice	32 pack
33 buzz	34 itchy	35 for a while
36 suffer from	37 do better	38 feed on
39 keep ~ in mind		40 go for a walk
41 at that moment		
42 stay away from		43 take ~ to ...

단어 TEST Step 3　　　　p.23

1 bug, 벌레   2 bite, 물린 상처   3 prevent, 방지하다, 막다

4 miss, 놓치다, 빼먹다   5 bump, 혹, 타박상

6 scratch, 긁다   7 lay, (알을) 낳다   8 protein, 단백질

9 buzz, 윙윙거리다   10 happen, 일어나다, 발생하다

대화문 TEST Step 1　　　　p.24~25

Listen & Speak 1-A (1)

look worried, wrong / worried, my cat is sick / I'm sorry to hear that, Why don't you take / I will

Listen & Speak 1-A (2)

How, class / lost by / I'm sorry to hear that, you do better next time / hope so, too

Listen & Speak 1-B

Let's go swimming / love to, I can't / Why not / to stop swimming for a while / sorry to hear that, can go next weekend / hope so

Listen & Speak 2-A (1)

look at, sunburn / hurts a lot, went swimming, without sunscreen / Make sure, wear sunscreen

Listen & Speak 2-A (2)

go shopping / going to play / Just make sure you wear a hat, going to be very hot / I will

Listen & Speak 2-B

any / under the sink / fruit flies around / put, trash / fruit waste / Make sure you don't put fruit waste in the trash can / keep, in mind, should also empty our trash can / good idea

Real Life Communication

what happened / a lot of mosquito bites / I'm sorry to hear that, How / went camping / Don't scratch them / itchy / with, make sure you wear long sleeves, go camping / thank you

대화문 TEST Step 2　　　　p.26~27

Listen & Speak 1-A (1)

Brian: You look worried, Jimin. What's wrong?

Jimin: I'm worried because my cat is sick.

Brian: I'm sorry to hear that. Why don't you take her to an animal doctor?

Jimin: Okay, I will.

Listen & Speak 1-A (2)

Jane: How was the soccer game with Minsu's class, Alex?

Alex: We lost by three goals.

Jane: I'm sorry to hear that. I hope you do better next time.

Alex: I hope so, too.

Tom: Let's go swimming this weekend, Yujin.

Yujin: I'd love to, but I can't.

Tom: Why not?

Yujin: I have an eye problem. The doctor told me to stop swimming for a while.

Tom: I'm sorry to hear that. Maybe we can go next weekend.

Yujin: I really hope so.

Listen & Speak 2–A (1)

Emma: Tim, look at your face! You got sunburn.

Tim: Yes, it hurts a lot. I went swimming at the beach without sunscreen.

Emma: Oh dear! Make sure you wear sunscreen next time.

Listen & Speak 2–A (2)

Mom: Hojun, do you want to go shopping with me?

Hojun: Sorry, Mom. I'm going to play baseball with Alex this afternoon.

Mom: Okay. No problem. Just make sure you wear a hat. It's going to be very hot this afternoon.

Hojun: Okay, I will.

Listen & Speak 2–B

Sujin: Dad, do we have any bug spray?

Dad: Yes, it's under the sink. Why?

Sujin: There are a lot of fruit flies around the trash.

Dad: Oh no! What did you put in the trash?

Sujin: Some fruit waste.

Dad: Fruit flies love sweet things. Make sure you don't put fruit waste in the trash can.

Sujin: I'll keep that in mind. I think we should also empty our trash can more often.

Dad: That's a good idea.

Real Life Communication

Ms. Wheeler: Junsu, what happened to your face?

Junsu: I got a lot of mosquito bites.

Ms. Wheeler: I'm sorry to hear that. How did it happen?

Junsu: It happened when I went camping last weekend.

Ms. Wheeler: Oh dear. Don't scratch them!

Junsu: I know, but they're really itchy.

Ms. Wheeler: Clean them with cool water. That'll help. Also, make sure you wear long sleeves when you go camping.

Junsu: Okay, thank you.

본문 TEST Step 1 p.28~29

01 It, hot, evening
02 for, walk in
03 Soon, sweating
04 thirsty, something cold, drink
05 At, something tiny, bit
06 catch, if, can
07 have you done
08 just finished
09 from, How, find
10 from, nearby
11 looking for, to
12 something sweaty, found
13 could, smell, from
14 sense heat, smell
15 why, survived for
16 all, like you
17 female, drink blood
18 feed on, plant
19 interesting, why, drink
20 protein, to lay
21 How, sharp teeth
22 don't, teeth
23 long, pointed mouth
24 So, your, easily
25 bit, bump, itches
26 sorry to hear
27 Make sure, don't
28 clean, with, wipes
29 never tried, before
30 reduce, itchiness
31 try, home
32 have to, soon
33 Where, going
34 going back to
35 lot, have suffered
36 How can, prevent
37 cool, wear, sleeves
38 keep, in mind

본문 TEST Step 2 p.30~31

01 It, hot summer evening
02 went for a walk
03 was sweating
04 thirsty, something cold to drink
05 something tiny, at, bit
06 if you can
07 have you done
08 just finished
09 Where, from, How, find
10 from, nearby river
11 was looking for, to drink
12 smelled something sweaty
13 How, smell me
14 sense heat, smell
15 why, have survived, millions
16 like you
17 female, like me drink blood
18 feed on
19 interesting, blood
20 the protein, to lay
21 How, drink blood, sharp teeth
22 teeth
23 a long, pointed mouth
24 So, can drink, easily
25 After, bit, got a bump, itches

26 sorry to hear that

27 Make sure, scratch it

28 clean it with   29 never tried that before

30 reduce the itchiness   31 try that

32 have to go   33 Where, going 34 going back

35 A lot of, have suffered

36 How can, prevent them

37 cool, wear, sleeves   38 keep, in mind

37 모기: 시원하게 지내고 소매가 긴 옷을 입어.

38 서준: 고마워. 너의 충고를 명심할게.

1 무더운 여름날의 저녁이었습니다.

2 서준이는 공원에 산책을 갔습니다.

3 곧, 그는 땀을 흘리고 있었습니다.

4 서준: 목말라. 뭔가 시원한 것을 마시고 싶어.

5 그때에, 뭔가 조그마한 것이 그에게로 날아와서 그의 팔을 물었습니다.

6 모기: 이봐, 나를 잡을 수 있으면 잡아 봐.

7 서준: 너는 누구니? 나한테 무슨 짓을 한 거지?

8 모기: 나는 모기야. 난 방금 저녁 식사를 마쳤어.

9 서준: 너는 어디에서 왔니? 너는 어떻게 나를 찾은 거야?

10 모기: 나는 근처 강에서 왔어.

11 나는 그곳에서 마실 피를 찾던 중이었지.

12 그러다가 땀 냄새를 맡았고, 여기서 너를 발견했어.

13 서준: 너는 어떻게 강에서부터 내 냄새를 맡을 수 있었지?

14 모기: 모기들은 열과 냄새를 매우 잘 감지해.

15 그래서 우리가 수백만 년 동안 살아남은 거야.

16 서준: 모든 모기가 너처럼 피를 마셔?

17 모기: 아니. 오직 나와 같은 암컷 모기만이 피를 마셔.

18 수컷 모기들은 과일과 식물의 즙만을 먹고 살아.

19 서준: 그거 재미있네. 그럼 너는 왜 피를 마시는 거야?

20 모기: 알을 낳으려면 핏속의 단백질이 필요해.

21 서준: 너는 피를 어떻게 마시는 거야? 날카로운 이빨이 있니?

22 모기: 아니, 나는 이빨이 없어.

23 하지만 길고 뾰족한 입이 있지.

24 그래서 나는 너의 피를 쉽게 마실 수 있는 거야.

25 서준: 네가 나를 문 다음, 부어오른 자국이 생겼어. 가려워.

26 모기: 그 말을 들으니 미안하군.

27 그것을 긁지 않도록 해.

28 또한, 그것을 알코올 솜으로 닦아.

29 서준: 알코올 솜? 나는 전에 그것을 한 번도 해 보지 않았어.

30 모기: 그것은 가려움을 줄여 줄 거야.

31 서준: 알았어, 집에서 해 볼게. 고마워.

32 모기: 나는 이제 가야겠어. 다음에 보자.

33 서준: 너는 어디로 가는데?

34 모기: 강으로 돌아가려고.

35 서준: 기다려! 많은 사람이 모기에 물려서 괴로워하고 있어.

36 어떻게 하면 모기에 물리는 것을 막을 수 있지?

1 It was a hot summer evening.

2 Seojun went for a walk in the park.

3 Soon, he was sweating.

4 I'm thirsty. I want something cold to drink.

5 At that moment, something tiny flew at him and bit his arm.

6 Hey, catch me if you can.

7 Who are you? What have you done to me?

8 I'm a mosquito. I've just finished my dinner.

9 Where are you from? How did you find me?

10 I'm from a nearby river.

11 I was looking for some blood to drink there.

12 Then I smelled something sweaty and found you here.

13 How could you smell me from the river?

14 Mosquitoes can sense heat and smell very well.

15 That's why we have survived for millions of years.

16 Do all mosquitoes drink blood like you?

17 No. Only female mosquitoes like me drink blood.

18 Male mosquitoes only feed on fruit and plant juice.

19 That's interesting. So why do you drink blood?

20 I need the protein in blood to lay my eggs

21 How do you drink blood? Do you have sharp teeth?

22 No, I don't have teeth.

23 But I have a long and pointed mouth.

24 So I can drink your blood easily.

25 After you bit me, I got a bump. It itches.

26 I'm sorry to hear that.

27 Make sure you don't scratch it.

28 Also, clean it with alcohol wipes.

29 Alcohol wipes? I've never tried that before.

30 It will reduce the itchiness.

31 Okay, I'll try that at home. Thanks.

32 I have to go. See you soon.

33 Where are you going?

34 I'm going back to the river.

35 Wait! A lot of people have suffered from your bites.

36 How can we prevent them?

37 Stay cool and wear long sleeves.

38 Thanks. I'll keep your advice in mind.

Let's check

1. look upset, wrong
2. lost, my favorite
3. sorry to hear that
4. Why don't, Lost and Found
5. a good idea

Let's Write

1. Health Guide
2. Sunburn
3. Have, suffered from
4. useful tips to prevent
5. Wear
6. Wear
7. Be smart, enjoy

Culture & Life

1. thin, light, to stay cool
2. refrigerator pants
3. colorful patterns
4. look very stylish

Let's check

1. Sora: You look upset, Minu. What's wrong?
2. Minu: I lost my hat. It was my favorite.
3. Sora: I'm sorry to hear that.
4. Why don't you go to the Lost and Found Center?
5. Minu: That's a good idea .

Let's Write

1. Summer Health Guide
2. Sunburn
3. Have you ever suffered from sunburn?
4. Here are some useful tips to prevent sunburn in summer.
5. 1. Wear sunscreen.
6. 2. Wear a hat.
7. Be smart and enjoy the hot weather.

Culture & Life

1. In summer, some people in Korea wear thin and light pants to stay cool.
2. They call them " refrigerator pants."
3. Refrigerator pants come in colorful patterns.
4. Some of them look very stylish.

Lesson 5

01 구역, 블록	02 반, 절반	03 삭제하다
04 사고	05 던지다	06 어딘가에
07 용	08 맨 아래 (부분)	09 용의자
10 거짓말하다	11 탈출하다	
12 ~ 밖에, 밖으로, 밖에		13 단서, 실마리
14 숨기다, 숨다	15 탐정, 형사	16 다행히
17 콩	18 두 번, 두 배	19 공간
20 ~의 안에, ~의 내부에		21 축하
22 장면	23 이상한	24 도둑
25 상	26 안전하게	27 설명하다
28 똑바로, 일직선으로		29 마침내
30 사라지다	31 접다	32 하나도 ~ 않다
33 해결하다	34 수수께끼	35 단추
36 마음껏 드세요	37 ~을 적다	38 ~을 뒤집다
39 도둑을 잡다	40 A를 B로 채우다	41 공짜로
42 ~이 일어나던 때에		
43 ~에 이르는데 성공하다		

01 button	02 scene	03 clue
04 throw	05 bottom	06 strange
07 explain	08 fold	09 cross
10 half	11 somewhere	12 delete
13 twice	14 finally	15 hide
16 lie	17 straight	18 accident
19 solve	20 disappear	21 bean
22 suspect	23 escape	24 luckily
25 congratulation	26 space	27 outside
28 prize	29 riddle	30 safely
31 detective	32 candle	33 thief
34 stamp	35 dragon	36 fill A with B
37 turn over	38 make it to ~	39 for free
40 at the time of	41 write down	42 catch a thief
43 help yourself		

1 enter, 입장하다   2 suspect, 용의자   3 bean, 콩
4 bottom, 맨 아래 (부분)   5 thief, 도둑   6 half, 반, 절반
7 clue, 단서, 실마리   8 cross, 건너다   9 delete, 삭제하다
10 bat, 방망이, 배트   11 accident, 사고

12 detective, 탐정   13 riddle, 수수께끼

14 escape, 탈출하다   15 hide, 숨기다   16 stamp, 우표

Listen & Speak 1 - A

want to play, that, bought / what, it / like, dragons, seahorses, need to use, to play / sounds fun, Can you explain how to use

Listen & Speak 1 - B

riddle, twice in a week, once, never in a day / I have no idea / get it, Can you explain why / year, no, day / get it

Listen & Speak 2 - A

look at / How did you make it / First, in half, make a triangle, Second, fold the top, bottom line, Third, both ends, to make ears, Then, turn, over / sounds easy

Listen & Talk 2 - B

detective / didn't see, this week, about / all of, disappeared / did, do / First, looked around, Then, suspects, Finally, found, thief / don't tell, watch, later

Real Life Communication

solve / First, a bag of beans, needs to cross a river / can only hold, one more / Are you saying, take, at a time / Can you explain how to move everything across, safely

Let's Check

smells, good / going to, for dinner, Help yourself / Can you explain how to make / First, fill, with, Then, add, on the top / delicious / Would, like / thanks

Listen & Speak 1 - A

Jimin: Do you want to play the new game that I bought?

Brian: Sure, what is it, Jimin?

Jimin: It's like a soccer game but the players are dragons and seahorses. You need to use these buttons to play.

Brian: That sounds fun. Can you explain how to use the buttons?

Jimin: Sure.

Listen & Speak 1 - B

Jack: Kelly, here's a riddle. You can see this twice in a week, once in a year, but never in a day. What is this?

Kelly: I have no idea.

Jack: It's the letter "E."

Kelly: I don't get it. Can you explain why?

Jack: Well, there are two "E"s in the word "week," one "E" in the word "year" but no "E"s in the word "day."

Kelly: Aha! Now I get it.

Listen & Speak 2 - A

Tom: Yujin, look at my paper fox.

Yujin: That's cute. How did you make it?

Tom: First, fold a paper in half to make a triangle. Second, fold the top of the triangle to the bottom line. Third, fold both ends of the bottom line to the top to make ears. Then, turn it over and draw a face.

Yujin: That sounds easy.

Listen & Talk 2 - B

Jane: Minsu, do you know the TV show about the student detective?

Minsu: Yes. I love that show, but I didn't see it this week. What was it about?

Jane: Well, all of the bikes at school disappeared.

Minsu: So, what did he do?

Jane: First, he looked around the school. Then, he met some suspects and asked questions. Finally, he found the thief. The thief was ....

Minsu: No, don't tell me! I'll watch it later.

Real Life Communication

Emily: Junsu, do you want to solve a riddle?

Junsu: Sure, what is it?

Emily: There is a farmer. First, the farmer buys a fox, a duck, and a bag of beans. Then, the farmer needs to cross a river.

Junsu: What's the problem?

Emily: The boat can only hold the farmer and one more thing.

Junsu: Are you saying that the farmer can take only one thing at a time?

Emily: Yes. Also, the fox will eat the duck or the duck will eat the beans if the farmer isn't there. Can you explain how to move everything across the river safely?

Junsu: Hmm ....

Let's Check

Minjun: Wow! Something smells really good, Mom. What is it?

Mom: We're going to have tacos for dinner. Help yourself.

37

Minjun: Can you explain how to make a taco?
Mom: First, fill your tortilla with vegetables and meat.
　　　Then, add some sauce on the top.
Minjun: Sounds delicious!
Mom: Would you like some cheese?
Minjun: No, thanks.

본문 TEST Step 1　　　　　　　　　　　　　　p.47~48

01 Welcome to, Escape　　02 enter, first our
03 solve, riddles, escape
04 be found, inside
05 are, ready, think　　　　06 hit by, on
07 Luckily, badly hurt, see
08 suspects, questioned by
09 reading, time, accident
10 said, was walking
11 was making breakfast
12 Who hit, explain
13 have, Write, down　　　14 move to, next
15 accident happened in　　16 made it to
17 much harder, escape
18 gets, from, clothing
19 reads, won, event
20 surprised, quickly opens
21 won our, event
22 have won, prize
23 During, choose, item, free
24 to, on　　　25 can't wait to　26 Truly yours
27 However, real, deletes
28 Can, explain why
29 There, usually, days　　　30 have, answer
31 Write, down, free

본문 TEST Step 2　　　　　　　　　　　　　　p.49~50

01 Welcome to　　02 enter the first room
03 need to solve some riddles
04 be found, inside
05 are, ready to think like　　06 was hit by, on
07 Luckily, wasn't badly hurt, didn't see
08 were questioned by
09 reading a book at the time of the accident
10 said, was walking
11 was making breakfast
12 Who hit, explain why
13 Write it down　14 can move to

---

15 accident happened in　　16 made it to
17 However, much harder to escape than
18 gets, from, clothing store　　19 reads, won
20 surprised, quickly opens
21 won our　　22 Congratulations, have won, prize
23 During, choose, from, for free
24 Come to, on　25 can't wait to see
26 Truly yours
27 However, thinks that, isn't real, deletes
28 Can, explain why
29 There are usually, days
30 have the answer
31 Write it down, are free to go

본문 TEST Step 3　　　　　　　　　　　　　　p.51~52

1 '탈출 탑'에 오신 것을 환영합니다.
2 당신은 저희 탑의 첫 번째 방에 들어갈 것입니다.
3 당신은 탈출하기 위하여 몇 개의 수수께끼를 풀어야 합니다.
4 단서들은 방 어딘가에서 발견될 수 있습니다.
5 그러면 당신은 셜록 홈스처럼 생각할 준비가 되었나요?
6 Doodle씨는 일요일 오후에 차에 치였습니다.
7 다행히 그는 심하게 다치지 않았으나 그는 운전자를 보지 못했습니다.
8 세 명의 용의자들이 경찰에게 심문을 받았습니다.
9 A씨는 사고가 일어난 시간에 책을 읽고 있었다고 말했습니다.
10 B씨는 그의 개를 산책시키고 있었다고 말했습니다.
11 C씨는 아침을 만들고 있었다고 말했습니다.
12 누가 Doodle씨를 치었을까요? 왜 그런지 설명할 수 있나요?
13 답을 가지고 있나요? 적어 보세요.
14 그런 다음, 당신은 다음 방으로 갈 수 있습니다.
15 단서: 사건은 오후에 일어났습니다.
16 축하합니다! 당신은 두 번째 방에 오는 데 성공하셨습니다.
17 그러나 두 번째 방은 첫 번째 방보다 탈출하기 훨씬 더 어렵습니다. 행운을 빕니다!
18 Jay는 그가 가장 좋아하는 옷 가게로부터 이메일을 받습니다.
19 제목은 "당신은 '행운의 날' 행사에 당첨되었습니다!"라고 적혀 있습니다.
20 Jay는 놀랍니다. 그는 재빨리 그것을 엽니다.
21 당신은 우리의 '행운의 날' 행사에 당첨되었습니다!
22 축하합니다! 당신은 특별한 상품을 받게 되었습니다.
23 '행운의 날' 행사 동안, 당신은 우리 가게에서 일곱 가지 상품을 아무거나 공짜로 선택할 수 있습니다!
24 11월 31일에 우리 가게로 오세요.
25 우리는 몹시 당신을 보기를 기대합니다.
26 안녕히 계십시오, Kay Brown
27 그러나 Jay는 그 행사가 사실이 아니라고 생각하고 이메일을 삭제합니다.

28 왜 그런지 설명할 수 있나요?

29 단서: 한 달은 주로 30일 또는 31일이 있습니다.

30 답을 가지고 계신가요?

31 그것을 적으면, 당신은 자유롭게 가실 수 있습니다!

1 Welcome to the Escape Tower.

2 You will enter the first room in our tower.

3 You need to solve some riddles to escape.

4 Clues can be found somewhere inside the room.

5 So, are you ready to think like Sherlock Holmes?

6 Mr. Doodle was hit by a car on Sunday afternoon.

7 Luckily, he wasn't badly hurt, but he didn't see the driver.

8 Three suspects were questioned by a police officer.

9 Ms. A said she was reading a book at the time of the accident.

10 Mr. B said he was walking his dog.

11 Ms. C said she was making breakfast.

12 Who hit Mr. Doodle? Can you explain why?

13 Do you have the answer? Write it down.

14 Then you can move to the next room.

15 Clue The accident happened in the afternoon.

16 Congratulations! You made it to the second room.

17 However, the second room is much harder to escape than the first one. Good luck!

18 Jay gets an email from his favorite clothing store.

19 The title reads "You won our Lucky Day event!"

20 Jay is surprised. He quickly opens it.

21 You won our 'Lucky Day' event!

22 Congratulations! You have won a special prize.

23 During our Lucky Day event, you can choose any seven items from our store for free!

24 Come to our store on November 31.

25 We can't wait to see you.

26 Truly yours, Kay Brown

27 However, Jay thinks that the event isn't real and deletes the email.

28 Can you explain why?

29 Clue There are usually 30 or 31 days in a month.

30 Do you have the answer?

31 Write it down and then you are free to go!

Listen and Speak 1-C

1. Try to solve

3. are under, gets wet, explain why

4. because, a sunny day

Let's Write

1. It, last

2. at home

3. Suddenly, heard a sound

4. went into, was broken

5. looked outside, was holding, was throwing

6. broke

7. can, explained

Culture & Life

1. famous riddle

2. needs to solve, go into

3. that, asks him

4. Which, walks on four legs

Listen and Speak 1-C

1. A: Try to solve this riddle.

2. B: Sure.

3. A: Four people are under one umbrella, but nobody gets wet. Can you explain why?

4. B: Yes! It's because it's a sunny day!

Let's Write

1. It was last Sunday.

2. Dohun was at home.

3. Suddenly , he heard a sound in the next room.

4. When he went into the room, the window was broken.

5. When he looked outside, Sujin was holding a baseball bat and Ted was throwing a ball to his dog.

6. Who broke the window?

7. How can it be explained?

Culture & Life

1. This is the famous riddle of the Sphinx.

2. Oedipus needs to solve it to go into Thebes.

3. This is the question that the Sphinx asks him.

4. Which creature walks on four legs in the morning, two legs in the afternoon, and three legs in the evening?